THE SOVIET-POLISH WAR AND ITS LEGACY

THE SOVIET-POLISH WAR AND ITS LEGACY

Lenin's Defeat and the Rise of Stalinism

Authored by
Peter Whitewood

BLOOMSBURY ACADEMIC
LONDON • NEW YORK • OXFORD • NEW DELHI • SYDNEY

BLOOMSBURY ACADEMIC
Bloomsbury Publishing Plc
50 Bedford Square, London, WC1B 3DP, UK
1385 Broadway, New York, NY 10018, USA
29 Earlsfort Terrace, Dublin 2, Ireland

BLOOMSBURY, BLOOMSBURY ACADEMIC and the Diana logo are
trademarks of Bloomsbury Publishing Plc

First published in Great Britain 2023
Paperback edition published 2025

Copyright © Peter Whitewood 2023

Peter Whitewood has asserted his right under the Copyright, Designs and
Patents Act, 1988, to be identified as Author of this work.

Cover image: Russian-Polish war - Propaganda poster for the
enlistment into the Red cavalry © JJs / Alamy

Bloomsbury Publishing Plc does not have any control over, or responsibility for,
any third-party websites referred to or in this book. All internet addresses given in this
book were correct at the time of going to press. The author and publisher regret
any inconvenience caused if addresses have changed or sites have ceased
to exist, but can accept no responsibility for any such changes.

Every effort has been made to trace the copyright holders and obtain permission
to reproduce the copyright material. Please do get in touch with any enquiries or
any information relating to such material or the rights holder. We would be
pleased to rectify any omissions in subsequent editions of this publication
should they be drawn to our attention.

A catalogue record for this book is available from the British Library.

A catalog record for this book is available from the Library of Congress.

Library of Congress Cataloging-in-Publication Data

Names: Whitewood, Peter, author.
Title: The Soviet-Polish war and its legacy : Lenin's defeat and the rise
of Stalinism / authored by Peter Whitewood.
Other titles: Lenin's defeat and the rise of Stalinism
Description: London ; New York : Bloomsbury Academic, 2023. | Includes
bibliographical references and index. | Summary: "An examination of the Bolshevik
defeat to Poland in the Soviet-Polish War (1919-20) and the rise of the repressive,
highly industrialised Stalinist system it encouraged"– Provided by publisher.
Identifiers: LCCN 2023026473 (print) | LCCN 2023026474 (ebook) |
ISBN 9781350238947 (hardback) | ISBN 9781350238985 (paperback) |
ISBN 9781350238954 (ebook) | ISBN 9781350238961 (epub)
Subjects: LCSH: Stalin, Joseph, 1878-1953. | Russo-Polish War, 1919-1920. |
Soviet Union–Politics and government–1917-1936. | Soviet Union–Foreign
relations–Poland. | Poland–Foreign relations–Sovet Union.
Classification: LCC DK4405 .W45 2023 (print) | LCC DK4405 (ebook) |
DDC 947/.048–dc23/eng/20230622
LC record available at https://lccn.loc.gov/2023026473
LC ebook record available at https://lccn.loc.gov/2023026474

ISBN: HB: 978-1-3502-3894-7
PB: 978-1-3502-3898-5
ePDF: 978-1-3502-3895-4
eBook: 978-1-3502-3896-1

Typeset by Integra Software Services Pvt. Ltd.

To find out more about our authors and books visit www.bloomsbury.com
and sign up for our newsletters.

For Felicity

CONTENTS

Acknowledgements	viii
Introduction	1
Chapter 1 WAR IN THE BORDERLANDS	9
Chapter 2 THE BATTLE OF WARSAW	37
Chapter 3 COEXISTENCE TO CRISIS	65
Chapter 4 STABILITY TO INSECURITY	93
Chapter 5 CAPITALIST ENCIRCLEMENT AND DICTATORSHIP	123
Chapter 6 TRANSFORMATION, A PACT AND NEW ENEMY	153
Conclusion	183
Notes	188
Bibliographic Abbreviations	225
Select Bibliography	226
Index	228

ACKNOWLEDGEMENTS

I have accumulated many debts in the years of researching and writing this book and without the support and assistance of others, the project would have been impossible. At the outset of the research, I was fortunate enough to attend the Hoover Institution Workshop on Authoritarian Regimes in summer 2016, hosted by Paul Gregory and Mark Harrison. Not only was this a valuable opportunity to work in the Hoover Institution's rich archives, but daily discussions with other workshop participants about Soviet authoritarianism gave my book project the momentum needed. A few years later I was able to revisit these themes when, alongside Lara Douds and James Harris, I edited a collection of essays on the emergence of the Stalinist dictatorship. Through another valuable workshop, I encountered a range of fresh arguments from each participant, shaping my thinking about the evolution of Stalinism. Later, when writing the manuscript, Arch Getty, James Harris, Olena Palko and Jim Cooper generously read chapters, offering incisive comments and sharpening my arguments. My PhD student, Patrick Stickland, working on early Anglo-Soviet relations, encouraged me to revaluate key issues in the diplomatic history of the Russian civil war era.

Early versions of parts of this book have been published elsewhere, as 'In the shadow of the war: Bolshevik perceptions of Polish subversive and military threats to the Soviet Union, 1920–32', *Journal of Strategic Studies* 44/5 (2021), and 'The International Situation: Fear of Invasion and Growing Authoritarianism' in Lara Douds, James Harris and Peter Whitewood (eds), *The Fate of the Bolshevik Revolution: Illiberal Liberation, 1917–41* (Bloomsbury Academic, 2020). The feedback from anonymous reviewers for both pieces was always helpful, and David R. Stone, as ever, provided perceptive comments, helping me better frame my work in these early stages.

As always true, a book is impossible without financial support. This came from the Hoover Institution, the Institute of Historical Research and from the School of Humanities at York St John University. I am indebted to the latter especially for giving me research leave in 2020, the necessary time to write the lion's share of the book's chapters and for funding numerous conference attendances down the years. The collegial atmosphere of the History programme at YSJ was essential to keeping me on track, and I owe thanks to all my colleagues. My research efforts were also greatly assisted by Aleksandra Maslova, Anastasiia Zaplatina and Ivan Balykin, who gathered additional archival documents in Moscow and Kyiv. My own trips to the archives were productive only because of knowledgeable archivists. The librarians at York St John expertly managed to track down rare books and texts in every case with the inter-library loan service. Rhodri Mogford, at Bloomsbury Academic, has been supportive and helpful from beginning to end.

Finally, my parents deserve renewed thanks for their continuing support and encouragement over a long period, and likewise to my wife, Carly, who has heard me talk about this book more than anyone else. Our daughter was born just as I began writing Chapter 1, and it is to her that this book is dedicated.

INTRODUCTION

In a phrase resonating still today, British diplomat and member of the Inter-Allied mission to Poland, Viscount Edgar Vincent D'Abernon, once described the Battle of Warsaw of August 1920, the dramatic climax of the Soviet-Polish war, as 'the eighteenth most decisive battle in history'. Had Vladimir Lenin and the Bolshevik Party secured victory, D'Abernon went on, Europe would have been left wide-open to further Soviet invasion, propaganda and subversion. This was nothing less than a turning point in the history of the twentieth century, determining the fate of Europe and western civilization.[1] Regardless of whether ranking battles in numerical order is a valuable exercise, claims by D'Abernon and others like him have lent an element of drama to the past for sure, and today still generate commentaries about the hypothetical consequences of the Soviet-Polish war, in both popular and academic works.[2] Yet to imagine that the Polish victory against Soviet Russia heroically stopped Vladimir Lenin's revolutionary wave hitting Europe is to accept that this was a likely prospect when, in reality, the chances of success were small from the beginning. In addition to glaring weaknesses in the Red Army, by 1920, there was little popular appetite for Soviet power outside of Bolshevik-held territory and a surge of popular labour unrest was already rocking Soviet Russia from within.[3] The truth was that even if events had swung towards a Soviet military victory at Warsaw in summer 1920, this would have only been temporary. In this scenario the core problem for the Bolshevik Party was the likelihood of massive, organized response from the Allied Powers. Even with populations weary after years of world war, and despite the reticence shown by the British and French governments for intervening in the Soviet-Polish war in the first place, a Bolshevik takeover of Warsaw in summer 1920 would cross a firm red line. In such circumstances, Allied armed forces would almost certainly have travelled to Poland, outmatching the Red Army, still in its chaotic years of early development and strained from several years of fighting in a vicious civil war. Vladimir Lenin's opportunities for the Soviet subversion of Europe, vanishingly small in the first place, would have been quickly closed off.

However unrealistic this proved to be, D'Abernon was right that Lenin had planned to use war against Poland as a vehicle to create conditions for another revolution.[4] The Red Army's counterattack from early summer 1920 was a concerted effort to spread revolution into Europe by armed force. In Lenin's vision, the Red Army would rapidly spearhead a revolutionary wave, 'sovietizing' Poland and, in turn, spark a second organic revolution in industrial Germany – a major strike for the communist movement in the very heart of Europe. For Lenin and other like-minded senior Bolsheviks (although some figures, including Iosif Stalin, harboured persisting doubts), this was the essential means for securing their own power in Soviet Russia. Without world revolution, so the thinking went, the Bolshevik revolution would be forever isolated and vulnerable to capitalist predation. Out of step with reality, Lenin's ambitions were driven by rising confidence in Moscow once the Red Army had managed to defeat other enemy forces in the wider civil war and then began pushing back the Polish Army in early summer 1920. The height of the Soviet-Polish war now seemed to be a moment when the face of Europe could be transformed. It was therefore the sudden evaporation of Lenin's revolutionary designs that gave the defeat such meaning for the Bolsheviks. In August 1920, Polish head of state, Józef Piłsudski, masterminded a stunning defeat of the Red Army at the Battle of Warsaw, leaving Lenin's plans in ruins and him unable to witness his anticipated second revolution. Not only a humiliation of Soviet military power, the shallow support among the Polish people for the Bolsheviks' revolutionary programme took many – though not all – in Moscow by surprise. Lenin's gamble failed on numerous fronts.

The Soviet-Polish war of 1919 to 1920 was just one of the many conflicts that erupted across the lands of the former Russian Empire after the Russian Revolution. During what is commonly known as the 'Russian' civil war – but, in reality, was a series of complex and overlapping struggles encompassing territories beyond Russia[5] – varied counter revolutionary forces, and chiefly the so-called White armies, led by a succession of ultimately weak and rivalrous imperial Russian generals, sought to overthrow the new Soviet regime. The Bolsheviks' political rivals, parties like the socialist revolutionaries, squeezed out of power after the October Revolution, harboured similar ambitions; while in wake of a collapsing empire, nationalist organizations, and especially those operating in turbulent Ukraine, struggled for independence. With shifting momentum from its beginnings in 1918, sporadic fighting stretched from Europe all the way into Central Asia and the Far East of the old Russian empire, some of this lasting into the mid-1920s. Yet the Bolsheviks' military position was increasingly unassailable far earlier into the conflict. General Anton Denikin's White Army came perilously close to Moscow in autumn 1919, but his defeat by the end of the year greatly reduced the chances of removing the Bolsheviks from power with armed force for the remainder of the civil war. For sure, the Red Army still faced frequent and sometimes serious attacks from armed peasant bands, notably during the widespread rebellion in Tambov during 1920 to 1921. White forces, under the reorganized leadership of general Petr Wrangel, and after retreating to Crimea under Red Army pressure, managed to launch fresh attacks to the north at the end of the Soviet-Polish war. Widespread desertion, mutinies and internal popular discontent with the Bolsheviks' increasingly dictatorial governance and emergency wartime measures, the draconian system of war communism, reached potentially dangerous levels by the early 1920s. Yet with their opponents perpetually divided and maintaining control of major urban areas, and with it, a large proportion of the population and military industry, the Bolsheviks' military superiority in Soviet Russia was cemented by 1921.[6]

At the tail end of the Cold War and forming one strand of a broader scholarly challenge to orthodoxies which came to define the study of Soviet history, so-called revisionist historians underlined how these bitter years of civil war, during which hundreds of thousands of people died or suffered terrible hardships, came to shape the nature of the Soviet regime and its evolution. On face value, the linkages between the civil war era and later Stalin period seem clear. In the years after the civil war, and particularly by the late 1920s, the Stalinist leadership used terror and violence more liberally and openly; the Soviet state was visibly characterized by rising centralization and bureaucratization; there was an inward turn towards nationalism and away from internationalism. All of this, the argument went, partly stemmed from this earlier civil war experience when desperate circumstances on the ground encouraged these very trends and behaviours. Rather than ideology or inherent authoritarianism in the Bolshevik Party playing central roles in the revolution's deterioration into dictatorship, it was the violence of the civil war – and the party's emergency wartime responses which persisted long after – which contributed to the emergence of Stalinism.[7]

It is hard to deny that the civil war had lasting effects on the Bolshevik Party and the nature of the Soviet regime, but arguments in this direction sometimes lack precision. It is not clear exactly how or through what processes the formative civil war experience contributed to the later Stalinist dictatorship. What connected the early and late 1920s is not always obvious, aside from the fact that Soviet wartime measures of the civil war era resembled, if sometimes closely, Stalin's radical and often destructive campaigns of industrialization and collectivization ten years later: the 'revolution from above' that propelled the rapid industrial transformation of the Soviet Union.[8] To bridge the gap more comprehensively then, this book argues that among the varied conflicts of the civil war the Soviet-Polish war was the most significant in terms of its later ramifications. Much of the focus in the pages below is given over to tracing the aftermath of this conflict domestically in the following decade.[9] One of the most important points of continuity across the 1920s, for instance, was how the Bolsheviks' perception of Soviet-Polish relations after their military defeat in 1920, and the near-constant anxieties about renewed future war which followed, shaped the core features of their emerging state. The purpose of this book therefore is to examine the Soviet-Polish war but also to concentrate on its material consequences. Rather than speculate about alternate histories, the pages below argue that the ways in which the Bolsheviks understood the war against Poland, and how they perceived their stunning defeat, pushed the early Soviet regime more rapidly towards the emergence of the Stalinist system.

The history of the Soviet-Polish war has been told numerous times down the years and classic accounts published decades ago remain some of the best guides.[10] The conflict's place in the wider civil war continues to be prominent in newer works, and especially in those emphasizing the complexity and multifaceted nature of this period of violence.[11] For these reasons, while the first two chapters of this book focus on the same events of the Soviet-Polish war, their purpose is to go beyond the detail of the military back-and-forth to examine how the Bolsheviks' later obsession with future war stemmed to a large degree from this moment. The argument developed in the pages below is that the Bolsheviks' stunning military defeat in summer 1920 placed Poland firmly at the centre of later Soviet security assessments of future war, and this had lasting effects. The ongoing perceived threat of future war, from Poland and other border countries supposedly influenced by powerful capitalist patrons, pushed the Bolsheviks towards rapid industrialization in the late 1920s, with the destruction of the collectivization drive following on its heels. The permanent war scare that defined much the 1920s – with Poland consistently deemed the Soviet Union's most likely adversary – had effects elsewhere. Inside the Bolshevik Party, a widely accepted vision of future renewed war deepened a trajectory towards strengthening authoritarianism and more quickly destroyed lingering democratic practices. This, in turn, helped cement Stalin's and the party majority's authority over any political opposition. Of course, there was never much scope for political challenge under the Bolshevik regime but what existed was curtailed more sharply in circumstances when the party majority – and the opposition included – believed the country was facing a future inevitable war of such a scale that would decide its fate. All of that said, it would be an exaggeration to claim that the Soviet-Polish war defined the very nature of the early Soviet system. What this book argues is that the loss of the war, stemming from Lenin's reckless adventure from early summer 1920, deepened and accelerated pre-existing trends already underway. To reformulate the argument discussed above more narrowly: the civil war was undoubtedly a formative experience for the Bolsheviks, but the Soviet-Polish war was the most consequential conflict over the long term.

The most common point discussed in this book, therefore, is the significance of Soviet-Polish relations for the Soviet Union in the decade after the Russian Revolution. For obvious reasons, a large and wide-ranging number of works are permanently in print on Soviet-German relations in the 1930s. There are far fewer on Soviet-Polish relations in the previous decade, even though the Bolsheviks often judged these in equally threatening terms.[12] It is also important to stress that while this book concentrates on how the Bolsheviks perceived Polish military and subversive threats, Poland was not deemed to be an independent actor in the world. Another central argument following below is that during and after the civil war years, and notably following the Soviet-Polish war, the Bolsheviks not only believed that Britain and France – the chief forces of the capitalist world – had manipulated Poland into war in the first place, but that they aimed to do this again in the future. Poland was consistently portrayed as a major threat to Soviet security but typically so as the core country in a wider coalition of anti-Soviet powers. At varying times in the 1920s this was said to include the Baltic states and Finland,

and Germany in the early 1930s, acting all the while under the malign influence of Britain, France and international capital.

How the Bolsheviks perceived the outside world and international relations has long been a mainstay of scholarship on Soviet foreign policy. Since the partial opening of Russian archives in the 1990s, which gave researchers access to extensive internal documents from the Soviet foreign ministry, upper party structures, military intelligence and security organs, greater insight into the conspiratorial view of the world that held sway in Moscow for much of the interwar years has been possible.[13] It is now clear that Bolshevik officials, under both Lenin and Stalin, frequently misinterpreted or exaggerated the dangers posed by the outside world, seeing threats where they did not exist and predicting wars which never arrived. This tendency was partly a product of the Bolsheviks' ideological positions which anticipated inevitable war between the communist and capitalist worlds in the absence of world revolution. Already influenced by a worldview predisposed to seeing anti-Soviet coalitions continually in the making, critical analysis of intelligence and security projections for the future then became more dependent on the views of one single person as Stalin cemented his hold on power. By the late 1920s, the general secretary, who rarely travelled outside the capital, was the most influential – though not the single – voice in deciding which intelligence was valuable and for what reasons. Sometimes operating solely with his instincts, it is not hard to imagine how Stalin's dominance over the party and government, combined with the self-interests pervasive to Soviet institutions themselves, shaped the type of intelligence materials gathered by agents on the ground and their presentation. Inaccurate intelligence and failures were no means unique to the Soviet Union in the 1920s, but the distance between perception and reality was often so much the greater here than elsewhere.[14]

Scholars have studied the misperception and the misinterpretation of foreign threats in the Soviet Union with varying focuses. On the one hand, it has long been recognized that the Bolshevik leadership's perception of outside threats in the 1920s provided a central rationale behind the industrialization drive and the first five-year plan.[15] More recently, a growing number of historians have analysed Stalin's and his close officials' misperception of external and internal security threats and drawn connections to dramatic escalations of state violence against the Soviet people, as during the Great Terror of 1937 to 1938. Whether this violence was intended to eliminate anyone the regime deemed an individual 'enemy' or constituted cleansing operations against 'unreliable' population cohorts in anticipation of future war, studying how the Stalinist regime misperceived the world provides more complete answers to what on face-value can seem like arbitrary and ultimately self-defeating actions. Focusing solely on a dictator seeking untrammelled power leaves too many questions unresolved.[16] Similar connections also, though not in a systematic way, have been drawn in other work between the regime's perception of dangers in the capitalist world and broadening authoritarian practices in the Bolshevik Party.[17] Another aim of this book, therefore, is to pull these strands together to show how the perceived Polish threat to the Soviet Union, coming from its place in a wider anti-Soviet coalition, was a core force shaping the nature of the Soviet state in terms of its industrialization strategy; the party's attitudes towards democratic practices; and the use of state violence, during the critical transitional decade of the 1920s.

To do the above, this book is structured in the following way. The first two chapters focus on the events of the Soviet-Polish war between 1919 and 1920. Chapter 1 examines the early and sporadic clashes between Polish and Soviet troops from early 1919, as each side moved into the space vacated by the German Army on the former eastern front. Józef Piłsudski escalated these low-level clashes a few months later after ordering a much larger invasion of Ukraine in April 1920 and for months the Bolsheviks' new Red Army was firmly on the backfoot until it managed to regroup for a counteroffensive in early summer. Chapter 2 picks up the war from this moment, detailing the Red Army's steady westward push, to which Lenin pinned his hopes for revolution. The chapter concludes with the disaster at the Battle of Warsaw, the consequence of poor and confused Soviet strategy but also the unrealistic premise of the entire offensive from the beginning, something eventually admitted to inside Bolshevik circles in the aftermath. The central theme running through both chapters is that from the start of the war, Lenin and the Bolsheviks were convinced that they were not just fighting Piłsudski's Poland. They exaggerated the roles played by Britain and France in providing critical support and direction to the Polish Army and saw them equally responsible for the Soviet defeat at Warsaw.

Chapters 3 and 4 form another pair, focused on the years after the war, following the signing of the precarious peace agreement, the Treaty of Riga in March 1921. Chapter 3 concentrates on Soviet-Polish relations in the period up to 1924, detailing numerous tensions and controversies in foreign affairs. Throughout the early 1920s, both the Soviet and Polish sides accused each other of sponsoring and financing the subversion of territory. These accusations had more than a grain of truth, but only the Bolsheviks perceived the subversion of their borders as strongly indicative of future war. The chapter concludes by examining how the Bolsheviks assessed the perceived military danger from Poland during the tense 1923 Ruhr crisis, underlining that while the Soviet-Polish war ended in 1920 and the wider civil war was more or less extinguished soon after, these were not years when the threat level meaningfully lowered. In the same way, Chapter 4 details Soviet-Polish foreign relations from 1924, a year that held out some promise of improvement for the Soviet leadership, given the new left-leaning governments elected in Britain and France. Yet none of this fundamentally changed the position of Poland as a perceived pressing danger on the border. Predictions of war only became more dire when Piłsudski, out of favour in Polish politics for some years, suddenly returned to power in May 1926 through a coup d'état. Alarms bells were ringing in Moscow once again as the perceived war danger ratcheted upwards.

The final pair of chapters explore how this long-standing perceived threat from Poland and the capitalist world shaped the nature of the Soviet regime. Chapter 5 concentrates on the corrosive effects that the Bolsheviks' perception of capitalist encirclement had on democratic practices in the party throughout the 1920s. Under both Lenin and Stalin, the permanent war scare closed down what limited opportunities still existed for dissent from the party line in the years after 1917. It is well-known that Lenin banned 'factions' in the party in 1921, yet an important piece of context was the widely shared view among Bolsheviks that renewed war was around the corner. That Lev Trotsky and his allies equally accepted this threat, even if they argued that more open party discussion was the essential response, only helped to place limits on their own freedom of action. The chapter concludes with analysis of the war scare which spread quickly throughout the Soviet Union in 1927, further ensuring that the party majority, now firmly led by Stalin, was unassailable. Examining Soviet-Polish relations in the late 1920s to early 1930s, Chapter 6 emphasizes how the Bolsheviks' expectation of future war – again with Poland as the central core of a future anti-Soviet coalition – provided a powerful rationale for the launch of the first five-year plan. Collectivization soon followed, during which the Soviet political police notably ratcheted up repression against Polish nationals. The chapter details, moreover, how the nature of the perceived existential threat was beginning to shift in these years. Although Stalin sought a non-aggression pact with Poland (finally signed in 1932), Adolf Hitler's Germany was steadily emerging as the danger it would become in the 1930s. For a time at least, both Poland and Germany were analysed in Soviet intelligence reports as co-dangers, potentially already working in collaboration. Still, the perceived security threat from Poland, as viewed from Moscow, was never entirely replaced, as the extreme state violence deployed against Poles in later years shows most clearly.

A final qualification is that this book is not a study of Soviet-Polish relations in which each side is given equal attention. Its intention is to analyse how the Bolsheviks judged their military adversary, Poland, in the war of 1919 to 1920 and throughout the following decade. Poland's changing political, economic and international position in this period is therefore essential to understand; without which, it would be impossible to show the degree that the Bolsheviks misinterpreted the outside world. But this book is chiefly a study of how war, and the misperception of future war, shaped Soviet affairs.

Chapter 1

WAR IN THE BORDERLANDS

On Germany's defeat in the First World War and the signing of the armistice, new scattered conflicts erupted almost immediately across the reordered map of central and east central Europe. The war in the east, unlike in the west, did not end in November 1918.[1] Struggles for territory between newly independent states on the former eastern front soon became a defining feature of the post-war years. This added to the chaotic situation even further east where, following on the heels of the Russian Revolution, Vladimir Lenin and the Bolshevik Party were deep in civil war against the counterrevolutionary White armies and rival socialist forces, amid widespread peasant revolts. Having clung on to power, by 1919, the Bolsheviks and the newly formed Red Army were steadily turning the tide, tightening their grip on the coalescing Soviet Russia. Further west in central Europe, and after over a century of partition among the German, Austro-Hungarian and Russian empires, a new independent Poland emerged on 11 November 1918 as part of the post-war settlement. But while the Treaty of Versailles settled Poland's western borders, civil war in Russia made it impossible to do the same in the east. The new Soviet and Polish governments, keenly aware of their vulnerabilities, thus watched each other with apprehension. As the German Army steadily exited the expansive and coveted borderlands, spanning from Wilno in the north to the Romanian border in the south, leaving a vacuum to be filled, conflict was only a matter of time.

From early 1919 both Soviet and Polish sides sent units probing forwards into the borderlands. Polish forces pushed towards western Belarus and Lithuania, seizing Białystok and Brest-Litovsk, and clashed with the Soviet western army, which in January had already taken Wilno from the recently established Republic of Lithuania, later to become the capital of the future – and short-lived – Lithuanian-Belorussian Soviet Republic. These clashes marked the beginnings of an undeclared war, although for now both sides were small in number and poorly armed.[2] For their part, the Bolsheviks were proceeding in line with optimistic plans for retaking the borderlands drawn up several months before, which envisaged the Red Army reaching as far as East Prussia and linking up with the German working class to foment another revolution.[3] This would ease the Bolsheviks' deepening fears that the survival struggle of their own revolution would only become more difficult if left alone among hostile capitalist powers. In 1919 escalating fighting with Poland stymied these unrealistic ambitions, but Lenin's commitment to breaking through to Europe to engineer another revolution never waned.

The Polish Army struck a major blow when it seized Wilno from Soviet control in mid-April 1919. In Warsaw opinions differed about whether the city should be incorporated into Poland, or its fate chosen by its people (although Jewish civilians were victims of shocking violence at the hands of Polish soldiers). Emboldened by the signing of the Treaty of Versailles in late June, which, for the time being, eliminated the German threat on their western border, the Poles then took Minsk, recently claimed by the Bolsheviks as capital of the Belorussian Soviet Socialist republic, and formerly Polish regions of Belarus by the summer. In fighting against Galician Ukrainians further south, the Poles struck out in an offensive from May, driving them into retreat. Most of East Galicia was soon occupied, including the strategic city Lwów. Polish forces similarly moved into the Volhynia region of Ukraine. The Polish offensive was then halted to concentrate on the defence of these new territories, much of it the lands of former Austria-Hungary.[4] Despite this string of victories, however, Poland was not yet a major preoccupation in Soviet foreign policy and Lenin's focus was elsewhere in 1919. He was far more concerned with the intentions of the Allied Powers, chiefly Britain and France; the status of defeated Germany and its revolutionary potential; and the ongoing struggle against the counterrevolutionary White armies.[5] Poland was a priority insofar as reaching a temporary armistice would allow more military strength to be diverted against the White General Anton Denikin, whose army was making strides in South Russia and seized Kiev and Orel in the summer and autumn. The Bolsheviks, moreover, feared that the Allied Powers might engineer an alliance between the Whites and the Poles, making the security situation even more precarious. In truth, there was almost no prospect of this as Denikin, like other White leaders, never gave strong guarantees about respecting the independence or territorial integrity of the new states that emerged from the collapsed Russian empire, including Poland. Despite tentative negotiations, the Whites and Poles failed to reconcile core differences.[6] That the Bolsheviks failed to appreciate these difficulties was characteristic of their perception of international affairs which imagined the Allied Powers manipulating smaller countries and actors easily at will. An armistice with Poland, they believed, would do much to counter this threat. A deal therefore needed to be done with new Polish head of state, General Józef Piłsudski.

In the decades before 1918, Lithuanian-born Piłsudski's chief priority was Polish independence. This eclipsed his weaker attachment to the class struggle, notwithstanding a long history of revolutionary activity in the former Russian empire, culminating in five years' exile in Siberia. Piłsudski later became a leading member of the Polish Socialist Party and during the First World War commanded a Polish legion in cooperation with Austria-Hungary against Russia, the focus of his strongest hatred.[7] With reputation enhanced, and after a period of difficult political negotiations following the war, Piłsudski became head of state in the new independent Poland, drawing power from his position as commander of the armed forces and serving in an uneasy political partnership with the prime minister, the famous pianist Ignacy Paderewski from the rival National Democratic movement. Piłsudski's focus was to now strengthen Poland's power and security in Europe and, critically, extend its influence further east. Along with other members of the Polish Socialist Party, and Paderewski, Piłsudski harboured a long-term vision for a 'Greater Poland' that would be ranked alongside other major powers and encompass the border states formerly belonging to his country before its first partition among the Russian empire, Kingdom of Prussia and Habsburg empire in 1772. Lithuania and Belarus were to be federated states and Ukraine detached from Soviet control and brought under Polish influence.[8] None of this would be easy and a botched coup attempt in Kaunas in August 1919, which failed to change the government and bring Lithuania into a federation, was a clear sign of trouble. Yet the central problem with Piłsudski's vision for Poland, aside from its unpopularity with the peoples targeted for incorporation, was the Bolshevik challenge in the same areas following failed efforts to create regimes in their own image from 1918. Despite the Polish military victories so far, achieving Piłsudski's ambitious federation required a more extensive military solution. Knowing he had to bide his time therefore, Piłsudski was content enough for the Polish government, for now, to pursue negotiations with the Bolsheviks in 1919.[9]

Another complication for Piłsudski's plans was the positions of Britain and France, who discouraged his ambitions in the east and believed Polish claims to be excessive. Supporting the White armies and restoring Russia as a reliable ally, with much of its former borderland territory intact, was the bigger priority early in the civil war. Neither government had much interest in supporting Piłsudski's military ambitions, especially when these were presented in unrealistic ways. In September 1919, for instance, Piłsudski and Paderewski made a fantastic proposal that the Polish Army could seize Moscow, but the British government dismissed this costly adventure, estimated at approximately £1,000,000 per day, and continued to pin hopes on Denikin.[10] Piłsudski directed similar efforts at securing French support for an offensive against Soviet Russia, to pre-empt what he saw as a rising danger should the Bolsheviks finish off the Whites and transfer military strength from the south. The French government was equally dismissive and mindful of staying aligned with Britain.[11] The effect of such rejections was to incentivize the Poles towards, temporarily, coming to terms with the Bolsheviks. Under the cover of Red Cross missions, secret talks between Soviet and Polish delegates took place in autumn 1919 in Mikaszewicze. Piłsudski produced conditions for a ceasefire, though not an armistice; however, by November nothing had come of the talks which collapsed shortly after.[12] In truth, neither side was committed to peace. Piłsudski was more interested in testing Lenin's sincerity and biding time for his offensive; the Bolsheviks had the same ambitions and refused, in particular, the Polish demand of ceasing military operations against the forces of the Ukrainian nationalist leader Symon Petliura, after the Red Army retook Kiev from the White forces in December.[13]

Before the secret talks in Mikaszewicze broke down, the Red Army's successes against Denikin's army from October 1919 had started to shift Piłsudski's calculations about the timing of military action against Soviet Russia. Because Denikin's offensive in the south was likely to end in defeat, joining other failed offensives by White generals Aleksandr Kolchak and Nikolai Iudenich,

Piłsudski now seriously considered a strike sooner than later, and critically before the Bolsheviks could transfer forces from the south. This would have to be done without serious support from the Allied Powers. When the Polish government appealed to Britain and France for military supplies, little was forthcoming.[14] While staunchly anti-communist politicians like British Secretary of State for War, Winston Churchill, backed Piłsudski, his government's position was to refuse material aid. The French extended 375 million francs of credit to Poland, but this was not sufficient for servicing a major offensive in the east.[15] Then in early December 1919, the Allied Supreme Council delivered a clear rebuff to Piłsudski's plan for a strike against Soviet Russia. It proposed a new eastern boundary to Poland's territory with Soviet Russia, running north to south near Brest-Litovsk, to bring the fighting to an end. Later known as the Curzon Line after one of its architects, British Foreign Secretary George Curzon, this approximated the former boundary between the Russian empire and Prussia following the third partition of Poland in 1795. Yet the line was unacceptable to the new Polish government led by Leopold Skulski, installed in the same month following a related dispute with the Allied Supreme Council about the fate of eastern Galicia, leading to Paderewski's resignation. (The Allied Supreme Council gave way on eastern Galicia in 1919, though it would reverse course in the following year).[16] Despite encompassing Polish ethnic boundaries, the Curzon line did not award Poland other coveted territories such as the Lithuanian-populated north Suwałki province or Wilno, and the new Skulski cabinet broadly shared Piłsudski's ambitions for power and influence in the east.[17] The more pressing problem with the new boundary, however, was that it was simply outstripped by the developing war. By December 1919 clashes between Polish and Soviet troops had moved up to 30,000 kilometres away in east, far beyond the proposed line.[18]

As Curzon made his intervention, the Bolsheviks launched a diplomatic offensive of their own. Alarmed by the new Polish government's firmer support for Piłsudski's territorial ambitions, and still fearing that the Allied Powers would try to 'unite the borderlands' against them, the Soviet government sent a peace proposal on 22 December 1919 to the Polish foreign minister, Stanisław Patek, in the name of his counterpart, Georgy Chicherin, People's Commissar for Foreign Affairs. Chicherin claimed that the Bolsheviks had felt compelled to send a peace offer after learning of remarks given by the Polish deputy minister of foreign affairs, Władysław Skrzyński, to the Polish Sejm in October that no Soviet peace proposal had ever been received. Chicherin pointed out that the Bolsheviks had given assurances of their benign intentions already months before in April and he was now presenting a formal offer 'to begin negotiations as soon as possible with a view to concluding a just and lasting peace'. But by December, seeing as two months had been and gone since Skrzyński's comments to the Sejm, as one historian notes, the episode was more likely a ploy to create problems for the Polish government in left-wing circles, gain favour with the working class and mobilize them against the upcoming Polish assault against Latgale, the last part of the embattled Latvian Socialist Soviet Republic.[19] The Polish government did not respond.

In a recurring theme in Bolshevik discussions of the war with Poland, Chicherin's December peace note heaped blame on the Allied Powers for hindering the very peace that could end hostilities serving 'only foreign interests'. The Bolshevik leadership hoped to drive a wedge between the Poles and the Allied Powers, but there was little confidence in Moscow that outside influences on Polish affairs could be overcome. In detailed reports on Poland from the same month, the Bolshevik Party's expert on Polish affairs, Iulian Markhlevskii, who had been central to brokering the Mikaszewicze negotiations of 1919, described how the Polish government could simply not afford to ignore British and French demands: '[Polish] finances are in a desperate condition, economic life is difficult to restore without the Entente […] to receive financial and economic support […] the Polish bourgeoisie will agree to fulfil all of its orders.' In Markhlevskii's view, it was doubtful that Piłsudski could resist demands to make war, even in support of the White armies whose leaders sought to consolidate former Russian territory at Poland's expense.[20] Similarly, People's Commissar for War, Lev Trotsky, wrote to Lenin at the same time describing how 'Anglo-French interventionists are now constructing their policy on an alliance of the border states and attach vast importance to a link-up between Denikin's troops and the Poles'. While certainly an ambition of more staunchly anti-communist officials in the British and French governments, like other Bolsheviks, Trotsky failed to appreciate the unbridgeable gap between the Whites and Poles.[21]

Polish and Latvian troops, commanded by General Edward Rydz-Śmigły, launched the anticipated assault on Latgale in January 1920, forcing the Red Army into retreat at the Battle of Dunaburg, seizing the city that would become Daugavpils in the new independent Republic of Latvia. In the aftermath of the battle, the Bolshevik leadership believed, rightly, that Piłsudski was planning a larger offensive and Chicherin presented this to Lenin as 'the most serious danger for the Soviet Republic'. He urged that nothing be done that might spark war.[22] The crux of the Bolsheviks' anxieties about an upcoming Polish offensive stemmed from the Soviet military's weak presence on the western front, the future theatre of operations north of the near-impassable Pripet marshes. Although total victory over Denikin's army was in sight by early 1920, this left numerous Red Army units in the south. Transferring north would take time and Soviet strength on the western front in January 1920 comprised just four infantry divisions and one cavalry brigade. Polish forces, by contrast, numbered approximately 300,000 soldiers by the end of 1919, with sizeable concentrations forming in Grodno and Wilno in the north, and Kamenets-Podol'sk in the southwest. Further reinforcements were expected.[23] Assessing this imbalance, the Soviet military leadership on the western front predicted that if the Poles launched an attack, they 'would reach Smolensk in a parade march'.[24] For the time being, and before the predicted Soviet reinforcements arrived in the first months of 1920, the peace offensive was therefore the key strategy. But with Poland in the position of strength, and the Bolsheviks almost universally mistrusted (Lenin would try to spread revolution to Poland by force just six months later), Chicherin's overtures were easily ignored. Moreover, antagonistic comments from the Bolshevik side worked to decay trust further. One week before the December 1919 Soviet peace offer was delivered, for instance, Trotsky boasted in an interview with *Internationale Communiste* that after Denikin had been defeated the Red Army would 'throw the full weight of our reserves onto the Polish front'. Even if just bravado, such comments undermined Chicherin's softer approach. In another hinderance, the French government – Poland's closet patron – cautioned the Poles against entering negotiations with the Bolsheviks and awarding them legitimacy.[25]

Taken together, with no response forthcoming to the December peace proposal and the Polish Army steadily advancing into the space vacated by Denikin's forces towards Soviet Ukraine, the Bolsheviks had little other choice but to send another note to the Polish government on 28 January 1920, which opened with the usual charges aimed at the Allied Powers: 'the supporters and agents of Churchill and Clémenceau, are straining all force at the moment to plunge Poland into an unreasonable, senseless and criminal war with Soviet Russia'. To assuage concerns of a hidden agenda, the note assured that the Red Army would not cross the front line and that there was no secret deal between Soviet Russia and Germany – a common point of rumour – or with any other power, that would threaten Polish independence or integrity.[26] The Soviet government then broadcast radio addresses to the peoples of the Allied Powers and Poland conveying the same message and calling upon the working classes to pressure their governments into abandoning 'reactionary imperialist' schemes. The Polish people, apparently, had nothing to fear from the Red Army and the Bolsheviks stressed their efforts to secure peace, underlining that communism would never be imposed from abroad by force.[27] These appeals, however, fell on deaf ears. The final calculation in Piłsudski's mind, as we shall see, proved that if military escalation was inevitable in 1920, it was in Poland's best interest to move quickly, rather than agree peace with an untrustworthy adversary that would not hold.[28]

The 'new campaign' against Soviet Russia

The Bolsheviks blamed the Allied Powers for coordinating a multi-pronged offensive against Soviet Russia from the very beginning of the wider civil war in 1918. This was not just rhetoric for propaganda purposes either. Writing to Lenin in August 1919, for instance, Stalin described how a 'single unified command' in the west was preparing operations against Soviet Russia from Riga, Warsaw and Kishinev.[29] In numerous Bolshevik forums across 1920, the Allied Powers were blamed for financing and steering the Polish war effort, representing the next phase in an ongoing anti-Soviet campaign.[30] It was true that Poland did not have complete freedom of action in these years. The Allied Powers exercised significant leverage through control of the post-war settlement and Britain, France and the United States, among others, had intervened in the civil war in support of the White armies to topple the Soviet government. The Bolsheviks never forgot the reality of foreign soldiers landing on Soviet territory. More directly, it was also true that French generals played a major role in organizing the new Polish Army.[31] For a political party already inclined to see the international order as rigged against them, the Allied intervention in the civil war resonated powerfully and fuelled a narrative that the revolution faced an existential threat from encircling capitalist powers, now manipulating border states like Poland into another war.

In truth, the reality of the Allied support given to their opponents was far away from this picture. It certainly lacked the careful coordination and unity that the Bolsheviks feared. In fact, by the end of 1919, the Allied Powers were preparing to abandon Denikin's army due to the high costs and poor results. French Prime Minister Georges Clémenceau now looked to use Poland, with Czechoslovakia and Romania, as *defensive* buffer states to stop the contagion of Bolshevism reaching western Europe; to create a 'barbed wire entanglement' and bulwark against Germany (but for Piłsudski would create an unsustainable position of 'neither war nor peace' on Poland's eastern border).[32] Significantly on 16 January 1920, the Allied Supreme Council then partly lifted the economic blockade of Soviet Russia that had been in place since 1918, signalling a shift in strategy. Rather than deploy military force or sponsor new interventions to reduce the threat of communism to Europe, a new approach sought to moderate the Soviet government through increased trade.[33] The blockade, after all, had hardly succeeded in saving Denikin's army. As British Prime Minister David Lloyd George, the architect of the policy, remarked to Parliament in February 1920: 'Commerce has a sobering influence in its operations [...] Trade, in my opinion, will bring an end to the ferocity, the rapine, and the crudities of Bolshevism surer than any method.'[34] By no means was Lloyd George's grasp of the nature of Bolshevism always well-assured, but he was right that post-war recovery and prosperity in Europe rested on access to Russian and Ukrainian agriculture.[35] At the very least, this required a stable trading relationship, even if the British wanted to avoid formally recognizing the legitimacy of the Soviet government.

While Lloyd George made steps towards the Bolsheviks, he took a sterner line with Poland, expressing on several occasions that its claims to territory in east central Europe were excessive, especially in areas not ethnographically Polish, such predominately Ukrainian, and oil-rich, eastern Galicia. 'Preposterous and not justifiable on any grounds', one internal British assessment noted. Lloyd George worried that unreasonable ambitions could spark new war in Europe and he was certain that Poland needed to compromise with its neighbouring states.[36] In late January 1920, as the Poles were weighing up how to respond to Chicherin's second offer for peace negotiations, Lloyd George told Polish foreign minister Patek plainly that Britain could not support a war.[37] During a conference of ministers in the same month, he doubted that the Bolsheviks even posed much of a danger, remarking that they had 'practically nothing to gain by over-running Poland, Germany, Hungary, Persia or Roumania, or even the Caucasus, except that they might gain control of the oil fields in the latter region'.[38] The Allied Supreme Council then adopted Lloyd George's position in a statement on 24 February that there would be no intervention to assist countries on the Soviet border unless 'Soviet Russia attacks them inside their own legitimate frontiers'.[39] And despite vocal Bolshevik protests to the contrary, only a small number of British arms were ever shipped to Poland in the first half of 1920, and done on the basis of pre-existing agreements or private contracts.[40] By contrast, with more riding on the post-war settlement in Europe being maintained, France delivered greater support and 80 million francs of military equipment was shipped to Poland in late February. New French premier, Alexandre Millerand, urged the Polish ambassador in France, Maurice Zamoyski, not to trust the Bolsheviks, and he told Patek that even peace might not fully eliminate the risk of a future Soviet attack (Millerand also made clear that the French would not try to halt any Polish assault).[41] Still, this was not a clear-cut message of support. Like his predecessor Clémenceau, Millerand, in the end, aligned with Lloyd George. There would be no encouragement of further fighting and certainly not for a pre-emptive Polish attack: a major blow for Piłsudski. Not only did the Allied Powers refuse to support a pre-emptive attack but even if peace was agreed, Poland would alone have to guarantee it, as the British and French would not enter the necessary diplomatic relations with a government they refused to recognize.[42]

On the one hand, the Bolsheviks relished the Allied Powers' change in strategy in early 1920 and the furore sparked in Poland. 'The news about the lifting of the blockade against Russia by the Entente came as a bolt from the blue in Warsaw […] the bourgeois press shrieked: how can it be that they force us to fight the Bolsheviks, while they wish to trade with them', the Bolsheviks' Polish Bureau recorded.[43] Chicherin's deputy in the Soviet foreign ministry (NKID), Maksim Litvinov, someone with more direct experience of British affairs than other Bolsheviks – and described by his superior as someone 'not by nature inclined towards optimism' – now saw a brighter future and believed that the blockade would soon be completely lifted and trade representatives permitted to travel to Britain.[44] Even so, this turn in the Bolsheviks' favour did nothing to eliminate deep concerns about an existential threat to Soviet Russia. In a speech on 24 January, for instance, Lenin remarked that while circumstances had improved with removal of the blockade, 'the bourgeoisie of the West will probably attempt to fight us again […] they are inciting the Polish whiteguards against us'.[45] Lenin made his thinking clear in public again in February with an address to the All-Russian Central Executive Committee, where he claimed Poland was being pushed into war and the situation had reached a 'very acute' stage. 'All the Entente states are crawling out of their skin to incite Poland into war with us', he remarked.[46] Chicherin also made a public declaration in February, broadly aimed at the working classes of Allied countries, and claimed that 'dark forces in Europe, these Clémenceaus, these Churchills, these Northcliffes, are diligently preparing a new attack on Soviet Russia'.[47] Again, while it is tempting to dismiss such comments as boilerplate rhetoric for public consumption, the same security concerns ran throughout the Bolsheviks' private communications. Although he was optimistic about future trade with Britain, Litvinov relayed to Chicherin just ten days after the blockade was partially lifted that the interventionist French Marshal Ferdinand Foch, who the year before had advocated using a coalition of border states against Soviet Russia to 'see the end of Bolshevism', was soon to arrive in Warsaw with other Russian anti-Soviet leaders to put together a force for an attack. Churchill and Foch were said to be working behind Lloyd George's back and even entertaining deploying German military forces against Soviet Russia.[48] Writing in private to Lenin at the end of January, Chicherin pointed to the same rising danger that 'interventionists, enemies of Soviet Russia, have concentrated attention on Poland as a weapon in the struggle against Bolshevism'.[49] Trotsky, too, warned Lenin of an 'imminent possibility of an attack by the Poles along the entire front'.[50]

That exaggerated security concerns like these remained potent in Bolshevik circles in the first months of 1920, despite the change in Allied strategy towards trade and away from intervention, was also, in part, because these contained more than a grain of truth. Advocates of intervention still held senior positions in the British and French governments and lobbied for military action against Soviet Russia on lines which resembled the Bolsheviks' worst-case-scenario: a broad-based anti-Soviet coalition. High-profile statesmen, like Churchill, British Secretary of State for War and Air, widely publicized his hostile views which the Bolsheviks could not help but notice.[51] Churchill was a vocal advocate of bringing Poland and other borders countries into an anti-Soviet coalition, to salvage Denikin's offensive and crush the 'Bolshevik peril' (however, even Churchill would start to feel pessimistic in early 1920 about whether an intervention could actually succeed as the White armies lost momentum).[52] Likewise, First Lord of the Admiralty, Walter Long, although a figure of declining influence, agreed with Churchill that 'overtures should be made to the Roumanians, Bulgarians, Serbians and others [...] in an offensive against the Bolshevists'. Others around the British War Office felt the same.[53] Moreover, on the Polish side in early 1920, Piłsudski had discussed creating 'a kind of League of Nations in the Near East of Europe for combatting the Bolsheviks' with the British ambassador to Poland, Sir Horace Rumbold. Patek, for a time at least, entertained the same proposal as Churchill: an alliance of anti-Soviet border countries under a 'great commander' like French Marshal Ferdinand Foch.[54] But while the French interventionists were stronger voices in military and diplomatic circles, their British counterparts struggled to gain support from government. Nevertheless, it did not take much to activate the Bolsheviks' deeply rooted conceptions of capitalist encirclement. This was a core preoccupation that magnified any evidence of anti-Soviet collaboration in the international order, even when official Allied policy was in retreat from intervention.

With tensions therefore still running high in upper party circles in early 1920, Chicherin's natural caution expressed itself once more and he urged Lenin that nothing be done to worsen Soviet-Polish relations and he seized upon anything potentially damaging. He was incensed, for instance, by inflammatory comments that surfaced from a member of the Ukrainian Revolutionary Committee, Vladimir Zatonskii, who, in a January press interview, suggested that a Soviet seizure of Right-bank Ukraine was a means 'to help Hungarian and German comrades finish off the Polish nobility'. This hardly helped efforts to convince Poland that the Bolsheviks had nothing but benign intentions. As Chicherin told Lenin, a declaration publicly recognizing Polish independence should be reissued and Russian and Ukrainian troops should not move beyond their current locations.[55] Similarly, on 24 February Chicherin again wrote to Lenin drawing attention to a recent press article from the party firebrand Grigory Zinoviev, Chairman of the Executive Committee of the Communist International, where he declared that independent Poland was attainable only through revolution. 'I will not say that this would be especially terrible', Chicherin noted, but at such a 'delicate diplomatic moment' it was not helpful for someone as high-profile as Zinoviev to be publicly linking 'the Polish question with calls for revolution'.[56] Chicherin made it clear to Lenin that if war erupted, given the importance of attracting support among the Polish working class, 'it is absolutely necessary that blame lies fully with the Polish government'.[57] There was little to suggest that Lenin was taking Chicherin's cautious approach on board, however. When he wrote to the Bolsheviks Ivar Smilga and Sergo Ordzhonikidze on the Caucasus front in late February about a 'desperate need of oil', Lenin called for a manifest to be presented to the local populations of Maykop and Grozny threatening to 'slaughter all of them' if oil wells were damaged or sabotaged. 'Poland is stepping up the pressure', he added.[58]

Beyond the strategy of the peace offensive towards Poland in early 1920, the Soviet military started preparing for military escalation and on 27 January, commander-in-chief of the Red Army, Sergei Kamenev, presented his plan to Trotsky. Because of ongoing engagements in the south and the Caucasus against the White forces, Kamenev did not propose a major assault. He sketched out instead a series of 'decisive and energetic strikes' to force Poland on the defensive. The projected start of this campaign was mid-to-late April in the direction of Minsk, when Kamenev judged Soviet strength on the western front to be at sufficient levels.[59] The Soviet military build-up began in earnest and a new southwestern front, below the Pripet Marshes, was formed from the existing southern front in January 1920 to guard against White and Polish attacks on Ukraine. In mid-February, Polish intelligence reported on the reinforcements arriving to the western front, by this point comprising 34,000 soldiers in Soviet infantry and cavalry units. Even so, progress was slow and Red Army troops proved difficult to spare. Head of the Bolshevik Polish Bureau, Stefan Bratman-Brodovskii, wrote to the central committee in mid-February to warn, like others before, that the Polish Army was in a position to reach Kiev and Smolensk and the Bolsheviks faced 'catastrophe in the case of a Polish attack'.[60] The Polish Bureau was wildly optimistic in other respects, however, when it described visible rising resistance among Polish workers to capitalist imperialism in the east, something which Soviet military success could only apparently encourage. In reality, such claims about the revolutionary potential of the Polish people in 1920 would prove entirely hollow.[61]

Exactly one month after Sergei Kamenev presented his strategic plan to Trotsky, Lenin ordered the revolutionary military council on the western front to prepare for war and called for a 'lightening transfer' of reinforcements. 'All the indications are that Poland will present us with absolutely impossible, even insolent conditions', he noted.[62] Another central strand of Kamenev's strategy had also emerged by this time: the linking of the western and southwestern fronts should future fighting move into Polish territory, creating a combined Soviet force to attack Warsaw. The Polish capital was a central objective early on, should circumstances turn in the Bolsheviks' favour.[63] Kamenev was optimistic, moreover, that the western front would prove to be the military theatre of least resistance and he described a 'number of indications' of apparent weakness among the assembled Polish forces. Yet the revolutionary military council on the southwestern front, commanded by Red Army officer and Stalin's ally, Aleksandr Egorov (and soon to include Stalin himself in May following transfer from the Caucasus), argued with Kamenev that it would be impossible to confine fighting to the western front and its leadership proposed a supporting strike from the southwest in the direction of Równe – Brest-Litovsk.[64] Several months later, at the climax of the Battle of Warsaw in August, Egorov and Stalin stuck to their plan and resisted Kamenev's strategy, a contributing factor in the disaster.

Although the Bolsheviks' attentions were focused on building up the western front in the first months of 1920, it was Ukraine, sitting on the secondary front in the southwest that would be centre of action in just two months' time from April. Vulnerability in the southwest had not been totally ignored in Moscow, especially as Kiev had only recently passed back under Soviet control. In February Chicherin called for more troops and supplies for the Ukrainian Bolsheviks but he stressed that they would have to defend themselves from Polish encroachment. He advised that Moscow create more formal distance with Soviet Ukraine as an independent republic, meaning any Polish attack would be seen, internationally, as an attack on a sovereign state and not against an appendage of Soviet Russia. (Similarly, proposed closer federation of Soviet Ukraine with Soviet Russia was postponed, though this stemmed also from Lenin's more conciliatory approach to managing local Ukrainian popular opinion).[65] The perceived danger from the Allied Powers to Ukraine loomed in these months. Head of the Soviet Ukrainian government, Kristian Rakovskii, warned Chicherin that foreign states could exploit poor relations between Ukraine and Poland to the point of war.[66] Yet when Piłsudski finally launched his attack on Soviet Ukraine in April, it was firmly in defiance of the British government, with only, at most, tacit French approval.

*

Fighting between the Red and Polish armies escalated again in early March 1920 when Polish forces commanded by Władysław Sikorski captured Mozyr', Kalinkovichi and Ovruch. The capture of Mozyr', located between Minsk and Kiev, was a significant victory and severed a vital railroad between the Soviet western and southwestern fronts. The Red Army launched an unsuccessful counterattack; momentum was firmly with the Poles.[67] In frustration, a close ally of Trotsky, Nikolai Muralov, serving on the revolutionary military council of the embattled 12th Red Army, sent a telegram to Kiev complaining about the 'harmful fiction' of Moscow's attempts to carry out negotiations with the Polish government in these circumstances, which had simply taken the opportunity to advance its forces. He pushed for resistance to be stepped up across the board.[68] Trotsky, for this part, interpreted the ongoing Polish assaults either as a means of strengthening a negotiating position or as a deliberate ploy to provoke the Bolsheviks into retaliation, gain public support and thereby 'create the political atmosphere for intervention in the grand manner'. The Bolsheviks, in short, needed better information and should avoid risky actions.[69] Nevertheless, with Soviet military strength limited on both fronts, the Bolsheviks had few options to choose from. No doubt to the further frustration of those like Muralov on the ground, Chicherin had little choice but to send another proposal for negotiations to Poland that stressed the usual lines that the Bolsheviks had only peaceful intentions and criticized a war 'disastrous for the interests of both nations'. A similar appeal followed to the Allied Powers, declaring readiness to enter negotiations with Poland.[70] But more visible signs of disagreement with the government's approach were appearing. Some Bolsheviks, like Chicherin's own deputy, Litvinov, and Trotsky's deputy, Efraim Sklianskii, warned that the latest Soviet peace offer was a sign of weakness. Sklianskii instead pushed for a mobilization campaign to both ready the Soviet people and discourage a Polish attack.[71]

The Polish government, by this time, had in fact drawn up peace conditions; however, these were never sent to the Bolsheviks as the Allied Powers rejected them almost immediately in March. Calling for an end to Soviet propaganda was one thing, but to demand that Soviet Russia return to the old 1772 borders, pay reparations, return property taken during the partitions and for national self-determination to shape control of territory in the borderlands was certain to wreck any negotiations. In a letter to Curzon, Rumbold, British ambassador to Poland, described the conditions as a 'gamble on the part of the Polish Government, which thinks that it stands to gain either way'.[72] But the nature of these demands, above all, revealed how peace talks were a low priority for Piłsudski. It seems likely that Piłsudski was honouring comments made to head of the French military mission in Poland, General Paul Henrys, when he described stretching out talks by pushing unacceptable demands until the Allied position became clearer (and presumably more to Poland's advantage). Foreign minister Patek, someone more supportive of negotiating with the Bolsheviks, tried to mount a defence of the Polish conditions as less onerous than the Allied conditions presented to Germany, but this was hardly reassuring.[73]

The Bolsheviks discovered the shape of the Polish demands from leaks to the foreign press, seemingly confirming Lenin's instincts that the Bolsheviks could only expect 'absolutely impossible, even arrogant conditions'.[74] Chicherin agreed: 'The Polish demands are clothed in such a crude form, which only does them damage [...] they are simply repeating the Brest [Litovsk] formula.' He advised ignoring them (in the end, the Bolsheviks offered no formal response).[75] Chicherin, however, offered a slightly more nuanced view of the relationship between the Allied Powers and Poland than sometimes seen from other senior Bolsheviks. For him, there was no point appealing to Poland's interests since its position was to try and 'blackmail the Entente on the basis of war against us'. This suggested he recognized that Poland exercised some leverage of its own, perhaps in threatening to launch war in circumstances not to the Allied Powers' choosing. Still, this did not change the perceived present danger and Chicherin more forthrightly argued it was necessary to prepare for a Polish attack, commenting to Lenin that he saw 'little chance of avoiding war' and that the Bolsheviks must be 'ready for the worst'; although he was optimistic that the Soviet peace offensive had proved to the Polish people they had nothing to fear from the Bolsheviks, despite the efforts of 'imperialists' to turn the mood against Soviet Russia.[76] The decision to not respond to the Polish conditions generated internal disagreement. Trotsky saw it as a mistake: silence would only encourage their enemies 'to think that we shall accede to their terms, and will make the Poles go further along a path which will inevitably end in war: in other words it is a provocation to war'. Sharing the view of Sklianskii and Litvinov, Trotsky argued that a firm response was essential for mobilizing Polish workers towards the Bolshevik cause, making it more difficult for Britain and France to push Poland into war. As he put it, 'It stands to reason that the final decision is in the hands of the Entente [...] But it is not true [...] that either the Entente or France can "make" Poland go to war. If the power of resistance of the Polish workers proves sufficient war will be frustrated.'[77] The Politburo seemingly agreed that mobilization was needed at home and abroad. Soon enough, the ongoing Soviet propaganda campaign was ratcheted upwards and significant spending devoted to explaining the 'true reasons' behind the war to the Soviet people and greater efforts made to influence Polish soldiers.[78]

Expecting war, the Soviet high command adopted an operational plan for an offensive in the west on 10 March 1920.[79] On the same day, Lenin telegrammed Polish Bolshevik and future member of the Polish Revolutionary Committee, Iosif Unshlikht, with a stark warning: 'The Poles, apparently, will fight. We are doing everything possible to strengthen defence. It is also necessary to intensify agitation in Polish.'[80] More confirmation came a few days later when Unshlikht and Iakov Doletskii, a member of the Bolsheviks' Polish Bureau, relayed the comments from the Polish Communist Party which was certain that Piłsudski and the Allied Powers were preparing a March or April assault. It reported that supplies, automobiles and weapons had been arriving from France for two weeks.[81] This fed neatly into Lenin's current preoccupations. Indeed, at this same time, he drew Trotsky's attention to information relayed by Chicherin, originally from the sympathetic British journalist Arthur Ransome, which claimed that 5000 French officers had arrived in Poland, including Marshal Foch.[82] Foreign assistance to Poland continued to loom large in Lenin's mind.

Preparations for war now continued apace. The Soviet military leadership and revolutionary military council on the western front were ordered to be ready with troops, and orders were given for the transfer of Semen Budennyi's elite 1st Cavalry Army to move to the southwestern front from the Caucasus.[83] Lenin urged that the maximum number of troops travel to the western front, the anticipated centre of action.[84] But the Red Army's weaknesses were impossible to avoid. In mid-April, the Politburo ordered that a 'significant number' of communists also travel to the western front to make sure an influx of 'raw recruits' – typically peasants who had evaded earlier drafts – were sufficiently ideologically prepared (Trotsky would later lament the poor results and the 'extremely great danger' on the front, alongside numerous other defects).[85] All the while, Lenin indulged in revolutionary optimism, evidently less cautious than other Bolsheviks about what the ragtag Red Army could achieve. Fantasizing about exporting revolution to Europe, in a telegram to Stalin on 17 March he exclaimed excitedly:

> We have just received news from Germany that fighting is under way in Berlin and that the Spartacists have seized a part of the city. It is not known who will win, but for us it is essential to speed up maximally the capture of the Crimea in order to have entirely free hands, as a civil war in Germany may force us to move west to aid the Communists.[86]

Although Lenin mistook the right-wing Kapp Putsch for a left-wing Spartacist revolt, his optimism about pushing west to further the cause of communism – and in doing so fight *through* Poland – was unmistakeable.

Lenin also primed the wider Bolshevik Party politically for the coming struggle at the ninth party congress held between late March and early April, another moment when the enemy was firmly identified as Poland and its capitalist backers. Lenin warned that Poland was benefitting significantly from outside assistance and 'receiving so many trainloads of artillery and promises of help in everything, if only she would continue the war with Russia'. The French were playing a major role and 'most zealous in egging Poland on'. Yet Lenin was most divorced from reality when he spoke about a growing revolutionary movement in Poland. 'The temper of the workers is rising more and more', he proclaimed. 'The Polish bourgeoisie and landowners are themselves beginning to wonder whether it is not too late, whether there will not be a Soviet Republic in Poland before the government acts either for war or for peace.' Apparently, it was precisely because Poland was in such 'desperate straits' that war was such a danger.[87] Lenin delivered a grave warning that the party 'must be prepared for anything', yet outside of the congress the Red Army was far from ready. The disparity with the amassing Polish Army was becoming more obvious, and especially in the southwest where the main attack would finally come. Just prior to the ninth party congress, Muralov reported again from the southwestern front, warning that the Poles had been able to concentrate a superior force because the Bolsheviks, given their weaker position, had ruled that the Red Army should not cross the front line. Soviet losses, Muralov complained, were not being reinforced.[88] From the end of March, the Poles made further advances east and on 8 April, Kamenev told the commands of western front and southwestern front to expect a larger attack in the coming days.[89]

In the meantime, on 27 March, the Polish government finally responded to Chicherin's offer of peace negotiations. But having declined to send a peace proposal of their own, and following internal division over the hard-line Polish conditions and the adverse reaction from the Allied Powers, this was only to suggest that negotiations take place from 10 April in the town of Borisov, 50 miles outside of Minsk, just inside Polish lines.[90] Seeing as Borisov was under Polish control, the Bolsheviks, in effect, would be negotiating in the presence of Polish troops. The proposal was even less attractive for the Bolsheviks as Piłsudski had insisted on a local ceasefire confined to the town, rather than a wider armistice. The latter, of course, would give the Red Army more time to prepare; on the other hand, if negotiations ever materialized, a local ceasefire would put the Poles in a stronger position having already pushed forward their offensive.[91] For the Bolsheviks, the choice of Borisov posed an additional problem as the town was close to where they intended to amass Soviet troops on the western front, quite possibly also part of Piłsudski's calculations.[92] For these reasons, Chicherin, unsurprisingly, rejected the proposal outright and the following day pressed Patek once more for a general armistice and for negotiations in a neutral country, or at least somewhere away from the front lines.[93] In a message to Lenin on 2 April, he argued that the Poles were seeking to 'blow up' the negotiations in public view and righty assessed that Piłsudski's choice of a local ceasefire was designed to deny the Bolsheviks breathing space. Indicative of the febrile atmosphere, Trotsky believed the Bolsheviks should accept Borisov as a venue, as the Poles might use a rejection itself as provocation for war. Lenin, in the end, agreed with Chicherin.[94] However, Patek in turn swiftly rejected Chicherin's push for a general armistice and for a change of location.[95] Chicherin then attempted to build pressure by accusing the Polish government of effectively giving an ultimatum and he sought mediation from the Allied Powers, but neither Britain nor France took up the offer. For its part, the Polish government suspected, not unreasonably, that the Bolsheviks were playing for time in order to strengthen their position on the western front. The back-and-forth dispute continued into late April.[96]

With war looming, the Bolshevik leadership continued to speculate about the mood among the Polish people. At the end of March, Lenin received information from the Polish Communist Party feeding a picture of anti-war sentiments building among the Polish people and even a growing revolutionary movement among the working class.[97] Later, on 22 April, Chicherin relayed to Lenin and Trotsky another report from the Polish Bureau, drawing attention to its similarly optimistic conclusions, namely, that the Soviet peace offensive was countering an impression that the Bolsheviks had aggressive designs. The Polish people were apparently looking sceptically on their government's own defensive slogans and these moods needed further cultivation for revolution to be achieved. While these judgements were generally rose-tinted, the Polish Bureau did make one prescient point: a major Soviet attack on Poland was likely to 'poison a significant part of the working class with defencism' and produce a wave of nationalist resistance. Lenin and Trotsky agreed with this assessment.[98] Seemingly wary of inadvertently stoking Polish nationalism, Lenin wrote to the party's secretariat in April with a directive that all press articles on Poland should be carefully scrutinized by managing editors so as to not 'fall into chauvinism' and how these should differentiate 'the Pans and capitalists from the workers and peasants of Poland'.[99] Stalin, never truly enthusiastic about a major Soviet offensive against Poland, made his doubts clear in a *Pravda* article published in May, criticizing the notion that class consciousness among Polish workers would become a stronger force than nationalism.[100] As we shall see, a few months later when the Red Army was finally in the position of advantage on the western front, a rush of revolutionary enthusiasm encouraged Lenin to abandon such cautions.

Another preparation for the upcoming war, on the diplomatic front, was efforts by both sides to secure allies, or at least neutrality, from neighbouring countries. The NKID secured peace with Estonia in early 1920 and Chicherin later suggested to Lenin in April that the Bolsheviks should give Lithuania, with whom diplomatic negotiations had provisionally been agreed, 'several millions of gold' to make sure that in the event of escalation of war with Poland it remained a reliable ally in the rear.[101] Elsewhere, the Bolsheviks failed to achieve much with Romania. Relations were already difficult because of the Bolsheviks' refusal to recognize the latter's control over Bessarabia and while there was some contact in February 1920, the Romanians played for time, hoping for a clearer Allied position on Soviet Russia to emerge.[102] For his part, Piłsudski made similar efforts, and in March convened a Warsaw conference with Romanian, Finnish and Latvian representatives to secure their cooperation in the war. Very little came of this. The Latvian government entered negotiations with the Bolsheviks, eventually agreeing to neutrality (and not before a difficult moment when the Bolsheviks made claims about a secret Polish-Latvian military convention in May, a suspicion with some truth).[103] In this way, by late spring, the Bolsheviks had managed to reduce the danger of concurrent assaults on the western front, but it was also true that they did not view such treaties as an iron-cast guarantee against the deep and malign influence of the capitalist powers.

Amid this flurry of activity, Piłsudski managed to secure one ally, however. On 21 April, he struck an agreement, the Treaty of Warsaw, with the exiled Ukrainian nationalist, Symon Petliura, who had resided in Poland since September 1919 after accepting an armistice with the Poles following complex fighting in Ukraine between nationalists, Polish and Soviet forces.[104] Petliura's partisan army resisted the Soviet authorities in Ukraine thereafter and the Treaty of Warsaw recognized him as the rightful leader of a sovereign Ukrainian People's Republic. In return, Petliura agreed to support a Polish military offensive against Soviet Ukraine under Polish command. The two sides provisionally agreed on a division of borderland territories with Poland gaining sovereignty over eastern Galicia and western Volhynia, while a free, independent, Ukraine would receive territories once belonging to the pre-partition eighteenth-century Polish commonwealth.[105] Petliura's military strength was comparatively small but, in spring 1920, the Red Army was hardly in a position to deal with multiple opponents.[106] Perhaps more significant, however, was the connection this alliance later formed in the Bolsheviks' minds after the Soviet-Polish war, between Polish subversion and Ukrainian nationalism, later to have far-reaching consequences.[107]

By this time, Piłsudski was no less convinced the Bolsheviks were planning to launch an attack of their own and he still saw a pre-emptive strike as essential. His plan, put into motion on 25 April, envisaged a Polish attack in the southwest to first seize Soviet Ukraine, and only after turn northwards towards the western front. Negotiations with the Bolsheviks could then be opened, but the Poles would have already gained significant advantages. Such a strike in the southwest had been central to Polish military planning from the end of 1919, although the Bolsheviks consistently failed to appreciate this, drawing their attentions instead to the western front.[108] Months before, in December 1919, Piłsudski discussed an attack on Ukraine to take place in April or May with Rumbold and the British High Commissar in South Russia, Sir Halford Mackinder.[109] Piłsudski several times spoke openly about the deficiencies in the Red Army. He calculated that the

Polish Army was not only better equipped for a spring campaign (especially after arms purchases from France), but that the Red Army would be exhausted after fighting the White armies through a harsh winter.[110] By April 1920, the plan had not fundamentally changed.

The spring offensive

Thinly dispersed Red Army forces on the southwestern front rapidly collapsed as ten divisions (nine Polish and one Ukrainian) pushed towards Zhitomir and Berdichev in late April. Exploiting the element of surprise and making good pace – covering 80 kilometres in just two days – Kiev was firmly in sight as the Red Army rapidly retreated beyond the Dnieper River. Polish cavalry, operating in the rear, seized vital rail and road junctions at Korosten, Zhitomir and Koziatyn.[111] Superiority in numbers made every difference in these early days. The Polish forces comprised three armies, with ten divisions, faced only the 12th and 14th Red Armies with seven divisions.[112] Making matters worse, communication between the two Red Armies was severed during the Polish attack and two Soviet Galician brigades defected after killing their political commissars.[113] On the first day of Piłsudski's offensive, the revolutionary military council of the 12th Red Army described a disastrous scene to the central committee. Hungry and poorly armed Soviet troops were 'melting from day to day'; some regiments were left with just fifteen to thirty soldiers. It had also proved impossible for Soviet officers to mobilize local Ukrainians who, after receiving weapons, formed some of the numerous partisan bands causing trouble in the Soviet rear. The revolutionary military council requested urgent reinforcements and estimated their forces could hold out for just ten days.[114] From Khar'kov, Kristian Rakovskii and Ian Berzin, the latter the future head of Soviet military intelligence, wrote to Trotsky describing the Soviet retreat and a 'catastrophic' situation on the southwestern front. Calling for reinforcements, they pressed Trotsky to convince Kamenev to divert strength from the western front, now that the southwest was unexpectedly bearing the brunt of the Polish attack. Trotsky recognized the seriousness of the situation, and in addition to a military response, he pushed the party leadership to adopt other 'drastic measures' and send a 'very significant' number of reliable political workers to Ukraine to help bring order on the ground.[115]

Temporary relief came to the embattled Soviet forces when Piłsudski halted his offensive, but this was only to prepare for the seizure of Kiev.[116] Despite efforts by the Soviet high command to transfer reinforcements, the Bolshevik leadership knew the city could not be defended. On 6 May the 12th Red Army withdrew, saving itself from destruction. As one historian notes, Moscow was likely cutting its losses and preparing to use the defeat to mobilize the Soviet people behind the wider war effort.[117] With the Red Army evacuated, the Poles easily took Kiev on 7 May, halting once again to transfer divisions for engagements further north.[118] The loss of Kiev was a disaster in many respects. Not only had Piłsudski captured the symbolic city, but in doing so, his forces gained new stocks of war materiel and had taken over

30,000 prisoners of war (although the victory left them potentially overstretched).[119] Furthermore, the hopes kindled among the Bolsheviks about rising support for peace among Polish workers were quickly dashed when Piłsudski's popularity surged at home to an all-time high.[120] 'The Polish government skilfully exploits its military advantage, inflating its cheap victories to unprecedented proportions', remarked the Polish communists.[121]

Lenin initially urged calm after the attack and expressed optimism that the Poles had taken a step too far and revolution in Poland would nevertheless eventually come from the escalating war. But the attack forced an unavoidable shift in the Bolshevik leadership's strategic priorities. On 28 April, Chicherin sent a message to London, to George Curzon, finally agreeing to seek peace with the last-remaining White forces amassed on the Crimean Peninsula, now under the leadership of General Petr Wrangel. Up to this point, Curzon had pushed for an armistice and negotiated peace settlement between the Bolsheviks and the Whites without success, but with greater Red Army strength needed against the Poles, Chicherin agreed to guarantee the safety of Wrangel's officers if they chose to stay in Soviet Russia or to facilitate passage abroad.[122] On the same day, the central committee approved the Soviet field staff's campaign plan, to begin on 14 May. This sketched out a counterattack on the western front in Belarus and North Polesie, with Red Army strength in the southwest providing crucial support. The young and ambitious officer, Mikhail Tukhachevskii, experienced in coordinating offensive operations, took control of the western front the following day, over the 4th, 15th and 16th Red Armies, comprising 90,000 men.[123] The Politburo ordered agitation and propaganda increased among the assembled troops.[124] Taken together, Kamenev was confident that the Red Army could halt the Polish advance and he saw special importance in a strike by Budennyi's 1st Cavalry Army against the right flank of the Polish-Ukrainian front, creating a breakthrough towards Równe and forcing the Poles to dangerously overextend themselves.[125] In order to cause more problems for the enemy, Trotsky supported Tukhachevskii's proposal of encouraging Lithuania to now seize Wilno to tie up the Polish Army and ease pressure on the Red Army's right flank. The Politburo agreed.[126]

Although Soviet strategy was evolving, there was no change to how the Bolsheviks explained the war in public after the loss of Kiev. Lenin vocally denounced the Allied Powers for the Polish attack. French imperialism had 'gained the upper hand in Poland's government circles', he remarked in a speech at the end of April. 'Poland is obviously getting all her military support from France, Britain, and the entire Entente.' The attack on Ukraine was a 'relic of the old plan that once united the entire international bourgeoisie'. Reflecting Lenin's optimism about the ripening potential for revolution in Europe, the capitalist powers had apparently instigated the war to 'deepen the gulf' between Soviet Russia and the revolutionary German proletariat.[127] Trotsky described the military escalation in similar terms. In theses published through the Revolutionary Military Council of the Republic at the end of April, he accused the capitalist powers of sponsoring 'new military adventures against Soviet Russia' in a quest for raw materials, to crush the successful 'foundations of the socialist economy' and curtail 'the stormy growth of proletarian revolution in Germany'. Like the other border countries, Poland had 'no independent policy of its own' and Trotsky optimistically reiterated that the war would only encourage the Polish working class to rise in revolution.[128] He incorrectly claimed shortly after, moreover, that Piłsudski's next targets were Khar'kov and Moscow.[129]

Beyond the public eye, this same narrative appeared in senior Bolsheviks' private correspondence amid the war in the southwest. When Stalin wrote to Trotsky in May to pour water over his suggestion that military alliances be forged with Latvia and Lithuania to support a military operation on the western front, not only did he argue that both countries believed the Bolsheviks were going to lose the war but noted how the 'Entente's hypnosis' remained 'extraordinarily strong'.[130] It was also true, however, that there was a correlation between the proximity of a source to Polish affairs and the sometimes-more nuanced picture produced. When Chicherin wrote to Lenin on 3 May, relaying the opinion of a frequent source on Polish affairs, the Polish communist Paweł Łapiński, the latter drew a different picture of relations between Poland and the Allied Powers. Łapiński detailed that the Allied Powers did not fully grasp the significance of Piłsudski's attack on Ukraine nor his ambitions in the east, which the Bolsheviks understood as going beyond the 1772 borders and would see all of Ukraine – and the entire of South Russia – turned into Polish colonies. Moreover, Łapiński pointed out, and as Chicherin well recognized, Piłsudski had started the campaign against the will of the Polish National Democrats, the influential political movement more closely aligned with the Allied Powers. Evidently taking some of this on board, Chicherin wanted Lenin's agreement to direct a joint protest note with Soviet Ukraine to Britain and France, covering Łapiński's points, to give a 'simple explanation of the facts'. Ultimately, this was still to lay blame with the Allied Powers for Piłsudski's offensive, even if they did not necessarily understand what forces had been unleashed.[131] Indeed, in another report from mid-May, Chicherin described how the Polish attack would have been impossible without outside financial and military support, although he recognized that there were differences in approach between the Allied Powers, not always clear to the outside world. Nevertheless, British and French responsibility was still collective and Chicherin amplified the conspiracies running through the party. 'Clearly, the Polish venture is a general attempt at intervention. The Entente is trying to disrupt our economic recovery. They hope at least to cut us off from the south, doom us to another season of military tension and bring us to ruin.' The French, moreover, Chicherin noted, were 'actively participating' and deploying instructors on the ground, attempting to strengthen their position in the east by turning Ukraine into a Polish protectorate. On Britain, Chicherin described a hostile change in tone, its government now evasive on the prospect of future trade with Soviet Russia and, in his view, looking to avoid a general agreement. If the French benefitted in the east from the Polish attack, moreover, Chicherin suspected the British might launch a 'parallel action, possibly in the north, possibly in the Black Sea, to compensate itself'.[132] Few escaped Chicherin's eye and Italy and Finland came under fire for playing roles in the 'new attempt at intervention'.[133] Despite the nuance therefore sometimes seen in private, and especially from sources away from Moscow, the core views of Soviet Russia's chief diplomat remained unchanged: the Allied Powers were as guilty as Poland for unleashing war.

In truth, Lloyd George was aghast at the Polish attack on Ukraine and had no intention of assisting Piłsudski or endorsing the more supportive French position. 'There are two nations in Europe who have gone rather mad, the French and the Poles [...] The Poles are inclined to be arrogant and they will have to take care that they don't get their heads punched.'[134] The supply of British rifles and artillery to the Polish Army on pre-existing contracts was unfortunately timed in this sense for the impression created. London dockworkers, acting with the Hands Off Russia! campaign, refused to load munitions directed to Poland (though in May, the British government managed to block Polish efforts to purchase 300,000 surplus Mauser rifles from Germany).[135] In another incident, King George V's telegram to Piłsudski congratulating him on the rebirth of Poland, sent on 3 May, a Polish public holiday, did nothing but aggravate the Bolsheviks' suspicions, even though it had been prepared prior to the Kiev offensive. In a public statement, the NKID described the King's message as 'clear evidence of the common views that exist between the governments of the Entente and the authors of the Polish offensive'.[136] Indeed, in a private message to Chicherin, referring to the King's telegram, Litvinov wrote of an 'international plot against Soviet Russia', originating in London and Paris, seeking to embroil the border states in war. 'It is possible that Lloyd George supports more peaceful methods of strangulation', Litvinov remarked, 'but he is powerless in the hands of the conservatives'.[137]

France, while more sympathetic to the Polish position, like Britain, did not provide much tangible support in practice during the spring offensive. The French military mission in Poland was involved in the planning of the Ukraine operation for sure, and the French government approved supplies to the Polish Army, totalling half of its rifles and machine guns, and much of the artillery. Alexandre Millerand's policy before the April offensive had been to discourage Poland from making war, but also not enter peace talks with the distrusted Bolsheviks either. This was an unsustainable position for Piłsudski to maintain in the long-term. It was 'impossible [...] to retain his army permanently on the Beresina [sic]', as he put it to Mackinder in January.[138] Yet more definitive French warnings to not attack were delivered only after the offensive in Ukraine began in April, suggesting that Millerand was never too inclined to rein in Piłsudski.[139] In any case, this was still some distance away from the presentation of France inside Bolshevik circles as a chief architect of the war.

*

The Soviet counteroffensive, as drawn up by the Soviet field staff, launched in Belarus on time on 14 May with Tukhachevskii taking command. The Poles expected the attack, yet it arrived sooner than anticipated. With Polish forces still concentrated in Ukraine and Soviet strength reinforced on the western front, Tukhachevskii was able to push the Poles back 80 kilometres as the Red Army advanced towards Minsk.[140] But while Soviet forces crossed the western bank of the

Berezina River one week later, they lacked the numbers to exploit their victories and then faced renewed Polish resistance from early June.[141] 'The situation on the Western Front is worse than Tukhachevsky or *Glavkom* think', Lenin wrote to Stalin.[142] Indeed, the Poles managed to recover much of their lost territory on the western front a couple of weeks later.[143] These difficulties did not come as a total shock to the Bolshevik leadership, still keenly aware of persisting weaknesses in Soviet military strength. Trotsky had few illusions that the war was going to be anything but challenging.[144] In the weeks before the Soviet counteroffensive, he described 'extraordinary paucity in man-power and resources' on the western front. And in view of the large number of peasants serving in the Red Army, who Trotsky described as former deserters, he called for an influx of Bolshevik workers and a propaganda offensive to 'shake and enliven' the inert front in anticipation of a protracted struggle.[145]

A second Soviet counterattack came in Ukraine, intended to destroy the Polish forces around Kiev headed by General Rydz-Śmigły. Here the 12th and 14th Red Armies, and the so-called Fastov army group, were to advance on Kiev and the 1st Cavalry Army, which had arrived in the southwest on 25 May, would operate in the Polish rear. However, facing stubborn resistance and the effective use of trenches, it took several attempts before Budennyi's 16,000-strong cavalry managed to break through further south and loop back around to destroy the Polish rear. An imbalance in strength between the Soviet and Polish armies remained clear in the southwest. In a report to Lenin from 17 May on the recent disaster in Ukraine, Muralov noted how the Poles had the superior numbers, military equipment, and provisions. Moreover, the Polish troops were motivated, he said, by a strong sense of nationalism. By contrast, Red Army soldiers were poorly equipped, suffering with lice and political instruction on the ground was often dysfunctional.[146] Trotsky also expressed concerns about the southwestern front to Lenin on 20 May and urged that Stalin be sent to oversee its improvement.[147] When the latter arrived at Kremenchuk, Stalin had gloomy news, describing Red Army troops as 'tired [...] and not always well-armed'. In order to avoid defeat, he wanted additional troops and a minimum of two infantry divisions.[148] However, in an early sign of competition for resources between the fronts, Trotsky refused to send the divisions and cited the complications in the west (Trotsky had made clear to Tukhachevskii that he saw special importance in the western front compared to others).[149] Stalin continued to press for reinforcements, arguing that weaknesses in Soviet infantry in the southwest meant it would be impossible to take Brest-Litovsk. He also pressed for a resolution to the 'Crimean question' to 'untie our hands' and release further reinforcements, by either coming to a truce with Wrangel or crushing his army.[150] Despite the problems that dogged the southwest, Budennyi's cavalry finally broke through the frontline on 5 June, capturing Zhitomir on 7 June, and Kiev five days after. However, as true elsewhere, Soviet forces struggled to sustain their victories and the cavalry was soon forced to withdraw.[151] Steady advances in the south combined with effective attacks by Budennyi's cavalry worked to steadily push the Poles westward; nevertheless, the Red Army lacked the strength to destroy its opponent.[152]

By this time, the war had almost totally consumed the Bolsheviks' attentions and the Politburo officially raised its priority over the conflict with Wrangel on 25 May (Stalin, however, continued to push for a solution to the Wrangel danger in the south). Supporting this wider shift towards the western front, the centrally coordinated propaganda drive was ratcheted up once again. The central committee declared that the Polish war was 'not just a partial task of the western front, but the central task for all workers and peasants of Russia'. Writing to the head of the council of defence, to all people's commissars and party committees, the central committee called for communists to be mobilized and for clearer propaganda to explain the danger to the Soviet people, and the need for 'heroic sacrifices'. It drew attention to the international scale of the enemies arrayed against Soviet Russia, pointing to secret transfers of French officers, supplies and even colonial troops through the German-Polish border.[153] Trotsky pushed for any such intelligence to be published in the Russian and foreign presses (a later Soviet note sent to Britain, France, Italy and America made accusations about French officers working in the Polish Army 'even in high positions', contrary to French denials).[154] The Soviet press, moreover, was instructed to 'not only [write] about our victories, soothing the masses, but about the enormous danger which threatens the country'.[155] Indeed, when the town of Borisov, the proposed site of peace negotiations one month before, was taken by the 16th Red Army on 25 May, it became a symbol of an increasingly destructive war. Three days later, the Poles launched an artillery assault, using chemical and incendiary weapons. Half the town caught fire and over 500 civilian deaths were recorded. Polish troops then set fire to the rest of Borisov in another artillery barrage, according to a Soviet report.[156] Immediately, Trotsky telegrammed Lenin and Chicherin about the need to make use of the burning of Borisov in propaganda.[157] The same applied to destruction in Kiev when retreating Polish soldiers destroyed passenger, freight, water and electric power stations. Trotsky was clear that France and Britain ultimately should take responsibility and Soviet diplomats should 'do all they can to ensure the most extensive use of the base outrages committed by the Polish authorities, placing direct responsibility for them on the British and French Governments. The aqueduct was blown up with French dynamite, the Cathedral with British guncotton, and so on.'[158] The Politburo had already ordered that seized British and French goods be used extensively in propaganda. In Chicherin's view, 'all of Lloyd's George's statements need to be examined in light of the explosions in Kiev and the Borisov fire'.[159] More dramatically, as Trotsky put it to editors at the Russian Telegraph Agency on 9 June, the ongoing conflicts, whether in Kiev or Zhitomir, were 'all only separate episodes of that gigantic struggle for life or death, which we and the Entente are involved in on the western front'.[160]

In a similar way, and with significance for future years, Stalin articulated his theory of the war in an extensive article published across two editions of *Pravda* at the end of May. Here he reiterated that the Allied Powers were coordinating the widespread anti-Bolshevik crusade and that the conflict with Poland was, in reality, a 'third campaign' against Soviet Russia, following the previously attempted, and failed, interventions by Kolchak and Denikin. 'The chief point is that without the Entente's support Poland could not have organized her attack on Russia, that France in the first place, and also Britain and America, are doing all they can to support Poland's offensive with arms, equipment, money and instructors.' Also significant, and foreshadowing the Soviet defeat outside Warsaw just a few months later, Stalin noted that the Poles' key strength was national unity. 'If the Polish forces were operating in Poland's own territory, it would undoubtedly be difficult to fight against them.'[161]

When Wrangel then, on his own volition and to British fury, launched a new assault from Crimea on 6 June, taking control of northern Taurida in southern Ukraine by the end of the month, this only further confirmed the Bolsheviks' vision of the war. The forces arrayed against them seemed ever-more united. A Politburo decree a couple of days before had already made inaccurate claims about a secret military agreement between Germany and Poland, and Polish collaboration with Wrangel. In mid-June Stalin even discussed with Kristian Rakovskii arresting the American Red Cross as an 'espionage organization' working for Poland.[162] Likewise, in a message to the revolutionary military council of the 1st Cavalry Army, Stalin called for the arrests of representatives of foreign military missions and European Red Cross organizations, as these were apparently the *de facto* leaders of the Polish forces and centres of espionage.[163] Trotsky, too, had sent a telegram to the Politburo drawing attention to information received from Leonid Krasin, the Soviet People's Commissar of Trade and Industry currently in London, suggesting an even wider attack was in preparation. Britain was apparently pressuring Finland, Latvia, Romania and other states into the military intervention. France, according to Krasin, was also separately pushing Romania into war (Trotsky had already warned Lenin about a supposedly secret Polish-Romanian agreement, and he pushed for a peace proposal sent to Romania, 'analogous to our February proposal to the Polish government').[164] Despite these multifaceted perceived dangers, however, Trotsky still saw a path to improving the Bolsheviks' position. Not only should they make stronger appeals to British popular opinion, but Trotsky underlined that the Bolsheviks should do what they could to encourage political moderates, non-interventionists, in the British government and avoid further antagonizing them with subversive Soviet operations in Asia and the Middle East. Lenin disagreed, seeing instead a single undeviating hostile anti-Soviet line running through British foreign policy.[165]

*

The opportunity to examine British hostility first-hand had already appeared after a Soviet trade delegation led by Leonid Krasin arrived in Britain in May for negotiations. Lloyd George, as we know, sought to stabilize trade relations with Soviet Russia to weaken the potency and threat of Bolshevism. In line with these priorities, at the first meeting with Krasin and his colleague, Nikolai Klyshko, Lloyd George was clear that Britain wished to resume trading relations, although diplomatic recognition of Soviet Russia was ruled out, something depending on, not least, the Bolsheviks' recognition of pre-revolutionary Russian debts. For Krasin, however, the key question was whether the two countries were in a position of 'war or peace'. This would prove a point of fundamental disagreement. Indeed, as part of wide-ranging discussions covering Soviet propaganda in the east of the British empire, the fate of remaining White forces under Wrangel and Russia's pre-revolutionary debts, the Soviet-Polish war was a central issue. Krasin made plain the position of the Soviet government that the Polish attack on Ukraine could not have occurred without Allied assistance, something Lloyd George entirely rejected. Krasin went on to claim that the Bolsheviks had only peaceful intentions towards Poland and that its priority was improving a trading relationship, itself hindered by the war. Lloyd George argued in reply that if the British government was giving assistance to the Poles, he would never have met with Krasin, and it would be dishonest to negotiate about future trade. He also pointed out that he told Patek back in January that the British government would not provide military support to Poland unless it was first attacked. Less convincingly, Lloyd George argued that this was the same position held by other powers – including France – but he was right that the Allied Supreme Council had not discussed assisting Poland at its recent San Remo conference.[166] Despite these differences, Krasin understood that Lloyd George wanted to change Britain's relationship with Soviet Russia. Writing to Lenin and Chicherin on 1 June, he described how the prime minister was 'ready to take serious steps in the direction of a *rapprochement* with us'.[167]

Moscow disagreed with Krasin's optimism. On the one hand, Lenin wanted to press the Bolsheviks' recent advantage over Poland following the Soviet counteroffensive. Chicherin wrote to Krasin again reiterating that Soviet policy with Britain remained the complete removal of the blockade and reconciliation, and due to the 'certainty of our victory over the Poles', these concessions were within the Bolsheviks' grasp. Krasin was ordered to take a firm line. The Bolsheviks should 'not be in a position of petitioners', Chicherin noted, 'from whom everything is demanded and who are not able to even put questions to the other side'. There would be no 'kowtowing and perpetual concessions' to the Allied Powers.[168] On the other hand, deeply rooted mistrust towards the British government also undermined the negotiating effort, something made worse by the events of the war. When Budennyi's cavalry carried out a successful operation on the southwestern front in early June and discovered five wagons of British weapons among the seized goods, in another note to the Allied Powers Chicherin criticized the 'financial, military and technical aid rendered by the Entente governments to the Polish government'.[169] But it was Wrangel's resumed offensive in June from Crimea, something the Bolsheviks were certain the British were responsible for, which soured the mood significantly. Chicherin relayed to Krasin a strongly worded message from Lenin after Wrangel's attack began, in which the party leader vented his fury: 'That scoundrel Lloyd George is deceiving you shamelessly; don't believe one word he says and deceive him three times over.'[170] Stalin, likewise, wrote to Lenin remarking that Chicherin 'will be glad of Wrangel's offensive because this gives him the opportunity and right to scold Curzon as a dishonest politician. It would be good, in a special note, to underline not only Curzon's insincerity, but also his powerlessness to keep his client Wrangel in his hands. If there is opportunity to humiliate England, why not do this.'[171] Like others, Chicherin saw the negotiations in London now in a different light and writing to Litvinov, accused the British of 'lulling us with conversations between Lloyd George and Krasin and conciliatory messages in the press' while Wrangel's army was being reorganized.[172]

The reality was very different and the British government, for several months, had ceased supplying coal and oil to Wrangel and blocked his efforts to purchase military supplies. In the end, and in a later note, Chicherin welcomed the British denial of involvement in Wrangel's new assault, but for him, this did not change the fact that this happened under British patronage, using supplied weapons, ammunition and coal. He now asked what the British intended to do about Wrangel if they were not involved in his fresh attack, as claimed (the actual result was a complete severing of relations between the British and Wrangel's army).[173] His view of the British government's actions much the same, Chicherin later remarked on 18 June in a telegram to Krasin that its policy 'strives to deceive us by alleged negotiations, eggs on Poland, at the same time declaring that she has nothing to do with them'.[174]

At the end of June, Krasin put forward Chicherin's proposal to the British government that the cessation of Soviet propaganda and the settlement of pre-revolutionary Russian debts could only occur if a formal peace treaty was agreed with the Allied Powers, including full recognition of Soviet Russia. Trade could be resumed in the meantime until a future peace conference, where Soviet Russia would receive proper recognition, could decide these outstanding issues. The British wanted the Bolsheviks to make concessions first, however, and in memorandum sent in reply on 1 July described a 'sincere desire to end the isolation of Russia from the Western World' and for trade to be resumed, but Soviet propaganda in the east of the British empire had to end and British prisoners in Soviet Russia immediately released. If no reply was received in one week, negotiations would be curtailed.[175] Chicherin revealed to Krasin shortly after that the Bolsheviks, in fact, had little intention of making serious concessions, certainly not on pre-revolutionary debts, and that they were encouraged by the British Labour Party's position that Russian debts should not stand in the way of the resumption of trade.[176] All of this created an impossible situation for Lloyd George. His strategy had been to moderate the Bolsheviks through the promise of trade, perhaps leading to a more stable peace settlement, but they had rejected the key preconditions, seeking formal recognition at the outset. And Lloyd George could not recognize or accept trading with the Bolsheviks at the same time as acquiescing in continued Soviet propaganda and the non-recognition of debts.[177] The negotiations were going nowhere. Krasin departed from Britain shortly after with the unanswered British memorandum.

For now, however, this was an acceptable enough outcome for Moscow. Chicherin acknowledged to Krasin that the British refusal to enter political discussions gave the Bolsheviks a freer hand for the time being and avoided getting tied up in complex discussions about debts.[178] Moreover, as he revealed to Trotsky, Wrangel's June offensive had turned out to be a 'convenient tool in our game', namely, on the one hand, encouraging the British government to think that the Bolsheviks might one day cooperate on the issue of pre-revolutionary debts, through feeding Krasin vague dispatches indirectly suggesting this, while on the other, providing reports about how the working classes, supposedly enlivened by British involvement with Poland and Wrangel, 'would never understand if [...] we acknowledge the English debts'.[179] With the collapse of the first round of trade negotiations, Chicherin was able to continue to chart this ambiguous course.

With the war going the Bolsheviks' way in the summer, the British government itself was also more strongly pushing for Poland to negotiate before its army was totally overwhelmed.[180] By mid-to-late June the Bolshevik leadership was certain that a Polish peace proposal was forthcoming. In telegrams from mid-June to Lenin and other senior Bolsheviks, Trotsky relayed intelligence describing the Polish Army in a 'catastrophic condition' and that he now expected 'a quick intervention from the Entente with the aim of concluding peace'. In the meantime, to press their advantage, Trotsky called for the Red Army to carry out an 'extraordinarily forceful operation' (Stalin agreed and suggested speeding up the offensive from Ukraine).[181] Moreover, in order to influence western public opinion in advance of negotiations – and chiefly present Soviet Russia as the innocent party – Trotsky wanted another propaganda push 'to exactly establish the facts and brand the subversive role of France, consciously and maliciously having prepared the Polish attack [...] and giving the general picture of Anglo-French facilitation of the Polish gentry and Lloyd George and Millerand's cheating of the working masses.'[182] He made the case once more to the Politburo, supported by Stalin, that peace negotiations be opened with Romania, since intelligence apparently pointed to 'France's attempts to drag Romania into the war'.[183] The Politburo, however, decided against a separate peace initiative. While Lenin was as wrong as others in thinking that 'Romania will probably attack', he argued that the Romanians would likely fall into line with Poland anyway if the latter made peace. 'We do not want to help them [Romania]', Lenin added, laying out the Politburo's position that Romania might use the opportunity to propose simultaneous negotiations with Poland, something to its potential advantage. For Trotsky, this was a 'profound mistake' and he warned once more about the risks of Romanian mobilization as the Red Army advanced in the southwest.[184]

While Chicherin agreed with many of Trotsky's suggestions, he wanted the Bolsheviks to consider seriously accepting a Polish peace offer, if now forthcoming. Considering the mounting problems in Soviet Russia, he saw major downsides in the opposite course. 'Phrases about Warsaw are good for agitation, but if victory will be bought with riots of starving people next winter, it is a too high price.' And critically, any propaganda campaign launched to shape western public opinion and 'expose the Entente's deceit' depended on whether a Polish peace offer was accepted or not. For Chicherin, above all, the present situation needed more clarity, not least the Allied position, which, in his view, was moving towards neither reconciliation nor further hostilities.[185]

On 24 June Stalin gave an interview to the newspaper *Kommunist* from Khar'kov, in which he underlined the mistake in thinking the Poles were defeated, and the war over. 'After all, we are contending not only against the Poles, but against the whole Entente, which has mobilized all the dark forces of Germany, Austria, Hungary and Rumania and is providing the Poles with supplies of every kind.'

The Polish Army had not yet disintegrated and, for Stalin, 'there is no doubt that more fighting is still to come, and fierce fighting at that'. In this way, 'boastfulness and harmful self-conceit' in the party about 'a march on Warsaw' was premature. Wrangel's attack, 'dictated by the Entente' had come like a 'bolt from the blue', reinforcing how Poland was just one lever at the disposal of the Allied Powers. Even at a moment of growing military advantage over Poland, therefore, the Bolsheviks' perception of an existential threat to Soviet Russia remained the same. In Stalin's view, the Allied Powers had simply adopted a new tactic and unleashed Wrangel's army in the south to 'upset all Soviet Russia's plans' and protect the weakened Polish forces.[186]

As we have seen throughout this chapter, such presentation of the Soviet-Polish war was not merely a propaganda device. Ever since the outbreak of hostilities in 1919, the Bolsheviks comprehended the war through the lens of international capitalist conspiracy and internal discussion mirrored public commentary. The Bolsheviks failed to grasp the reality of the war and the nature of relations between the Allied Powers and Poland. Yet Britain and France were by no means blameless in perpetuating the bloody Russian civil war and had sought to topple the Soviet government. But by 1920, neither was seeking to push Poland into war in the manner that the Bolsheviks believed, even if they held leverage as major powers in Europe and could pressure Poland into aligning with their interests.[187]

The Bolsheviks could be forgiven for misinterpreting the often opaque and ambiguous Allied position in 1920 and they were hardly unique either in misinterpreting international affairs or misunderstanding the dynamics of military conflict. Senior figures on the Allied side, and some close to the Polish government, easily endorsed conspiracy theories of their own. Since the outbreak of the Russian civil war in 1918, many British and French officials had given credence to the idea that, for their own gain, Germany was secretly assisting the Bolshevik cause. And these same conspiracies rolled on during the Soviet-Polish conflict. It was true that figures like German General Hans von Seeckt proposed the idea to his staff officers in early 1920 that Germany should jointly attack Poland with Soviet Russia, and then both move against Britain and France. But none of this came to pass, owing to the colossal risks. The German government, moreover, had already spurned Lenin's offer of negotiations the year before. The Reichswehr assisted the Red Army in purchasing large numbers of locomotives and vehicles, but this came too late to influence the war.[188] However, Churchill and his circle around the British War Office in 1919 and 1920 endorsed exaggerated theories about 'Germano-Bolshevik activity' and at times incorrectly accounted for the Red Army's victories as 'in large part due to the assistance of German staff officers'.[189] Elsewhere, the head of the French military mission in Warsaw, General Paul Henrys, expressed confidence in wildly inaccurate intelligence from a certain German Captain Schirinsky in January 1920, which he sent to the French Minister for War. This claimed that 'the Germans have numerous Staff Officers and N.C.Os. in Russia', including 400 of the former and 3000 engineers. There apparently existed 'a complete skeleton army in the whole of Soviet Russia', thanks to which the Red Army was able to defeat the White armies.[190] At this same time, the 'sleuth-hounds' at the British

Political Intelligence Department were examining information purporting a high-level German conspiracy operating in Russia. This apparently involved 'daily pro-German intrigues' in Denikin's army to bring about an armistice with the Bolsheviks, thereby giving the Red Army a freer hand to crush Poland, then culminating with Germany declaring war on Soviet Russia in alliance with the White armies and Turkey. Even though this 'intelligence' soon drew doubts, and the source was described as 'so unbalanced and excitable as to be totally unreliable' and 'a dangerous lunatic', the Foreign Office continued to investigate nevertheless.[191] Running in other directions, British intelligence, at various times, relayed equally absurd claims about pro-German sympathies among the White forces. The foreign press, namely *Gazeta Warszawska*; the *Daily Herald*; and *Der Neue Tag*, carried stories in early 1920 about a supposed Anglo-German conspiracy to use German soldiers against the Bolsheviks. The *Daily Herald* claimed that a 100,000-strong German Army was being prepared for a major offensive in spring, to cover the left flank of Poles.[192] While on the Polish side, Patek told Churchill's military secretary, Sir Archibald Sinclair, in January 1920 the opposite again, that the Germans were 'undoubtedly behind the Bolsheviks in Russia'.[193] Later in mid-June, Polish General Tadeusz Rozwadowski told another of Churchill's colleagues, General Sir Edward Spears, that before the Polish Army was able to slow the Red Army's advance in early summer, '70,000 German troops were concentrated ready to break through and join hands with the Bolsheviks'.[194] It is entirely possible that the Poles were knowingly playing upon a fear of revanchist Germany to encourage stronger action from the Allied Powers against Soviet Russia; but then, as was true in British and French circles, fears of Germany resurgent could easily skew thinking among many.

What these few examples indicate is how conspiracies and misapprehensions abounded in 1920 and it is false distinction to contrast the 'rational' western powers and 'irrational' Bolsheviks. One difference, however, was the degree that such conspiracies were ingrained in the Soviet government compared to elsewhere. What also mattered most in the Bolsheviks' understanding of the Soviet-Polish war – and something with major significance in the years after – was not just the wider backdrop of a perceived capitalist conspiracy against Soviet Russia but, more specifically, the perceived danger that unions of hostile border states were always somewhere being engineered. This would be a central lesson taken from the Soviet-Polish war and the Red Army's dramatic defeat at the Battle of Warsaw.

Chapter 2

THE BATTLE OF WARSAW

European capitals watched with increasing anguish as the Red Army turned the tide in the Soviet-Polish war in early summer 1920 and began streaming across the western front. Poland's future seemed suddenly uncertain, and with it, the continental security arrangement established by the Versailles Peace Conference. As Tukhachevskii notoriously declared to Red Army soldiers assembled on the western front on 2 July: 'Turn your eyes to the West. In the West the fate of the World Revolution is being decided. Over the corpse of White Poland lies the road to World Conflagration.'[1] In the months after the Russian Revolution, the Soviet government had proclaimed that the Polish people had an 'inalienable right to independence', although Lenin, evidently, saw no contradiction in using military force to ensure that their future was a Soviet one.[2] But despite rising optimism among the Bolsheviks in 1920, there was never a credible chance of 'sovietizing' Poland, let alone sparking revolution elsewhere in Germany. Swept up in the revolutionary drama of summer 1920, Lenin, more than any other Bolshevik, let the prospect of bringing down the Versailles system cloud his judgement. He gambled everything on breaking through to Europe in the short window of opportunity he was convinced existed between July and August. Like others, Lenin ignored the growing warning signs about the Polish people's lack of revolutionary zeal and the gathering problems in the Red Army's overstretched offensive. In the face of Piłsudski's successful counterstrike in mid-August, the entire Bolshevik endeavour came crashing down at the gates of Warsaw.

This chapter will explain why Lenin and the Bolsheviks took the risk of attempting to sovietize Poland in summer 1920 and how, in a stunning turn of fortune, the Soviet offensive dramatically collapsed. Poor strategy; confused last-minute directives; and straightforward insubordination, each contributed to the Bolsheviks' defeat. Even though the Bolsheviks later admitted some of these errors in a bad-tempered post-mortem, they remained convinced that the Allied Powers had played a much bigger role in the Polish Army's successful resistance than was true. This exaggeration of Allied responsibility for the failure of a poorly conceived offensive left behind a legacy that would help shape the path of Soviet Russia in the years after.

The 'sovietization' of Poland

The Red Army launched its major offensive on the western front on 4 July into Belarus, striking out towards the Berezina River. Outnumbering the Poles, in a matter of days the 16th Red Army was able to make the crossing. Meanwhile in the southwest, the 1st Cavalry Army was busy carrying out its trademark mobile warfare and seized Równe by mid-July, adding another city to Budennyi's tally. Before long the Polish military had been forced back to the very starting point of its offensive against Ukraine from April.[3] The Red Army then took Minsk on 11 July; Wilno was captured three days later, and then Grodno. On 11 July, in discussion with the commander of the southwestern front, Egorov, the supreme commander-in-chief, Kamenev, described how the Polish Army was in full retreat across all fronts, from north to south.[4] Under Soviet pressure, they would retreat 600 kilometres during June and July, with some Polish forces seeing losses as high as 40 per cent.[5]

Military success against Poland concentrated the Bolsheviks' minds towards taking decisive action against Wrangel, whose army was still engaged in southern Ukraine in northern Taurida. Wrangel's army had proved difficult to subdue and was a growing threat to the Don and the Kuban regions. It was also a danger to the rear of the Soviet armies arrayed against Poland.[6] In early July, therefore, Trotsky called for a 'crushing onslaught' in the south, even if this risked a British bombardment in reprisal (such was Trotsky's misunderstanding of British priorities).[7] In the same vein, writing in *Pravda* on 11 July, Stalin delivered another warning that it was dangerous to assume that the wider war was over and 'all that remains for us to do is to "march on Warsaw"'. This 'harmful self-conceit' not only ignored existing Polish reserves and unwavering support from the Allied Powers – who were now apparently doing their utmost to 'embroil Rumania in war with Russia' – but Wrangel, Stalin argued, was working 'hand in glove' with Poland (in private he repeated similar comments to Lenin about this supposed collaboration).[8] As with Denikin months before, there was some limited cooperation between the Poles and Wrangel, but this was never to the degree that the Bolsheviks, Stalin included, imagined and unreconcilable issues, such as Piłsudski's support of Petliura in Ukraine, undermined effective cooperation.[9] Nevertheless the Bolsheviks were certain that military success against Poland was in jeopardy without Wrangel's destruction, something which would also represent another blow against the Allied Powers, the perceived architects of their troubles. With this in mind, and with his eye as ever on propaganda, Trotsky contacted the editors of *Pravda* and *Izvestiia*, Nikolai Bukharin and Iurii Steklov, in early July to criticize the inaction of the Soviet press in exposing the 'vile behaviour' of the Alllied Powers in southern Ukraine. It had to be 'hammered into the head' of each French worker that the Allies had used the 'slogan of diplomatic mediation' as cover for continued support of Wrangel, giving the White general opportunity to regroup and attack. The French government's ongoing role in Poland's war effort therefore needed to be further exposed. 'Criminally little', lambasted Trotsky, had been done on this so far. With the Bolsheviks anticipating Allied diplomatic intervention in the war now that momentum was firmly with the Red Army, Trotsky argued it was imperative to 'decisively compromise the role of England, and the Entente in general, as a mediator between us and our enemies'.[10]

The anticipated diplomatic intervention emerged during the Spa conference in Belgium in early July, where the Allied Supreme War Council convened to discuss Germany's disarmament and reparations payments. And as the conference coincided with the Red Army's gathering offensive on the western front, finding a way to bring the Soviet-Polish war to a close was another live issue. Under Red Army pressure, a new coalition government in Poland – formed after the Skulski cabinet resigned during the Polish retreat from Kiev – knew there was no choice but to appeal to the Allied Powers to help bring about peace. New Polish foreign minister, Prince Eustachy Sapieha, discussed a diplomatic intervention with the British ambassador to Poland, Sir Horace Rumbold, prior to the conference and his predecessor, Patek, made the first appeals for assistance at Spa. The new Polish prime minster, the National Democrat Władysław Grabski, also made the journey to Belgium. Although he initially pushed for soldiers and equipment to be sent to Poland's aid, Grabski could not escape how his weakening position made peace on Allied terms unavoidable. Back in Poland, Piłsudski, by contrast, was still pushing for a renewal of the Polish war effort – 'war can be won if the country wants war', he claimed. But the Polish political right, led by the National Democrats and emboldened by the disaster unfolding on the western front, had already called for his resignation. Grabski, as a leading member, was no less a critic of the Kiev campaign. Piłsudski, increasingly isolated, was a diminished voice in the recently formed Polish State Defence Council. Beyond moments of bravado, he admitted that his grand vision for a Polish federation in the east lay in tatters.[11]

An Allied-negotiated peace would come at a heavy price for Poland. Lloyd George made it clear to Grabski that assistance was only possible if the Poles abandoned imperialism in the east and excessive claims to the border regions. In effect, the Allies would control the final peace settlement, the biggest implication of this being the use of the territorial line of December 1919 as the boundary between Poland and Soviet Russia, which, as we know, the Polish government resisted. Wilno, moreover, would immediately be handed back to the Lithuanians (although the city, soon under Soviet control, was shortly afterwards 'returned' to the Lithuanians in exchange for neutrality in the war). The future of eastern Galicia and other disputed territories, including Teschen (with Czechoslovakia) and Danzig (with Germany), would be decided within the Allied Supreme Council.[12] Piłsudski was exactly right to see this as the death knell to Polish federalism. The British government did give a guarantee against Soviet aggression and promised to assist Poland if it was invaded, but Lloyd George's formulation of 'with all means available' was hardly iron cast.[13] And in the British prime minister's vision, all the above was to be agreed at a peace conference in London, under Allied control, involving Soviet Russia and other eastern European and Baltic nations. Grabski managed to secure some minor concessions. The stopping distance from the armistice line was increased to 50 kilometres and assurances were given – empty as it turned out – that Wilno would not fall into Bolshevik hands. But Grabski had no choice but to agree to Lloyd George's fundamental conditions.[14] For further support, an Inter-Allied mission was dispatched to Warsaw, but in the words of one historian, this advisory body was a 'symbolic substitute for material aid'.[15]

There were still some influential voices calling for stronger action against Soviet Russia at the time of the Spa conference, notably on the French side. Marshal Foch wanted 'significant aid' and 'all possible assistance to the Polish Army' including the secondment of French officers.[16] But his government had bigger priorities at Spa than Polish affairs. Fearing Germany resurgent, the French placed a higher premium on maintaining the post-war settlement than Lloyd George, who privately accepted that Warsaw might even be overrun. For this reason, Millerand wanted to establish a common front with Britain to enforce German reparation payments. With French security so closely wrapped up in a strong Anglo-French bond – and seeing a risk in deploying French troops once again to Soviet Russia when the previous civil war intervention had witnessed outbreaks of mutinies and desertions – Millerand was inclined to support Lloyd George's handing of the Soviet-Polish conflict. This meant no military assistance for Poland. More optimistic than the British that the Poles could hold out against the Red Army, however, Millerand granted additional credits to Poland and made efforts to unblock supply routes.[17]

Lord Curzon duly sent the British proposals for an armistice and a London peace conference to the Bolsheviks in a note on 11 July, the so-called Curzon ultimatum. The British government, as Curzon detailed, intended to pursue negotiations for a definitive trade agreement with Soviet Russia and an armistice between Soviet Russia and Poland. The Red Army was required to halt its offensive east of the Bug River and Curzon laid out the details of the proposed London conference, under the auspices of the Peace Conference, to negotiate peace settlements between Soviet Russia, Poland, Lithuania, Latvia and Finland. A second armistice would be negotiated between the Bolsheviks and Wrangel, and the latter's army was to withdraw to Crimea, itself to become a neutral zone (Wrangel was to be present at the London conference but not participate as an equal member). Behind these proposals lay a military threat. If the Bolsheviks took 'action hostile to Poland in its own territory the British Government and its Allies would feel bound to assist the Polish nation to defend its existence with all the means at their disposal'. Considering Lloyd George's aversion to using force, this was only ever an empty threat. Nevertheless, applying pressure, Curzon wanted a reply within a week.[18]

Curzon's note sparked a storm of internal discussion in Moscow. Although the resurrected demarcation line between Poland and Soviet Russia was more generous to latter, Curzon's proposals for an armistice with Wrangel and Crimea's conversion into a neutral zone were entirely unacceptable and fuelled conspiracies that the British planned to annex the territory. On receiving the proposals Lenin immediately telephoned Stalin on the southwestern front, where he was a political commissar, and asked for his opinion, while also ordering him to 'furiously intensify' the offensive against Wrangel. In Lenin's words, the British proposal was 'a piece of knavery aimed at the annexation of Crimea […] The idea is to snatch victory out of our hands with the aid of false promises.' As he put it to Efraim Sklianskii, Trotsky's deputy in the war department (who was likewise impelled to accelerate the war against Wrangel), the British position was 'annexation of Crimea for a truce with Poland'.[19]

In a more clear-eyed way, Lenin saw through the British threat of intervention should the Red Army advance into Polish territory. He was convinced that two years of Soviet survival in the civil war proved that the Allied Powers were 'powerless to crush us militarily, powerless to utilize its troops', a message reiterated by Soviet officials on the ground, Nikolai Klyshko and Fedor Rotshtein, in the trade delegation in London who dismissed the British warnings. But while Lenin appreciated how the risk of Britain once again undertaking direct intervention was receding, he continued to overestimate its ability to control and incite smaller countries, like Poland, against Soviet Russia.[20] Stalin, for his part, was as bullish as Lenin during these days. In his reply to the party leader, he described that: 'the Polish troops are completely falling apart [...] the Poles are experiencing a collapse from which they will not soon recover'. Stalin agreed that Curzon was trying to rescue Poland with an armistice, protect Wrangel and ultimately take control of Crimea. If Poland was defeated, he claimed, all of this would fall apart. 'You are completely right to say that they want to snatch victory from us.' Stalin made several suggestions for the Soviet response to Curzon: first, in line with the earlier peace offensive, the Bolsheviks should write about Poland only in vague language, using 'general phrases about the peacefulness of Russia' and second, underline that if Poland wanted the war to end, it should seek negotiations independently. 'This will buy time', he added. Third-party mediation between the Bolsheviks and Wrangel was out of the question. This domestic matter would be resolved by the Bolsheviks. Buoyed by the Red Army's military successes, Stalin was inclined to take a tough line. 'I think that imperialism has never been so weak as now, at the moment of Poland's defeat, and never have we been as strong as now.'[21]

Elsewhere there was a spectrum of opinion about the Curzon note. On the one hand, leading Bolshevik Lev Kamenev, writing from London with the Soviet trade delegation, feared that accepting Curzon's conditions would not resolve anything and another war against Poland would simply erupt soon after, and no later than the following spring. The way forward was the 'sovietization of Poland' and to achieve this, according to Kamenev, was through the southwest rather than via Tukhachevskii's presently successful western front. (In contrast to December 1919, the British offer of July 1920 proposed more generous territory for Soviet Russia in Galicia, explaining this rising interest in the southwest). Kamenev argued that the Red Army needed to occupy Lwów to enable a 'peasant movement' to penetrate Poland – a deeply optimistic reading of the local peasants' revolutionary potential. Lwów was the 'gateway to Hungary', where a short-lived Soviet republic under Bela Kun's revolutionary government had lasted for just six months from March to August 1919. To eliminate any future danger that Poland posed to Soviet security, Kamenev believed the country had to be so thoroughly defeated and an armistice so punishing that it faced similar circumstances to Germany after 1918.[22]

Trotsky at this moment, by contrast, was more accommodating than others, chiefly because he doubted that a Soviet-style Polish revolution was feasible. Mindful still of different positions in the British government, he had not changed his view about encouraging the moderate tendency towards Soviet Russia and capturing public support in the west. He argued the Bolsheviks should agree to British mediation (though not mediation by the Allied Powers, as Curzon actually proposed) and guarantee the inviolability of Poland's borders, while stressing the Bolsheviks' benign intentions. Like others, he was firmly against outside mediation in the war with Wrangel, a domestic Russian matter: 'Crimea is not an independent state.'[23] In line with the Bolsheviks' fundamental understandings of the war, Trotsky argued that any armistice with Poland must hinge on Britain and France, the war's enablers – 'the countries that set Poland on us and nurtured its offensive' – also agreeing to end hostilities. Such an outcome, he believed, would appropriately apportion blame, and prevent Britain from presenting itself as an honest mediator.[24]

Like Trotsky, chief diplomat Chicherin also had doubts about Poland's revolutionary potential, warning against the rising enthusiasm for sovietizing the country by force. Utopian dreamers like the party theorist, Nikolai Bukharin, he argued, were thinking with 'agitational formulas' rather than 'concrete information'. Chicherin instead wanted the Bolsheviks to reap the advantages of the British offer now on the table. On 13 July he noted that this would award Soviet Russia 300 versts (320 kilometres) from Minsk to Brest-Litovsk, effectively 'for free'. From the new line, Poland could still be pressured to accept Bolshevik conditions and if it refused, the offensive could always begin once again. Putting himself in the minority, the proposal for Wrangel's surrender also suited Chicherin, who saw few downsides in securing his capitulation. However, he was against the war being discussed at a London conference and wanted a narrower Soviet-Polish conference either held in Warsaw or another Polish city. Making sure negotiations with Britain and the border states remained separate would remain a core and long-running principle of Soviet foreign policy. A general conference, including the Baltic states and Finland, moreover, risked allowing the Allied Powers to become 'the supreme arbiter in our relations with our neighbours'.[25] This mattered as Chicherin still worried about the formation of a more extensive anti-Soviet military union and, for him, 'rude refusal' of the British offer might encourage the raising of such a force.[26] As he put it to Lenin, the Allied Powers were still capable of arming Poland with 'masses of pilots and aeroplanes'; they could force Romania, Finland and possibly Latvia into war. Moreover, if the full lifting of the economic blockade was further postponed this would create further damage.[27] As he put it to his deputy, Litvinov, the party was divided between those content with compromise, 'to limit themselves to a half-victory of gaining peace'; while the others, typified by Bukharin and Zinoviev, were 'adventurers' lacking foresight and long-term thinking. Litvinov shared his worries. Although he believed that the Allied Powers were pushing for an armistice to give Poland a breathing space to rearm, he also pointed out that rejection of the British proposals would 'revive the charge against us of imperialism and give water to Millerand's mill'.[28]

From the military establishment, Sergei Kamenev made the case that the Bolsheviks should agree to negotiations, but he pressed for operations to continue at the same time to maximize Soviet advantage.[29] Like others, Kamenev was certain that the British were planning to use Wrangel's forces in southern Ukraine to attack the Soviet rear 'or as a bargaining chip with which to cheat the Soviet government of its victory over Poland at the conference table'.[30] Victories were therefore necessary on both western and southwestern fronts. On 15 July, he notified the Politburo that Red Army troops would soon infringe the borders of Poland and to expect a response (like Chicherin, Kamenev speculated about a coordinated attack from the border countries at Allied behest). He estimated also that the Red Army could sustain 'two months of intense fighting' before getting into 'extremely difficult conditions' in supply and transport. Even so, two months was apparently sufficient to defeat the Polish Army, capture Warsaw and defeat Wrangel. Yet if Romania alone launched an offensive – threatening the flanks of Soviet armies on the southwestern front – victory could be put in serious doubt.[31] For this reason, Trotsky soon ordered Kamenev to plan for Romania's entry into the war, at Allied bidding, and he again pushed for a peace proposal to be sent to its government. The French successfully discouraged the Romanian government from negotiations and, in any case, Romania adopted a neutral position by the summer.[32] However, it is striking that, even at a point when the war was moving in the Bolsheviks' favour in July, and when concerns that Britain and France could repeat the direct interventions of 1918 to 1919 were diminishing, unfounded fears about a new, and more extensive, anti-Soviet coalition of border states attacking Soviet Russia continued to be the undercurrent shaping the party leadership's strategic thinking.

Despite the varied viewpoints on display about how to respond to Curzon, during a plenum of the central committee on 16 July, the Bolsheviks naturally followed Lenin's lead and formally rejected the British proposals, although the door was held open for a separate Polish approach for bilateral negotiations. The central committee arrived at the position that Soviet Russia would 'help free the proletariat and working masses of Poland and Lithuania from their landlords and capitalists'. In practice, this meant accelerating the offensive and mobilizing Polish communists for Poland's sovietization. As member of the central committee, Evgeny Preobrazhenskii, captured in his notes of the plenum, Lenin remarked that the Bolsheviks 'needed to test with Red Army bayonets whether Poland was ready for Soviet power. If not, it will always be possible under one or another pretext to step back.'[33]

In the days before the plenum, Lenin asked the Polish and Lithuanian Bolsheviks, Feliks Kon and Vincas Mickevičius, to report on the situation in Poland and to relay this to Stalin, who still doubted Poland's revolutionary potential, even if he was confident in the Red Army's military advantage in the war. In their account, Kon and Mickevičius were certain that concerns about an 'explosion of nationalist feeling' among Polish workers, and at least some of the peasantry, were 'groundless' and they sketched out a picture of active labour militancy among the Polish working class (it was true that trades union membership was strong and strikes common to Poland, which broke out again in summer 1920). Kon and Mickevičius noted, however, that other parts of the peasantry, and especially the wealthier, could easily turn against the Bolsheviks because of the likely violence and chaos resulting from sovietization and the still-powerful influence of catholic priests. The Polish communists themselves were also apparently split on the consequences of the Red Army entering Poland. In their final judgement, the two estimated that counting on proletarian revolution in Poland in the near future was 'risky'.[34] Lenin had sought similar advice elsewhere from Polish Bolshevik and future member of the Polish Revolutionary Committee, Iosif Unshlikht, about the prospect of revolution in Poland. Unshlikht was vague in reply and avoided a precise timeline, but he optimistically noted that with the Red Army advancing as it was, revolution was 'most likely within a short time'. Lenin, evidently, agreed.[35]

Discussion in the central committee plenum, however, had forced more doubts about the sovietization of Poland to the surface. Trotsky pointed out that, even in retreat, the Polish Army was still in good shape. Creating Soviet Poland would not be easy, and it would take time to transfer sufficient Red Army forces. Trotsky believed the Polish working class supported the Bolsheviks' cause, but the same could not be said of the much larger Polish peasantry, where hatred of Russia ran deep. Trotsky was again pushing for the party to accept the British offer of meditation, to drive a wedge between Britain and France. Refusing this, he argued, would only embolden Millerand and encourage Lloyd George to come around to the more hostile French way of thinking. As war commissar, it is likely that Trotsky's caution was cemented after hearing Sergei Kamenev's prediction that the Red Army's offensive on the western front could be maintained for two months, and only if the Allies did not engineer a new intervention. In contrast to Lenin, Trotsky's calculations were made through military priorities, rather than revolutionary politics.[36]

Others in the central committee, with deeper knowledge of Poland, likewise cautioned against its sovietization, including secretary of the Communist International, Karl Radek, and the Polish communists, Markhlevskii and Feliks Dzerzhinskii. And Stalin, still serving at the front, believed it was better to concentrate on the destruction of Wrangel's army and, as we have seen already, two months before expressed concerns that a key strength of the Polish Army was its national unity which would not be weakened by class conflict (it is worth noting that Lenin evidently ignored Stalin's advice, even though he had recently positioned him as the party's expert on the national question).[37] 'Our attack will provoke only an explosion of patriotism and throw the proletariat to the side of the bourgeoisie, ' Markhlevskii remarked; while Aleksei Rykov, head of the Supreme Council of the National Economy, warned that the effort to sovietize Europe 'by means of such units, as Budennyi's [cavalry], will only compromise us in front of the European proletariat […] It is easy for us to turn the wheel, but to turn millions [of people], who we taught to think we are leading only a defensive war and want peace as quickly as possible will be impossible.' He warned also that supplies were running low. 'We do not give bread, but we want the Red Army men to go to Berlin.' According to Preobrazhenskii, Lenin 'pounced' on Rykov for ignoring 'all the objective information' about Soviet successes and the supposedly supportive mood among British workers. Reportedly also 'very angry' with Radek, he accused him of 'defeatism'.[38] None of these objections did anything to change Lenin's decision to take the risk or stop the sovietization of Poland from gaining necessary party support.

The Soviet reply to the British government, sent by Chicherin on 17 July, therefore formally rejected British mediation in the war and the proposed general peace conference in London. Negotiations could take place, but only directly between Soviet Russia and Poland.[39] Chicherin's note, of course, said nothing about the acceleration of the Red Army's offensive.[40] But such secrecy was hardly required. The Allied governments were already alarmed about the Red Army's progress in July and the continuing collapse of Polish resistance. Defences were crumbling at the Neimen and Shara Rivers and Red Army troops were breaking through the Slonim region, between Minsk and Białystok (which would be taken on 20 July). From the southwestern front, Stalin predicted that if the Poles were unable to establish a new defensive line at the Bug River – the final defensive line before Warsaw – they would need to fall further back to the Vistula. Considering the rising probability of the Polish government now requesting direct negotiations which the Bolsheviks would now struggle to refuse, Stalin's advice to his close ally Kliment Voroshilov, a political commissar with the 1st Cavalry Army, was 'to rush your army forward'.[41]

Stalin anticipated things correctly. Even though unhappy with much of Chicherin's reply to Curzon, the British government dropped its proposal for Allied mediation and advised the Poles to immediately begin direct negotiations with the Bolsheviks. Such moves were already in motion. One of the first actions of another new Polish government, a national coalition formed by Piłsudski on 22 July in response to the country's deteriorating military position, and headed by Wincenty Witos from the Polish People's Party (Piast), was to send a radio message to the Bolsheviks offering to open negotiations, establish an immediate truce and agree an armistice (although Piłsudski, still resisting peace efforts, pushed for delays to allow reorganization of the Polish Army).[42] To the Bolsheviks, the British government continued to threaten, half-heartedly, to 'give to Poland the assistance and support' and break off trade negotiations if the Red Army advanced into Polish territory once the request for armistice talks arrived. But Lenin was willing to take the risk for the prize of revolution in Europe.[43] Indeed, Sergei Kamenev signed a directive one day after Witos's offer came through, calling for the Red Army to gain as much territory as possible in the next few weeks in the direction of Warsaw 'in order to inflict a final defeat on the enemy' and seize the city.[44] Trotsky likewise ordered Soviet forces to continue the offensive at full pace to prevent the Allied Powers from reorganizing the Polish Army and Wrangel's forces, bringing Romania into the war, and launching a new attack in an effort to protect the Versailles system.[45] This suggested also how this moment was seen as fraught with new dangers. In private, and evidently still harbouring some doubts about the strategy, Trotsky made clear that rejection of the Curzon note would bring forth a 'new tide of assistance' for Poland and Wrangel, including attempts to draw in Latvia and Finland. Reserves were to be prepared in the case of Romania's entry.[46]

Litvinov revealed other potential new dangers, describing how recent intelligence showed that the American government, for six months, had extensively supplied the Poles with military equipment after issuing a promissory note for 4 million dollars to purchase leftover supplies in France. Outside of Britain, Litvinov did not see the same scope for the working class to 'paralyse [Allied] intrigues' in the other border states.[47] As the offensive pushed on, doubts remained.

Despite these concerns, with the course set from the top, Trotsky pushed for better coordinated propaganda to achieve the sovietization of Poland in the shortest possible time. The Bolshevik organization bureau convened a meeting to discuss carrying out propaganda in territory occupied by the Red Army and resolved to create a special bureau of Polish Bolsheviks for coordination on the ground. All able-bodied male Polish communists aged between eighteen and forty (excluding those in Siberia or working in sensitive industries) were to be mobilized.[48] Trotsky, moreover, optimistically proposed to the central committee that propaganda could be bolstered by popularizing the names of well-known Polish Bolsheviks among local Polish people, including Dzerzhinskii, the head of the merciless Cheka. Perhaps lacking much else to work with, the central committee approved Trotsky's idea and tasked the unlucky Bolshevik Polish Bureau with implementation.[49]

Amid these hurried preparations, the second congress of the Communist International opened in Petrograd on 19 July, moving to Moscow days later where assembled delegates gazed upon an expansive map of Europe, hung across the wall, updated daily with red flags tracking the Red Army's progress towards Poland. With electrified rhetoric, Lenin's opening speech proclaimed that 'the unification of the world-wide proletariat is being created' and he looked ahead to the formation of an 'international Soviet republic'.[50] His main congress theses avoided controversy in stressing how foreign communist parties had a 'duty to accelerate the revolution' in Poland while the Red Army's future role was concealed. The congress was, after all, an open forum, and the Bolsheviks anticipated resistance from moderate delegates. In other business with far-reaching ramifications, Bolshevik delegates pushed through motions on unity, thereby subordinating foreign communist parties to the Communist International's executive committee, in line with the so-called twenty-one conditions. Overall, Lenin was delighted with the result, and with military events moving in the Bolsheviks' favour, he again took the opportunity to muse about the brighter revolutionary future. 'The situation in the Comintern is splendid', he remarked in a telegram to Stalin on 23 July. 'Zinoviev, Bukharin, and I, too, think that revolution in Italy should be spurred on immediately. My personal opinion is that to this end, Hungary should be sovietized, and perhaps also Czechia and Romania.'[51] Although sceptical about invading Poland, Stalin indulged Lenin's vision of revolutions breaking out across Europe. With the military situation against Poland still promising in mid-to-late July, despite the enemy 'crawling like flies' on Budennyi's cavalry army, Stalin replied that 'it would be a sin not to encourage revolution in Italy', and certainly if more pressure could be applied to the capitalist world. As to Poland, Stalin believed the Allied Powers were seeking a breathing space 'to rearm the Polish Army, to create cavalry and then again attack, possibly in union with other states'.[52] This was the moment to push the Soviet advantage.

Revolutionary aspirations started to directly feed into Soviet military strategy on both fronts. On the same day as Lenin wrote to Stalin about revolution in Europe, Sergei Kamenev ordered the 1st Cavalry Army to undertake an attack on Lwów instead of travelling northwest to join Tukhachevskii's offensive towards Warsaw. With Polish forces hastening a retreat from Ukraine towards Lwów, an opportunity had opened to strike another blow and keep the enemy divided. Pressure in the southwest was also a means of deterring Romania from entering the war, on suspected Allied encouragement.[53] However, with Lenin now foreseeing new revolutions beyond Poland – and with Lwów deemed the 'gateway to Hungary' – the rationale for changing the 1st Cavarly Army's objectives neatly aligned with his vision.

The main Soviet offensive on the western front was also reaching a critical point in late July with the large third Cavalry Corps, commanded by Gai Dmitrievich Gai, engaged in fierce fighting for Grodno, close to the former Curzon line. Crossing this would be an unmistakeable challenge to the Allies.[54] Confidence among the Bolsheviks, however, was riding high on the assumption that revolution could be sparked in Poland before Britain or France could organize an escalation of the war. To ensure this, however, the Bolsheviks knew they had to engage with Poland in direct negotiations, even if only for appearances sake. Their strategy was to string out early discussions with Poland to create one delay after another. For example, Tukhachevskii, as commander of the western front, was responsible for arranging a meeting place for armistice talks, but in a message to the Poles on 24 July – in fact written by Chicherin and signed in Tukhachevskii's name[55] – this claimed that because of the Belarusians' hostility towards Poland and the dangerous behaviour of retreating Polish soldiers, both posing difficulties for negotiations at the front line, Polish representatives would not be able to cross the latter until 30 July. A meeting place, the town of Baranowicze, was eventually agreed upon, but the Bolsheviks had successfully contrived a delay.[56] In the meantime, the revolutionary military council of the southwestern front – Stalin, Egorov and Ian Berzin – was quick to telegram the 12th and 14th Red Armies, and 1st Cavalry Army, to stress that the news of forthcoming armistice talks should not reach the Red Army rank-and-file and potentially slow the momentum of the offensive. 'The situation obliges you to hit harder and strive to continue the offensive without the slightest delay.'[57] As Stalin put it again elsewhere to Voroshilov and Budennyi: 'Of course, you understand that we are forced to agree [to the Polish offer for negotiations, PW]. On the basis of this, the swiftest offensive is required from you in the direction of Lwów.'[58] By this point, the Curzon line had been well-surpassed, but in banking on direct negotiations actually taking place and the war coming to a peaceful end, neither Britain nor France forcefully responded.

Knowing that negotiations were inevitable once delaying tactics had been exhausted, senior Bolsheviks discussed demands to put forward at the end of July. However, so hard-line were the proposed conditions that if accepted, willingly or not, this would be major interference in Poland's domestic affairs. Headline terms included the Polish Army being almost entirely demobilized (reduced to 50,000 soldiers and 10,000 in officer and administrative roles) and all military industry dismantled. To avoid a resurgence of Poland's 'militaristic politics', Polish workers were to be armed with weapons surrendered by the Polish government. All remaining weapons and military supplies would be passed to the Bolsheviks, and war correspondence between the Polish government and Allied Powers openly published. Soviet Russia would receive significant territory west of the 1919 Curzon line.[59] Despite his doubts about the whole enterprise, Stalin suggested hard-line measures of his own: land would pass to Polish peasants to encourage the 'liquidation of the landlord class', a chief culprit in the war.[60] Nevertheless, there was some restraint on display in other quarters, from the same individuals. Trotsky argued that it was a mistake to force the Polish government to agree to free transit of Soviet goods and literature through Poland. This would give the impression – not unjustly – that the Bolsheviks considered the country a pipeline for propaganda across Europe and might lead to discontent in Hungary, Romania, Germany and beyond.[61] How far to openly push revolutionary policies was a point of tension, but even if Warsaw was not actually captured, the Soviet conditions were designed in such a way that radical, potentially revolutionary, changes would be the end product nonetheless, or so the Bolsheviks hoped.

The delayed Soviet-Polish negotiations meanwhile ran into further problems when the Polish delegation arrived at the agreed meeting point of Baranowicze on 1 August and discovered that their Bolshevik counterparts wanted to conduct simultaneous armistice and preliminary peace talks, the purpose being to eliminate opportunity for Poland to reorganize its defences. Only authorized to discuss an armistice, the Polish delegation was forced to return to Warsaw to obtain a new mandate.[62] This delay was dragged out further when the Bolsheviks insisted that meaningful talks could not begin until 4 August as initial contacts could only have a 'preparatory character'. Increasingly frustrated, the Poles were reluctant to further engage with the Bolsheviks and only did so when pressured by the British government.[63] Although themselves the guilty party in the breakdown of the talks, the Bolsheviks nevertheless saw their suspicions confirmed that the Poles, all along, only wanted an armistice – and not peace – to rearm and launch a new offensive.[64] Supposed technical problems with the Moscow radio station receiving a Polish response on 5 August, accepting the Soviet terms for simultaneous negotiations, then stretched things out further. The Poles now pointed to 'flagrant proof of wilful delay' on the Bolsheviks' part, while the latter blamed bad weather for interfering with the radio signal and took the opportunity to accuse the other side of 'systematic and malicious' evasion.[65] With initial talks failing to get going, British ambassador to Poland, Sir Horace Rumbold, worried that the Bolsheviks might 'succeed in spinning out the armistice negotiations' in order to reach Warsaw.[66] The date finally agreed for a Polish delegation to cross the front line was moved to 14 August, all the while the Red Army pushed its way forward.[67] Midway through this series of events, Stalin messaged Budennyi and Voroshilov to stress they should 'hit Lwów now that you have time'.[68]

As negotiations with Poland faltered, Soviet military strategy was reorientated once again in early August. The struggle against Wrangel's army in the south, proving more challenging than anticipated, required reinforcements. Stalin described 'rabid attacks' by Wrangel's forces to Lenin at the end of July, which were

2. The Battle of Warsaw

now moving northeast in an effort to reach the Donbas and Kuban. Further Soviet losses were inevitable, Stalin warned, unless reinforcements arrived quickly.[69] Such was the threat there was some talk in the central committee of arranging a swift peace with Poland to ease the pressure. As Lenin put it to Stalin: 'The Wrangel danger is becoming enormous' and 'opinion is mounting in the Central Committee that peace with bourgeois Poland should be concluded immediately'. Stalin was critical of the prospective peacemakers and wanted the offensive towards Lwów – of which he was an integral part – maintained at full pace. 'Our diplomats sometimes very successfully wreck the achievements of the Red Army', he remarked.[70] Time and time again, Stalin would go on to demand more strength against Wrangel in the south, but as far as the attack on Poland was concerned, even though he still had misgivings about forced sovietization, Stalin did not want to concede a premature peace while the Red Army held the advantage. The momentary wavering in the central committee, however, while reflecting increasing pressures on the Bolshevik leadership, in the end went nowhere. Its membership agreed on 5 August to prosecute the war against Poland to total victory. Yet it remained true that if the war in the south went even further against the Bolsheviks, some, notably Trotsky, were ready to agree an armistice with Poland as a last resort.[71]

The proposed solution to the growing Wrangel problem was to split the Red Army's objectives on the southwestern front. Two armies would now deal exclusively with the Whites, creating a new southern front, with Stalin heading a new revolutionary military council, and Egorov assuming military command. The remaining three armies, including the 1st Cavalry Army, the 12th Red Army and 14th Red Army, would merge with the western front, thereby coming under Tukhachevskii's wider command, but still operating within the wider Polish offensive and remaining in position towards Lwów. But this new arrangement created ambiguity about the objectives of the three armies now under Tukhachevskii's leadership, which were supporting the wider Soviet attack against Poland at the same time as the Lwów offensive was gaining life of its own. Moreover, no direct order was issued for the 1st Cavalry Army and 12th Red Army to support Tukhachevskii until over a week later, by which time, with the Battle of Warsaw fast approaching, the Lwów offensive was firmly in motion.

Critically, therefore, this reorientation in military strategy did not actually send reinforcements to Tukhachevskii's offensive towards Warsaw. In fact, Kamenev's confidence in the western front was such that on 31 July he requested that Tukhachevskii divert his 48th division against Wrangel and he followed up a few days later with a request for two further divisions. Tukhachevskii refused to shed any more strength, citing difficulties on the western front (reinforcements were taken instead from the 12th Red Army on the southwestern front). Kamenev was overconfident and, although Tukhachevskii's forces took Brest-Litovsk on 1 August, the Red Army faced stubborn resistance after Poland's new chief of the general staff, General Tadeusz Rozwadowski, organized successful operations at the defensive line of the Bug and Narew Rivers and retreating forces under General Lucjan Żeligowski also launched a renewed attack in the Narew Basin.[72] The change of Soviet strategy and new division of the armies of the southwestern front, moreover, stretched the Soviet war effort to near-unsustainable levels. The field of battle now comprised around 200 miles, north to south. And this was further extended by Tukhachevskii's own plan to push three of his four armies to the north, to East Prussia and Lithuania, to travel around Warsaw and encircle the city. The manoeuvre would enable an attack from the rear, at the left-flank of the Polish armies and Tukhachevskii believed it essential to victory. The fast pace of the advance, he hoped, would leave no time for the Poles to regroup. But this all risked Tukhachevskii' own left-flank, comprising his sole remaining army, becoming dangerously exposed. It did not augur well that Red Army soldiers on the western front were worn out from the quick pace, with some armies having lost 40 per cent of numbers through desertion and stragglers.[73]

Preparation for the establishment of Soviet Poland was also moving quickly. On 23 July the Politburo formed the so-called Provisional Polish Revolutionary Committee (Polrevkom), staffed with senior Polish Bolsheviks and officially headed by Markhlevskii, although Dzerzhinskii was in the driving seat. Intended as the central organ for Poland's sovietization, the Polrevkom was to act as its temporary government in anticipation of workers taking power themselves. Smaller revolutionary committees had already been established on the front line as the Red Army moved forwards and were most widespread in Belarus. Travelling a matter of days behind the Red Army, the Polrevkom arrived in Minsk on 25 July, then Wilno on 27 July and reached Białystok on 30 July, where it declared a Belorussian Soviet Socialist Republic, nominally independent from Soviet Russia. The Polrevkom then set itself up in the opulent Branicki Palace to deliver various revolutionary proclamations, covering the establishment of local revolutionary committees to the nationalization of land and industry. A new Polish Bureau was also formed in Right-bank Ukraine and an eastern Galician revkom created on 1 August in Tarnopol, western Ukraine. The latter declared Soviet power in Galicia, but without control of Lwów this meant little in practice.[74] The Cheka was also deployed to the western front and Dzerzhinskii mobilized all Poles in its special departments (with primary duties in military security). In view of the proximity of the Polish-German border to the north of Białystok – and its 'political importance' – Dzerzhinskii requested a special intelligence organ be attached to the Polrevkom and pointed to German and Allied intelligence agents supposedly operating in the area.[75]

Despite this raft of activity, Polrevkom's measures and revolutionary edicts struggled to gain traction with local Poles (perhaps out of desperation, Lenin pushed for its manifesto to be distributed from the air). The fact was, this improvised committee had few links outside Moscow and no direct connection to Warsaw, where the workers' movement itself was divided and the communist party weak. The trail of destruction and local requisitions – 'outrageous poaching', as Lenin put it – left in the wake of the Red Army's advance did few favours to the Bolsheviks' revolutionary message. Tellingly, Dzerzhinskii, soon enough, appealed to Moscow for a Cheka battalion to be urgently sent to Białystok to provide additional security.[76] The Polrevkom's policies were simply too far-reaching and detached from local priorities. There proved little appetite among the local population for revolutionary change (as some senior Bolsheviks had accurately predicted). Dzerzhinskii's push for a Polish proletarian Red Army, for instance, only netted 175 Poles to a volunteer regiment.[77] In light of this, Stalin's call for the Polrevkom to ensure soviets be immediately formed in the ranks of the embattled Polish Army and the 'most counterrevolutionary generals' arrested was a serious overestimation of its influence and perhaps a sign too that he was finally being swept up, like Lenin, in anticipation of military victory.[78] In another telling trend auguring poorly for the future, the mobilization of Polish communists to the various fronts proved chaotic and disorganized. Some sent to carry out propaganda and agitation were unable to speak Polish, hardly the foundation for exporting revolution.[79]

*

Away from the fighting, Lev Kamenev and Leonid Krasin, representing the Soviet trade delegation, arrived in London on 4 August to meet with Lloyd George. That the Bolsheviks were deliberately delaying armistice negotiations with Poland to deepen their military advantage made for a difficult encounter in Downing Street. Lloyd George was straight to the point and accused the Bolsheviks of lacking sincerity, claiming to want peace but breaking previous assurances. Unless the Soviet government came to the negotiating table, he threatened, the British would assist Poland and supply its military. A naval blockade would resume in the Baltic Sea (despite there being no British naval base in the Baltic).[80] In reply Kamenev stated, unconvincingly, that the Soviet offensive, ongoing after Polish appeals for an armistice, was because the Bolsheviks needed a stronger guarantee against future attack. To ensure that Poland was unable to resume war after signing an armistice, Kamenev argued, a wider range of issues had to be decided, going beyond current military operations, and namely, the future demobilization of the Polish Army and the ceasing of weapons and munitions manufacture. According to Kamenev, the Polish delegation's inability to discuss such issues, because of a narrow negotiating mandate, was the true cause of the delay and the Soviet offensive had rolled on. Chicherin wrote to Lloyd George with much the same explanation the following day, emphasizing the importance of going 'beyond narrowly military negotiations', especially in light on the 'incessant and systematic assistance' given to the Poles and Wrangel and the risk of a ceasefire simply becoming a space to rearm and attack.[81] Lloyd George was not convinced by any of this, and privately feared that the Red Army would soon reach Warsaw.[82] Further discussions took place two days later, and to avoid total breakdown and the risk of outside intervention counterproductive to the Soviet offensive, Kamenev and Krasin provisionally accepted a British plan for a ten-day truce between Soviet Russia and Poland.[83] Lloyd George wanted an 'authoritative statement' from the Bolsheviks on the proposed truce by 8 August when he was scheduled to meet Millerand at the Lympne conference. He reiterated his threat of military action, pointing out to Krasin and Kamenev that British ships were already en route to the Baltic Sea.[84]

The Bolsheviks still suspected that the Poles might use a truce as a breathing space to rearm. Kamenev was immediately suspicious, describing the proposed truce as a 'trick' and recommended to Moscow that the Red Army improve its strategic situation before Lloyd George's deadline.[85] But as the Bolsheviks had already secretly decided in the central committee to prosecute the offensive against Poland to victory, voicing concerns about Poland taking advantage of a truce was nothing but hypocritical. Lenin, moreover, was certain Lloyd George would not follow through his threats of military action and blockade. It was clear to all that the British government, for several weeks, had done nothing meaningful in response to the Red Army's gathering offensive and Lenin was confident that the Allied Powers were still unable to send their own troops to Soviet Russia. Other Bolsheviks more familiar with British affairs, like Litvinov, worried that the trades unions and the threat of a general strike in retaliation for military intervention would not always act as restraining forces on the British government, without which, apparently, 'Churchill's hands would finally be left free'. Indeed, from the London trade delegation, Klyshko and Rotshtein warned in early August that forced sovietization of Poland could damage support among the British labour movement.[86] But for now, Lenin saw (rightly) that repeated direct British or French intervention was off the table. The party leader shared the concerns of other leading Bolsheviks about a new and wider military intervention involving the militaries of other border states, engineered by the Allies, but he was likely as much influenced by rising optimism in the Soviet high command that Warsaw could be taken quickly in the current window of opportunity, delivering a decisive blow against the Versailles order.[87] For this prize alone, the gamble was still worth it. Lenin, for these reasons, remained in a buoyant mood after receiving Lloyd George's threats of military action, writing to Stalin on 7 August that successes against Wrangel would remove doubts in the central committee about pursuing the offensive on the western front. 'Much still depends on Warsaw and its fate', he noted.[88]

Stalin, for his part, gave more credence to the British threat of intervention. On 8 August, he and Egorov warned the commanders of the 13th and 14th Red Armies, and the Soviet Navy, that the British and French navies might carry out action in the Baltic and Black Seas and the two stressed that intelligence be improved. But rather than warn against economic blockade (Lloyd George's only real leverage), Stalin suggested counteractions be prepared against the possible landings of troops.[89] Perhaps simply undue caution on Stalin's part, but others, including Trotsky, also saw reason to worry. On 6 August he suggested to Chicherin and Nikolai Krestinskii that Lev Kamenev inform Curzon that if the British attacked, the Bolsheviks would harden their 'diplomatic and military politics' in the east, in Persia, Turkey and India.[90] From the high command, Sergei Kamenev expressed even more strongly unfounded concerns – based on press reports – and claimed that in addition to dispatching vessels to the Baltic, the Allies planned to send troops through Latvia, Lithuania, Germany, Italy, Austria, Czechoslovakia and Romania to assist Poland.[91]

Lenin's calculation proved correct and Lloyd George's priority, as ever, remained peace not escalation. The British prime minister made it clear to his cabinet, and the French government, that he would wait for the results of armistice negotiations before taking further action against Soviet Russia (which he still wanted to do everything to avoid). The French position was more hard-line and envisaged applying pressure on Soviet Russia by fully restoring the economic blockade, assisting Wrangel and organizing other border states.[92] The British provisionally agreed to these measures, although Lloyd George made everything conditional on the outcome of the Soviet-Polish negotiations, unless the Red Army pushed into Polish territory in the meantime.[93] Yet Lenin was still assuming the Red Army would make progress faster than the Allies could mount a response. After receiving more information from the Soviet trade delegation in London about growing working-class resistance to any sign of British efforts to go to war, he believed he had necessary time.[94]

Lloyd George's threats did produce one concrete result. Lev Kamenev handed the Soviet peace conditions to the British government on 9 August, sent to Poland the following day, with negotiations to begin at Minsk shortly after. In discussions behind-the-scenes, Kamenev had pushed for the Soviet conditions to be now presented to the British. Partly a response to Lloyd George's application of pressure, Kamenev understood, too, that the prime minster was 'seeking a way out' of the conflict. There was also the prospect of creating a new wedge between Britain and France around the Soviet conditions, something which happened quickly considering how demanding these proved to be. Litvinov sided with Kamenev on these issues, admitting to Chicherin that 'artificially delaying negotiations with the Poles' had been a mistake. The Bolsheviks, he argued, in hindsight should have presented conditions earlier and so demanding that 'their fulfilment would require long enough to allow us to occupy the left bank of the Mlava [River], and even Warsaw'. But in current circumstances and with initiative in defining armistice terms slipping away to the British, the Soviet terms needed to be presented there-and-then. Furthermore, anticipating hostile international reaction to the Soviet occupation of Warsaw, Litvinov pressed Chicherin for a preliminary peace to be at least concluded with Poland before its sovietization.[95] This presupposed that the Polish government would accept what was on offer – an unlikely prospect. Indeed, outside this discussion of when, how and in what manner, the Soviet terms should be handed over, other Bolsheviks displayed the same instincts about the value of draconian conditions. For Stalin, ensuring that it would be 'impossible for the bourgeoisie of Poland to recover' was essential.[96]

The Soviet terms, of course, proved to be impossible for Poland to accept. Demobilization of the Polish Army to 50,000 soldiers and the dismantling of military industry were flagrant interferences in the country's internal affairs. The Bolsheviks refused an armistice line any further east than the former Curzon line and the proposed neutral zone from which Polish troops would depart actually included Warsaw.[97] However, Lloyd George (perhaps not appreciating the reality of the latter point) put to the cabinet that the terms were not as severe as the conditions imposed by the Allies on Germany and Austria and therefore were acceptable. He ruled out engaging in war to achieve better conditions and advised the Polish government that the British could not provide assistance if it rejected them.[98] The French vigorously disagreed, and, with that, the Bolsheviks had split the Allied Powers, a core aim of their security policy. The Millerand government went on the formerly recognize Wrangel as the legitimate head of government in South Russia on 11 August, widening the gap even further; but nevertheless, the French still resisted sending significant troops to Poland.[99] The Polish government understandably reacted to the Soviet terms with fury. Describing these as 'humiliating', Sapieha entirely ruled out demobilizing the Polish Army or agreeing to any interferences in Poland's internal affairs. He vowed that the Poles would continue to defend themselves.[100]

What Lloyd George did not know, however, was that Lev Kamenev, on his own initiative, had omitted two key conditions from the Soviet terms: arming of the Polish workers, which had been obscured as the Polish government relinquishing surplus weapons beyond required for a smaller army and 'civic militia', and the freedom to transit goods and people through Poland, creating a path to Germany. Kamenev had worried that these unmistakably revolutionary objectives might prove unpopular with British labour movement, still regarded as essential for restraining the imperialist impulses of the British government.[101] Even though Klyshko and Rotshtein reported the opposite from London, that, in their view, arming the Polish working class would be a popular proposal, it seems that Kamenev was unmoved.[102] Unsurprisingly, back in Moscow, Chicherin was unhappy with Kamenev's freelancing. He wanted all the Soviet conditions widely publicized and explained to him that arming the working class was a guarantee of peace 'unprecedented in history'.[103] Still, Kamenev did not want to take the risk. Britain and France were at odds over the conditions as already presented; anything more demanding might jeopardize this. He also pointed to popular support building for the Bolsheviks' position among the British left, 'unheard of in scale and unity' and amenable to the so-far published conditions. Kamenev pushed Chicherin to agree that any future Soviet-Polish peace agreed at Minsk would accord with the already presented Soviet terms. He made clear at the same time that Poland would most likely reject the Soviet conditions anyway, meaning little was to be gained from revealing the fuller picture.[104] For now, with Kamenev having effectively made the decision himself, to some dissatisfaction in Moscow, the two potentially incendiary conditions remained concealed.

In a similar episode, as the Soviet conditions were presented to Lloyd George, the Politburo approved Trotsky's proposal for sending 100 or so German communists to the western front, suitable for carrying out propaganda and agitation (and presumably in anticipation of the Red Army's future crossing through Poland's western border into Germany).[105] This idea, however, was a step too far for Chicherin this time, who warned the Politburo that forming special German detachments so close to the Polish-German border would be interpreted by the German government and western powers (not unreasonably) as making 'a preparatory step' towards world revolution. This would 'extraordinarily complicate' diplomatic relations, he noted. Trotsky's proposal, moreover, ran counter to the unofficial assurances given by Viktor Kopp, the Soviet representative in Berlin, that the Bolsheviks would cooperate with Germany to allow plebiscites in its former territory now incorporated into Poland, should a 'Polish Bolshevik government' be established in Warsaw. Indeed, two days later, Chicherin assured the German foreign minister that the Red Army would respect the 'old German boundary' as it advanced.[106] Taken together, it was no secret that the Bolsheviks saw Poland as the bridge uniting 'Soviet Russia with proletarian Germany'; but at the same time, they sought to aggressively deny that Poland would be sovietized by force of arms. If revolution happened to break out, it would be organically guided by the working class, even if supplied with Soviet weapons. In essence, although earlier disagreements about the plan for sovietizing Poland (and if the opportunity arose, Germany) had been overcome, new fault lines were emerging about how this would be achieved and how quickly to force the pace of revolutionary change in public view without provoking a more serious Allied response. All of this played out as the Battle of Warsaw drew closer.[107]

Towards Warsaw and defeat

On 10 August Tukhachevskii issued an order for the final Battle of Warsaw, setting the stage for the anticipated victory.[108] However, at this very moment, Sergei Kamenev's confidence began to waver. Even though the commander-in-chief still planned a decisive strike on the western front, he worried that Tukhachevskii's strategy of sending three of his armies to the north of Warsaw left insufficient forces east of the city and his left-flank exposed. Kamenev wanted two of his armies redeployed south to provide cover. Tukhachevskii resisted and maintained that his strength was needed in the north, arguing that this was where the main Polish defences were amassing.[109] This was not actually true. The main Polish counterattack eventually came south of the city and would puncture the vulnerable spot between the increasingly strung-out Soviet fronts. Tukhachevskii's insistence on this risky northward advance was driven by wider strategic and revolutionary goals. One calculation was preventing the Allied Powers from supplying Poland through Danzig and the Polish corridor, the last viable channels since Germany declared neutrality on 20 July (though, in truth, any supplies that managed to get past British dock workers would be so small as to have barely any impact).[110] And second, the possibility of restoring both territories to German ownership represented a bigger tantalizing prospect and another means of chipping away at the Versailles order.[111] Seeing as Tukhachevskii was actually in the field, Kamenev decided to give him the benefit of the doubt about where Polish troops were amassing and he made adjustments to the wider strategy. To protect what he saw as Tukhachevskii's vulnerable left flank, he sent an order to Egorov calling for the 1st Cavalry Army and 12th Red Army to cease operations towards Lwów and move north, to strike towards Lublin in support of Tukhachevskii's attack, closing the distance between Warsaw by half. The 12th Red Army would need to make its transfer by 13 August; the cavalry army, two days later.[112]

Egorov and Stalin, still in charge of the revolutionary military council of the southwestern front, took two days to reply, citing problems with deciphering Kamenev's message, but in the end, resisted transferring their forces. Stalin argued that the 1st Cavalry Army was too deeply engaged towards Lwów and simply could not move north.[113] On the same day as Kamenev sent his order, Stalin telegrammed Voroshilov and Budennyi asking for urgent clarification about when the attack on Lwów would begin. It is unclear whether this was sent before or after Kamenev's order went out, but either way, Stalin's commitment to staying on course in the southwest was plain to see.[114] In this dispute, Stalin proved correct on balance. By the time the 1st Cavalry Army managed to extricate itself from difficult fighting and travel northwards, it was too late to make any difference to Tukhachevskii's attack, though this did not alter the fact of Stalin's insubordination.

Lenin now also intervened further muddying the waters, and inadvertently gave Stalin cover to ignore Kamenev's order. In the backdrop of Lloyd George calling for the Poles to accept the Soviet conditions for armistice negotiations, Lenin immediately wrote to Stalin on 11 August describing the 'big victory' achieved (even though he mistakenly believed the British had accepted the revolutionary proposals Lev Kamenev obscured). Believing that Britain had, in effect, ordered its instrument of war – Poland – to stand down, Lenin pressed upon Stalin that victory would be complete 'if we finish off Wrangel'. This would deliver in Lenin's mind the decisive blow against the Allied Powers and he urged Stalin to take Crimea.[115] But this produced mixed messages at a crucial moment. Kamenev ordered forces in the southwest to travel north to support Tukhachevskii, while Lenin pushed for greater efforts against Wrangel in the south. Stalin was therefore given the very opportunity he needed to resist the transfers north and take shots at Kamenev at the same time. In his reply to Lenin, aside from noting he did not believe Lloyd George's statement to the Polish government, Stalin railed against the slow pace of reinforcements to the southern front. Kamenev was 'sabotaging the organization of victory over Wrangel' and did not show 'one tenth of a desire' to beat his army as he did Poland.[116] For Stalin, as he had made clear during the July central committee plenum, it was fruitless to try to seize Warsaw with Wrangel's army still active. Lenin's confusion of the strategy was only temporary. He realized his error two days later and like Kamenev now appreciated the risk of leaving Tukhachevskii without sufficient reinforcements. Furthermore, his suggestion of conscripting Belarusian peasants to bring up numbers was hardly going to match the strength of the now-absent 1st Cavalry Army.[117] Confusion at the top was not the only reason why successfully capturing Warsaw was looking in doubt by mid-August. There were further warning signs about Polish public opinion as the battle drew near. The regular source of Polish intelligence, Paweł Łapiński, for instance, wrote to Chicherin on 12 August commenting on rising 'extreme nationalism' and anti-Russian sentiment in Poland, especially from the Polish peasantry.[118] Having just returned from the western front, the Bolshevik Ivar Smilga wrote to Lenin and Trotsky on the same day, with a similar warning. 'Going beyond the Vistula in the absence of a powerful revolutionary movement in Poland will lead us to disaster', he explained.[119]

Yet by mid-August, there was no stopping the momentum of the Soviet offensive. The wheels of the war machine were in full flow and the Battle of Warsaw began. In its early days, fighting took place 20 kilometres northwest of Warsaw in the vicinity of Radzymin, a small but strategically significant town on the edge of the Vistula bridgehead. The 16th Red Army and 21st division of the 3rd Red Army easily took Radzymin on 13 August, but the town soon changed hands numerous times over subsequent days.[120] Confusion also still reigned in wider Soviet military strategy. On the first day of fighting, Kamenev reiterated that the 12th Red Army and 1st Cavalry Army were needed on western front.[121] But even though Egorov now informed the 1st Cavalry Army of Kamenev's decision, he neglected to say anything about stopping the advance towards Lwów. Stalin, moreover, continued to complain to Lenin about Kamenev's inattention of the southern front and pushed for a 'clear decision' about whether Wrangel would be taken on decisively or not.[122] Yet Lenin's attentions, for the moment, were firmly focused on Warsaw. On 15 August, in a message to London, in which Lenin advised Lev Kamenev about writing a joint statement with a member of the British Communist Party on the subject of Poland free of landlords and capitalists, he added: 'keep in mind that we hope to take Warsaw on 16th'.[123] More problems came on this very day, however, when Tukhachevskii ordered the 1st Cavalry Army and 12th Red Army to support his offensive, which had moved into fierce fighting at Wkra River following a counterattack by Władysław Sikorski's Polish forces from the area of the Modlin fortress. The main Soviet attack was repulsed 50 kilometres north of Warsaw.[124] But Budennyi then questioned the validity of Tukhachevskii's order as this had not been countersigned by a political officer. A new countersigned order took another two days to arrive by which time it was too late to transfer the 1st Cavalry Army, which was once again firmly engaged at Lwów. The 12th Red Army belatedly turned northwards but was soon bogged down in difficult terrain.[125]

Confused strategy from the beginning, ego-driven foot-dragging and some blatant insubordination were all on display in the run-up to the main Polish counterattack, which began on 16 August, the day Lenin had anticipated Red Army soldiers entering the streets of Warsaw. Alongside a renewed push around the Wkra River, led by Sikorski's 5th Army, Piłsudski now sent five divisions through the weakest point between the Soviet fronts, only defended by the small formation, the Mozyr Group, much depleted in strength following the pursuit of the Poles from Kiev. By this point, such was the overstretch in Soviet lines that the Polish armies met almost no resistance and quickly travelled through the chasm between the Soviet fronts, sparking confusion and panic among Red Army soldiers. Furthermore, so unreliable were Soviet communications that Tukhachevskii learnt of the counterattack two days after it began. He quickly ordered a temporary retreat on 18 August for regrouping, but fearing being cut off and encircled by the Polish counterattack from the south, soldiers under Tukhachevskii's command were already withdrawing in chaotic scenes.[126] Amid the confusion, Egorov, on the southwestern front (who had heard about Piłsudski's counterattack from the Lublin region at least one day before Tukhachevskii) ordered the 14th Red Army to take Lwów in the shortest possible time. This was partly in response to Soviet intelligence that Romania was concentrating two armies in Bessarabia, but it shows once again the priority some still awarded to the southwest even at this critical moment.[127] A few days later, on 20 August, Budennyi's 1st Cavalry Army finally moved north away from Lwów, but it could do nothing to halt the disaster unfolding outside Warsaw.

The key to Piłsudski's counterattack was to skilfully exploit the forces at his disposal, combined with the good fortune of Soviet strategic errors. In the two weeks before the Battle of Warsaw he organized a fiendishly complex withdrawal and regrouping of Polish military strength to create a striking force in the southwest of Warsaw that would deliver the hammer blow.[128] With reinforcements in the southwest keeping Budennyi's cavalry busy, Piłsudski also left just enough strength to tie down and delay the Soviet advance towards Warsaw (which he mistakenly assumed would be an offensive in a straight line rather than Tukhachevskii's wheel to the north of the city). Regardless, when the main Polish blow struck through the centre of increasingly stretched out Soviet fronts, driving at the left flank of Tukhachevskii's armies, the battle was decided at this moment. This was personal vindication for Piłsudski, who, all the while, had been subjected to French pressure and rising criticism at home as the mood turned against his entire military campaign – with efforts launched to weaken his powers as commander-in-chief.[129] Moreover, the information feeding back to Moscow during the counterattack revealed how far the Bolsheviks miscalculated the revolutionary potential of the Polish people. Travelling with the Polrevkom and now in the town of Wyszków, just 60 kilometres outside Warsaw, Dzerzhinskii wrote to Lenin on 17 August to report on the situation on the ground and the mood among local Poles. Polish workers, he claimed, were apparently awaiting the arrival of the Red Army in Warsaw, but the much larger Polish peasantry was, even in Dzerzhinskii's optimistic reading, indifferent to either side. Dzerzhinskii also described the serious preparations underway in the city. Men and women were being rounded up to dig trenches; barricades were constructed in the streets; a campaign of 'state terror' targeted leading workers; communists were being arrested. Polish cardinals and religious leaders compared the Bolsheviks to the antichrist.[130] This was not a city that was going to fall easily. In a message to Sklianskii, however, on the same day, Lenin piled on the pressure anyway, exclaiming that 'if the military department or the Supreme Commander *is not refusing* to take Warsaw, *it must* be taken'. A truce would be 'idiotism' and he urged Warsaw be taken in a matter of days.[131]

Yet by 19 August, the Polish Army had successfully pushed the Red Army out of the Vistula bridgehead and the military situation was firmly turning against the Bolsheviks. Lenin made one-last desperate attempt to spark revolutionary fervour among local populations (though this as much could have been an effort to hinder Polish reoccupation of the border regions in recognition of defeat). He wrote to Radek calling for the Polrevkom to enact 'merciless defeat of the landlords and kulaks faster and more energetically' and for the peasants to be given land freely. He pushed for an uprising among Galician peasants and for 'thousands of communists' and 'a significant number of old and experienced workers' to be sent to the 'Polish-Wrangel front', describing the disaster as a 'temporary setback'.[132] But even Lenin, by now, must have understood that the revolutionary committee could not effectively mobilize local people, let alone effect revolutionary change. The party leader was certainly not alone in entertaining fantasies of a successful fight back. On the same day, Tukhachevskii and Smilga advised signing an armistice and regrouping strength, claiming that the Red Army had the numbers for a new strike. Other Bolsheviks, including Chicherin, suggested this was still possible.[133] Soon enough, however, Lenin adopted a more defeatist tone. In a message to Lev Kamenev in London on 20 August, he admitted: 'It is hardly likely that we will take Warsaw soon. The enemy has concentrated his forces there and is advancing. It is quite clear that Lloyd George and Churchill have appointed the rôles and that Lloyd George, under cover of pacifist phrases, supports the actual policy of the French and of Churchill.'[134]

Away from the action outside Warsaw, the armistice negotiations at Minsk had begun on 17 August. Initially, neither side had any idea about what was unfolding 300 miles away, and in truth, they were only in Minsk to keep the Allied Powers, and primarily Britain, on side. The Poles knew there was no chance of meaningful assistance if they did not engage in negotiations; the Bolsheviks wanted to discourage any form of intervention and their suspicions were still running high. Trotsky had speculated to Chicherin, Krestinskii and Lenin a few days before that Polish evasion in the negotiations, or at least how the Bolsheviks saw it, was due to the Allies concentrating troops or alternatively because France and Poland were still seeking to draw Britain into the war by underlining the 'impossibility of coming to terms with us'.[135] For Lenin, Britain remained central to his calculations. 'I hope that England will be unable to fight, and without her, everything falls to the ground', he wrote to Lev Kamenev.[136] Still, the Bolsheviks had no intention of negotiating in good faith at Minsk and considering their apparent position of strength at the outset of the Battle of Warsaw, they planned to simply present terms as an ultimatum and had hardened their demands in the days before.[137] And when the Soviet proposals were finally presented in Minsk on 17 August, it became clear to all that they contained those omitted from the list previously given to Lloyd George, including the establishment of a revolutionary workers' militia. The British reacted with scorn, later describing a Bolshevik effort to overthrow Poland's democracy and substitute it with 'the despotism of a privileged few who may have absorbed the doctrines of Bolshevism'.[138] But as news of the Red Army's defeat started to reach Moscow on the first day of the negotiations, everything suddenly changed. With the military situation dramatically shifting, Chicherin warned Lenin that the Poles would not accept their conditions (he also believed that the Poles had purposely delayed the start of negotiations to allow a striking force to be built outside Warsaw for the counterattack).[139] The Minsk talks broke off and both sides agreed that negotiations would resume in the neutral territory of Riga in September. The Bolsheviks' leverage had evaporated.

With the loss at Warsaw sinking in, the Politburo, on Stalin and Trotsky's initiative, reorientated Soviet military priorities towards the south against Wrangel, effectively abandoning the offensive in the west.[140] In the meantime, in the southwest, Budennyi's cavalry, along with the 12th Red Army, was engaged in a final offensive to break through Lublin to hit Piłsudski's armies from the rear. But with Tukhachevskii's armies in retreat, the Poles could now focus more power in the southwest. Budennyi was temporarily encircled and forced into a humiliating retreat. The Polish Army then pushed further east, retaking Volhnynia and eastern Galicia. A final significant clash came at the Niemen River in mid-late-September, where Tukhachevskii was regrouping his strength. Although the Red Army managed some renewed resistance, Tukhachevskii was again forced back. The Poles then pushed forwards towards Minsk, ending up at the culminating point of their first offensive.[141] In a repeat of history, some Bolsheviks worried that without an armistice in place, the Poles would again take Kiev as the Red Army was withdrawn to the southern front to combat Wrangel's army. Trotsky was concerned that the Polish high command might order another push forward and give Poland greater leverage in future peace negotiations. In early October, the Revolutionary Military Council of the Republic called on Red Army forces on the southwestern front to deliver a 'crushing strike' against Polish forces approaching Kiev, but by now, this was wishful thinking.[142]

During the tail end of fighting, Polish and Soviet negotiators worked in Riga from September on the armistice and preliminary peace agreements. As Chicherin had put it to Lenin in late August, the Bolsheviks were faced with a choice: 'whether to change the basis of our politics towards Poland or break off negotiations'.[143] A sense of vulnerability was deepening. On 25 August, Litvinov warned Chicherin that the 'unexpected Polish success made Lloyd George go to Canossa, to Millerand. The French are celebrating the victory and are already plotting about using the Polish attack as the starting point for a new intervention.'[144] Litvinov advised agreeing peace quickly and concentrating military strength against Wrangel. The Bolsheviks chose this path. After weeks of difficult negotiations, an armistice and preliminary peace came into effect on 18 October.

Aftermath

There was no question that the Red Army suffered a stunning defeat in August 1920. The losses on the Soviet side far exceeded the Polish with, at the upper end, perhaps 25,000 killed and twice as many captured in the disaster outside Warsaw. Elite units, which had proved so devastating in early summer, like Gai's 3rd Cavalry Corps, experienced humiliatingly internment after fleeing into East Prussia. The outcome was more of a blow considering the weak state of the enemy. In the words of Polish chief of staff, Tadaeusz Rozwodowski, to the Inter-Allied mission in early August, the Polish Army was 'an entirely new and improvised organization deficient in training and experience and lacking officers with the necessary professional qualifications'.[145] The Polish Army, without doubt, benefitted from French expertise and the several hundred French officers who arrived in Warsaw. It also had the experience of a veteran contingent which had served in the First World War.[146] But it remained a young and inexperienced military force, not dissimilar to the Red Army. The outcome was therefore decided by failings elsewhere. When Lev Kamenev wrote to Moscow following the battle and remarked that 'the policy of the bayonet, as usual, has broken down "owing to unforeseen circumstances"', this was too generous an explanation, as these were entirely clear.[147] The Bolsheviks were never blind to Red Army's deficiencies, from its dwindling manpower and reinforcements to unreliable communications and overstretched supplies, so much so that its soldiers ended up living off the land at the expense of the Poles they claimed to be liberating. The Bolsheviks took a major risk in launching an attack on Poland and there was plenty of blame to go around in an acrimonious internal debate which erupted soon after the defeat. Yet few directly criticized Lenin for his role in the disaster, even though he was chief culprit of the ill-considered revolutionary war.

In a lengthy address at the ninth party conference one month after the Battle of Warsaw, Lenin delivered in some respects a frank account of the war and why the decision was taken to attack Poland. The party leader was disingenuous when he claimed the Bolsheviks had been sincere about peace in early 1920; however, Lenin's words rang true when he described the Curzon ultimatum of July as the central turning point. 'We faced the question of either accepting this proposal, which would have given us an advantageous border and thus [allowed us to] assume a position that was, generally speaking, purely defensive, or [else] to exploit the élan of our army and the advantage we enjoyed to help in the sovietization of Poland.' With some justification Lenin noted how the Bolsheviks had taken advantage of 'the splits emerging between the various counties of the Entente', meaning a new united anti-Soviet force could not be easily formed. For him, this left one road ahead: to 'exploit the military situation to launch an offensive war [...] to assist the sovietization of Poland', which he later labelled 'the center of world imperialist politics' and 'linchpin of the whole Treaty of Versailles'. As we have seen, this was the core rationale for Lenin's gamble in the summer and the Red Army duly crossed the Curzon line. The failed war was therefore framed within the backdrop of a momentous struggle against capitalism and imperialism, and, for Lenin, the Red Army's defeat ensured that Poland would 'remain entirely in the hands of international imperialism against Russia'. Even so, he argued, the plan to force revolution in Europe had been the right choice.[148]

Accounting for the disaster, Lenin also explained that he had mistakenly believed the working peoples of the west would rise in support of the offensive (although he still saw some scope for proletarian uprisings in Germany and Britain). Furthermore, the Bolsheviks' efforts to 'test the true mood' of the Polish masses had not been good or deep enough, failing to breakthrough to the centres of the industrial proletariat. The Red Army consequently 'encountered a great national surge of petty bourgeois elements'. In private conversation elsewhere, with German communist Clara Zetkin, Lenin described how the Polish people had viewed the Red Army as 'enemies, not brother and liberators'. But none of this should have come as a surprise. Like others in the central committee, Lenin had been told the warning signs that the Polish people were not ready for revolution, but he chose to ignore them. Radek, castigated for defeatism in the July plenum of the central committee, was right to raise doubts as Lenin now admitted to Zetkin. It is possible that Lenin had been swayed by optimistic reports coming out of Poland from the likes of the Polish Communist Party about supposedly strong anti-war sentiments and even a gathering revolutionary movement among the

Polish working class – or these at least gave confidence to his instincts. But equally, Lenin knew, like others, that the Polish communists, few in number, had weak connections to Polish society; its reports from Poland were often inconsistent. To put it simply, Lenin knew the risks and miscalculated (he admitted to plenum he had no knowledge of 'military science'). And he was not going to repeat the same mistake twice. Although Lenin implausibly claimed the Red Army had the potential to carry on the war after the summer, 'the thought of the agonies of another winter of war was unbearable'.[149]

In another speech delivered to a group of industry workers, just before the October armistice was agreed, Lenin spoke again about the practical problems that had undermined the Soviet summer offensive, namely that the Red Army 'lacked just a little strength to reach Warsaw', whereas the Polish Army had been 'supported by a wave of patriotism in Warsaw'. It is not hard to understand why Lenin sought to downplay the mistakes of military overstretch – something under the Bolsheviks' control – when speaking in public. It was, of course, false to say 'just a little' extra power would have propelled the Red Army into the Polish capital. At the same time, Lenin underlined the global nature of the conflict. He described Poland as 'the Entente's cat's-paw […] a buffer state which is to guard against German contact with Soviet communism […] a weapon against the Bolsheviks'. The significance of the Soviet-Polish war, he argued, was that it 'proved to be a more direct war against the Entente than previous wars had been'. Now that the Bolsheviks were once again temporarily on the back foot, 'French and British imperialism is inciting Poland to make a fresh attempt to overthrow the Soviets'. The wider 'war against the Entente' was also clear in the ongoing conflict against Wrangel. International imperialists were 'attempting to strangle the Soviet Republic with both hands'.[150]

Other leading Bolsheviks, like Stalin, made contributions in the difficult raking over of the disaster. Because of his and Egorov's refusal to follow Sergei Kamenev's orders on the eve of the Battle of Warsaw, to divert the 1st Cavalry Army and 12th Red Army further north in support of Tukhachevskii, Stalin was at risk of being tainted by the defeat. In the first instance, he made a swift denial of responsibility for the delay in transferring the 1st Cavalry Army and then resigned his military posts on 1 September, after already being put on leave by the Politburo.[151] What comments Stalin offered beyond this were mostly focused, as in previous months, on the high command's misconceived strategy, a central part of the post-mortem. And given the reality of his insubordination, it is hardly a surprise Stalin sought to spread blame to others.[152] At the ninth party conference, therefore, Stalin criticized Kamenev's decision to transfer the 1st Cavalry Army to the western front. He claimed that Lwów could have been taken had Budennyi stayed his course, a victory needlessly thrown away. Stalin's criticism was indirectly aimed at Lenin when he complained how the party leader was trying 'to spare the command' and he wanted the military leadership to take responsibility for letting the Red Army fall into overstretch and exhaustion. 'If the command had warned the TsK [central committee] about the actual state of the front, the TsK would have undoubtedly temporarily abandoned the offensive', he remarked. Overconfidence within the high command about taking Warsaw, Stalin argued, not unreasonably, had swayed opinion in the central committee towards launching the attack in the first place. 'I was, it seems, the only member of the central committee who ridiculed the current slogan about a "march to Warsaw" and I openly warned comrades in the press against enthusiasm for success, from underestimating the Polish forces.'[153] At another meeting, of the Moscow City Committee of the Communist Party, Stalin pursued his criticism of the high command's 'incorrect plan of attack', although meaningful debate about Soviet military strategy was thereafter increasingly confined to military forums.[154] Tukhachevskii naturally became an object of blame for the manner of his risky offensive, creating rifts in the high command. Stalin's ally Egorov, later in 1922, for instance, objected to Tukhachevskii receiving command of the western front because, as he put it to Stalin, it was 'completely unacceptable on all sides to put again into post of command of the western front, a person who has already failed'.[155]

Because Trotsky was so integral to the military command that Stalin blamed for the disaster, he pushed back against this explanation of defeat. At the ninth party conference, Trotsky pointed out that the central committee had received the very same intelligence as the high command and attacking Warsaw was a shared decision (referring also to Stalin's insubordination, Trotsky accused him of having 'undermined me and the central committee'). Falling in line with Lenin and minimizing his earlier doubts about the revolutionary potential of Poland, Trotsky claimed the offensive had been the right strategy all along and the Bolsheviks had a duty to 'probe the enemy' and test the revolutionary waters in Europe.[156] Trotsky also, like Lenin, cast blame at malevolent Allied interference. In early September, he claimed the war was the result of a Polish 'bourgeois-gentry government obedient to the will of the French stock exchange'.[157] Another exaggeration, though not without a grain of substance. It was true that, at the end of August, the Quai d'Orsay attempted engineer a final offensive by Poland, Romania and the White forces to topple the much-weakened Soviet government. But the main direction of French government policy was facing the other way: to ensure that Piłsudski did not occupy too much territory in the east, potentially creating new future conflicts with other states. Both Britain and France encouraged Poland to make peace using the Curzon line.[158]

Like Stalin's comments in the aftermath of the war, other Bolsheviks highlighted the unrealistic expectations that had held sway in the party about a new revolution. Chicherin, already a critic of the so-called revolutionary dreamers, told Litvinov that the Red Army's offensive failed because it advanced too quickly and 'psychological considerations were put above strategic'. Yet rather than give Piłsudski credit for the counterattack, Chicherin claimed that 'French generals' were responsible for exploiting the weaknesses in the Red Army's flank.[159] Voroshilov, one of Stalin's key allies, unsurprisingly sided with him, and expressed similar sentiments in private to another likeminded Bolshevik, Sergo Ordzhonikidze, in early September: 'We expected uprisings and revolutions from the Polish workers, but we got chauvinism and stupid hatred towards "Russians."'[160] Feliks Kon, member of the short-lived Polish Revolutionary Committee, pointed out the fundamental misapprehension of the true circumstances in Poland, noting, like others, that Polish peasants had responded passively to the Bolsheviks' revolutionary appeals. With the benefit of hindsight, Kon did not express much surprise, considering Poland's past in the Russian empire when 'the Russia soldier was an instrument of power for 150 years under the tsarist regime'.[161]

The fallout from defeat at Warsaw, in this way, opened some genuine reflection about Soviet strategic errors and logistical weaknesses, and some senior Bolsheviks, Lenin included, admitted overestimating a revolutionary mood in Poland. Still, doubts about invading Poland had hardly gone unsaid in the months before and Lenin could have chosen a different path. Ultimately, he was responsible for the Soviet defeat; the gamble had failed. But while some space opened for more candid discussion of the war with a changed tone, there was little deviation from the long-running deeper explanation of the war: the evolving capitalist conspiracy against Soviet Russia. This was no less the primary undercurrent to party discussion in the war's aftermath. As the next chapter shows, this continued to shape opinion about the emerging peace settlement and internal assessments about future Soviet-Polish relations years after. At the ninth party conference in September 1920, Lenin warned that another conflict in the coming winter could not be ruled out, precisely because Poland was still a central cog in a wider international anti-Soviet coalition. This was 'in all likelihood […] predetermined […] We realize that a winter campaign will cost many lives […] because Wrangel and Poland, no matter how much they quarrel, still form part of the same international front.' It is possible that Lenin was knowingly raising the prospect of another damaging war to prime the party towards accepting the difficult concessions necessary for peace. However, he also warned, incorrectly, that the chances of peace were not high and, as the next chapter shows, a permanent war scare now set in from 1920, lasting far beyond the peace negotiations at Riga.[162]

Chapter 3

COEXISTENCE TO CRISIS

As the preliminary peace and armistice came into effect at midnight on 18 October, fighting between Poland and Soviet Russia finally ground to a halt. Yet the formal ending of war was not a watershed moment. While the armistice curtailed military action, mutual distrust remained stubbornly high. In the first years after the war, this was predominately driven by uprisings and attacks by nationalist organizations in the border regions, which both the Bolsheviks and Poles tried to leverage to their advantage. The arming and financing of such third-party groups infringed the spirit of the preliminary peace and threatened to wreck precariously balanced Soviet-Polish relations. But while both governments were quick to volley complaints through foreign ministries, it was only the Bolsheviks who regularly made the leap to interpreting attacks in the border regions as a precursor to renewed war. Peace established with Poland did little to dent the Bolsheviks' siege mentality.

The reality was that such anxieties about the resumption of war were misplaced. The NKID received reports on a regular basis about the Polish government's turn away from military action in the early 1920s. These included detail of how the influential National Democrats sought to consolidate Poland's existing influence, not extend this further east. It was true that Piłsudski was no less committed to pushing back Soviet controlled territory and still coveted influence over Soviet Ukraine and Belorussia, but he was an increasingly marginalized figure in political life.[1] The Bolsheviks, for the most part, though not always consistently, understood these shifts in political influence and foreign policy. It was at a deeper level where they saw the danger. They feared that the real enemy – the western capitalist powers – had not abandoned their crusade against communism and would find new ways to manipulate Poland again into war. Such suspicions were sustained not only by fresh security concerns about internal subversion in the border regions but through the difficulty of interpreting a complex and fluctuating international situation through an ideological lens. These anxieties about war would reach another peak in 1923 when the Ruhr crisis shook western Europe and the Bolsheviks again accelerated plans for a European-wide conflict.

Towards lasting peace and subversion in the borderlands

The armistice in October 1920 did little to change how the Bolsheviks and their security organs viewed the severity of Polish subversive threats to Soviet territory. Feliks Dzerzhinskii, head of the Cheka, in fact drew a direct link to the summer catastrophe outside Warsaw. In an order published in October, he claimed that enemies were exploiting the Red Army's defeat, as well as other weak points such as the struggling post-civil war Soviet economy, in an effort to topple the government through engineered local uprisings.[2] From an array of perceived dangers, however, the Cheka's attentions during autumn and winter 1920 to 1921 focused more than anything on the activity of the Polish Military Organization (POV). Originally Piłsudski's creation in the First World War, and founded to carry out sabotage and intelligence operations, the POV remained active in the western border regions until 1921. After the armistice, therefore, Cheka operatives were quick to report apparent POV infiltrations in Ukraine's major cities, with groups unearthed in Kiev, Odessa, Khar'kov, the Volhynia region, among other places. Espionage and the planning of uprisings to disrupt the Soviet rear were marked out as central dangers. In some cities, the Cheka claimed victory over the organization; in others, active operations were underway with apparent successes reported from late 1920. The deputy of the Cheka's special departments on the southwestern front, for instance, notified Dzerzhinskii at the end of November that POV organizations had been crushed in the Khar'kov, Poltava, Pavlograd and Aleksandrovsk regions.[3] Nevertheless, new investigations soon began, running in 1921.[4]

A second subversive danger, rising up the Bolsheviks' agenda after the armistice, and with bigger implications for diplomatic relations, was the nationalist organizations operating in Soviet territory with Polish support. Indeed, just one week after the armistice came into effect, head of the government in Soviet Ukraine, Kristian Rakovskii, complained to Moscow about the Polish military's ongoing support of anti-Soviet groups loyal to Petliura and the self-styled 'peasants' general', Polish-Belarusian Stanisłav Bułak-Bałakhovich. He made several complaints over October and November.[5] However, in the first weeks after the armistice, the preliminary peace permitted the support of third-party organizations until the exchange of ratification documents; and only later would a firmer obligation to cease supporting such groups be enshrined in a definitive peace treaty.[6] The Bolsheviks themselves had few grounds for protest, given their own support of separatist movements in the Polish borderlands, one part of a deliberate Soviet strategy to gain a stronger foothold further east. Sensitive and oil rich East Galicia, where Poles were in a minority and Polish sovereignty not formerly awarded until 1923, was a priority target (the situation became so tense in the region that Polish troops were dispatched in summer 1922).[7] Unsurprisingly, the Bolsheviks denied accusations of subversion, choosing to blame attacks on Polish territory on 'local gangs' or claim that uprisings in the borders were driven by spontaneous resistance oppression (something true to an extent on both sides).[8] Accusations of subversion cannot be separated from efforts to gain leverage in the ongoing peace treaty negotiations, and none of this augured well for future relations.

The Bolsheviks had fully expected hostility from Polish-supported anti-Soviet organizations following the end of the war and this was marked out as a particular weakness in the preliminary peace. In a debate on its ratification held in late October 1920, where Chicherin defended the compromise arrangement – justifying territory conceded to Poland for the abandonment of its government's federalist schemes in the border regions – he acknowledged that peace with Poland would not actually extend to local anti-Soviet leaders. The threat was underlined more forcibly by Comintern secretary, Karl Radek, who drew attention to remarks given to the press by the Piłsudski ally and former Polish minister of foreign affairs, Leon Wasilewski, admitting that Petliura, Bułak-Bałakhovich and the former Russian deputy minister for war-turned counterrevolutionary terrorist, Boris Savinkov, would continue fighting even though Poland planned to ratify the peace. Radek was certain, not wrongly, that these prominent anti-Soviet leaders would not suffer a loss of Polish support.[9] Indeed, just before Petliura's and Bułak-Bałakhovich's forces duly left Poland on 2 November on the exchange of the ratification documents, the Polish government had equipped them already for continued fighting in the border regions.[10]

For these reasons, the activity of anti-Soviet groups quickly became a preoccupation for various Soviet institutions. Inside the NKID, Chicherin warned Soviet diplomat Adolf Ioffe in early November 1920 that Bułak-Bałakhovich was preparing a 'serious attack' from Polish territory, with forces in Pinsk apparently supplemented by White émigrés arriving from across Europe and the French acting in support. Soviet military intelligence estimated his army to number 23,000 and reported the supply of locomotives and over 100 wagons from Poland. Elsewhere it was claimed that Petliura planned to use his territory as a bridgehead for a strike, again with Polish support.[11] In total, the Bolsheviks recorded thirty apparent infringements of the preliminary peace in November and December alone.[12] Alongside the usual diplomatic broadsides, Trotsky called for a propaganda campaign to expose the Polish government's 'deceitful conduct'.[13]

It needs to be stressed, however, that the NKID was reasonably well-informed about the true shape of the Polish political landscape between 1920 and 1921 and understood that propping up anti-Soviet organizations was becoming a divisive political issue. Chicherin was sent reports describing how the National Democrats – still with significant political leverage – were moving away from this strategy.[14] Nevertheless, as would prove true in the future, Chicherin struggled to evaluate the material that crossed his desk consistently. In late November, for instance, he remarked to the Soviet plenipotentiary in Latvia and member of the Soviet peace delegation, Iakov Ganetskii, that he did not attach much seriousness to Savinkov and Bułak-Bałakhovich, but this came only weeks after he had described a threat of a 'serious attack' in the border regions to Adolf Ioffe. In December, Chicherin bemoaned the contradictory Soviet intelligence he was receiving.[15]

But like other officials within the NKID, Chicherin was confident – and correct – that Poland's military and its intelligence services, the second department of the Polish general staff, were chiefly to blame for funding anti-Soviet groups.[16] Consequently, the NKID rarely accused the Polish government of directly funding anti-Soviet groups and instead blamed it for not sufficiently cracking down on rogue institutions. Chicherin was also alert to how this problem jeopardized his goal of putting Soviet-Polish relations on surer footing. Looking for a way to diffuse the issue early on, therefore, he suggested to Trotsky in December 1920 that the Bolsheviks offer an amnesty to the supporters of Petliura, Savinkov, Bułak-Bałakhovich and other anti-Soviet leaders (who, after suffering military defeats at the hands of the Red Army in the weeks after the armistice, were forced to retreat to Poland and interned in accordance with the now-active preliminary peace). Ioffe and Jan Dąbski, the chief Polish negotiator at Riga, had already discussed the idea and Chicherin made the case to Trotsky that this would drain a body of 25,000 interned soldiers who might otherwise be used against Soviet Russia in a new spring offensive.[17] An amnesty, in the end, only materialized in November 1921, and with little impact; all the while, around 16,000 members of the Ukrainian People's Republic (UNR) remained in Polish internment camps.[18]

Amid mutual accusations about subversion on both sides of the border, negotiators at Riga finally agreed the terms for a lasting peace treaty, the Treaty of Riga, signed on 18 March 1921 by delegates from Poland, Soviet Russia and Soviet Ukraine. Establishing a new border more generous to Poland than the 1919 Curzon line, the treaty recognized Polish control over eastern Galicia and Wilno and territory in between; the Bolsheviks, although losing out in the territorial settlement, were given the border regions of Ukraine and lands across eastern Belarus.[19] The treaty also included a series of agreements on non-aggression and non-interference in each other's affairs; prisoner exchanges; financial compensation; the return of Polish property stemming from its history in the Russian empire, among other conditions. The Bolsheviks shouldered most obligations, many of which would go unfulfilled, including a 30 million ruble settlement owed to Poland. Not only for this reason, but the NKID held out little optimism that this definitive treaty would improve relations or put an end to attacks from anti-Soviet organizations. That the agreed border left over one million Poles in Soviet Russia raised the spectre of ongoing Polish espionage and subversion.[20] Indeed, in the week before the treaty was signed, Chicherin drew Ioffe's attention to what he described as the 'enormous development of Polish espionage', something 'acquiring an especially serious character', and interpreted this alongside the 'plans of our enemies' focused on sparking uprisings in Soviet territory.[21] One month later, Chicherin then forecast an 'energetic struggle against the presence of White guard organizations in Polish territory' and he wrote to Trotsky requesting evidence from the war department revealing ongoing Polish collaboration with anti-Soviet groups, something to use as ammunition in future disputes.[22] The NKID would go on to send multiple protest notes to the Polish government about what it saw as threats to the Treaty of Riga after March 1921.[23] The government of Soviet Ukraine likewise called on the Polish government to do more to curtail Ukrainian nationalists, highlighting in April how anti-Soviet gangs crossed the border to carry out riots, murders, lootings, arson and pogroms and sought 'to provoke a new war between Poland and Ukraine'. On another occasion, Soviet diplomats in Ukraine complained that they would not consider the Treaty of Riga fulfilled unless those trying to start war were stopped.[24]

Considering how Soviet efforts to foment anti-Polish sentiments in eastern Galicia and Polish Volhynia were still active, the Bolsheviks' accusations about Polish subversion were as cynical as ever, but this does not mean they were totally off the mark. As much as the Polish government had moved away from funding anti-Soviet organizations in 1921, Piłsudski, who was still influential in military and intelligence circles, sought ongoing support for military organizations like those of the UNR, while a parallel initiative was emerging, focused on cultivating broader popular support for autonomy in Soviet Ukraine and Belorussia.[25] Just weeks after the Treaty of Riga was agreed in March, Piłsudski solicited French support for more resources to be funnelled to Savinkov with an eye to his grander ambitions of separating Belarus and Ukraine from Soviet control and the wider Polonization of the eastern borderlands. Without approval of the government, Polish intelligence services secretly committed to increasing support for Petliura's and Savinkov's operations.[26] On the Soviet side, the foreign department of the Cheka (INO VChK) intercepted materials sketching out such apparent secret collaborations. One piece of intelligence from summer 1921 claimed that Savinkov's organization, the Russian Evacuation Committee (REC), was in direct contact with Piłsudski and other Polish officials. It was said that REC had lobbied Piłsudski and deputy minister of foreign affairs, Stepan Dąbrowski (someone typically unsympathetic to the émigré cause) to allow the training of new anti-Soviet groups on Polish soil for deployment in Soviet Russia.[27] Another intercepted letter revealed that Savinkov had also written to General Władysław Sikorski requesting support for his brother's organization, operating in Soviet Russia, which he claimed could provide valuable military intelligence (the same request was made to Józef Beck, a chief in the second department).[28] Moreover, in May the INO VChK reported to Chicherin about the formation of Belarusian partisan groups under Bułak-Bałakhovich in Polish territory, apparently still working with the Polish authorities.[29]

Such intelligence, even if the accuracy was difficult to determine and outcomes unclear, was more than enough to sustain Bolshevik concerns about Polish subversion. The reality of border attacks kept conspiracies – real or imagined – at the forefront of minds in Moscow. All of this too naturally increased the Bolsheviks' scepticism towards the Polish government's denials of subversive operations. In August, for instance, new Polish chargé d'affaires and Piłsudski ally, Tytus Filipowicz, failed to convince the new Soviet representative in Warsaw, Lev Karakhan, that the Polish government was only giving 'refuge' to anti-Soviet leaders in the same manner that Polish revolutionaries were sheltered abroad before the First World War (political asylum was permitted in the preliminary peace). Chicherin's response, however, was scathing: 'This is not political refuge at all. It is the continuation of the civil war and the continuation of war in a new form.' Recently appointed Polish minister of foreign affairs, Konstanty Skirmunt, who, in contrast to his predecessor, Sapieha, opposed supporting anti-Soviet organizations, made a similar case to Karakhan and tried to convince him that the Bolsheviks were exaggerating Savinkov's significance. Even if the Polish military was in contact with Savinkov, Skirmunt argued, anti-Soviet actions were not necessarily in preparation.[30] However, due to his political resistance in Warsaw, the second department began to keep Skirmunt in the dark.[31]

The temperature was raised further in August 1921 when Soviet military intelligence reported on supposed plans of the Polish and Romanian governments to send the remaining forces of Savinkov, Petliura and Bułak-Bałakhovich across the border to disrupt the Soviet grain harvest. Chicherin expressed alarm about the possible strike, describing it as a danger of 'paramount significance'.[32] 'It would be tantamount to a new declaration of war from Poland', the NKID warned.[33] Chicherin made clear to Karakhan that an invasion by such a mass of Savinkov's and Petliura's forces would bring about a break in Soviet-Polish relations. Applying pressure once more, the NKID sent a note to the Polish government making clear that the Bolsheviks would not honour obligations in the Treaty of Riga without a solution to the problem of border attacks.[34] Karakhan was told to ready himself to leave Poland if its government rejected NKID demands to expel a list of anti-Soviet leaders and Chicherin aired further accusations about Poland in public view.[35] In this case, Chicherin was right that an attack on Soviet Ukraine was in preparation, but, as ever, he exaggerated the scale of the danger (when the feared attack took place later in November, it was easily repulsed). As proved to be the case in previous months, the closer NKID personnel were to the ground, often the clearer their understanding. Karakhan, for one, simply did not believe that 1000s of soldiers were about to descend on the borders posing the threat Chicherin described. In fact, Karakhan stressed to Chicherin that if the Bolsheviks made too much noise about border attacks and uprisings this would only hinder efforts to resolve disputes with Poland, whose government was threatening to sever relations if the Treaty of Riga was not implemented.[36]

What appeared a breakthrough came on 7 October when Soviet and Polish diplomats Jan Dąbski and Karakhan struck a secret agreement, the Dąbski-Karakhan protocol. The Polish government agreed to expel Savinkov and thirteen other anti-Soviet leaders on the condition that the Bolsheviks begin to fulfil the Treaty of Riga, pay the first instalment of gold and allow re-evacuation commissions to begin work. The agreement was not without controversy and in Poland some quarters saw it as too lenient on the Bolsheviks. It was certainly unacceptable to Piłsudski and his allies who resisted the normalization of relations (Dąbski, in the end, was forced to resign in the political fallout). Even so, the agreement represented another unmistakable move by the Polish government away from supporting anti-Soviet organizations and Skirmunt, notably, saw a new opportunity to improve relations with Soviet Russia and secure fulfilment of the Treaty of Riga.[37] Yet the Dąbski-Karakhan protocol started badly when Savinkov, who the Bolsheviks viewed with symbolic importance, failed to be expelled from Poland on time, prompting alarm within the NKID.[38] Waiting for confirmation of Savinkov's expulsion, Chicherin feared a sudden downturn in Soviet-Polish relations. Spooked by the delay, he described to Karakhan that Polish inaction had to be seen against a backdrop of 'a rising interventionist wave' and warned that the Poles intended to break off relations. Karakhan was certain, not unreasonably, that Piłsudski and the Polish military were doing all they could to break the agreement.[39]

Savinkov and other anti-Soviet leaders were eventually expelled on 30 October, although Petliura remained in Poland in secret for another two years.[40] Despite this progress, the protocol did not eliminate the danger as far as the Bolsheviks were concerned and Karakhan even admitted to Chicherin that it was never a 'radical solution'.[41] Little changed, therefore, in the Bolsheviks' threat perception. The day after the expulsions from Poland, for instance, Chicherin warned again about an upcoming attack on Soviet Ukraine and that supporters of Savinkov and Bułak-Bałakhovich were apparently planning a march on Kiev, supported by the Polish military.[42] An attack did take place shortly after in November when Yuriy Tiutiunnik, a leader in the UNR, one of the number forced to leave Poland, immediately embarked on an insurgent campaign in Soviet territory. The Red Army easily quashed this poorly planned assault by 1200 partisans, but the episode, although far smaller than predicted, did little to inspire confidence in Moscow that the Poles were living up to their side of the bargain. This was particularly true when the Bolsheviks pointed to hard evidence revealing the Polish military's assistance to Tiutiunnik. Fresh accusations about Polish-supported organizations in Soviet Ukraine and Belorussia thus persisted.[43] Running in the opposite direction, however, and as a corrective to the NKID's concerns, Soviet intelligence recorded a general weakening of anti-Soviet activity in the border regions following the Dąbski-Karakhan protocol, going into 1922.[44] In this sense, Karakhan had been right to question whether the protocol would achieve much, and it seems that Tiutiunnik's disastrous offensive actually did more to curtail clandestine Polish support of anti-Soviet organizations. In its aftermath, the Polish political right expressed marked unhappiness about the entire affair and the Polish military decided to withdraw support for future operations. Economic cooperation with the Bolsheviks was instead pushed higher up agenda. By the end of 1921, Chicherin allowed himself some optimism for establishing better relations with Poland, now that the 'splinter' of Savinkov had been removed.[45]

Beyond the NKID, the GPU, as the chief security organ of the Soviet state, continued reporting on anti-Soviet groups coming from Polish territory throughout 1922 and 1923.[46] By autumn 1923, the Ukrainian GPU claimed to have almost eliminated organizations headed by Petliura, Tiutiunnik and Savinkov. GPU operatives also declared fresh discoveries of Polish espionage organizations, some apparently working together with French support.[47] The GPU was undoubtedly a powerful voice in shaping the Bolsheviks' perceptions of internal dangers, but its claims needed to be treated with a level of scepticism not often seen in these years. Polish intelligence, like its Soviet counterpart, undeniably sought to infiltrate state institutions and its agents were in the process of rebuilding a network in Soviet Ukraine from 1922. Despite operating at a lower level than the GPU assumed (and rarely operating competently), Polish intelligence ran an array of operations, many under the cover of newly established Polish diplomatic representation.[48] The Polish general staff and second department, as we have seen, secretly supported anti-Soviet organizations which continued to plot attacks, even with dwindling supporters.

But the reality was that most Polish espionage cases recorded in Soviet Ukraine during this period were exaggerated or entirely fictitious and the political mood in Poland was still moving away from interventions with proxy organizations.[49] The GPU, it must be remembered, had a strong interest in proving its value in the early 1920s when some senior Bolsheviks were questioning its outsized role now that the civil war was coming to an end. Presenting a starker picture of subversive threats than the NKID or other institutions was the simplest way to do this. And the tone was set from the top. From Dzerzhinskii's point of view, for instance, attacks like those carried about by Petliura's bands were unambiguously part of a Polish plot to disorganize the Bolsheviks before a wider intervention.[50] But even if the GPU's vision lacked the nuance sometimes detectable elsewhere, its security assessments were on the extreme end of a spectrum shared with others. That Soviet Russia was in a state of siege and assailed from all sides was a widely accepted article of faith with almost no dissenters.

The roles assigned to Britain and France in the amorphous picture of secretly coordinated anti-Soviet groups and intelligence plots were especially exaggerated in the years after the Soviet-Polish war. The Allied Powers featured regularly in Soviet reports as prime instigators of the ongoing threats to the border regions. At the time of the October 1920 armistice, for instance, Trotsky pushed for a protest note sent to the British government about the French undermining the peace through creating a 'new front from [the forces of] Petliura, Bałakhovich, Savinkov'.[51] Soviet military intelligence, also in October, claimed incorrectly that 'many English and French officers' could be counted among the forces of Bułak-Bałakhovich and Lucjan Żeligowski (the forces of the latter seized Wilno, on Piłsudski's encouragement, in October 1920, establishing the short-lived Republic of Central Lithuania, soon controversially incorporated into Poland, along with the city).[52] Later in December 1920, in a telegram to Chicherin, Krasin detailed that the French government intended to funnel 5 million francs to Poland to form a new army from anti-Soviet organizations to deploy against Soviet Russia.[53] Similarly, Soviet military intelligence highlighted plans, apparently drawn up inside the French general staff in Warsaw, envisaging using an army of 125,000 soldiers to advance on Kiev while Bułak-Bałakhovich and other rebel leaders pushed forward through the Polots-Vitebsk-Smolensk line with an army of 115,000 soldiers.[54] All the while, French officers working with the Polish military were apparently organizing a new Russian army from the forces of Petliura and Bułak-Bałakhovich, to be 100,000 strong by spring and ready to deploy.[55]

This picture of malevolent Allied conspiracy was clearly out of touch with reality. The French government, as we have seen, was more strongly anti-Bolshevik than the British (and reflected as such in Soviet intelligence), but both were steadily reconciling themselves with existing alongside the Soviet government. Efforts to send arms and war materiel to Poland after the Battle of Warsaw, including some from within the British government and its military, were only limited in scope.[56] Savinkov, without doubt, spent much of his time coming up with new plots against the Bolsheviks and was generally well-received in British political circles. Churchill later described him as an 'extraordinary product – a Terrorist for moderate aims' and in a message to Curzon at the end of October 1920, remarked that 'the Prime Minister thinks more of Savinkov than of any other anti-Bolshevik Russian [...] and we have had several long confabulations and lunches at 10, Downing Street'. Even so, good words were not concrete, well-funded, support (and, according to Churchill, other officials such as the British representative in Warsaw were looking to 'put a spoke in Savinkov's wheel').[57] The fact was the British Foreign Office cut ties with Savinkov a few months after the Soviet-Polish war ended, in late 1920, and the French were also winding down their support. Other prospective anti-Soviet leaders were similarly given the brush off by the British War Office in 1921 on the grounds that it was 'inconceivable' that the government could both negotiate an open trade agreement with Soviet Russia and 'give a secret undertaking to the organizers of an anti-Bolshevik army'.[58] But as far as the Bolsheviks were concerned, the two were not mutually exclusive.

Peaceful co-existence and inevitable war

The Bolsheviks were not alone in thinking the armistice and preliminary peace agreed in October 1920 would fail to prevent another war. The Polish minister of foreign affairs, the Polish chief of the general staff and the British minister to Poland, among other statesmen, immediately cast doubt on whether a new war could be avoided.[59] But in Moscow, this had quickly become the prevailing mood. One of the most outspoken Bolsheviks, Karl Radek, for instance, launched a public attack on the inadequacies of the preliminary peace in the pages of *Pravda* just days after it was signed and raised the threat of new war. The preliminaries were 'a piece of paper which we do not know will have significance tomorrow', he remarked at a later party meeting.[60] The Red Army leadership was also uncertain about what the future might hold. On the day the armistice was agreed, Sergei Kamenev detailed in a set of theses that there was little guarantee peace would last. The Bolsheviks should be 'fully prepared for the resumption of the struggle'. He advised moving quickly to finish off Wrangel's forces in the south while there was still time. Lenin agreed.[61]

The party leader presented the international situation as a mixed picture in addresses given in November and December 1920. On the one hand, Lenin crowed about the 'gigantic victory' achieved over the Bolsheviks' enemies. Despite disastrous defeat to Poland in the summer, he described economic crisis in the capitalist world and rising popular resistance to imperialism. The Russian Revolution had survived, and the alliance of enemy states was crumbling. 'Among the states which have preserved the bourgeois system and border on Russia, there is no other country but Poland on which the Entente can rely in a long-term plan of military intervention.' With the armistice secured and the collapse of capitalist designs to overthrow the revolution, as Lenin put it, 'something more than a mere breathing-space' had been achieved. Yet Lenin was clear that the Soviet armed forces were still 'incomparably weaker' than those of the capitalist powers. And while he pointed to a potentially lengthy period of stability, the duration of this breathing space was still unknown (Lenin also claimed to be in possession of 'facts' showing another planned assault in the spring). Because the Bolsheviks viewed the international order in terms of hostile alliances, the strategy for defence was to exploit divisions emerging between the capitalist powers 'to hamper their struggle against us'. This was key to Soviet survival. 'We have so far been victorious only because of the most profound discord among the imperialist powers [...] a most deep-seated and ineradicable conflict of economic interests among the imperialist countries [...] has stultified their efforts to unite their forces against the Soviets.' Lenin warned, however, that 'the deeper and more formidable the communist movement grows, the greater will be the number of new attempts to strangle our Republic'.[62]

Despite the antagonism embedded in his rhetoric, Lenin's reference to a breathing space was an early sign of the reshaping of Soviet Russia's relations with capitalist countries towards a period of temporary 'peaceful coexistence'. Driven by necessity more than anything, the Bolsheviks aimed to exploit their apparent breathing space for improving economic and diplomatic ties with the west. It was otherwise unthinkable that their precarious state would recover from the double shock of civil war economic collapse and famine spreading through Soviet territory.[63] None of this meant the abandonment of the Bolsheviks' revolutionary ideals nor efforts to spread propaganda abroad. While the Politburo saw increased trade with western powers as a means of strengthening Soviet Russia and as a precursor to diplomatic recognition, this was also essential for future challenges against capitalism.

Stalin was another senior Bolshevik to discuss the threatening outside world in public at the time of the armistice with Poland. At a conference of communist organizations of the Don and the Caucasus at the end of October 1920, like Lenin, he reiterated that because of a growing workers' movement in the west and rising anti-colonial nationalism in the east, the Allied Powers were no longer in 'a position to hurl against Russia its own, that is, British, French and other, forces'. They still had no choice but to rely upon the armies of other countries, but these could not be completely controlled. The Soviet peace with Poland itself was evidence of 'the frictions that exist, and will continue to exist, between the Entente and the national interests of the countries whose armies the Entente is using'. Stalin struck a confident tone, remarking that 'in 1920, the chances of Russia being defeated are incomparably less than they were two years ago'. Even so – and like Lenin also – Stalin looked ahead to inevitable future conflicts with the capitalist states, who had reconciled only 'grudgingly, to the peace we have concluded with the Poles'.[64]

It would be several years until Stalin was able to directly shape Soviet foreign policy, but his vision of future war in the early 1920s was hardly an outlier. Aligned with Lenin in public, behind-the-scenes his view typically accorded with Soviet military intelligence, the central organ for assessing foreign threats. Military intelligence correctly recognized that Poland could not go to war without substantial assistance from more powerful countries and this, in any case, would be an unpopular move at home when the government was attempting to stabilize the economy. The Allied Powers needed Poland for war, but the latter was not ready (back to Stalin's 'frictions'). Nevertheless, military intelligence forecast that major conflict between Soviet Russia and Poland was inevitable at some point in the future and that the latter was already preparing for it.[65] And an evolving picture of such dangers was recorded in its weekly intelligence summaries. In early November 1920, for instance, one intelligence survey claimed that a union of France, Poland and Wrangel's forces was a likely future enemy and Piłsudski saw the armistice as nothing more than pause before resuming a campaign to Moscow.[66]

Because Soviet diplomats were at the forefront of efforts to improve relations with the western powers, vital to the revival of the Soviet economy, more so than others, the NKID tended to downplay talk of new war and emphasized the importance of creating new lines of trade.[67] Stronger trading links with Poland were also seen as an effective means of putting further distance between Poland and the Allied Powers.[68] For this reason, Chicherin was a firm advocate of Lenin's turn towards *realpolitik* and bringing Soviet Russia out of isolation. He was no less commented to long-term revolutionary objectives and staunchly opposed the Versailles order (as the later Soviet-German partnership of the 1920s would prove); and like other Bolsheviks, he was preoccupied with the risk of renewed war.[69] But in the near term after the October 1920 armistice, and in contrast to the types of material coming out of the GPU, the NKID received a stream of reports from its sources describing consensus in the Polish government for quickly achieving a lasting peace treaty, even if negotiations would prove prolonged and difficult.[70] 'A new war would be a stunning surprise for Polish society', the frequent source, Polish communist, Paweł Łapiński, wrote at the end of 1920. The country was experiencing a 'colossal fatigue of war' and was preoccupied with the upcoming plebiscite in March 1921, mandated in the Treaty of Versailles to decide the fate of Upper Silesia, the disputed border region between Poland and Germany. (The Polish government believed peace with the Bolsheviks would strengthen its hand, though controversy over the plebiscite results and violence on the ground led the League of Nations to simply divide the region.)[71] According to Adolf Ioffe, the mood in Poland was one of 'confusion and despair' and, if anything, it was the Bolsheviks who risked exacerbating tensions with an 'alarmist tone' in the Soviet press that could ignite Polish militarism. 'It is possible that we have already gone too far and created assumption about the inevitability of war in several [Polish] circles.'[72] Chicherin was seemingly swayed by reports from the likes of Łapiński. As he wrote to Krasin at the end of December 1920, a moment when his optimism was already rising following Savinkov's expulsion: 'According to all information, Poland is dominated by a peace-loving mood and an aspiration to conclude peace. It can hardly be expected to resume a military adventure against us in spring.'[73]

Chicherin also knew from his sources that Piłsudski, the most dangerous Polish figure to Soviet power to date, was increasingly isolated in political life after the war. NKID reports detailed his declining prestige and worsening reputation. Described as 'isolated military dreamers', his circle had been transformed in the public eye from 'national heroes to the culprits of all economic and financial disasters'.[74]

Piłsudski was an 'increasingly impotent decoration in the Polish Republic', as one report put it.[75] In December 1920, Piłsudski still entertained achieving his federation with a new war to seize Kiev and Minsk, but he admitted to his fellow officers that 'Poland does not want it ... it has been exhausted by the longer war, and its army worn out and ... impoverished'.[76] Moreover, the new Polish constitution of March 1921, shaped by the National Democrats, was designed precisely to avoid a powerful presidency that might see Piłsudski restored to influence and able to again wage war. He did not enter the running. The new constitution, however, injected significant instability into political system, contributing to the fall of fourteen governments between November 1918 and May 1926.[77]

The NKID also received dispatches detailing that France, the most anti-Soviet western power, was also pushing for peace. Łapiński reported to Chicherin in November 1920 that the Quai d'Orsay was advising the Polish government not only to conclude an armistice but to solidify peace with Soviet Russia. Łapiński then noted in December that the French ambassador to Poland had ruled out a new intervention.[78] Because Chicherin was convinced, like other Bolsheviks, that Poland was too small a country to have independent foreign policy, these conciliatory signals from France were significant. However, as was often the case, intelligence proved contradictory and could easily swing in the other direction. In early November, the usually well-informed Ioffe warned of a French-devised attack force in preparation in the territory held by Lucjan Żeligowski, comprising guerrilla organizations and Wrangel's White forces. Chicherin took this apparent danger seriously. Yet revealing of uncertainties in assessments of near-term security threats, a few weeks later Ioffe then cast doubt on such 'open intervention', aligning again with coalescing thinking inside the NKID that European powers were prioritizing trade with Soviet Russia and there was no mood for war inside Poland.[79] In January 1921, Łapiński reported to Chicherin that Poland's allies, France included, were now pushing for peace.[80]

None of this meant that the NKID doubted the hostility in the wider international capitalist system towards Soviet Russia.[81] But it was right to reflect on France's evolving position from the end of 1920. With the Bolsheviks looking like undisputed victors in the civil war, like the British, the French political elite were beginning to accept that coexistence was unavoidable. Diplomatic recognition was ruled out due to outstanding tsarist debts to France, but so was a new intervention.[82] The French government sought instead to construct a barrier of states on Soviet Russia's European borders to halt the spread of Bolshevism to the west (though not necessarily weaken Russia).[83] Improving relations between Poland and Czechoslovakia, and bringing the former closer to the 'Little Entente', the defensive alliance of Czechoslovakia, Romania and the Kingdom of Serbs, Croats and Slovenes (future Yugoslavia) was not suggestive of France planning another major war; though antagonism between Poland and Czechoslovakia over the disputed Teschen border region doomed their cooperation anyway. Going against core Bolshevik assumptions about power relations in the capitalist world, some NKID reports now underlined how the Polish government resisted French efforts to exert control over its foreign policy.[84] Outside of the civil war years, more nuance was creeping into Soviet assessments of international relations.

It was the Politburo, not Chicherin's NKID, that was the real centre of power and decision-making in Soviet foreign policy; however, even here, one of Lenin's influential advisors on Polish affairs, Julian Leszczyński, presented the same message about the low risk of renewed war at the end of 1920. Leszczyński, who participated in the peace treaty negotiations at Riga, reported to the central committee twice at the end of December to underline that peace was essential for Poland to prevent financial catastrophe. He noted also that neither France nor Britain would support 'adventurism of Polish imperialists'.[85] And without this, war was 'unthinkable'. Admittedly, Leszczyński saw any kind of peace with Poland – a bourgeois state – as only ever temporary and believed the country had unfulfilled imperialist designs.[86] But for now, the party's expert on Polish affairs was convinced that Soviet Russia was safe from attack.[87] Such confidence, however, would be short-lived.

It is telling of the Bolsheviks' deep-seated insecurities that despite the numerous sources casting doubt on the prospect of renewed war with Poland, there was growing unease about a sharpening international climate from 1921, nevertheless. A marked sense of vulnerability crystalized again. This was best summarized in a report Ioffe sent from Riga to Moscow in early January 1921, in which he reflected on the previous months. 'After the defeat of Wrangel, we seemed as strong as ever', he wrote: the capitalist powers wanted to trade with Soviet Russia and there was growing acceptance that the Bolsheviks could not be deposed by force. Yet Ioffe now believed 'the mood had changed'. As yet, little had come of trade negotiations with Britain; White émigré forces abroad were apparently 'stirring' and France 'loudly promises to help Poland'. He described 'thunderous applause' in the French parliament when Piłsudski was invited for a state visit to Paris. Ioffe believed all of this would shape the thinking of Polish political leaders towards Soviet Russia, especially as France, so he argued, was trying to undermine the ongoing peace negotiations by spreading rumours of Soviet militarism. Chicherin separately wrote to Ioffe, expressing similar concerns about a sudden change in the international climate, and pointed to stronger anti-Soviet agitation in the foreign press and radio. He noted claims made abroad about anticipated Soviet attacks against neighbouring countries and likewise suspected French influence behind-the-scenes. In the month before, Chicherin had worried about an 'invisible hand' in another country spreading rumours that the Bolsheviks intended to break off negotiations with Poland.[88]

This growing unease about the international situation at the outset of 1921 was then accelerated by a new alliance between France and Poland, signed on 19 February, the product of Piłsudski's visit to Paris.[89] The alliance became central to future Polish foreign policy. And whatever relationship was agreed with Soviet Russia at Riga, Poland was no less critical to French foreign policy in the east and not only as a barrier against Bolshevism. Yet the February 1921 alliance was chiefly designed as another pressure point on Germany, should it challenge the new European order, with responding joint military action agreed with Poland.

A secret military pact followed a few days later that mandated Poland to maintain an army of at least thirty infantry divisions and nine brigades of cavalry. This opened the way for cooperation between the Polish and French general staffs with a promise of a 400 million francs loan for Polish rearmament. A separate pact between Romania and Poland was signed soon after on 3 March, also under French influence, yet in this case, its focus was more consciously designed to further the cause of anti-Soviet alliances.[90]

That the Bolsheviks saw a fresh alliance between two hostile powers, one a recent combatant and the other its chief patron, with alarm is hardly surprising. But there were important caveats in the detail. The French government promised only to supply Poland with arms if it was attacked *unprovoked* by Soviet Russia. It was also clear in ruling out 'adventurous Polish policy' in the east. And because of Prime Minister Aristide Briand's general lack of enthusiasm for the alliance, it was left to his successor Raymond Poincaré to ratify the treaty, and not until one year later.[91] Still, caveats like these could never fully counteract the Bolsheviks' ingrained tendency to view treaties and alliances, and especially those between potential belligerents, as part of a global conspiracy against communism. This was especially true when concerns were rising once more in the party about dangerous new international connections. Chicherin, notably, had already stressed to Ioffe at the beginning of the year that it was essential to avoid a scenario where Poland entered a French-devised alliance against Soviet Russia.[92] He also received information that figures close to Piłsudski sought a French guarantee that Poland would not be drawn into a new war against Soviet Russia (suggesting this was a possibility) and other reports describing how former Polish prime minister and current finance minister, Jan Steczkowski, had apparently warned that French influence in the separate Polish-Romania alliance could lead to conflict. To make matters worse, Chicherin was generally unclear in early 1921 whether Romania was pursuing war or peace.[93] Elsewhere, Soviet military intelligence analysed the Franco-Polish alliance with a stronger element of French control than was true (it was not only Briand but other senior French military figures, including Ferdinand Foch, were unenthusiastic about a formal alliance, seeing Poland as too weak a military power).[94] Although the treaty provided only for the 'concert' of defence questions and no plans were ever drawn up for joint military action in wartime, Soviet military intelligence claimed that the Polish supreme command had been subordinated to the French general staff and that major Polish military manoeuvres were scheduled for April, under French leadership.[95] The Bolsheviks later received other intelligence suggesting a wholly uneven partnership between France and Poland. In May, the Cheka's foreign department intercepted a purported letter from the French ambassador to Poland, André de Panafieu, sent to the Polish cabinet in which he explained that because of the new alliance, France 'reserves the right to influence the principle political decisions of the Polish government, both in the realms of foreign and internal policy'. It was important, therefore, that the appointments of Polish ministers of foreign and internal affairs have his approval.[96] While this letter almost certainly reveals an ambassador exceeding his remit (and if anything, the alliance gave France far more economic than political leverage, especially in concessions in eastern Galicia and Upper Silesia[97]), the Bolsheviks could be forgiven for assuming that ambassadors spoke with the voice of their governments.

With anxiety growing about the nature of Franco-Polish relations, Lenin once again castigated France in public view. In speeches given in February 1921, the party leader openly accused its government of pushing Poland to war:

> If the Poles once again yield to the pressure of the French imperialists, then, I repeat the effort to conclude peace may be frustrated [...] we all know from a number of sources and reports that attempts are being made and enormous efforts are being exerted to this end, and that the foreign capitalists are spending millions upon millions to organise another invasion of Soviet Russia in the spring [...] we must reckon with the possibility of war on a much larger scale than some people imagine. Those who say that we need not put so much into defence are wrong, because our enemies are resorting to all sorts of machinations and intrigues to break up the final peace with Poland.

The way Lenin characterized Poland's place in the international order was becoming familiar: a pliable border state, vulnerable to manipulation and sold to the capitalists 'lock, stock, and barrel'.[98]

But, as ever, in contrast to Lenin's boilerplate rhetoric from Moscow, Soviet officials on the ground managed more nuance. While Ioffe had described 'darkening international horizon' and like others was pessimistic in early 1921, at the same time, he saw events with a clearer eye: 'I do not attach serious importance to either the Polish-Romanian or Polish-French agreements, but nevertheless these agreements are a fact, and a fact directed in a certain part against Germany, but even more against us.'[99] Then in another message to Lenin, Chicherin, Trotsky and other Bolsheviks at the end of February, Ioffe was clear that there was no serious risk of intervention. Britain would conclude a trade agreement in the near-term (which it did in March, representing *de facto* diplomatic recognition) and France sought to isolate Soviet Russia, not invade. 'We have concluded peace with all the border republics [...] who will support a Polish attack on us?' Ioffe stressed that Poland had everything to lose and nothing to gain from war. Frustrated that his reports were having little impact in Moscow, he added: 'All of this is so clear that I'm starting to fear that the TsK [central committee] is not reading my reports at all.'[100] It does seem that the Politburo was ignoring Ioffe's advice. In April it decided against withdrawing troops from the western front, pointing to the ongoing risk of eruption of a new European war.[101]

Perhaps the only positive outcome from the growing apprehension in the party leadership in early 1921 was that definitive peace with Poland was finally agreed in March, on an expedited basis. What was taken to be a deteriorating international climate was an unavoidable background pressure and an internal naval revolt at Kronstadt in February raised the stakes further. The central committee ordered negotiations with Poland concluded with speed and the Treaty of Riga was signed on 18 March.[102] The treaty, on face value, did much to regulate Soviet-Polish relations. It was a landmark moment, even if both sides soon found themselves wrapped up in new arguments about its implementation. Still, during the spring and summer, Chicherin's judgements about Poland's intentions continued to veer from one extreme to the other. For instance, in a message sent to Soviet plenipotentiary in Lithuania, Sergei Aralov, in May Chicherin described a marked downturn in relations. Apparently due to rising antagonism with Germany over Upper Silesia, Poland had 'thrown itself completely' to the French, strengthening the 'war party' inside Poland.[103] Shortly after, however, he performed a *volte-face*, writing again to Aralov to acknowledge his earlier 'gloomy' judgements. Poland was now, apparently, moving again towards 'peaceful and more realistic politics'. Lev Karakhan's recent approval as Soviet representative in Warsaw and Jan Steczkowski's emergence as a candidate for prime minister – a 'realist politician' – had apparently created room for optimism.[104]

Chicherin's ongoing difficulty in understanding the shape of Soviet-Poland relations was most clear when he was driven to the point of exasperation over delays in granting formal diplomatic representation to Soviet Russia. He had erroneously complained in May to the Polish government that diplomatic representation was an 'indispensable part' of the Treaty of Riga and blamed the 'war party' in Poland for undermining progress (in truth, the delays were chiefly a response to Bolshevik foot-dragging in implementing the Treaty of Riga).[105] In a message to Lev Aleksandri, an NKID official in Latvia, Chicherin labelled Polish politics as 'absurd': the Treaty of Riga risked being torn up at a time when Poland's relations with Germany had almost degraded to war.[106] He later lost patience entirely in July when, owing to a local boycott by Polish property owners, the building offered to the Bolsheviks for an embassy turned out to be an unsuitable hotel. 'An impossible slum with the filthiest reputation.' Chicherin vented to the Soviet plenipotentiary in Latvia, Ganetskii:

> I do not understand the attitude of Poland. Is it peace or war on their part? They sabotage the restoration of relations for so long by engaging in conspiracies known to us and trying to wage a struggle against us with the hands of the Savinkovites, and when at last we got them to invite the embassy, they push this agreement to nothing [...] We thought that Poland would have genuine peaceful relations with us, meanwhile, the Polish government seems to deliberately prevent this.[107]

The dispute about the Soviet embassy, even though resolved by September, was another sign of how Chicherin and other officials in the NKID failed to make sense of Poland's behaviour. Admittedly, like any other governments' intentions, these were not openly transparent. But much of Chicherin's confusion stemmed from the stream of Soviet intelligence and assessments about Polish affairs, themselves often contradictory, which the NKID struggled to analyse consistently. More so than those working in other Soviet institutions or in the party leadership, NKID officials were more inclined to take seriously information countervailing the dominant narrative, but they were still hamstrung by the Bolsheviks' overarching ideological interpretation of international relations that instinctively exaggerated competition between capitalism and communism and the prevalence of threatening anti-Soviet alliances. While some accurate assessments about Poland, as we have seen, could emerge from the information-gathering machine, the opposite was more often the case.

*

Delivering a speech at the third congress of the Communist International, held between June and July 1921, Lenin proclaimed that the 'international bourgeoisie' was prepared to attack 'at any moment'. While previous efforts to 'strangle Soviet Russia' had failed, forcing the capitalist powers 'to grant her recognition, or semi-recognition, and to conclude trade agreements with her', another assault was only a matter of time. Soviet Russia remained encircled and international capital was 'waiting and watching for the moment when circumstances will permit it to resume the war'.[108] Lenin pushed the same line in private, and wanted Chicherin or Trotsky to give a 'threatening' press interview in response to what he saw as rising French aggression and for Tukhachevskii to be dispatched to Minsk in a show of force. Chicherin disagreed, arguing that such provocative steps would only play into the *leitmotifs* of their enemies: namely, to escape difficult domestic circumstances the Bolsheviks were preparing an attack of their own against neighbouring states. 'Bullying' tactics such as these, Chicherin explained, would only unite their enemies and strengthen the 'war party' in Poland and the formation of a hostile Baltic union. The Soviet press, in his view, needed to make clear that the French were using accusations of Soviet aggression to help assemble a hostile coalition, to push smaller states into the arms of Poland 'which France in turn pushes towards a military path'.[109]

We have seen already how Soviet-Polish relations nosedived in summer 1921 amid accusations about Polish-supported anti-Soviet organizations and the Bolsheviks' refusal in turn to implement the Treaty of Riga. But these were also months when a post-civil war famine gathered pace across Soviet territory, having the effect of heightening fears of invasion. The famine devastated vast swathes of Soviet territory in the Volga region, the Urals, Ukraine and Transcaucasia, leaving millions of dead. This tragedy deepened the sense of vulnerability already palpable in the Soviet government and not only because the Bolsheviks were forced to accept humanitarian relief from foreign sources, such as the American Relief Administration. Various materials, from surveys of the foreign press to NKID sources, claimed that foreign governments planned to exploit the famine to overthrow Soviet power and pointed to a possible joint Polish-Romanian attack (Polish intelligence reported on a Soviet military build-up in August in anticipation of war with Romania).[110] According to the NKID, the French government expected the Bolsheviks to crumble in the crisis and was pushing for local anti-Soviet resistance, and apparently also encouraging Polish representatives to begin negotiations with exiled Whites in Paris in anticipation of the formation of a new Russian government.[111] This type of material was soon circulated at the upper reaches of the Bolshevik Party.[112]

It was true that western governments recognized opportunity to renew financial claims against Soviet Russia and to connect these to famine aid. This fed immediately into the Bolsheviks' insecurities. In September 1921, the NKID accused France of encouraging Poland and Romania to deliver ultimatums, along with one of its own, demanding settlement of claims against Soviet Russia, backed with the threat of force.[113] But a conspiracy of foreign powers and relief agencies, jointly working to overthrow the Soviet government, was only ever in the Bolsheviks' imagination. Nevertheless, in another note to the British, French, Italian and Belgian governments in September, Chicherin delivered such accusations: 'Every day brings us new evidence of interventionist plans forged by some governments against the Soviet Republic. The policy of the French government in Poland and Romania, expressed in preparations for the war against Russia […] is sufficiently proven by the facts.'[114] To Viacheslav Molotov, he repeated these same concerns in private correspondence, claiming that if Wincenty Witos's government did not resist outside pressure, it would become 'a humble instrument' of 'the interventionist policy of France'.[115] Witos was soon to resign as prime minster, to be replaced by Antoni Ponikowski, but changes in government did not always concern the Bolsheviks. As Molotov then warned the party committees, an 'extremely chauvinistic clique' in Poland 'fulfilling the order of French imperialism' was the danger and he described a 'possible beginning of a new interventionist war'.[116]

It was amid this downturn in foreign relations that Chicherin welcomed the Dąbski-Karakhan protocol in October, which, as we know, eased the dispute about the Bolsheviks' fulfilment of the Treaty of Riga but it also helped dampen down fears of war. As Chicherin put it to Karakhan, 'the interventionist mood is thickening in the west […] The agreement with Poland deprives the interventionists of a weapon'.[117] But the danger was not extinguished entirely (the Cheka's foreign department soon enough suggested war against Poland and Romania could erupt in the spring).[118] Indeed, as much as the Bolshevik leadership was starting to realize that the Polish government was not seeking war independently, in their minds, Piłsudski, the outsider, remained a danger and the Allied Powers were still pushing for intervention.[119] In November 1921, Trotsky took aim at a shadowy military clique in Poland, headed by Piłsudski, and stressed that the Red Army needed to be prepared for the worst.[120] Elsewhere, Litvinov recommended that the Bolsheviks arrange a defensive alliance with Germany as Poland was likely to remain a '"sword of Damocles" hanging over our heads'.[121] In the meantime, in another effort to put distance between Poland and the Allied Powers, the Bolsheviks agreed to discussions towards a trade agreement, following an earlier Polish proposal. These began in March 1922 yet quickly broke down due to a dispute over Soviet transit rights.[122]

Stalin delivered another public warning about the risk of future war in the pages of *Pravda* at the end of 1921. 'We should not forget', he wrote 'that these countries, especially Poland and Romania, are arming themselves heavily due to the Entente and preparing for war […] they now, like before, constitute the immediate reserves of imperialism'.[123] But it was also important to account for the fact that another war had not yet arrived. Lenin provided the explanation at the ninth all-Russian congress of soviets, also in December, suggesting that it was more difficult for the capitalists to launch fresh attacks because of broad sympathy towards the Russian Revolution from the world's workers and peasants. Nevertheless, he warned, the Soviet people 'must remember that we are always a hair's breadth away from invasion'.[124] A similar explanation emerged later at the eleventh party congress, held between March and April 1922. The congress underlined that Poland and Romania had represented real and direct threats in autumn 1921, but Soviet military preparations and effective diplomacy had apparently ensured peace.[125]

The eleventh congress coincided with the international conference held at Genoa between April and May 1922, spearheaded by Lloyd George to agree a new political and economic settlement for Europe; to better integrate the outcasts, Germany and Soviet Russia; and avoid future military conflict. Seeing the conference as another attempt to forge a united front against Soviet Russia, Lenin did not attend (GPU reports about a Polish assassin potentially awaiting at Genoa were another discouragement).[126] A change of leadership in France, which brought Raymond Poincaré to power as French premier in January 1922, did not help put the Bolsheviks in the mood for cooperation at Genoa either. Poincaré soon ratified the Franco-Polish treaty of February 1921, left dormant by Briand, and General Maxime Weygand travelled to Poland to assist in the organization of the Polish Army.[127]

In line with Lenin's position set in Moscow, negotiations in Genoa stalled when the Bolsheviks refused to acknowledge pre-war tsarist debts in return for western loans and investments. As is well-known, in tune with Litvinov's advice at the end of 1921, they instead went on to agree the Treaty of Rapallo with Germany in April, opening the door to diplomatic recognition, most-favoured nation status and the renunciation of mutual claims.[128] A secret military collaboration began later in August, providing the Bolsheviks with access to much-needed technology and technical assistance, while the Germans were able to train troops and develop weapons in Soviet territory. When news of the treaty broke at Genoa itself – something potentially destabilizing to the entire Versailles system – the conference limped on without meaningful results. The Polish prime minster, Antoni Ponikowski, resigned, and Poland fell into political chaos lasting for months.[129] Soviet Russia's security position, however, undoubtedly emerged enhanced from Genoa, even if the alliance with Germany soured relations with the western powers.

Parallel Bolshevik efforts were also ongoing to forestall other potentially hostile alliances in Europe during these months. In early 1922, at the outset of the Genoa conference, the NKID warned the Polish government to not participate in or agree to any kind of anti-Soviet arrangement during a meeting of representatives from the Baltic states held in Warsaw in March. This meeting's aim was to establish a common line for the Genoa conference, which for all participants, and especially Poland, was potentially revisionist.[130] But to some Bolsheviks, this pre-meeting in Warsaw itself was a danger. Litvinov wrote to Trotsky to claim – with the usual line – that under French influence, the Poles were seeking to create a 'Baltic or

Finnish-Polish military union'. Such alliances, as we know, were the standard preoccupation in the Bolsheviks' security assessments. As Litvinov put it, even if Poland was not seeking war, it might find itself drawn into one because of its alliance with Romania.[131] The complexity of these perceived international alliances had an almost inner anti-Soviet logic of their own. But Litvinov exaggerated the threat posed by the Warsaw conference. Its participants were undoubtedly worried about Soviet aggression, especially following the mobilization of the Red Army on the border with Finland in late 1921, but rather than establish a military union, Poland, Estonia, Latvia and Finland signed the Warsaw Accord, in which Article VII provided for only consultations on joint defence should one of the four be attacked (and seeing as Finland did not ratify, it never came into force).[132] Moreover, at a follow-up conference in Riga at the end of March, and this time including Soviet representatives, the tone differed. Subjects under discussion were deeper economic cooperation, disarmament and even *de jure* recognition of Soviet Russia.[133]

Because the Politburo had prioritized bilateral relations with Germany at Genoa rather than take a step towards reintegration into the international order, intelligence reports about a forthcoming military attack, coordinated in the west, continued unabated. Sergei Kamenev wrote to Stalin at the end of April, for instance, highlighting how recent intelligence indicated that Poland and Romania were considering launching military action in late spring or early summer.[134] This news was followed up two weeks later with another report from the OGPU's foreign department that described 'serious discussions' in Latvia about a possible conflict between Poland and Soviet Russia.[135] Soviet intelligence agents reported various worrying signs over the summer, including supposed French-Polish-Romanian military cooperation, the movement of Polish troops to the borders of Ukraine and the possibility of a new attack if conditions were right to spark the internal collapse of the Bolshevik state.[136] But the core conclusions of Soviet intelligence were largely unchanged since the end of the Soviet-Polish war: Poland would find it difficult to wage war independently; its government needed to improve economic relations with Soviet Russia to meet the demands of industry; war would be unpopular at home, and impossible during a financial crisis.[137]

There were, as ever, outliers pushing more urgent scenarios. In September 1922, Oleksandr Shumskyi, Soviet Ukraine's ambassador to Poland, warned Mikhail Frunze, commander of the Ukrainian military district and future head of the Red Army, about Poland's own 'systematic preparations' for war.[138] But the predominate view in the Bolshevik leadership by late 1922 coalesced around Poland possibly going to war, and Britain and France as being essential for making this a reality. It was therefore hardly reassuring that Soviet intelligence also detailed in October that the French government planned to give Poland and Czechoslovakia 200 million francs to purchase military materiel. The conciliatory Lloyd George's resignation in the same month created further uncertainties.[139] For Lenin, at least, Allied pressure was beginning to intensify on Poland. As he wrote to Chicherin in October: 'They [the Entente] *will* hazard an intervention in spring, if they can *force* Poland: nothing can be done to prevent this except strengthening our defence capacity.'[140] This was to directly repeat his unfounded remarks from the year before.

Amid this now-routine back-and-forth in the Bolsheviks' estimations of the war threat, and as was often the case, some modest improvements in Soviet-Polish relations were recorded. At the end of September, Chicherin visited Warsaw and met the new prime minister Julian Nowak, appointed at the close of Poland's political crisis in 1922. Both men expressed worries that Romania and Turkey might come into conflict, which could then draw in Poland and Soviet Russia. The two agreed that they should work together to 'maintain and enforce peace in Europe' and made a commitment to restart trade negotiations (these would fail again). In an interview with *Izvestiia* later in October, Chicherin spoke optimistically about the advantages of improving ties with Poland.[141] But while these advantages were plain to see, incremental improvements in Soviet-Polish relations were easily crowded out by the Bolsheviks' intelligence, from varied sources, pointing to an opposite picture of a coming and devastating future war. This noise would only become louder, and almost totally consuming, in 1923.

The Ruhr crisis

When French and Belgian troops occupied the Ruhr industrial region on 11 January 1923 following the failure of the German government to meet its reparations payments, and days later, after chancellor Wilhelm Cuno called on the Ruhr population to engage in passive resistance, a crisis accelerated in the heart of Europe. Watching attentively from abroad, the Bolsheviks recalculated their assessments of future war and, at the very least, the leadership now suspected that Poland might, in short order, take advantage of the upheaval to seize the German regions of East Prussia and Upper Silesia (in the view of Soviet intelligence this would be at French behest).[142] The worst-case scenario was European-wide conflict with France pushing the Polish Army once again to the east. The subversive designs of the German Communist Party (KPD) were a further complication to the unfolding crisis. Its leaders sought to exploit the chaos by not only resisting the French occupation but agitating to bring down the German 'bourgeois' government. As we shall see, the Bolsheviks went on to give the KPD full backing in the summer after being caught up yet again in visions of upending the European order. Still, they could not shake grave concerns that even if revolution took hold, the Polish Army would immediately invade Germany to forestall the creation of a second revolutionary state on its borders. The Red Army would then be compelled to defend its new socialist ally. The Ruhr crisis, in this respect, held out the possibility of the long-anticipated revolution in Germany, but with it came significant dangers.

In the weeks before the occupation of the Ruhr, Soviet intelligence agents kept a close eye on any potentially threatening troop movements across the now Soviet Union's western borders and agents in Ukraine were tasked with obtaining Polish, Latvian and Estonian rail mobilization plans.[143] With an eye trained already to the west, the spectre that the Soviet Union could be pulled into another war was quickly reflected in intelligence at the outset of the Ruhr crisis. One report from January, for instance, claimed that the French general staff accepted that war against Germany would, by extension, develop into a war against the Soviet Union.[144] In response to the unfolding crisis, Trotsky wrote to Nikolai Bukharin, editor of *Pravda*, and Iurii Steklov, editor of *Izvestiia*, to insist that more needed to be done in the Soviet press to emphasize the 'seriousness of the international situation as a result of the French occupation of the Ruhr'. The situation would turn 'catastrophic', he argued, if Poland intervened, threatening 'all the peoples of Europe, and first of all, Russia'.[145] Trotsky added that his views aligned with the mood in the Politburo, which soon approved a commission to travel to Germany for negotiations on military cooperation and mutual defence. Trotsky estimated that Poland was now likely to launch war against Germany, and this might only be delayed by mere months.[146]

The worrying intelligence continued to filter in. The foreign department of the GPU detailed in March that the occupation of the Ruhr had apparently refocused the Polish general staff towards the prospect of war against the Soviet Union, having convinced themselves (not entirely unrealistically) that the Bolsheviks would intervene if Poland went to war against Germany. Soviet military intelligence held the same view: a majority within the Polish general staff, it reported, now believed that another war should be launched to overthrow Soviet power.[147] During these months, both GPU and Soviet military intelligence agents drew attention to Polish military preparations around the Ukrainian border and in major Polish cities, including preparations for new mobilizations; the reinforcements of Polish troops; and assessed the possibility that these could be sent to Kiev. According to these materials, Polish railways were already being adapted to match those in Ukraine.[148]

The wider Red Army was then primed when supreme commander, Sergei Kamenev, and chief of staff, Pavel Lebedev, sent directives to the command of the western army group and to forces in Ukraine warning that Soviet troops 'might, in the near future' need to defend the borders. The array of possible future enemies Kamenev identified included White émigré formations – organized by the Allied Powers – and Poland, Finland, Estonia, Latvia, Lithuania and Romania.[149] The Red Army war-gamed possible conflicts, taking the view that armed conflict was inevitable.[150] Rumours about a forthcoming conflict also started to spread throughout the Soviet population and the GPU stepped up efforts in March to purge the west and southwestern border regions of the Soviet Union of supposedly 'harmful elements' that might support enemies of Soviet power. Poles were specifically targeted.[151] All of this, moreover, was taking place during another sharp downturn in Soviet-Polish relations following the GPU's arrest of the head of the Polish repatriation delegation in Minsk on espionage charges.[152]

As was nearly always the case, not every piece of intelligence pointed in the direction of war. More closely matching the reality of circumstances, one Soviet intelligence official reported to Trotsky in March something the Bolsheviks had heard time and time again: Poland was not in a position, economically, to go to war against Germany and the Soviet Union; the French government knew this and was concerned that Polish defeat could undermine the entire Versailles system.[153] The reality was that much of Poland was in a state of devastation in 1923, with masses of buildings, transport hubs and farm land destroyed in earlier conflicts. Several million people remained displaced from their homes.[154] But while such intelligence provided a corrective, its impact on Bolshevik thinking – if there was any – appears almost zero. It was true that Trotsky chose to openly cast doubt on the possibility of a Polish attack on Germany in a March interview with British journalist, Arthur Ransome; and Litvinov did the same in private conversation with other diplomats.[155] But considering the Bolsheviks' later behaviour and the alarmist tone that ran through internal commentary about forthcoming war, it is likely that both men were seeking to mask Moscow's deepening concerns about a coming conflagration and ease international tensions as part of a wider Soviet peace offensive.

Some, like Chicherin, worried that the Bolsheviks were making a strategic error in prominently siding with Germany during the crisis. This, he argued, would alienate France, undermining promising improvements in relations (future French prime minister, Edouard Herriot, visited Soviet Russia for a month in September 1922 as head of an economic mission and came away advocating stronger economic ties).[156] It was also unclear to Chicherin what the Bolsheviks would get in return. As he put it to Stalin: 'You told me recently: "We have thought enough about foreign interests, it is time we thought about our own interests."'[157] Stalin gave Chicherin short shrift, accusing him of a 'sad misunderstanding' of the situation with France where there was no prospect of a beneficial agreement. There was, instead, only 'credits in several millions from France to Poland and Romania – this is the basis of an agreement, only not with Russia, but against Russia'. Stalin, as we shall see below, was pessimistic about whether a German revolution was in fact feasible, but still, for him, Chicherin did not grasp the severity of the unfolding crisis in Europe.[158] The alarm was now sounding in major party forums. Comintern head, Zinoviev, warned of an imminent danger of war at the twelfth party congress in April, while Lev Kamenev pushed for higher investments to strengthen the borders.[159]

As far as the Bolsheviks were concerned, by early summer, the pendulum had swung even closer towards war when the British government delivered another ultimatum, in Curzon's name, to the Soviet government in early May. Among a litany of complaints about damage done to British interests by Soviet hostile behaviours, the central accusation focused on subversion in India and Central Asia. The British government gave the Bolsheviks ten days to cease otherwise the Anglo-Soviet trade agreement would be severed. Arriving amid the high tension of the Ruhr crisis, the ultimatum sparked a severe reaction inside the Bolshevik Party and a slew of articles appeared in the Soviet press on the imminent war (Trotsky admitted in private that these were useful also in preparing the population for a future draft).[160] However, looking to diffuse tensions quickly and appreciating their vulnerability, the Bolsheviks conceded to most points in the British ultimatum, even if Comintern propaganda continued on a lower scale.[161]

The situation looked even worse, however, as the British ultimatum arrived when Marshal Foch was in Poland on an official visit exploring the coordination of the French and Polish armies.[162] This resulted in no concrete measures, but Foch's visit was denounced in the Soviet press as further evidence of imperialism and, behind-the-scenes, Soviet intelligence reported on fresh French efforts to coax

Poland into the Little Entente and deepen the Franco-Polish alliance in the event of war against Germany and the Soviet Union, enabling Poland to fight war on two fronts. Yet in another fleeting moment of measured analysis, it rightly described this as a defensive arrangement: French efforts to create stronger alliances in Europe were a guarantee against a Soviet attack and the primary goal remained the deterrence of German aggression.[163] Soviet intelligence, furthermore, reported that Foch admitted that France should find ways to pressure the Soviet government to collapse during the crisis, but it stressed that he did not mean to go as far as military methods.[164]

The more level-headed analysis, as usual, failed to make much impact, lost amid reports claiming more dangerous trends. Indeed, political flux in Poland over the summer, when General Sikorski was ousted as Polish prime minster in May, abruptly ending his short-lived government, and its replacement by a new centre-right coalition headed by Wincenty Witos, added to the Bolsheviks' perception of rising unpredictability in the crisis. While supportive of French action in the Ruhr and seen as pro-French, Chicherin, initially, characterized the Witos government as conservative and opposed to foreign aggression. There was some renewed Polish momentum towards rapprochement, and particularly in trade relations.[165] The Bolsheviks should also have taken comfort in Piłsudski's resignation from his last substantive post as chief of the general staff in June. A critic of the Witos government, Piłsudski resigned when the army was brought under firmer control of the ministry of war and when his allies were ousted from the government and second department. Witos, notably, ended the subsidies still being provided to UNR forces in Poland. Piłsudski would spend the next three years on the outskirts of Warsaw, and on the borders of political life, in a manor house in the town of Sulejówek.[166]

Nonetheless, there was noticeable skittishness among some Bolsheviks about the new government's intentions. When Witos delivered a speech to the Polish People's Party conference in July, for instance, he referred to the future advancement of Poland using the phrase: 'we will not move to the west but should move to the east'. This set off a furore in Moscow and inside the NKID, where Witos's words were misinterpreted as an expression of future aggression. 'How can the Polish government insist on our fulfilment of the Treaty of Riga while it threatens to expand to the east', Viktor Kopp proclaimed.[167] *Izvestiia* published a front-page article from Radek criticizing the remarks, noting that the Witos government appeared no different than Piłsudski's.[168] The NKID convinced itself that Witos was adopting a more 'anti-Russian' position to see off possible challenges from Piłsudski and his allies, who continued to wield influence behind-the-scenes. The government 'feels very fragile and may not survive the upcoming parliamentary storm', Kopp stressed.[169] In August, however, it became clear that Witos had referred simply to economic expansion. 'Witos did not really talk about political advancement in the east, and we hurried in Moscow to evaluate this speech', noted Leonid Obolenskii from the Soviet embassy in Poland, drawing attention to Radek's hastily written *Izvestiia* article.[170] Evidently, the Bolsheviks' long-standing tendency of seeing Polish actions in the worst possible light was only exacerbated by the rising drama of 1923.

International tensions rose again in mid-August when the Cuno government was brought down by a growing strike movement in Germany, propelled by worsening economic crisis and skyrocketing inflation. This was a crucial moment and the Politburo now fully committed itself to exploiting the crisis, throwing its weight more emphatically behind the KPD's attempts to ignite revolution. Fearing that the fall of the Cuno government might also enable the assumption of power by the political right and Germany's entry into an anti-capitalist coalition, money, advisors and weapons were sent to the KPD.[171] Trotsky, Bukharin and Zinoviev now emerged as some of the strongest advocates for supporting the nascent revolution. Zinoviev, caught up in visions of a union of the Soviet Union and future Soviet Germany, produced a set of draft theses in mid-August describing a maturing crisis with 'decisive events' imminent. He called on the KPD to seize opportunities 'quickly and resolutely' and warned of the possibility of a European war if the German revolution became a victim to the western powers.[172] More starkly, at a plenum of the central committee a few weeks later, Zinoviev claimed that if the German revolution was crushed, the next step would 'undoubtedly be a campaign against the USSR'.[173] Trotsky saw the same danger, writing to his deputy in war department, Efraim Sklianskii, that 'victory for the working masses in Germany' increased the risk that the world bourgeoisie would 'crush the proletarian revolution and drown communism in rivers of blood'. Such an intervention into Germany 'would only be the first step to a strike against the Soviet Union'.[174] Among the less enthusiastic, Stalin still doubted that the German communists were ready for revolution, though he was more open to the possibility than before. With Lenin increasingly outside party life following a second stroke in December 1922, moreover, Stalin was becoming the preeminent voice in foreign policy. And his position about the genuine risk of war was aligned with other Bolsheviks. As Stalin detailed in a note on Zinoviev's theses: 'If we want to help the Germans – and we want to and should help – we need to prepare for war, seriously and comprehensively, for the matter will ultimately be about the existence of the Soviet federation and about the fate of the world revolution in the near future.'[175]

A central problem, and a major reason behind the Bolsheviks' anxieties in 1923, was that the Red Army was in no condition to fight a major war. The Polish Army, with Allied backing, would be a force to reckon with, something obvious to the leadership for months. Earlier in January, Soviet intelligence laid out clearly that although having suffered from scarce funding, the Polish Army had benefitted from years of French assistance and had mastered a wide variety of weaponry.[176] Then in February, the head of the collegium of the chief administration of military industry, I. N. Smirnov, sent a report to the Politburo describing his 'party duty to tell the central committee the hard truth about the state of defence of our republic and about our unpreparedness from the technical and production side'. Smirnov was blunt: the army could not be armed or supplied for major war on the western front. Available weaponry was not sufficient to fight Poland alone and Smirnov warned of the collapse of overloaded factories.[177] Other weaknesses in Soviet defences were highlighted elsewhere. Dzerzhinskii described problems in Soviet transport infrastructure in June and the inability to efficiently move troops. He concluded that Poland would be able to carry out a successful short strike towards Kiev, in a worrying repeat of recent history.[178] A report prepared for the Politburo commission on Soviet defence in the month before painted a similarly depressing picture: the Red Army was falling behind the Polish Army and needed urgent strengthening.[179]

Facing the prospect of war on undesirable terms, the Bolsheviks launched a doomed effort in October to secure Polish non-intervention in German affairs and permission to transit goods through Poland to Germany (claimed to be foodstuffs, but the intention was most likely to supply weapons). The proposal was for Poland's frontiers to be guaranteed and in return, the Poles would be given a free hand in East Prussia and Danzig in exchange for Soviet compensation in the Baltic region.[180] Spearheading these efforts, Viktor Kopp made parallel attempts to secure neutrality from, and transit rights through, Latvia and Lithuania. However, the Poles understandably refused transit rights at a time when the Bolsheviks were still foot-dragging in their fulfilment of the Treaty of Riga.[181] The whole endeavour was unrealistic from the outset and indicative of the Bolsheviks' weak position. As Leonid Obolenskii put it to Kopp, for the Poles to discuss transit arrangements in the circumstances of autumn 1923 'would be political madness'.[182]

Despite the weak Soviet military and international postion, the war machine swung into action from late summer, nevertheless. On 18 September 1923, the Politburo ordered Red Army units on the western front, the Ukrainian military district and in air defence, strengthened.[183] Revolutionary Military Council of the Republic ordered the number of political officers on the western front increased on the following day.[184] In October, student communists were called up as political officers on the western front and demobilized Red Army men returned to the ranks.[185] As these measures rolled out, the Soviet press was increasingly filled with stories of war and intervention.[186] Between 24 October and 26 November, moreover, the Soviet defence commission met nine times, indicative of intensifying planning for war.[187] Closer to the ground, industry officials in Soviet Ukraine secretly prepared in November for the evacuation of enterprises and factories in the border regions, should war suddenly erupt.[188] Factories near the border employing Polish workers were scrutinized for evidence of counterrevolutionary activity following GPU suspicions of arson attacks, soon attributed to Polish spies. The GPU recorded an increase in the second department's operations, whose agents, for their part, were sending reports home on the hurried Soviet preparations for new conflict.[189]

War, of course, did not erupt in 1923 and the much-anticipated revolutionary uprising in Germany, which began more concertedly from late October, attracted little support in the end. Even a stronger show of strength in Hamburg fizzled out almost as soon as it began and by the end of the year, the crisis had drawn to a close. As three years before, when the Red Army was approaching Warsaw in 1920, the Bolsheviks placed too much faith in a German revolution in 1923, and they misperceived the threat of war. This time, the latter was the greater miscalculation. Even after the German revolutionaries had clearly failed, the war threat remained on the Bolsheviks' radar. In theses produced for a joint plenum of the central committee and central control commission, convened as the Hamburg uprising was falling to pieces, Stalin interpreted the failure as a step towards war and claimed that intervention from Poland and France was still likely.[190] Soviet military planning, as we have seen, continued into November, even though Poland was at that time paralysed by a general strike with economic turmoil forcing the collapse of the Witos government one month later.[191]

Although Soviet intelligence tended to present the opposite, there is no evidence that Poland planned a military strike on Germany in 1923, and this was less of a prospect against the Soviet Union. There were certain influential groups in Poland, particularly centred around the military and intelligence services, enthusiastic for the French occupation of the Ruhr (and perhaps even for another war), but the Witos government took a cautious approach and wanted to maintain neutrality and stabilize relations.[192] In fact, despite its concern about the formation of the Soviet Union and the implications of greater centralization in Soviet foreign policy, the Witos government went on to recognize the new state in December 1923.[193] And with Piłsudski further from the centre of power, anti-Soviet voices in Poland were weakened at the very moment that the Bolsheviks took the threat of war most seriously. The 1923 war scare reveals, in this way, how precariously the Bolsheviks viewed their position in the world and the degree to which they misperceived the nature of foreign threats. They certainly received intelligence more closely reflecting reality that Poland had little to gain from starting another conflict. As one report put it in mid-October, during the climax of the crisis: 'a social and political-economic catastrophe in Germany could trigger a new European war. This war would not be as grandiose as the Great European [war], but nevertheless for Poland it would be deadly. The world war brought political independence for Poland, but in the near future, war could destroy Poland.'[194] But such intelligence did not gain much purchase among leading Bolsheviks or dampen down the war scare.

This misperception of a war threat in 1923 was also characteristic of the previous three years, following the end of the Soviet-Polish war. Anti-Soviet organizations, those headed by Savinkov, Petliura and Bułak-Bałakhovich, were a major headache for both sides during the negotiations towards the Treaty of Riga and throughout its half-hearted implementation. For the Bolsheviks, clandestine support given to these groups by the Polish general staff and the second department made the problem more pressing. Even so, they saw the danger in outsized terms. Border raids were not a precursor to an invasion, despite whatever unrealistic ambitions anti-Soviet leaders fostered. The Polish ministry of the treasury in fact began to starve the émigré fighters of funding and once Tiutiunnik's rash intervention was quashed in November 1921, support in Poland for interventions of this type quickly fell away, to be replaced by the softer encouragement of separatism in the Soviet border republics, where some local actors aspired to maintain looser connections with Moscow.[195]

While showing some ability to accurately assess the landscape of Polish domestic and international politics in the early 1920s, the Bolshevik leadership, the NKID, military intelligence and the security organs could just as easily misperceive the nature of Polish foreign policy and frequently misunderstood the country's relationship with the western powers. Contradictory intelligence and a worldview rooted in global ideological competition bore much responsibility for this. Even the central NKID, less inclined than other Soviet institutions to exaggerate the war danger, struggled to assess Poland's behaviour consistently, with Chicherin jumping from one position to another in the early 1920s and failing to reach consistent judgements. While further away from Moscow, NKID officials on the ground often saw things with a clearer eye. Taken together, from 1920 to 1923, as far as most senior Bolsheviks were concerned, the danger had come full circle with the Ruhr crisis. The years after the close of the Soviet-Polish war, therefore, did little to ease the Bolsheviks' deep sense of uncertainty and lack of clarity in relations with Poland and the western powers. The fear of invasion was sustained, where no such meaningful threat existed.

Chapter 4

STABILITY TO INSECURITY

Despite the high tension sparked during the Ruhr crisis and the Soviet leadership's deepening conviction that a Polish military response would follow a revolution in Germany, there was, of course, no war in 1923. The failure of the so-called German October brought the Bolsheviks' revolutionary enthusiasm suddenly back down to the ground. What did not change after 1923, however, was the steady feed of Soviet intelligence predicting a future military attack. Though in contrast to the immediate years after Soviet-Polish war, the senior party leadership, military and intelligence establishments by in large were no longer as convinced that renewed war against Poland was imminent, even if this was no less accepted as a future inevitability. From the mid-1920s, during a period cautiously welcomed as a new breathing space characterized by infighting among capitalist enemies, Soviet officials continued to analyse the international situation carefully for signs of the future inevitable war and the intensity of this perceived foreign threat waxed and waned. The Bolsheviks, naturally, felt more at ease when short-lived left-wing governments came to power in Britain and France in 1924, but this temporary respite was soon followed by a return to conservative anti-Sovietism. New security arrangements in Europe, moreover, isolated the Soviet Union further by weakening the already precarious Soviet-German partnership.

In these years, Poland maintained its place at the core of the Bolsheviks' imagined anti-Soviet coalition. Exaggerated accounts of banditry and Polish espionage in the border regions cemented the vision of the country as a key hostile adversary. The fact was, however, that even after Piłsudski returned to power in a military coup d'état in May 1926, Poland was not suddenly placed on a collision course with the Soviet Union. Contrary to Stalin's and other senior Bolsheviks' assumptions, Piłsudski had no intention of launching a new war or position Poland as a cog in an anti-Soviet bloc. The gap between this reality and Soviet assessments of subversive and military threats was widening.

'Hidden war' in the border regions

The failure of the 'German October' delivered a crippling blow to the Bolsheviks' hopes of another revolution taking root in western Europe. The fantasy of overturning governments across the continent, so pervasive from 1917, never recovered. A separate failed uprising in Bulgaria in September 1923, also on Bolshevik encouragement, led to equally disastrous results. Bulgarian communists suffered terribly in a vicious state crackdown. In all, the weakness of the European revolutionary movement could not have been clearer and no further concerted efforts were made to engineer a seizure of power in Europe on the model of the Russian Revolution. The Bolsheviks instead began to see the survival of their system, and the very path to a communist future, as dependent on the growing power of the Soviet Union itself.[1]

Notwithstanding the disaster in Germany in 1923 and the implications for future revolution in Europe, the Soviet Union's position in the international order in fact gained some stability in 1924. Political change sweeping through Britain and France proved to the Bolsheviks' advantage. By the middle of 1924, both Stanley Baldwin's and Raymond Poincaré's hostile conservative governments were replaced by left-wing alternatives: James Ramsay MacDonald's Labour Party in a minority government, and Edouard Herriot's radical and socialist coalition, *Cartel des gauches*. The new British Labour government was the quicker of the two to signal a change of course in foreign relations. Even though it went against MacDonald's cautious instincts, the government granted unconditional *de jure* diplomatic recognition to the Soviet Union in February 1924.[2] From the world's preeminent imperial power, this was a landmark moment. The Soviet Union had taken a major step forward out of international isolation. Although it would wait another decade to be realized, MacDonald invited the Soviet Union, alongside Germany, to enter the League of Nations. In economic relations, a new draft Anglo-Soviet commercial agreement was then worked up in summer 1924 and, generous to the Bolsheviks, this postponed negotiations about compensation for property seized during the Russian Revolution and difficult questions about outstanding pre-revolutionary debts (although the treaty was never ratified following the fall of the MacDonald government later in the year).[3] Elsewhere optimism was rising in Bolshevik circles about the prospect of improving relations with France and perhaps striking a concrete Franco-Soviet pact. The Herriot government, like its predecessors, no less prioritized relations with Britain and Germany, but it was also seeking improved relations with the Soviet Union and its better integration into Europe. Signalling a major shift in strategy, Herriot dropped the creation of an eastern alliance as a core priority and, in the face of substantial domestic opposition, diplomatic recognition of the Soviet Union followed in October.[4] By the end of 1924, the Bolsheviks had not only established formal relations with Britain and France – their long-time preoccupations as members of the capitalist Entente – but a string of other countries likewise forged diplomatic ties across the year.

Improving Soviet relations with Britain and France alarmed the Polish government, now under the leadership of Władysław Grabski, which feared for the stability of its 1921 French alliance. There were sufficient grounds for concern. Against the wishes of the French general staff, Herriot sought to weaken France's Polish commitments, in the past typically associated with the political right. While in Britain, MacDonald's efforts to reconcile France and Germany inevitably squeezed Poland further. Internal calculations for Poland's security in Europe started to shift in response. Following the wider political mood, the Polish government anticipated reconciliation between Germany and the western powers, and the former's political and economic reintegration into Europe. Fearing fresh international backing for German claims of territorial revision on the Polish-German border, it began to see the rationale for *rapprochement* with the Soviet Union. In Moscow, some senior Bolsheviks saw similar dangers and opportunities, likewise shaped by Germany's moving allegiances. Following the party's risky commitment in the Ruhr crisis and the failure of revolution in Germany, Chicherin did not sugar coat the 'deeply hostile' character of Soviet-German relations at the outset of 1924. Amid a downturn that might see Germany more closely align with the west, improving Soviet-Polish ties was the obvious way to compensate, something Bolshevik representatives also chose to highlight to German officials as discouragement behind closed doors.[5]

Improving Soviet-Polish relations to counter drifting Germany was far from a straightforward task. Clashing territorial claims in the Soviet-Polish border regions were still rolling and contentious in 1924; the Bolsheviks, moreover, were ramping up the pressure to undermine Polish authority at this very time, with a new propaganda campaign castigating the mistreatment of minorities under Polish rule. Presenting themselves as defenders of minority interests, the Bolsheviks played upon Article VII of the Treaty of Riga which obliged both sides to allow national and cultural freedoms among minority groups. As ever, while much of this was plain propaganda, there was some truth to the Bolsheviks' complaints. Belarusians and Ukrainians living in Poland, although given freedom to exercise religion and language, lacked similar rights across the state administration and in the justice system.[6] Still, to gain maximum leverage, the campaign exaggerated the picture of persecution.

More provocatively – and seemingly running entirely counter to the project of improving Soviet-Polish relations – in July 1924, at its fifth congress, the Comintern called for Ukrainian and Belarusian territories under Polish, Romanian and Czechoslovakian control to be handed over to the Soviet Union. Shortly after, and in line with Soviet Ukraine's territorial claims once the Conference of Ambassadors recognized the Soviet-Polish border in 1923, Kristian Rakovskii, now chargé d'affaires in London, provocatively denounced the Polish 'annexation' of eastern Galicia as conflicting with the self-determination of its people following a high-profile Anglo-Soviet conference in August 1924.[7] Working in the other direction, there were signs elsewhere of marginal improvement in Soviet-Polish relations. Negotiations started for a new railway agreement and consular convention, the former concluded in April 1924; stalled trade negotiations experienced some revived momentum.[8] And the new Polish representative to the Soviet Union, Ludwik Darowski expressed optimism about the prospect of better relations.[9] On the Soviet side, there were some signs of a risk-adverse spirit when Stalin and Grigory Zinoviev, both leading members of the ruling party, sought to keep a lid on the spiralling diplomatic arguments of the summer, having resisted the Comintern's radical position on unifying Polish-controlled Ukrainian and

Belarusian territories. Stalin, at least for now, suggested to Dmitri Manuilskii, a member of the Comintern's executive committee, a 'humbler and more careful' approach, even if, in the end, 'all of these torn parts will join with the USSR when their times come'.[10] But as before, modest steps forward and the evidence of some restraint in upper party circles were easily drowned out by the old and still fractious arguments about subversion in the border regions, and ongoing armed skirmishes.

At the thirteenth party congress held in Moscow in May 1924 – the first since Lenin died in January after long illness and extended incapacitation – Zinoviev delivered the main political report to assembled delegates and examined the shifting international situation. The recent death of the party leader had sparked fear and significant alarm throughout the Soviet Union and rumours about the outbreak of war had spread quickly among the people.[11] Adjusting to new internal and external circumstances, Zinoviev's report presented a mixed picture of the international environment. On the one hand, he interpreted the elections of social democratic parties in Britain and France as evidence of the power of the Second International and the international labour movement. On the other, at least according to Zinoviev, the rise of such left-wing governments was, in truth, the work of international capital, seeking to control and manage the growing workers' movement. Gains abroad were thus immediately caveated. Nevertheless, Zinoviev made clear that the threat of war against the Soviet Union had lowered. Even if international capital was exploiting the new British and French governments, the stronger position of the European working classes enabled better popular resistance to future capitalist designs for aggression via proxy states. 'The current French government, no matter how it develops, cannot openly give weapons and arms to Romania against us. It cannot arm Poland against us [...] It is difficult for MacDonald to directly raise them against us.'[12] Such optimistic thinking about the power of the British left was partly a legacy of the 1920 war when London dockworkers refused to load munitions for dispatch to Poland (even though this occurred only in isolated cases).[13] The true strength of the western working classes aside, the fact remained that the imminence of war, accepted as a near certainty in Bolshevik circles just months before, was no longer presented this way in any major party forum. These were not just reassuring words given to a political congress either. Tangible changes were underway far from Moscow. One month earlier, the western front had already been converted to peacetime status in recognition of the lower risk of war and the failed revolution in Germany.[14]

With Lenin dead, Stalin, now preeminent in the Bolshevik Party, spoke regularly in public about the improving international circumstances of the Soviet Union in 1924. 'Poincare and Curzon, have, to put it plainly, come a cropper, they have been thrown overboard', he proclaimed in June. Drawing on Lenin's theory of imperialism and in another reassuring note, Stalin claimed that inherent rivalries between capitalist powers, driven by their never-ending quest for resources, stymied the formation of an anti-Soviet front. The capitalist powers were 'incapable of developing further without plundering the defeated countries and colonies, without conflicts and clashes among themselves over division of the loot'. And because the masses increasingly rejected war, 'growing resentment' was rising among the working people against such 'bellicose imperialism', another trend to the Soviet Union's advantage. Back home on the domestic front, Stalin pointed to the ever-increasing stability of Soviet power: this was 'as firm as a rock' with the Soviet Union attracting 'mounting popularity' overseas.[15] Taken together, while the Soviet people could not afford to abandon their vigilance, Stalin did not describe an imminent external threat.

None of this, of course, ruled out the possibility of conflict in the longer term and this was no less an accepted certainty in Bolshevik circles, manifesting in public and private. In August 1924, for instance, the Soviet government launched a mobilization campaign timed for the tenth anniversary of the First World War. By its end, the memory of the global conflict was muted, and the campaign focused more strongly on the possibility of future war, choosing to emphasize the destructive power of new technologies, like military planes and gas attacks. Some, like Trotsky, chose this moment to deliver stark warnings to the Soviet people that they needed to be ready to defend themselves.[16] Likewise, writing in the journal *Bolshevik* in September, Stalin revealed to its readers how the danger of future war remained very real, even if the signs were hidden from public view. As Zinoviev had done at the party congress, Stalin claimed that the international bourgeoisie had moved 'from a policy of frontal attack to a policy of compromise, from open imperialism to hidden imperialism, from Poincare and Curzon to MacDonald and Herriot'. In this way, the British Labour Party and *Cartel des gauches* were simply 'a cloak to cover the nakedness of imperialism [...] to dupe the masses with high-sounding phrases about peace in order to prepare for a new war'. The capitalist powers, Stalin argued, intended 'to fool the masses with highfaluting talk about "friendly" relations with the Soviet Union, about various "treaties" with the Soviet government, in order to establish still closer relations with the counter-revolutionary conspirators who have been kicked out of Russia, with the aim of bandit operations in Byelorussia, the Ukraine and Georgia'.[17] Ongoing raids in the border regions, therefore, were telling signs of this future military threat. Stalin's public commentary on foreign affairs, as usual, aligned with the intelligence crossing his desk. Going against the optimism expressed in the NKID about potentially improving Soviet-Polish ties, Soviet military intelligence reported in May 1924 on apparent efforts in Polish military and political circles to pursue a 'more active foreign policy towards the USSR'. Other intelligence, among various examples, included a report detailing how a member of the Romanian general staff visited Poland to 'enlist the support of Poland in the event of a conflict with the USSR'. The Bolsheviks' habit of misreading defensive alliances as offensive collaborations was as strong as ever.[18]

The political police, now reorganized as the union wide OGPU, shared Stalin's concerns about a 'hidden war' against the Soviet Union and more so than other Soviet institutions. Even though the crisis of 1923 had dissipated, OGPU operatives expended more energy in the mid-1920s towards rooting out Polish subversives in the border regions, something Polish officials on the ground could not fail to notice. The Polish consulate in Kiev, for instance, reported on intensifying surveillance of its personnel and efforts to break informer networks from the beginning of 1924.

Polish diplomats were certain that this 'feverish activity' had been accelerated from the centre.[19] (They were right and Dzerzhinskii pushed his subordinates for more vigilance against spies from Poland, Romania, Latvia and Estonia in these months.)[20] And as it had done in the past, the OGPU continued to exaggerate the scale of Polish intelligence operations and judged the danger in outsized terms, although there was enough truth behind its security concerns to maintain these as live issues. In the mid-1920s and with mixed success, Polish agents had certainly tried to forge contacts with domestic anti-Soviet organizations. One Polish agent in Ukraine, for instance, collaborated in early 1924 with an organization of former officers from the Imperial Russian Army that, according to Polish sources, numbered 1600 members across various cities (with 412 characterized as 'active').[21] The Kiev GPU arrested another Polish agent, a certain engineer, Michał Węgliński, in March 1924 for belonging to a Polish intelligence station code-named A.9.[22] The Kiev GPU then arrested several people working for Polish intelligence later in June, including former general of the Imperial Army, Viktor Belavin, and former lieutenant and still-serving Red Army officer, Aleksandr Ivanov. Belavin was also in contact with the A.9 intelligence station and had been left exposed following the arrest of its courier, Janina Krzeczkowska.[23] Another case had seen Polish agents attempt to contact an anti-Soviet network, named 'M', to secure proffered intelligence about the Red Army. 'M', however, turned out to be the creation of Soviet counterintelligence, a strand of the wide-ranging clandestine Trust Operation that ran successfully until 1926 and designed to entrap foreign intelligence agents and émigré counterrevolutionary organizations.[24] The OGPU had no reservations in broadcasting such dangers to the wider party and public. In an interview given to *Kommunist* in October 1924, head of the Ukrainian GPU, Vsevolod Balitskii, elaborated at length on the threat presented by Polish spies operating in Soviet Ukraine. Large numbers of Polish subversive organizations were apparently active in the republic and official Polish representatives, some operating with diplomatic immunity, were said to be coordinating the 'overwhelming majority'.[25] An editorial in the same issue, styled as a warning to Poland, urged its government to stop 'playing with fire' and underlined how the international system had changed from the years 'when we had all of bourgeois Europe against us'.[26]

Not to deny the reality of Polish espionage and subversion, and especially along the border, the fact was that the OGPU leadership presented this as growing in strength when it was in fact in decline. Much of the Polish second department's intelligence network in Ukraine was shut down in the mid-1920s, and not only because of stronger OGPU pressure. When the mass repatriation from Soviet territory of Polish citizens, refugees and POWs, caught up or captured in the Soviet-Polish war, finally came to an end in 1924, an important means of concealing intelligence activity was lost for good.[27] But this made no difference to the OGPU's presentation of the Polish subversive threat, which became even starker in later years as we shall see. In early 1925, to take one example, Polish intelligence officials reported on the cases of ninety Poles and Ukrainians arrested in Soviet Ukraine because of political views or supposed anti-Soviet activities. The Soviet authorities went on to accuse 90 per cent of espionage. Based on its sources, however, Polish intelligence regarded less than half of these charges as accurate.[28] Polish intelligence was undoubtedly still active in Ukraine after 1924, and whether the GPU actually believed in each and every espionage case or not, the culminative effect of its reporting was to produce a more threatening picture.

Alongside Polish espionage, anti-Soviet groups operating in the border regions remained a central focus for Soviet security and intelligence organizations. Internal reports underlined more frequent acts of disruption and threats to the borders, typically presented as backed by Polish intelligence. In January 1924, for instance, Soviet military intelligence reported on a concentration of forces led by Bułak-Bałakhovich and the Belarusian nationalist Anastas Antsipovich on the Polish side of the border, totalling 1260 people.[29] The Polish government, it was claimed, had organized a stockpile of weapons.[30] Other Soviet reports claimed much the same and Polish officers were said to be coordinating bands of Polish soldiers elsewhere in the western border regions. One report from the summer identified twenty-six anti-Soviet groups, apparently totalling around 200,000 people.[31] This type of information arrived in Moscow at an already tense moment, amid mutual accusations between Soviet and Polish diplomats about the mistreatment of national minorities on either side of the border.[32] Adding fuel to the fire, Polish officials, for their part, accused local Soviet personnel of involvement in ongoing border raids; a charge quickly returned.[33] At the third congress of soviets, head of the government, Aleksei Rykov, decried 'an almost unbroken series of bandit raids from across the Polish frontier'.[34] It is hardly surprising that none of this eased the NKID's goal of establishing better relations and a trade agreement with Poland to counterweight Germany's shifting alignment in Europe.

By 1925 Poland featured even more prominently in high-level Politburo discussions about the secret coordination of anti-Soviet groups and the OGPU, continuing its line, drew attention to apparently 'intense work by Polish intelligence' to subvert the border regions.[35] By this point, head of military intelligence, Ian Berzin, was also discussing these very subjects with new head of the Red Army, Mikhail Frunze (who had taken over following Trotsky's ousting as People's Commissar for Military Affairs in January as Stalin turned the screws on the political opposition). According to Berzin, Bułak-Bałakhovich commanded the largest and most effective anti-Soviet force in the area though he pointed to other threatening groups operating in Ukraine. In another indication of future danger, Berzin noted that Symon Petliura's UNR and the Romanian government had struck a military agreement, with the former to receive money and weapons for a future attack on Soviet Ukraine.[36] The Politburo, in response to this picture of anti-Soviet activity, pressed in June for stronger border defences and for an enhanced OGPU presence.[37]

It is worth stressing once more that the Bolsheviks' concerns about Polish-supported guerrilla organizations continued to contain more than a grain of truth. In fact, there was a stronger basis here than in the consistently inflated Polish espionage threat. Most importantly, from the autumn of 1925, Piłsudski's supporters coordinated so-called Promethean operations in the border regions, which gathered momentum when rumours about the marshal's potential return to power began to circle in Poland. Promethean operations typically centred on the creation of Ukrainian and Belarusian committees on the ground in the border regions, working together with émigré centres, to cultivate stronger nationalist and anti-Soviet sentiments among local people. On the other side, the Bolsheviks had parallel initiatives to gain influence and leverage of their own. Alongside the campaign claiming significant Polish mistreatment of Belarusian and Ukrainian minorities, the Bolsheviks launched a wider policy of so-called indigenization (*korenizatsiia*), which more liberally awarded cultural freedoms to non-Russian minorities in the border regions to promote the benefits of living under Soviet power (and ideally attract supporters beyond). The establishment of the Marchlevsk Polish Autonomous Region in the Ukrainian border region in July 1925, where inhabitants enjoyed expanded cultural and national autonomy, was emblematic of the policy and designed precisely to draw Polish support to the Soviet project.[38] Both sides, in this way, actively sought to subvert the loyalties of peoples living in the border regions through non-interventionist methods. However, contra the Bolsheviks' impressions, it is important to stress that until Piłsudski seized political power in May 1926, Polish Promethean operations remained limited in scope and the government remained opposed to any sort of direct action.[39]

The Polish government was not alone in looking to avoid risky interventions. Some senior Bolsheviks expressed similar caution about border clashes escalating into much larger, and counterproductive, armed conflicts. Deputy head of the OGPU, Genrikh Iagoda pointed out, for instance, how local protests on the Soviet side of the border, often following press reports of Polish raids, were needlessly destabilizing. In a message to Stalin's close associate and personal secretary, Lev Mekhlis, Iagoda warned that the 'extreme belligerence' in some local demonstrations might create 'extremely serious difficulties in the practical implementation of the accepted party line for business rapprochement with Poland'. He recommended that local campaigns against border raids cast blame elsewhere, and in a familiar direction to powerful off-stage forces. The Soviet press, according to Iagoda, ought to underline how nefarious circles in Poland were acting 'against the interests of their country, are agents of British politics' who 'aimed at disrupting the *rapprochement* between Poland and the USSR'.[40]

In seeking to place blame with malevolent capitalists, it is unlikely that Iagoda was solely looking to protect precarious Soviet-Polish relations at a time when Bolshevik policies were pointing in two directions, towards *rapprochement* and subversion. It is almost certain he believed serious international conspiracies were still at work in Poland. From the materials passing through the OGPU's leadership, it is unmistakably clear that it was convinced that Britain and France wielded outsized influence on the border states. A report sent to Dzerzhinskii, held in his personal papers, for instance, described how 'the growing aggression of the British government against the USSR' made likely that 'the state of tension at our borders is a protracted one [...] under English pressure on our other western borders (Finland, Estonia, Latvia and Lithuania), diversionary acts are being prepared against us'. It recommended urgent reinforcement of the Soviet borders, additional funds released for border security, stronger intelligence and the potential deployment of soldiers.[41]

A further complexity, however, was the deepening tensions between the OGPU and Soviet military intelligence about the febrile situation on the border, stemming from the latter's aggressive tactics deployed from summer 1924. Without the OGPU's knowledge, Soviet military intelligence, for some time, had been running terrorist operations (known euphemistically as 'active intelligence') in the border regions. Frunze and Iosif Unshlikht, who oversaw the operations, and were evidently less troubled by the corrosive impact on Soviet-Polish diplomatic relations, saw these as valuable methods of fomenting unrest on the borders of Soviet Ukraine and Belorussia in the hope of encouraging spontaneous local insurrections into Polish territory.[42] One notorious example of this strategy was the Red Army raid in early August 1924 against the town of Stołpce inside the Polish border. Its primary goal was to free a group of imprisoned communists, but several Polish policemen and citizens were killed in the action, leading to a rush of condemnation from Poland, which then strengthened border defences and created a new military border defence corps. Following the standard line, the NKID blamed local partisans for the attack and denied central coordination, but behind closed doors the Politburo sternly criticized military intelligence's actions.[43] And the leadership was not oblivious to how this episode in 'active intelligence' undermined ongoing trade and border negotiations with the Poles.[44] A similar incident then took place six months later at the city of Iampol' in January 1925 when Polish border guards clashed with a group of Soviet military intelligence agents. When forced to retreat across the border, the latter, still dressed in Polish military uniforms, were then accidentally met with fire from Soviet border guards. This chaotic fighting sparked further bad feeling between both sides, and Soviet and Polish officials began another round of accusation and counteraccusation.[45] In private, while Dzerzhinskii reassured his colleagues that the Poles had no hard evidence against the Bolsheviks from the incident, he was scathing about the 'irresponsible actions of Razvedupra [military intelligence]' for risking sparking war between the Soviet Union and its neighbouring states.[46] The Politburo agreed with Dzerzhinskii and brought 'active intelligence' operations to a swift end (military intelligence prepared for another uprising in Volhynia regardless, until its plans leaked).[47] The priority in the party elite remained doing everything to avoid accelerating the timetable to war.

With 'active intelligence' on the borders effectively ended, and in another shift of priorities, the Politburo now called for stronger focus on preparing for future war in Soviet territory and for potential foreign occupation. In March 1925 it discussed creating diversionary and partisan groups in the border regions, which in wartime would activate to slow down an invading army.[48] At the same time, the ongoing public relations disaster surrounding the Stołpce raid underlined the importance of long-term diplomatic engagement over short-term insurgent operations (although this did not always soften Soviet diplomatic stances). The focus of strategy for the border regions swung back towards the softer line of cultivating political sympathy from minorities on the Polish side of the border. By

August 1925, the Soviet Union and Poland agreed to resolve the border attacks, and in doing so provide stronger guarantees for stopping guerrilla organizations crossing into each other's territory. This took much heat out of the issue, although it failed to eliminate future clashes in coming months.[49]

A central priority for the Politburo during 1924 to 1925, then, was to avoid low-level border clashes escalating into extensive armed conflict. And for a while, since the more-conciliatory Aleksander Skrzyński replaced Roman Dmowski as Polish foreign minister in August 1924, Chicherin and his new counterpart managed limited progress in improving Soviet-Polish relations. The common fear of a new German settlement in Europe and the threat this posed to both Poland's and the Soviet Union's security remained a strong motivating factor. Good words were expressed on either side in late 1924. Alongside Chicherin's calls for better Soviet-Polish relations, Skrzyński delivered a statement to the Sejm noting that Poland would not launch an attack on the Soviet Union nor be compelled to by another power. In early 1925, he proposed that the Soviet Union join a multilateral non-aggression pact with Poland, Romania and the Baltic states, although this proved a step too far for the Bolsheviks who refused to sign anything other than a bilateral pact, seeking security arrangements beyond the League of Nations and associated multinational agreements.[50] The Poles, of course, had their own priorities and resisted the Bolsheviks' preferred solution. As much as Germany's move towards the west changed Poland's security position in Europe, a bilateral pact with the Soviet Union – and the damage this would inflict on relations with the western powers – was too high a price to pay.[51]

The core problem for the Bolsheviks in the mid-1920s was the failure to establish a consistent approach in managing Soviet-Polish relations and tentative diplomatic progress in one area was easily undermined with disputes and mutual accusations elsewhere. While he extolled the virtues of improved relations, Chicherin, just as quickly, pointed to ongoing border conflicts, like the Iampol' attack, as undermining trust. It was not difficult for the Poles to make the same argument. But the Politburo's responses to low-level clashes and disputes were sometimes far in the extreme. One controversy that erupted at the very moment when the Politburo was making efforts to curb active intelligence in 1925 demonstrates this most clearly, underlining an unclear approach. In March of that year, two Polish communists living in Poland, Walery Bagiński and Antoni Wieczorkiewicz, both former officers from the Polish Army who had been convicted of planning sabotage and acts of terrorism, were murdered by their guardsman on the way to the Kolosovo border station as part of a prisoner exchange.[52] Seeing as the Polish authorities were responsible for the safety of the pair, Chicherin pushed the Polish government for a comprehensive investigation, but the Politburo's reaction went into overdrive.[53] It ordered the OGPU to strengthen counterintelligence and for the Soviet courts to take the hardest line with any person accused of counterrevolutionary crimes and espionage for Poland, with the most severe punishments implemented. A propaganda and press campaign sprang into action around the two murders, hardly conducive to calming relations after the Iampol' incident.[54] Notably, in the pages of the Soviet press, responsibility was pinned on

Polish 'landlords and the military' and 'agents of western capital' seeking war with the Soviet Union.[55] A familiar pattern reasserted. Although the Bolsheviks sought stability in relations with Poland for strategic reasons, their instincts towards seeing conspiracies where none existed and a tendency of reverting suddenly to hard-line responses, cut in the opposite direction. This contradictory approach persisted as forecasts for future war became stronger in 1925.

The future cataclysm

The Soviet Union's improved international position in 1924 turned out to be a temporary respite when Britain returned to its position of hostility in the following year. But even when MacDonald was still in power, Anglo-Soviet relations began to dip in summer 1924 once the major powers adopted the Dawes Plan in April. Named after the American banker, Charles Dawes, instrumental in its design, and created on the initiative of the United States, the Dawes Plan provided Germany with a new mechanism for paying reduced reparation payments with foreign loans, and its industry was permitted access to British and American capital. This recognized the importance of German economic recovery to continental prosperity, and there were winners and losers in the arrangement. Although not without significant downsides, Germany benefitted from lower reparation payments; while for France, once put into action, the Dawes Plan eliminated the benefits accrued from the Ruhr occupation and formalized the withdrawal of French troops, completed by the middle of 1925. Enforcing reparation payments through military occupation was ruled out in nearly all circumstances. For this reason, the Dawes Plan was a factor in Poincaré's fall from office and weakened an already-weak Herriot government.[56] Inside the Soviet Union, the Plan set alarm bells ringing because of the way it moved Germany into closer alignment with western Europe. Stalin not only saw rising Anglo-American influence in 1925, but through the lens of capitalist encirclement, the Dawes Plan for him was further evidence of a deteriorating international climate.[57]

However, it was the fall of MacDonald's Labour government at the end of 1924 which completed the Bolsheviks' new sense of isolation and reanimated British anti-communism. Amid opposition to the unratified Anglo-Soviet trade agreement (which British business and a wide spectrum of domestic political opinion regarded as too lenient), and the scandal of the forged 'Zinoviev letter' in the run-up to the 1924 general election, the MacDonald campaign had been critically damaged days before the British people went to the polls. The Zinoviev letter, purportedly sent from the head of the Comintern to the Communist Party of Great Britain, whipped up political and social furore about the subversion of Britain and the British Army when published in the *Daily Mail*. It was impossible for MacDonald to avoid a major political hit through association with supposed communist conspiracies.[58] And once Stanley Baldwin formed a new Conservative government in November 1924, the negotiations undertaken with the Bolsheviks and the Anglo-Soviet trade agreement were soon cast aside. The Baldwin government went on to adopt a tougher line with the Soviet Union and relations quickly deteriorated.[59]

When the German government then signalled commitment to joining the League of Nations in December – and seemingly dropped its stance that the Soviet Union needed to enter at the same time – the spirit of the Treaty of Rapallo weakened further. Unofficial Soviet-German discussions at the end of 1924 resulted in some assurances that each country would still put pressure on Poland regardless of Germany's changing status in the west. The influential German diplomat, Count Ulrich von Brockdorff-Rantzau, told Chicherin in private that if Germany joined the League this would not entail abandoning a future effort to push Poland back to its ethnographic borders (even though a central requirement of entry was respecting other countries' territorial integrity).[60] By promising to keep up the pressure on Poland, Brockdorff-Ranztau and other like-minded figures in Germany, wanted to discourage reconciliation between the Soviet Union and France – a repeat of the old First World War alliance – and the future possibility, even if unlikely, of Soviet recognition of Poland's western border.[61]

The NKID struggled to take the German assurances at face value, even though the Soviet-German secret military collaboration was deepening and despite the onset of a damaging German-Polish tariff war from summer 1925. It also recognized that Germany not only lacked the means of force to revise the German-Polish border and relied instead on commercial pressure. Soviet diplomats knew, also, that a strong current for *rapprochement* with the west – and particularly with Britain – ran through the German government for advancing the cause of revision of the Treaty of Versailles. At the end of 1924, when Chicherin offered a bilateral pact to Germany, partly to ensure it did not enter a new anti-Soviet combination or recognize Poland's borders, the Germans did not reply for five months and then rejected the offer. The strategic problems now emerging as Rapallo deteriorated were increasingly laid bare.[62]

Such political shifts abroad gave fresh momentum to the Bolsheviks' security concerns about clandestine anti-Soviet plots in motion. Even at the tail end of the largely sympathetic MacDonald government, Chicherin had warned the central executive committee that more western support was being funnelled to the project of a Polish-Baltic union.[63] Two months after the election of the Baldwin government, the potential dangers were framed more starkly. Shortly after, in January 1925 Dzerzhinskii ordered Mikhail Trilisser, the head of the foreign department of the OGPU, to report on 'all the machinations of England against us since the fall of MacDonald'. He wanted this put before the Politburo and suggested the creation of a special 'secret committee' to counter British subversion.[64] Elsewhere, within the NKID, Viktor Kopp described to Soviet representatives in the Baltic states how Poland was working 'extremely energetically' to establish a Baltic bloc. Even though Kopp admitted that Latvia, Finland and Lithuania showed little interest in such a formation – and Britain also was apparently unenthusiastic about Polish dominance – Chicherin, still reeling from the fallout from the forged Zinoviev letter, wrote to the central committee, pointing to a 'united front of bourgeois governments against the USSR, largely resuscitated as a result of the intensification of imperialist and reactionary tendencies'.[65] Parallel to deteriorating Anglo-Soviet relations, the French stance towards the Soviet Union was moving in a similar direction. In early 1925, the Herriot government sought to align more closely with the new British government's position towards the Soviet Union. Herriot's successor as prime minister, the more hostile Paul Painlevé, then cemented this direction of travel (something later maintained under subsequent premier Aristide Briand).[66] Like Chicherin, the recently installed Soviet ambassador to France, Leonid Krasin, soon reported to Moscow about strengthening 'reaction in Europe' and preparations for a new anti-Soviet offensive.[67]

As the international environment returned to the Bolsheviks' picture of traditional hostility, the Soviet military leadership was preoccupied with potential threats based on intelligence and a series of improbable conspiracies. Head of the Red Army, Mikhail Frunze, pushed for significant increases in Soviet defence spending at the outset of early 1925. In a report produced in January on the state of the Red Army and its mobilization preparedness, he stressed that since coming to power the new British government had 'sharply increased the activity of all anti-Soviet groups in the west' and was challenging Soviet influence in the east. These alarming developments, Frunze added, were accompanied by the rising military power in the capitalist states and expanding military budgets, something 'especially intense among our immediate western neighbours'. On Poland specifically, still widely regarded in Bolshevik circles as a chief British and French proxy state, Frunze drew attention to the growth of its peacetime army from 300,000 to 375,000 soldiers, despite ongoing domestic economic problems. A 400 million francs loan, he reported, agreed with France in 1923, was being used to buy equipment and rearm the Polish military (Polish military spending, it was true, was running at nearly 30 per cent in the 1920s).[68] 'The Polish government takes an energetic role in the financing of military industry, seeking to attract as much foreign capital as possible', Frunze outlined. 'In the aviation industry, which is already particularly advanced, French capital is already playing a role.' Frunze added that 'the same intense activity is observed in Romania', the second dangerous proxy state, which, according to him, had also increased its military strength and was purchasing equipment from France (Frunze pointed to 6000 new rifles).

When Frunze turned to the state of the Red Army, however, the picture was nearly entirely negative. 'Unfavourable economic conditions', he went on, had witnessed a cut in peacetime strength from 610,000 to 562,000 in the previous year. With the forces of the Baltic states included, Frunze estimated a combined potential enemy coalition totalling ninety-four divisions and fielding eighty, with the remainder securing the German and Hungarian borders. But the Red Army could field no more than seventy-eight divisions from a total of ninety-one, with several divisions unable to redeploy from the Caucasus, Turkestan and Siberia. The Red Army was not just outnumbered but also possessed inferior military technology. Only fifty-one of ninety-one divisions, according to Frunze, were even combat ready. Twenty-nine territorial divisions existed only 'on paper'. The conclusions were stark: arming at pace in Poland, Romania and the Baltic states made 'a new attack against us by the Entente and its vassals fully possible'. Ultimately Frunze used his report to argue for increased funding for Soviet defence to bring the army and navy to 'full mobilization readiness' over the next five to seven years.[69] As he put it in another speech to the Moscow garrison, 'nothing but the development of our military power will prevent our enemies from attacking us'; while at the third congress of soviets in May, he described the 'frantic pace' behind an international campaign against the Soviet Union: Poland, Romania, Latvia and 'even tiny Estonia' were arming and in receipt of British credits. Still, and in line with the consensus, Frunze did not warn of imminent war. 'I believe that not a single country in the bourgeois world, including England, will have enough gunpowder to organize an armed intervention against us.'[70] Nor was Frunze painting a foreboding picture simply to lobby for investment. Like other senior Bolsheviks, he saw future war as inevitable, even though not imminent.

Stalin shared Frunze's worries and he outlined the threat of future war at a plenum of the central committee, also in January 1925, the purpose of which was to establish a budget for military spending. 'I have taken the floor in order strongly to support Comrade Frunze's proposal', Stalin proclaimed. 'The danger of intervention is again becoming real.' In North Africa and the Balkans, Stalin argued, the imperialist powers were vying for influence. Although a rising 'colonial movement' in the east was resisting imperialist exploitation, this was 'bound to turn the ruling strata of the Great Powers against us'. Stalin summarized: 'all this shows that the preparation and regrouping of forces is taking place all over Europe [...] All this forms the pre-condition for a new war.' In an echo of Lenin's unfounded optimism years before, Stalin, at one moment, pointed to a 'revolutionary' situation developing in Britain because of the 'incipient split' between the General Council of the Trades Union Congress and the British Labour Party. Yet in 1925, this might just give the British government another reason to turn against the Soviet Union.[71]

It was in these years that Stalin publicized one of his most famous formulations: 'Socialism in One Country', arguing that socialism could be constructed in the Soviet Union alone, before spreading further afield and culminating in world revolution. To a large degree, Socialism in One Country was a political attack against Trotsky's rival theory of permanent revolution and became a common theme in the party infighting of the 1920s. But Stalin's vision of the Soviet Union's place in the world revealed much about his perception of the international order and its inherent dangers. One of his central public claims in 1924 and 1925, for instance, was how the stabilization of capitalism after the First World War coincided with growing 'contradictions between capitalist groups'. For Stalin, a resulting global struggle for markets and resources demonstrated that 'imperialism is incapable of resolving the contradictions that are corroding it, for it is capable only of alleviating them for a time with the result that they break out again later on and manifest themselves with fresh destructive force'.[72] The capitalist international system, at its core, was deeply unpredictable. Yet despite its underlying instability, Stalin still did not foresee imminent war. 'The pre-conditions for war are maturing [...] war may become inevitable, not tomorrow or the day after, of course, but in a few years' time.' Stalin threw his support behind Frunze's appeal for higher military spending for this very reason, concluding at the January 1925 central committee plenum: 'I think we must resolutely and irrevocably meet the demands of the war department'.[73] With Stalin's intervention, Frunze's increased 405 million rubles military budget was approved.[74]

Another key strand in Stalin's presentation of international affairs was the threat of a new international anti-Soviet coalition, a perceived danger frequently analysed in party, military intelligence and OGPU circles as we have seen from the civil war era onwards. Even though a growing list of countries had formally recognized the Soviet Union by the mid-1920s, this danger remained potent in the minds of the leadership. Stalin outlined to the Moscow organization of the Bolshevik Party in May 1925, for instance, that 'the stabilisation of capitalism may find expression in an attempt on the part of the imperialist groups of the advanced countries to strike a deal concerning the formation of a united front against the Soviet Union'.[75] In tune with Lenin's vision of the international order, Stalin claimed that natural contradictions and rivalries between capitalist powers would no doubt make the formation of such an anti-Soviet capitalist coalition more challenging; and exacerbating these tensions therefore remained a central Bolshevik task. But there was little confidence that the divisions among their enemies would hold back the danger for good.[76]

Persisting assumptions about new anti-Soviet coalitions in the making meant that almost any meetings between representatives from countries bordering the Soviet Union generated deep suspicions inside the Bolshevik leadership. At the same time as Britain was returning to a hostile position, for instance, representatives from Poland, Estonia, Latvia and Finland met in Helsinki to sign a general arbitration treaty in January 1925. Notwithstanding a report from the British ambassador to Riga that the discussion also produced a secret agreement relating to a 'united front against Bolshevism', this was a long way from a concrete coalition, at least as how the Bolsheviks imagined it.[77] A later meeting in Riga in March saw more pointed discussion about mobilization and operational plans between Polish and Estonian military representatives, Finnish observers, a representative from Romania, and members of the French military mission. While this certainly appeared more threatening, the Politburo's response was to prepare for the creation of a very real anti-Soviet force. It ordered a new commission formed of representatives from the NKID, OGPU and the military to examine information about the Riga meeting and 'the role of England'. The Soviet press howled in protest and the resolutions of the May third congress of soviets characterized the meeting as more evidence of international aggression towards the Soviet Union.[78] Interpreting a new stage in the formation of an anti-Soviet bloc – with Britain, once again, depicted in internal documents as taking a leading role in establishing 'anti-Soviet bridgeheads' on the western borders – in April, the Politburo approved applying economic pressure on the Baltic states and sought to worsen relations between Poland, Lithuania and Germany. Improving the military and mobilization preparedness of the Red Army again rose up the agenda.[79] Elsewhere, at a meeting of the Politburo in Soviet Ukraine in June, and claiming that Ukraine might in the future be used as a bridgehead in a war between Poland, Romania and the

Soviet Union, Stalin's close ally, Lazar Kaganovich, pushed for stronger counter-diversionary work from the Ukrainian GPU and more political police personnel and border agents deployed to the region.[80]

Assessments from Soviet military intelligence elaborated these perceived dangers in finer detail in summer 1925. In a report to Frunze, head of military intelligence, Berzin, and A. M. Nikonov, responsible for its research and analysis, described how the British government was apparently forging an anti-Soviet bloc from the border states to launch war when conditions were to its advantage. 'For the USSR, in general, unfavourable trends are developing faster than favourable ones', the two noted. In fact, in their estimation, three hostile blocs were in preparation or already existing under British direction, created in response to Soviet subversion in India and the east of the British empire. This included a Polish-Baltic bloc (said to exist already), a Romanian-Balkan bloc and western European bloc, to potentially include Germany. Referring to excerpts from British government materials, which in truth described little more than an ambition to improve relations between other powers to counter Soviet aggression, Berzin and Nikonov's report went on to describe the apparent alignment of the Polish-Baltic bloc with France and claimed it could be sent into war against the Soviet Union with French sanction alone. For now, however, disagreements between Britain and France on the status of Germany were said to be stymying hostile anti-Soviet designs. Another identified danger was that economically weak Poland could fall under the influence of 'Anglo-American capital', a force that was supposedly less restrained about military action. Ultimately, Berzin and Nikonov's gloomier worst-case scenario saw the right-wing National Bloc coalition return to power in France and with Franco-Soviet rapprochement proving disappointing, the prospect of an anti-Soviet bloc stretching from the 'Baltic to the Black Sea' (a realization of Piłsudski's 1920 programme).[81] Yet despite these overlapping security predictions, in 1925 military intelligence still did not see major war arriving any time soon. Regardless of Poland's military spending and its foreign loans, military intelligence knew that the Polish economy was struggling and that one of its government's core priorities was securing the western, not eastern, borders. Stronger British or American influence on Poland would increase the danger, for sure, but this did not mean *imminent* war would follow.[82] Military intelligence was certain that the Soviet Union's most likely enemy remained Poland, but the circumstances for war had not yet aligned.[83]

The OGPU, for its part, saw the very same dangers of new anti-Soviet coalitions in the making and the risk of war in the future. Iagoda wrote to Dzerzhinskii in July 1925 with a raft of material suggesting that preparations for an intervention were firmly underway. The 'most irreconcilable elements in Polish government circles', apparently under French influence, believed that overthrowing the Bolsheviks was necessary 'to protect the entire civilized world'. Elsewhere, the British were said to be planning the deployment of émigré White forces against the Soviet Union and the activity of the Ukrainian émigré organizations had also been intensifying. Iagoda noted that 'the ongoing course towards intervention by the Entente should remain the subject of the greatest attention of party and all relevant Soviet organs'.[84]

The Bolshevik leadership was evidently taking this on board and seriously, with subsequent adjustments to military and industrial planning. To take one example reflecting the heightened perceived threat to the Soviet Union's western border, Stalin wrote to Molotov, also in July, to note that in view of a potential military threat, building new factories in the west, in St Petersburg or in Rostov-on-Don, had to be avoided. Not only were interior regions in need of industrial capacity, but these were also 'the most convenient rearguard for us in the event of military complications'.[85]

As the worrying intelligence poured in, Soviet defence capabilities came under greater scrutiny. The Red Army's chief of staff laid bare shortcomings in the Red Army's performance in a July report, where he rated the organization of one-third of divisions as poor; and even where this was better, equipment and armaments, such as artillery, were in unacceptably short supply. In view of the higher number of divisions that could be fielded by 'our most likely adversaries Poland and Romania' and other countries on the borders acting in concert, this was only another significant disadvantage.[86] The Politburo's defence commission, moreover, had already pointed out that the Polish Army could mobilize in fourteen days, while the Red Army took thirty; another reason why Dzerzhinskii pushed over summer 1925 for the military and OGPU to prepare partisan warfare operations to disorganize and delay the opening stage of an attack.[87] In this way, while the Bolsheviks saw major conflict as something in the future, they were acutely aware of their weaknesses.

It was for this reason that improving diplomatic and economic relations with Poland was still a core priority in 1925, even if this was regularly undermined by border clashes and the chances of success diminishing. Indeed, at the congress of soviets held in May 1925, Chicherin argued that peace with Poland was still the essential strategy. He described how a 'major military offensive' against the Soviet Union was possible only with the participation of Poland and pointed to efforts by some in the Polish government to seek peace. It was the other side of Polish politics, according to Chicherin – the 'adventurist, imperialist, militaristic' interests – who were working in the other direction.[88] That the Politburo set up a commission around this time to examine means of reaching *rapprochement* with Poland suggests that Chicherin's aspirations for better Soviet-Polish relations still resonated in the party leadership. But anxious of the rumours that their old enemy Piłsudski could return to power and rejuvenate Polish militarism, the same Politburo commission discussed other more forceful measures 'to disorganize Piłsudski's warmongering clique'.[89]

From late summer 1925 there was a noticeable uptick in diplomatic activity. On his way to Berlin, Chicherin visited Warsaw in September with an offer of a non-aggression pact, including a guarantee for Poland's eastern border. While this was equally designed to dissuade Germany from striking closer relationships with the western powers, it marked the beginning of a long series of Soviet-Polish negotiations, successful, as we shall see, only in 1932. Chicherin's efforts failed at the outset because the NKID still insisted on a bilateral pact while the Poles pushed for a multilateral pact with the Baltic states and Romania. Poland's negotiating position had not changed and the importance of organizing a wider security bloc was obvious. Not only would it play the leading role, but the existing 1921 military convention with Romania had to be factored into negotiations with the Soviet Union. However, there were other obstacles in striking a multilateral pact beyond Soviet resistance to the idea. As ardently opposed was Lithuania. Its government expressed almost zero enthusiasm for joining a defensive alliance when the acrimonious dispute about control of Wilno was as strong as ever, after the city had been incorporated into Poland in 1922.[90] And the Poles knew that their alliance would fail without Lithuania's involvement and that Latvia and Estonia would not join by themselves. The Bolsheviks, however, failed to fully grasp the reality of these obstacles; they also failed to appreciate the nature of – unrealized – Polish plans for a defensive alliance. This was not an already existing Baltic bloc or nascent staging area for the landing of troops in a British-inspired war. But as far as the Bolsheviks were concerned, defensive alliances were only ever cover for offensive alliances.[91]

Germany, as we have seen, was no less a priority in Chicherin's offer of a non-aggression pact to Poland in 1925 and stopping its drift towards the west was crucial for Soviet security. Since 1924, German assurances about maintaining pressure on Poland had become vaguer and Brockdorff-Rantzau's comments to Chicherin on the subject had drawn mixed understanding at home. Yet striking the right balance in relations with Poland and Germany was challenge beyond the Bolsheviks' and NKID's abilities. Neither country accepted the Soviet Union agreeing a pact with the other. Indeed, the German foreign minister, Gustav Stresemann, was clear in 1925 that a new Soviet-Polish treaty would rule out a separate Soviet pact with Germany.[92] Internal NKID materials from 1925 reveal some appreciation of the fine balance needed. While it was said to be 'beneficial' to give Germany the impression that Soviet-Polish relations were improving, it was important to 'not give the German government the impression that we have already concluded a deal with Poland […] for this would free the hands of the supporters of an exclusively western orientation in Germany'.[93]

The NKID's failure to balance Germany and Poland was most clear when the former entered the League of Nations in September 1926. However, the writing had been on the wall in 1925 once the Treaty of Locarno was agreed, setting Germany's western trajectory firmly in motion and further isolating the Soviet Union. Concluded in October 1925 and signed in December, the Treaty of Locarno established a new security settlement in western Europe; ensured the demilitarization of the Rhineland; and guaranteed Germany's western borders as stipulated in the Treaty of Versailles, including formalizing the loss of certain territory to France. That Germany was not obliged to give similar guarantees on its eastern borders, for Poland, kept alive the future prospect of territorial revision to its disadvantage. At the heart of Locarno, however, was a multilateral security pact between Germany, France and Belgium, including an obligation for Britain and Italy to support and assist signatory countries should they be attacked. The Bolshevik leadership was certain that Locarno was designed to break Germany's alliance with the Soviet Union and pave the way towards the formation of a stronger

British-controlled anti-Soviet bloc. Zinoviev claimed this much at the fourteenth party congress in December 1925, while Stalin warned that Germany would never reconcile to its lost territory and that war was the inevitable result. More pointedly, he accused the western powers of hypocrisy 'when by shouting and singing about peace they try to cover up preparations for a new war'. At its core, according to him, Locarno was a 'plan for the disposition of forces for a new war and not for peace'. Earlier certainties that rivalries between capitalist powers would play to the Soviet Union's advantage were beginning to fade.[94] The intelligence crossing Stalin's desk, such as Dzerzhinskii's reports of British efforts to resolve the Polish-German tariff war and border disputes, only further reinforced a sense that the Allied powers were seeking to entrap the Soviet Union.[95]

As much as Locarno posed undeniable problems for the Treaty of Rapallo, in truth, it was some distance from an anti-Soviet alliance. British political leaders saw a chance of driving a wedge between Germany and the Soviet Union, for sure, though this was not the overriding goal of the treaty.[96] And running in the opposite direction, October 1925 saw a new commercial agreement between Germany and the Soviet Union; and in the following year, both sides signed the German-Soviet Neutrality and Non-Aggression Pact, the Treaty of Berlin, pledging non-aggression and neutrality for a five-year period should either country be attacked by a third party. As part of this, Germany was obliged to not enter anti-Soviet combinations. If anything, the Treaty of Berlin underlined how Germany was unwilling to totally abandon its Soviet ties and sought to heal the damage from Locarno, even if its government had self-interested motives and kept its options open in the east and west.

For their part, the Bolsheviks saw the Treaty of Berlin as a strike against capitalist encirclement, while in Poland, a muted British and French response deepened a growing sense of isolation, provoking anger and surprise.[97] With Germany now potentially given a freer hand in the east, and in the context of improving Franco-German relations, Poland's relationships with Britain and France suffered. Going some way to assuage Polish concerns, a Franco-Polish guarantee was agreed in December 1926, but even then, a meaningful response to German aggression could easily become tied up in the slow mechanisms of the League of Nations.[98] Locarno was unaltered, and Poland had little choice but to reconcile to weaker support in the west.

As to the implications of Locarno on Soviet-Polish relations specifically, the new Soviet plenipotentiary in Poland, Petr Voikov, who arrived in Warsaw in the previous year to pursue a trade agreement, reported on this issue in autumn 1925. Reflecting the Bolsheviks' common assumptions, Voikov described how the British government aimed to drive a wedge between the Soviet Union and Germany. Locarno would be the basis for then offering Poland economic incentives and territory to join an anti-Soviet bloc with Germany, thereby strengthening a wider anti-Soviet alliance immeasurably. For this reason, Voikov argued – and considering Poland's still weak finances – it was essential to improve Soviet-Polish trading relations.[99] If economies were more closely intertwined, the costs of a Polish attack would be higher. Voikov's assessment was perfectly in tune with the strategy

Chicherin had pursued for several years, but Locarno suddenly telescoped the challenges of balancing Soviet-German and Soviet-Polish relations. While there were still some questions about whether Poland coming under British influence was a completely fixed direction of travel, Moscow judged Voikov's assessment as reasonable.[100]

At the fourteenth party congress in December 1925, the mood of the main speeches was again one of reassurance. Chicherin proclaimed that it was necessary to expose 'the phoney character of British pacifism' and strike better relations with countries posing serious security threats, namely Poland, which he characterized again as 'the key to any attack on us'. Mirroring internal intelligence assessments, Chicherin did not consider a western-inspired anti-Soviet bloc to be completely formed or even especially unified, describing tensions between the United States and Britain. At least in this public forum, Chicherin saw no reason to panic: 'our position with respect to the west is growing stronger and in the east the struggle against imperialism is taking giant strides forward'.[101] Stalin struck a similar note, pointing once more to deep contradictions between capitalist countries, between the imperial centres and colonies, between the workers and the bourgeoisie, which raised challenges in collective action against the Soviet Union. According to one historian, Stalin adopted this reassuring tone at the congress partly in response to the succession struggle gripping the party after Lenin's death in early 1924. Concerned that radical foreign policy positions put forward by the political opposition, namely pressure for direct action to foment revolution in Britain where labour unrest was building, risked accelerating a military clash with the Soviet Union, Stalin chose to emphasize stability in the international order. Certainly, behind-the-scenes, outside the congress, the picture presented to Stalin was more worrying. Dzerzhinskii sent him intelligence over following weeks, supposedly revealing further British efforts to bring White émigré organizations into a common anti-Soviet struggle, with Japanese participation also possible.[102] Indeed, while Stalin often spoke about a period of 'temporary equilibrium' and 'peaceful co-existence' in public in the mid-1920s, his warnings about the threat of future war never altered. At the December congress he delivered his routine prediction on these lines, this time that the capitalist powers would one day 'strive to convert our country into an appendage of the capitalist system, that they will try intervention against us, but that we shall repel them'.[103] Just six months later, when Piłsudski returned to power in Poland, Stalin's claims about temporary stability in the international order seemed to ring hollow and the future predicted war, for some, appeared closer than previously anticipated.

The May coup d'état

Reassurances given about the international situation at the fourteenth party congress quickly evaporated when the Polish military threat assumed outsized proportions after Piłsudski returned to power in May 1926, the subject of rumours and chatter inside Poland and abroad for several months. At the beginning of the year, the Bolsheviks identified a coup d'état as a strong security threat, portraying Poland under Piłsudski in familiar terms: central to a future anti-Soviet bloc with the likelihood of war higher. While rumours abounded in early 1926, the NKID decided to offer another non-aggression pact. This stipulated that neither Poland nor the Soviet Union would join 'combinations hostile to the other side'. However, the Polish government continued to reject a bilateral agreement, instead seeking ways to counterbalance the geopolitical shifts in the west stemming from the Treaty of Locarno. Its preference remained a multilateral agreement with the Baltic states (although not Lithuania), and including the Soviet Union, to essentially create a parallel 'Eastern Locarno'. Neither side would budge from their positions and poorly timed inflammatory rhetoric from the Comintern, concerning Poland's supposed function as a revolutionary bridge to the west, hardly helped smooth the path of the NKID's offer.[104] When Germany then applied for membership of the League of Nations in February 1926 and Poland and Romania signed a Treaty of Alliance in March, including secret protocols concerning mutual support in the case of war with the Soviet Union (of which Stalin was well-apprised), the anxieties in Moscow about the wider implications of another downturn in Soviet-Polish relations only deepened. In early 1926, striking pact with Poland seemed as distant as ever.[105]

In these uncertain months, Soviet plenipotentiary in Poland, Petr Voikov, was an essential source of intelligence about the possibility of a coup d'état and he delivered regular reports to the central NKID in Moscow from Warsaw. For much of the second half of 1925, Poland had struggled with a serious financial crisis, another government collapsed when Grabski resigned in November, and popular support behind Piłsudski was building for him to restore order.[106] This same momentum continued into the next year. On 4 March 1926, Voikov reported to Semion Aralov, founder of Soviet military intelligence and member of the NKID collegium, that there was 'opinion in a wide range of circles that Poland stands on the eve of a state coup or at least a great clash between right and left'. The threat of a political takeover was not solely from Piłsudski either. After a long period of political crisis and turmoil, the National Democrats, Voikov reported, considered seizing power themselves and installing general Józef Haller as head of state.[107] In this unclear situation, some Bolsheviks in Moscow even entertained hope that the forces of the Polish left, spearheaded by its communist party, might successfully exploit a potential 'revolutionary situation' in the country, comparable to 1917. Nothing betrayed unrealistic idealism better than placing faith in the chronically weak Polish communists who, in the end, and to Moscow's later consternation, threw their support behind Piłsudski, having identified his supposedly democratic and revolutionary credentials.[108]

As rumours swirled throughout spring of Piłsudski's preparations for a coup d'état, in reports to Moscow, Voikov, by contrast, consistently downplayed the prospect of this happening any time soon. A seizure of power, he reported on 22 March, was 'a permanent threat, but hardly a threat that could be carried out quickly'. Piłsudski, crucially, had not yet consolidated enough political support.[109] Voikov did not think much of Piłsudski's political abilities either. He was 'a warrior and only a warrior' with delusions of grandeur: 'not jokingly [he] imagines himself as the very first marshal in the world and in his circle speaks only about his military glory and about his military abilities. There is basis to suspect that not all is well in his head.'[110] These doubts notwithstanding, Voikov acknowledged that much of Polish society anticipated political change of some kind and in the context of serious ongoing economic problems, this might come to pass sooner than expected.[111]

Whatever Voikov's views on the timing of a coup d'état, he was clear that Piłsudski 'continues to remain our enemy' and someone with unaltered hostile views about the Soviet Union.[112] Plugged into Polish politics more than others, Voikov also reported on the diminishing chances, to the point of impossibility, of a striking a Soviet-Polish pact since the Treaty of Berlin came into effect.[113] All in all, there was more than enough basis for the NKID collegium to unanimously agree that Piłsudski's return to power would pose 'a great danger'.[114] That Britain was pushing Piłsudski back into power, moreover, was commonly accepted. In the pages of *Izvestiia* in April, Chicherin mused that Britain was playing 'a complicated game with the aim of isolating the USSR and unifying in one form or another all the leading governments against this country'.[115] Berzin, head of military intelligence, predicted a fascist coup from either Piłsudski or the Polish political right, but believed the former in power would push Poland closer into Britain's orbit. (Soviet diplomats tried to confirm rumours of British influence, but the reality was that although Piłsudski took France's signature of the Treaty of Locarno as a betrayal of long-standing ties, he was cautious about cultivating closer Anglo-Polish relations.)[116] Showing how seriously the threat was now taken, and given the weaknesses of the Polish Communist Party, the Polish commission of the Politburo decided to establish an entirely new commission at the end of March with representatives from military intelligence, NKID and OGPU to provide a constant flow of information about Poland.[117] The OGPU elsewhere undertook a range of preventative measures. Dzerzhinskii wrote to the head of the counterintelligence unit of the OGPU, Artur Artuzov, to ensure that leaders of the largest industrial trusts and regional economic councils were informed about the subversive tactics employed by the Polish general staff. And as he had urged during other times of crisis, Dzerzhinskii wanted Poles barred from working in the most critical sectors of the economy.[118] The border regions, moreover, were to be swept for smugglers and contraband networks, which, according to Dzerzhinskii, harboured intelligence organizations.[119] As a result, amid this heightened scrutiny of Polish citizens, the OGPU unearthed further cases of apparent Polish subversion across Soviet territory, with reports going to the highest level. In April 1926, for instance, second deputy of the OGPU, Iagoda, wrote to Stalin about intelligence agents from Poland and the Baltic states – working on the orders of the British government – carrying out acts of sabotage and espionage.[120]

Contrary to Voikov's predictions in the spring, Piłsudski made a move in mid-May but initially not to seize power. Entering Warsaw on 12 May with supporters from the military, he demanded to be restored to military command and pressured President Stanisław Wojciechowski to dissolve Wincenty Witos's newly formed centre right coalition, elected after the fall of Aleksander Skrzyński's short-lived government one week earlier (another casualty of the escalating currency crisis). Because Witos had done much to diminish Piłsudski's influence in 1923, the marshal saw him leading another government as impermissible. Events now quickly unfolded and caught on the back foot, Voikov sent a flurry of reports to Moscow, most often to Boris Stomoniakov, member of NKID collegium recently given responsibility for Polish affairs. Voikov expressed surprise at what was unfolding in Warsaw and described quickly changing circumstances on the ground:

> The Marshal does not expect resistance and refuses to go along with any agreement as long as Witos's cabinet exists. The marshal's soldiers are moving across the bridges in Warsaw and occupying Warsaw after the shooting on the Kierbedź Bridge. The National Democrats are not prepared for the coup so, more or less, no significant troops have been sent to the bridge and no barricades are even being built.[121]

Following two days of turmoil, and several hundred deaths, Witos and Wojciechowski eventually resigned to avoid further bloodshed, opening the way for Piłsudski to take power. A final twist, however, came when the Sejm elected Piłsudski as president, conferring legitimacy on the May coup d'état. However, he rejected this still-relatively weak position in favour of the more powerful roles of commander-in-chief and minister for war (Piłsudski's ally, Ignacy Mościcki, was elected president). Still, from this point on, Piłsudski was *de facto* head of state. He eschewed traditional party support and strengthened executive power and control over parliament.[122] Reflecting a certain sense of unease in Poland, rumours abounded in the Polish press about Soviet troops amassing at the border.[123]

From Moscow, Voikov faced pointed criticism for downplaying a seizure of power in Poland in the near term in his earlier reports. Writing on 22 May, Stomoniakov remarked on the NKID's 'big surprise' in watching Piłsudski seize power, considering Voikov's categorical reassurances to the contrary. 'Evidently, you need to pay more attention to information than has been the case.' Voikov defended himself by underlining how he had never denied that a coup d'état was 'technically possible' and reported – not unreasonably, considering how events played out – that Piłsudski was not yet ready to take power.[124] The May coup d'état, nevertheless, definitively put an end to still-lingering hopes about the prospect of a Polish revolution from the Left. With little sign of a repeat of the dramatic events of 1917, the Bolsheviks started to work through the security implications of Piłsudski's return, presented starkly as Poland's descent into fascism.[125] Inside the NKID Stomoniakov believed Piłsudski would revive his ambitions to coordinate Poland with the Baltic states, to expand Polish influence east and seek territorial revisions. In essence, a return to his programme of 1919 to 1920. Like others in the collegium – and based on an unfounded rumour dating back to the Locarno conference – Stomoniakov suspected the German-Polish border would now finally be settled, with transfers of the Polish corridor and Danzig to Germany, for which Poland would receive Lithuanian territory, such as Memel, in compensation. Lithuania, in turn, would regain Wilno from Poland.[126] For Stomoniakov, this series of predicted settlements with Poland's rivals (in reality, unacceptable to Piłsudski), would create space for more 'active politics against the USSR'. Stomoniakov highlighted, furthermore, how intelligence from Riga, received just before the May coup d'état, revealed that the Polish government had sought, at a minimum, neutrality from Estonia, Latvia and Finland in any future Soviet-Polish war and had offered to arm them if attacked by Soviet forces. Like the Bolsheviks' own negotiations with the Baltic states, the Polish offers went nowhere fast, but the central NKID nevertheless quickly identified what it claimed as the secret influence of capitalist powers behind-the-scenes in the creation of a new Polish-Baltic military front. Voikov was instructed to pay special attention to connections between the new Polish government and the west and to concentrate on Britain specifically.[127] Elsewhere, this was in line with sharpening Anglo-Soviet antagonism after the Soviet trades unions supported the British general strike. Unknown to the Bolsheviks, however, this curtailed the beginnings of a shift inside the British government towards seeking better relations with the Soviet Union and trade and credit talks.[128]

From Voikov's point of view on the ground, however, and going against the grain in Moscow, the Bolsheviks did not need to expect a sudden deterioration in Soviet-Polish relations, even with Piłsudski back in power. In a report dated 8 June, Voikov detailed how the new Polish minister of foreign affairs, August Zaleski, had reassured him that his government had no plans to coordinate a hostile front with the Baltic states or 'act in one way or another against Russia'. Voikov was convinced, writing to the NKID that 'there will not be a sharp turn towards a sharp deterioration in relations with us, at least for the time being'. Voikov suggested, moreover, that Piłsudski had abandoned the territorial ambitions he once pursued, casting doubt on the rumours that he was seeking to solidify relations with Germany with territorial concessions. 'I consider that there is no evidence at all for such grand plans', he remarked. On Piłsudski's ties to the British government, and again challenging consensus, Voikov said he had no reason to suspect a British hand in the coup d'état and, at most, accepted only the possibility of unofficial involvement. He noted also that the British government had some doubts about Piłsudski's ability to manage the economy and had reacted negatively to his refusal of the Polish presidency.[129] Still, despite the caveats, Piłsudski's orientation towards Britain remained an 'extremely alarming phenomenon' and Voikov agreed with the collegium that the British would surely look to exploit the May events in some form. With striking a Soviet-Polish non-aggression pact increasingly difficult, Voikov believed the best way forward was quick and meaningful improvements in economic relations with Poland, though this was hardly a new strategy and had achieved little so far. 'It is only possible to conquer Poland from this side', Voikov argued.[130]

In contrast to his misreading of the May coup d'état, Voikov's assessment on Piłsudski's future intentions was far more accurate. His priority was for Poland to remain a neutral power between the Soviet Union and Germany, especially as relations with the latter had become more uncertain after the Treaty of Locarno.[131] He wanted to concentrate on strengthening his country internally and to avoid another counterproductive war against the Soviet Union. Piłsudski delivered this message in person on 13 July, when he reassured Voikov that he had no interest in conflict or seizing Soviet Ukraine and Belorussia. Taking the opportunity to point out that he had already fought, and won, a war against the Bolsheviks and had 'no need to seek revenge', Piłsudski stressed that Poland was not susceptible to outside pressure and he had no plan to create a 'political barrier' with the Baltic states.[132] On the other hand, and going unmentioned to Voikov, Piłsudski was no less committed to using Promethean campaigns to subvert Soviet influence in the border regions. Once back in power, he accelerated the programme and agreed additional covert funding. Various anti-Soviet organizations were also reactivated in Poland after May 1926. Although Symon Petliura was assassinated in Paris in that very month, Piłsudski maintained military collaboration with the Ukrainian nationalist forces. Months later, at the end of February 1927, as the Soviet-Polish non-aggression pact negotiations started up again, the army of the Ukrainian People's Republic was clandestinely reformed on Polish soil, seeking to prepare the ground in Soviet Ukraine for a future invasion coinciding with a popular uprising in Ukraine (a frequent Bolshevik security fear).[133] Such plans were unrealistic and out of step with Piłsudski's long-term strategic thinking, but this did not change his openness towards accommodating anti-Soviet forces. Still, none of these measures were comparable to preparations for another full-scale Polish military attack on the Soviet Union, as in April 1920. To the NKID, Voikov also relayed Zaleski's 'absolutely categorical' statement that Poland was not seeking war. 'Poland, after 10 years of war and after 100 years of captivity, needs peace.'[134]

This consistent message running through Voikov's reports – that the Bolsheviks should not overreact to Piłsudski's return to power – did not find a willing audience in Moscow. Perhaps the plenipotentiary's reputation had suffered too much damage after brushing aside the earlier rumours of Piłsudski's plan to bring down the Polish government. But even without his misreading of the May events, Voikov might still have struggled to get his voice heard. We have already seen how Soviet diplomats on the ground sometimes struggled to be taken seriously at the centre. During the negotiations for the Treaty of Riga in 1921, Adolf Ioffe complained with exasperation that his reports were not being read with care. That the capitalist world was bent on destroying the Soviet Union and planned to deploy proxy states in future war was a deeply rooted conviction in the party. It was difficult to break this down from the outside, even by those closest to the sources of intelligence and sometimes-reliable information. Despite Voikov's reports to the contrary, Stomoniakov still suspected that Piłsudski planned to construct a 'Polish protectorate' over the Baltic states. And in late May he gave the plenipotentiary the task of convincing Polish politicians and influential groups in society that the Polish government's policies towards Latvia and Estonia were 'objectively directed towards the organization of new war with the Soviet Union'.[135] Similarly, two weeks later on 15 June, the NKID collegium suggested to Aleksei Rykov's defence commission that, in order to stymie Polish grand designs, new treaties should be concluded with the Baltic states and a propaganda campaign launched against Piłsudski to isolate Poland from its neighbours, forestalling the formation of an anti-Soviet bloc.[136] Soviet military intelligence followed with a similar line, estimating that Piłsudski would unconditionally break with the efforts of his predecessors to improve relations with the Soviet Union, producing an inevitable rise in Polish militarism. It followed the broad consensus that Poland would move closer towards Britain's orbit, which would assist in building its military power. Nevertheless, although the danger of war was deemed higher from May 1926, this cataclysm was typically forecast further into the future. In military intelligence's view – something Stalin mirrored – there would be no major war until spring 1927 at the earliest.[137]

The OGPU stood out as an exception in 1926, more convinced than others that Piłsudski was set on the path of war, and critically, on a tighter timeframe. Shortly after the May coup d'état, Dzerzhinskii wrote to Iagoda on 25 June and articulated the standard Bolshevik conspiratorial assessment of recent events: 'Piłsudski's coup, as it is obvious to me now, is an expression of the nationalist forces in Poland directed against "Russia", that is, us, entirely supported by England. Therefore, of course, we must devote all our forces to preparing defence. The Poles' object of seizure will be Belorussia and Ukraine'. Dzerzhinskii wanted a range of measures put into place, including strengthening intelligence against Polish espionage; monitoring popular opinion; cultivating sympathies in the border regions; and the monitoring of the Red Army (where the OGPU recorded a new rush of apparent Polish espionage cases).[138] Iagoda expressed the same opinion, having produced with Arthur Artuzov, a wide-ranging assessment of the Polish danger in late May. The pair focused on the British government as the true power behind-the-scenes supporting large scale intelligence operations and separatism in Ukraine and Belorussia. Piłsudski was the British 'guard dog' in eastern Europe, as the two put it, and his goal was to bring Ukraine and Belorussia into federation with Poland. Iagoda and Artuzov ordered counterintelligence strengthened (particularly because the Polish Military Organization might be reactivated); more attention focused on Ukrainian and Belorussian intellectual elites; and the surveillance of foreign representatives with possible connections to Polish intelligence. They judged Ukraine, in particular, as 'strategically significant as a bridgehead for military action'.[139] The Belorussian and Ukrainian republic GPUs, moreover, recorded positive responses to the coup d'état among national minorities in their territories – groups instinctively viewed as potential fifth columnists – and broad-based popular anticipation of war between the Soviet Union and Poland.[140] A meeting of OGPU leaders on 8 July resolved to concentrate counterintelligence against the renewed Polish threat to the western borderlands and to work with military intelligence in preparing for war.[141]

Throughout July 1926, the last of month of his life following a long period of ill-health, Dzerzhinskii maintained his focus on the military danger from Poland. In his vision of war, however, the timeframe was shorter than in the assessments drawn up inside military intelligence. He personally impressed his concerns upon Stalin on 11 July, warning that Piłsudski was planning war. 'A whole range of information speaks with undeniable (for me) clarity that Poland is preparing a military attack on us with the goal of separating Belorussia and Ukraine from the USSR.' Dangers could apparently be seen from several directions. Romania, Dzerzhinskii reported, was soon to receive an 'enormous mass of weapons' from Italy, including submarines; there had been an uptick of White émigré activity in the Baltics and Caucasus.[142] To Iagoda, he suggested moving political police archives to Moscow as they lay too close to the increasingly threatened border. White guard and bandit groups needed to be excised from the area.[143] An OGPU order from 17 July echoed Dzerzhinskii's common demand that in the context of 'the preparation of hostilities against the USSR' Poles needed to be removed from work in military industry.[144] Fearing it was already too late, Dzerzhinskii expressed his concerns to Iagoda that nothing had been done to enact the Politburo decision from 1925 to organize diversionary groups in the border regions in the event of foreign military occupation.[145] Dzerzhinskii was still raising questions about diversionary groups and the importing of necessary defence materiel just days before he died.[146]

While the Bolsheviks convinced themselves that the threat of war against Poland had become more concrete, its government, in tune with Voikov's reports of Piłsudski's benign intentions, communicated to Chicherin on 14 July, via its chargé d'affaires, that it wanted to resume negotiations towards its favoured multilateral pact, including the Baltic states. Even though such a pact would go some way to improving the Soviet Union's deteriorating international situation, Chicherin reaffirmed his line that only bilateral negotiations were acceptable.[147] Evidently, no pact was deemed better than a multilateral agreement, even amid the anxieties sparked by the May coup d'état. In August the NKID pushed again for a bilateral pact, but Piłsudski, like his predecessors, refused anything that excluded the Baltic states. When arrangements were made for Zaleski to visit Moscow in August, raising hopes inside the NKID, Voikov soon dampened the mood in relaying that the Polish foreign minister had no interest in negotiating quickly and would not sign anything there and then.[148] Zaleski, in the end, backed out, citing needing time to prepare for an assembly of the League of Nations; while Chicherin suffered with his poor health.[149] All the while tensions continued to run high in the background. War alarm tests were conducted twice in Soviet Belorussia during the same month.[150]

Another complication in these tentative Soviet-Polish contacts of the summer was Lithuania, and specifically, the Bolsheviks' suspicion that Piłsudski was planning an attack on the country. Polish troops had recently been on manoeuvres in the area, and reports filtered into Moscow of them gathering at the Polish-Lithuanian border.[151] In reality, such an attack was an unfounded security scare, yet it gave the Bolsheviks the encouragement they needed to agree a provocative Soviet-Lithuanian non-aggression pact, thereby aligning Lithuania more strongly against Poland. Voikov warned the central NKID against going down this road, especially if the pact gave recognition of Lithuania's control over Wilno. This was certain to make Piłsudski less cooperative 'and move [him] from defence to attack'. Highlighting the distance in thinking between Voikov and the Moscow centre, however, Sergei Aralov, another influential voice inside the NKID collegium, was sanguine, suggesting to Voikov that he did not see why the Bolsheviks always had to adopt a soft approach with Poland. 'As in war, so in politics, the best defence is attack.' Aralov, moreover, noted that the NKID collegium did not believe Piłsudski was likely to sign a non-aggression pact with the Soviet Union anyway, even without a controversial Soviet-Lithuanian agreement. A pact with Lithuania was attractive to the NKID for several reasons. Not only did it weaken Polish influence in the Baltic region by creating another dividing line, but for the NKID, it delayed 'the creation of a bridge between Poland and the Baltics'.[152] In the end, both Aralov and Voikov were proved right. The Poles rejected another offer from the NKID for a non-aggression pact on 24 August and largely fruitless discussions continued for the next few months. When the NKID then went on to sign a non-aggression pact with Lithuania in September, including provocative recognition of Lithuanian control of Wilno, this sparked a torrent of Polish protest.

As to how Stalin judged the threat of war in the months after Piłsudski's coup d'état, he continued to align with Soviet military intelligence, which as we know, doubted the prospect of war until at least 1927, rather than agree with the more alarmist Dzerzhinskii. At the end of 1926, in a speech to the fifteenth party conference in November, and on the question of whether capitalist states were able to attack any time soon, Stalin remarked that it 'remains to be seen' and he fell back to his – and Lenin's – earlier position that much depended on the workers of the capitalist countries, who he claimed would not support war against the Soviet Union. 'It is on this sympathy that the international position of our republic now rests. Without it we should be having now a number of fresh attempts at intervention.' Stalin's other unchanged core view was that the Soviet Union remained in a dangerous position of encirclement. 'But if the capitalist world is not in a position to undertake armed intervention against our country just now', he remarked, 'that does not mean that it will never be in a position to do so. At any rate, the capitalists are not asleep; they are doing their utmost to weaken the international position of our republic and to prepare the way for intervention.'[153] For Chicherin, currently navigating a public relations disaster after the secret military collaboration with Germany had been exposed to the world, Stalin's foreboding rhetoric was a problem. 'All the foreign press and governments consider you the leading figure in the USSR', he wrote to the general secretary, 'and each of your words is considered as a government manifesto'. Stalin's tendency to make threatening statements, Chicherin pointed out, such as 'either they will beat us, or we will beat them', was counterproductive. 'Where is our policy of peace?', he asked.[154]

As we shall see in later chapters, however, Chicherin's 'policy of peace' would be eclipsed by one of rapid militarization. While it was true that Stalin agreed with Chicherin that better relations with foreign powers were essential to future Soviet economic development, it was also true that major conflict against Poland and the capitalist powers was widely accepted in the party as an even more likely prospect after May 1926. The Red Army high command now lobbied for higher levels of investment, spearheaded by Stalin's long-time ally and new head of the Red Army, Kliment Voroshilov, and chief of staff Tukhachevskii. The two took up the mantle as chief advocates of higher military spending following Mikhail

Frunze's death during surgery in October 1925. In line with months of intelligence, Tukhachevskii stressed on numerous occasions that the Red Army could not win a prolonged conflict against the combined forces of Poland and the border states, with British backing. The Soviet defence commission agreed and ordered 'urgent measures for strengthening the defense potential of the USSR'. Even so, with the state's finances restricted, the funds released by the Politburo – 700 million rubles – were below what Tukhachevskii felt necessary.[155] In a stark assessment of Soviet defence capability drawn up for the Politburo, Tukhachevskii underlined the grave threat facing the Soviet Union: 'Neither the Red Army nor the country is prepared for war. Our meagre material stocks for mobilization for fighting are scarcely sufficient for the first period of war. Subsequently, our position will worsen (especially in conditions of blockade).'[156] In a matter of years, this would quickly change.

Chapter 5

CAPITALIST ENCIRCLEMENT AND DICTATORSHIP

Acrimonious Soviet-Polish relations in the years after the 1920 war, during which the Bolsheviks focused much of their energy on the future round of conflict with the capitalist world, coincided with a crucial part of early Soviet history: Stalin's rise to power and the cementing of authoritarian practices inside the Bolshevik Party. Lenin, as we have seen, fell into serious ill-health at the close of the civil war in 1921 and, from there on, was steadily forced to withdraw from party affairs, unable to consolidate the revolution the Bolsheviks had struggled so hard to defend. Lenin's physical condition quickly deteriorated thereafter. In May 1922, following a cerebral haemorrhage, he suffered some paralysis on the right-side of his body and struggled to communicate. A third stroke in March 1923 left him unable to speak entirely. Lenin died on 21 January 1924.[1]

It is uncontroversial to say that Lenin's withdrawal from party life and later death created the necessary space for Stalin to gather power and influence. And how Stalin managed to defeat his rivals in a political succession struggle is one of the oldest questions in Soviet history. Going back decades, historians explained this in various ways, from highlighting Stalin's control of the party machine and his position as general secretary, allowing him to use the power of appointment to cultivate loyalties throughout the party hierarchy; to the basic errors, missteps and, at times, the simple arrogance displayed by Trotsky and other opposition figures.[2] This chapter will not go over these same arguments, some of which have been challenged in more recent work; the chapter will not reproduce an outline of Stalin's growing political power in the 1920s either.[3] It will show instead how the Bolsheviks' anticipation of war specifically, and their perception of deteriorating international relations in the 1920s, helped authoritarian practices embed more easily in the party and contributed to the closing down of democratic discussion, debate and dissent. Importantly, this process was not just the product of one single person's worldview. As we know already, beyond Stalin, numerous senior Bolsheviks working in institutions, such as the NKID, Soviet military intelligence and the GPU/OGPU, saw future war as an inevitability and Poland was almost universally depicted as an aggressor state, the central cog in their capitalist encirclement. Stalin's rise to power, as much as this was a consequence of careful manoeuvring and his abilities as a politician, cannot be fully understood without appreciating how a much wider shared expectation of future war adversely shaped democratic practices inside the Bolshevik Party.

Before the stark deterioration in his physical health, and ahead of the succession struggle, Lenin set a clear precedent that wartime imperatives should curtail democratic practices. This was in the early months of 1921 when the Bolsheviks faced serious domestic crises on multiple fronts in the final year of the civil war. Most seriously, because of the failure of the emergency wartime economic programme, war communism, to reliably deliver adequate food supplies, strikes and popular unrest were hitting all major urban areas. Soon enough the Bolsheviks' traditional base of political support, the working class, articulated its discontent with calls for free elections and an end to state repression. This growing anger in the cities coincided with the peak of peasant unrest against Bolshevik government in the provinces, an ongoing struggle from the turbulent years of civil war, contributing now to a widespread domestic crisis in 1921.[4]

Against a backdrop of rising popular disaffection, Lenin and his supporters drew pointed criticism from smaller political groupings inside the Bolshevik Party: the so-called Workers' Opposition and Democratic Centralists. For several years, both had critiqued the leadership because of its obvious failure to live up to the central promise of the 1917 revolution, namely, to construct a democracy for the benefit of the working class. Instead, democratic practices in the party had eroded; the bureaucracy expanded; revolutionary energies and autonomy were stifled; and ordinary workers had not been given adequate representation in senior party bodies and committees.[5] Lenin's response was to claim that such problems could not be fixed immediately for a number of reasons, not least because the workers of Soviet Russia lacked adequate experience of governance; but, according to him, the threatening international situation also made dictatorship necessary. Indeed, as we know, 1921 was not just a year of severe domestic crisis. This was a time when fears were running high inside the party leadership about a renewed Polish military attack on Soviet Russia, incited by the French government. And Lenin saw convergence of these two dangers, internal and external. In an article published in *Pravda* in January 1921, for instance, he argued that 'the Entente capitalists will surely try to take advantage of our Party's malaise [political disputes, PW] to mount another invasion […] We need have no fear of this because we shall all unite as one man, without being afraid to admit the malaise, but recognising that it demands from all of us a greater discipline, tenacity and firmness at every post.'[6]

This line of argument resurfaced in Lenin's opening speech to the tenth party congress two months later. Here he proclaimed that past discussions and disputes had been an 'amazing luxury' for a party shouldering such responsibilities – that is, keeping the flame of communism alive in a hostile international environment while 'surrounded by mighty and powerful enemies uniting the whole capitalist world'. Lenin once again argued that foreign powers were taking advantage of internal disputes, with foreign presses spreading rumours of Bolshevik weaknesses: 'discussion means disputes; disputes mean discord; discord means that the Communists have become weak; press hard, seize the opportunity, take advantage of their weakening. This has become the slogan of the hostile world'. In his closing speech to the congress, Lenin reiterated the need for unity:

We must have no doubts in our own mind when we look at our Party as the nucleus of world revolution, and at the campaign which the world syndicate of states is now waging against us [...] We have sized it up, and we have exactly sized up our own disagreements. We know that by closing our ranks at this Congress we shall emerge from our disagreements solidly united, with the Party much stronger and marching with every greater resolution towards international victories.[7]

The tenth party congress was a significant moment in the history of the Bolshevik Party in enshrining the so-called ban of factions. Splinter groups like the Workers' Opposition and Democratic Centralists were officially proscribed and criticizing the party line carried the threat of expulsion. Party members were encouraged to be alert to future cases of factional activity and its dangers. Lenin did concede that 'platforms' encompassing different viewpoints might still emerge in the party on particularly contentious issues, but formal political factions were officially ruled out (although members of Workers' Opposition and the Democratic Centralists, though much-weakened, continued to argue their causes).[8] While the perceived external military threat to Soviet Russia was not the sole cause of the ban on factions, it was certainly true that Lenin placed a higher premium on party unity in a hostile international environment. Others, like Nikolai Bukharin, felt the same and at the congress stressed the importance of ideological unity in the face of the external danger.[9]

Another significant internal driver of the ban on factions was the stunning mutiny at the Kronstadt naval fortress, twenty miles off the coast of Petrograd, which erupted as the congress was in session. For obvious reasons, the rebellion compelled a sense of urgency behind strengthening party unity and was an essential backdrop to the decision to ban political factions. The Kronstadt sailors had been some of the most loyal supporters of the revolution and were now demanding free elections to revolutionary councils (soviets) and an end to the Bolsheviks' monopoly on power. Seeking to quash the prospect of an uprising against the Soviet government – a 'third revolution' coming after those of February and October 1917 – Red Army troops suppressed the Kronstadt rebels with severe force. While predominately an internal crisis, even here, the party's discussion of the Kronstadt rebellion is difficult to untangle from the Bolsheviks' perceptions of a hostile international environment. In Lenin's closing speech to the tenth party congress, he drew connections between the Kronstadt rebels and the international bourgeoisie – the 'world press syndicate' and 'financial magnates' – apparently trying to bring down Soviet power through encouraging internal rebellions.[10] The Soviet government's official communication about the revolt, in tune with the hierarchy of international dangers at that time, blamed 'French counterrevolution' for its instigation.[11] Highlighting unremitting pressure from the international bourgeoisie on Soviet Russia and widening the field of culprits behind the Kronstadt mutiny, the resolution of the tenth congress on party unity read as follows:

The way the enemies of the proletariat take advantage of every deviation from a thoroughly consistent Communist line was perhaps most strikingly shown in the case of the Kronstadt mutiny, when the bourgeois counter-revolutionaries and whiteguards in all countries of the world immediately expressed their readiness to accept the slogans of the Soviet system, if only they might thereby secure the overthrow of the dictatorship of the proletariat in Russia.[12]

It would be wrong to dismiss this framing as rhetoric alone, designed to set up a division between embattled Soviet Russia and its powerful foes in the outside world for propaganda purposes; to explain away faults, weaknesses and the increasing, and unmissable, use of persecution and violence in the new revolutionary state. The truth, as shown above, was that fears about a new military attack were genuine and potent in the Bolshevik Party. And Lenin was not alone in framing the Kronstadt rebellion as a moment when the enemy within had successfully collaborated with powerful international bourgeois forces without. Head of the Cheka, Dzerzhinskii, saw the same connection, as did other senior Bolsheviks.[13]

Lenin reiterated the need for a dictatorship with similar justifications at the third congress of the communist international, held between June and July 1921. 'This dictatorship is essential as long as classes exist, as long as the bourgeoisie, overthrown in one country, intensifies tenfold its attacks on socialism on an international scale.' Describing dictatorship as a 'state of intense war' and following the line of argument presented in other forums, Lenin claimed that resistance from the working classes around the world was the only restraining force on the international bourgeoisie, even though war could 'never be ruled out'.[14] In this context, free political organization in Soviet Russia was not possible. As Lenin explained shortly after in a letter from August to the oppositionist and left communist Gavriil Miasnikov – who headed the so-called Workers' Group, associated with the Workers' Opposition – 'to place in its [the world bourgeoisie's, PW] hands yet *another* weapon like freedom of political organisation (freedom of the press, for the press is the core and foundation of political organisation) means facilitating the enemy's task, means helping the class enemy'.[15] Miasnikov soon after was expelled from the party in 1922.

Similar arguments were aired at the eleventh party congress held between March and April 1922, the final congress with Lenin's involvement before he suffered a cerebral haemorrhage in May. The congress convened at the tail end of several months of pressure on factions in the party, enlivened by a separate political controversy about the introduction of the New Economic Policy (NEP) in March 1921. NEP, the mixed market economic system, essential to Soviet Russia's post-civil war recovery, liberalized internal trade but was unacceptable to many on the left of the party. For them, this was an unforgivable compromise with market forces and step backwards into capitalism. While challenges from the political left on this score, although still vocal, were less pronounced since the ban on factions, party unity, nevertheless, occupied a central theme at eleventh party congress.[16] During the proceedings, senior Bolsheviks cast calls from critics of the party majority for stronger democratic practices as impermissible in a dangerous international environment. Criticizing Aleksandr Shliapnikov, for instance, the leader of the Workers' Opposition, Lenin argued against the principle of free political organization and emphasized the threat of war as the primary danger:

> I have indicated the three conditions under which it will be possible for us to hold on: first, that there shall be no intervention; second, that the financial crisis shall not be too severe; and third, that we shall make no political mistakes [...] Of course, even today the bourgeoisie may attempt another armed intervention, but they will find it much more difficult than before; it is much more difficult today than it was yesterday. To ensure ourselves the opportunity to learn we must make no political mistakes. We must waste no time playing with the unity of the Party, as Comrade Shlyapnikov is doing. We cannot afford games of that kind.[17]

Not yet the leading figure of political opposition, Trotsky was as strident in his criticism of disunity in the party and claimed at the congress that hostile states were turning this to their advantage. Focusing on the key dissenters, he argued that it was not an 'accident that the radio station of the Polish government sent extracts from comrade Miasnikov's pamphlet out to the whole world'. The writings of Aleksandra Kollontai, another high-profile figure associated with the Workers' Opposition, according to Trotsky, were also being quoted abroad.[18] Some awareness beyond Soviet Russia of oppositionist pamphlets should not have been remarkable. But in the context of perceived capitalist encirclement, for the party majority, this was a dangerous trend. In its final resolutions, the congress deemed the activity of the Workers' Opposition impermissible for several reasons: continuing difficult domestic economic circumstances, the presence of 'capitalist elements' in Soviet Russia, the spread of famine and the threat of invasion.[19]

*

After Lenin experienced a third haemorrhage in March 1923 and no longer played a meaningful role in political life, the divides in the Bolshevik Party grew and sharpened in the early stages of the succession struggle. Trotsky moved into outright political opposition later in the autumn, setting the stage for years of rancorous political clashes, in the first instance against Stalin, Grigory Zinoviev and Lev Kamenev who had assumed *de facto* party leadership as a ruling triumvirate in Lenin's absence. And while these larger cracks appeared at the top, political pressure continued to fall further down the chain on smaller opposition groups, still pushing for stronger democratic norms inside the party. But permitting genuine inner-party democracy and greater freedom of speech in a hostile international environment was no less a contentious issue as before. The twelfth party congress in April 1923, the year of the dramatic Ruhr crisis, was another moment when political factions came under attack for this very reason.

The run-up to the twelfth party congress proved highly charged after Miasnikov's Workers' Group circulated an anonymous platform calling for the removal of Stalin, Zinoviev, and Kamenev from their positions. A manifesto from another political grouping, Workers' Truth, called for stronger trade unionism and workers' rights. This was more measured for sure, but both were an undeniable challenge to party norms in advance of the congress.[20] With opposition groups therefore already an issue at the forefront of delegates' minds, and with Lenin absent, Kamenev, in opening comments to the congress, sketched out the outlines of the international position of the Soviet Union and engaged with the question of party unity. Enemies, he argued, menaced the country on all sides, internally and internationally, and unity in the party was essential. The Bolsheviks were in the position of the 'most shelled post' in the world proletarian revolution.[21] Zinoviev, another member of the ruling triumvirate, also raised the threat of war, warning that because imperialist powers were looking to take advantage of Lenin's illness, not 'the slightest ambiguity, or misunderstanding' on party unity could be permitted.[22] The final member of the trio, Stalin, framed the case for party unity in a way that he would repeat often in the future. Responding to accusations from the trade union official and Workers' Opposition sympathizer, Iurii Lutovinov, who called for more open discussion and wider democratic engagement in the party (and provocatively compared the Politburo to an 'infallible Pope'), Stalin argued that the party itself had simply become too large to allow such broad open discussion.[23] In 1923, the Bolshevik Party stood at nearly 500,000 members, a steep rise from the approximately 24,000 members in 1917.[24] Making a comparison to circumstances before the revolution, Stalin claimed that the Bolsheviks found themselves in a similar position in 1923 as they had been in 1912, the year the Bolsheviks formed their separate party and had been forced to operate in the underground in tsarist Russia to evade the authorities. In Stalin's presentation, in both years the Bolsheviks were surrounded by opponents; the difference in 1923 was that the encircling enemies were on an international scale. Moreover, and in keeping with ongoing Soviet security concerns of the early 1920s, Stalin proclaimed that there was no reason to doubt that preparatory work for a blockade or intervention was not underway, another important reason why open discussion in the party could not be permitted, especially when this concerned the most important issues of the day: war and peace. Attacking the suggestion of allowing more liberal discussion in the party, Stalin added: 'We cannot talk about questions of war or peace on the streets […] we need to remember that in an environment when we are surrounded by enemies, a sudden blow, or unexpected manoeuvre, decides everything.'[25]

As strikes erupted in several cities once again in summer 1923, this time over unpaid wages, the threatening international situation still loomed as the backdrop to the party majority's treatment of the smaller opposition groups, who had now gained a slightly stronger foothold in the factories given rising levels of militancy.[26] In a signal that the party majority intended to apply further pressure, Dzerzhinskii was appointed the head of a special commission in September, ultimately to quash factionalism in the party. The GPU was to keep an eye on oppositionists, and party members were obliged to make their own reports if necessary. Like other senior Bolsheviks, Dzerzhinskii was conscious of not giving an impression of political weakness in a threatening international climate. In notes prepared for a report to an upcoming plenum of the central committee, also in September, he detailed how the problem of opposition groups – namely, the Workers' Truth and Workers' Group – had to be urgently resolved in view of the nature of the international situation.[27] And at the plenum itself, Dzerzhinskii attacked the activity of the two factions. 'We should say that our enemies are very interested in this subversive work, and not only interested, but they are using it', he remarked.[28] Elsewhere at this same plenum, and in another nod towards the tense situation at the heart of Europe in 1923, Zinoviev called for 'absolute unity' in the party due to the mounting crisis in Germany.[29]

It was during this dramatic moment overseas, as the revolutionary movement in Germany reached its climax and failure, that Trotsky moved into opposition to the party majority, beginning with a series of open letters and writings, later coming under the title *The New Course*. In the first instance, Trotsky's criticisms were partly in response to the creation of the Dzerzhinskii commission, but the triumvirate's expansion of the Revolutionary Military Council of the Republic, stacking it with Trotsky's political opponents, including Stalin and Voroshilov, compelled him to speak out. Suffering poor health, in a letter to the central committee on 8 October Trotsky bemoaned the 'extraordinary deterioration' in party life should the Dzerzhinskii commission's recommendation for party members to turn informers be necessary. In what became a central motif in his case against the party majority, he underlined how it was the triumvirate's own authoritarianism and dissatisfaction among workers and peasants with Soviet economic policies that had created a situation where hostile factions were now multiplying. Trotsky pushed for stronger central planning as the remedy on the economic front and criticized weak inter-party democracy in highlighting the practice common to the party's secretariat, where Stalin reigned supreme, of appointing secretaries from above: individuals chosen for loyalty rather than ability. For Trotsky this only propelled the stultifying bureaucratization of party life and, for him, it followed that political factions were operating outside of formal channels. Trotsky's critical letter prompted the Politburo to promulgate a resolution on party democracy, but by this point, the spirit of his opposition had burst into the open. On 15 October, the so-called Declaration of the Forty-six, a platform signed by Trotsky's supporters and sympathizers, emerged in the public realm. This restated the essence of Trotsky's critique, pointing to the party leadership's worsening authoritarianism and economic mismanagement.[30]

The triumvirate misunderstood Trotsky's 8 October letter and the Declaration of the Forty-six, viewing them both as a coordinated political attack, when in fact they were only loosely related. Nevertheless, Stalin, Zinoviev and Kamenev were intent on doing whatever necessary to stop Trotsky from taking Lenin's mantle. Encouraging factionalism was a common accusation in these months, one that Trotsky threw at the triumvirate and it returned in kind. Although the Revolutionary Military Council of the Republic was now tilted against him, Trotsky was still war commissar, raising the stakes of his move into opposition. It was hard to say he was widely admired in party circles, but Trotsky was undoubtedly a capable Bolshevik and organizer, and some in the party feared his personal ambitions.[31] But a more pressing reason why Stalin wanted to shut down Trotsky's high-profile criticism was Lenin's so-called letter to the congress, the explosive document, later known as his 'Testament' that sent shockwaves running through the party. Written one year earlier when the party leader's relationship with Stalin was sharply deteriorating, Lenin's letter called for his removal as general secretary (Trotsky, too, fell under Lenin's critical eye as he weighed up the contenders for power). The ruling triumvirate's response to Trotsky's political opposition, in this way, was shaped by several priorities, not least Lenin's damning words about Stalin; but it is also true that the perceived threats of invasion and capitalist encirclement, unbroken since the early 1920s, played important roles in circumscribing Trotsky's freedom of action.

The party majority soon launched a political attack against Trotsky at an extraordinary joint plenum of the central committee and central control commission on 26 October, when he and the forty-six sympathizers were subjected to fierce criticism for undermining party unity at a critical moment for the party and world revolution.[32] The perceived military danger to the Soviet Union once again formed part of this condemnation. Stalin proclaimed, for instance, that 'we are on the eve of war' and criticized Trotsky for generating dangerous distractions. 'Instead of assisting in the discussion of these serious problems, you are pestering us with platforms', he remarked. One resolution from the plenum roundly condemned Trotsky and his supporters, noting that 'we have already entered a period that can be called direct combat' and referred to events in Germany and the possibility of war against Poland. 'Factional discussion' was prohibited at this very moment.[33]

Trotsky denied the various accusations against him, including that he wanted to seize control of the party or, as some suspected, that he aspired to be a military dictator, or even that he led a group of 'Trotskyists'.[34] There was much to this, and Trotsky's opposition and that of his sympathizers formed an amorphous collective. Yet on the charge that political factionalism was dangerous when war threatened, like in previous years, Trotsky still agreed with this position. The crucial point, however, was that he did not see his criticism of the party majority as constituting full-blown factionalism. Trotsky's argument was that broader democratic participation and weakening bureaucratism were the only ways to eliminate the emergence of factions in the first place. Nevertheless, Trotsky put himself in a difficult position in continuing to accept the premise that factionalism was dangerous when the party saw a credible risk of war.

Following the clashes at the October joint plenum, the party majority temporarily conceded to broad discussions on workers' democracy at the end of 1923, which played out in the pages of the Soviet press.[35] The international situation still impinged on considerations of party democracy in these months, even if the temperature had cooled after the collapse of the 'German October'. In a speech given in December 1923, for instance, and on the subject of when and how the Soviet Union would reach the utopian commune society imagined in 1917, Stalin accurately described this as 'a long way off'. The Soviet people not only needed a 'higher level of culture' to make the transition, but for Stalin 'peace conditions must be fully guaranteed all around us so as to remove the necessity of maintaining a large standing army, which entails heavy expenditure and cumbersome administrative departments'. Furthermore, and responding to the recent discussions on party democracy in the Soviet press, Stalin described how during wartime 'fear of defeat drew the Party together into one whole, and some of the disruptive elements in the Party were compelled to keep to the general line of the Party, which was faced with the question of life or death. Now these bonds have fallen away, for we are not now at war.' Stalin's comments reflected the waning of the perceived external danger in the aftermath of the failed German revolution. This would eventually pick up again later in 1924, as we have seen; but before then, he argued that even in the absence of a direct military threat, 'restrictive measures' on the party were nevertheless necessary given the revival in strength of the bourgeoisie in Soviet Union as a by-product of NEP.[36] But on a point of principle, that the party should be unified in the face of war was something that still resonated with him, as it did those on the other side of the party. The argument put forward by Trotsky's ally and the economic specialist, Evgenii Preobrazhenskii, was not fundamentally different. Precisely because the Soviet Union was no longer deemed to be in danger at the end of 1923, it was possible to have more open debate in the party (though two months earlier during *The New Course* controversy, Preobrazhenskii had then argued that freer discussion was vital to navigate a threatening international environment). Another critic of the party majority, the Democratic Centralist, Timofei Sapronov, held the same view: with no real threat to Soviet power, there was a real risk the party would lose touch with the working class.[37] From various wings of the party, the status of the international situation and the nature of threats to the Soviet Union helped to shape the debate about the party's democratic practices.

We have seen already how the Soviet Union's international position showed some improvement in 1924 following British and French diplomatic recognition, but also how Stalin and his allies viewed conflict with the capitalist world as inevitable and saw the Soviet Union as existing under conditions of hostile capitalist encirclement. Despite outward appearances, they saw international capital wielding powerful influence over the new left-wing MacDonald and Herriot governments. Iron unity, therefore, and especially in a party the size of the Bolshevik Party, was essential. At a central committee plenum in January 1924, and taking advantage of Trotsky's temporary relocation south for convalescence, Stalin launched into another long tirade against the oppositionists, accusing them of lacking sufficient discretion in their conversations, and supposedly openly talking about Politburo decisions, which then became known to the 'people on the street'.[38] At the thirteenth party conference in the same month, while claiming the recent and relatively open discussions on party democracy in the Soviet press were 'a well-aimed thrust at those of our ill-wishers abroad who have long been rubbing their hands in glee over our discussion', Stalin, at the same time, made his views obvious about the impossibility of party democracy in the context of possible war and criticized those who made a 'fetish of democracy, regarding it as something absolute, without relation to time or space […] for there are times when its implementation is neither possible nor advisable'. For Stalin, one key condition for democracy was as follows:

> I have already said that there is another group of conditions, of an external nature, and in the absence of these democracy in the Party is impossible. I have in mind certain international conditions that would more or less ensure peace and peaceful development, without which democracy in the Party is inconceivable. In other words, if we are attacked and have to defend the country with arms in hand, there can be no question of democracy, for it will have to be suspended [...] But what Trotsky suggests is profoundly erroneous; it runs counter to Bolshevik organisational principles, and would inevitably lead to the disintegration of the Party, making it lax and soft, converting it from a united party into a federation of groups. Living as we do in a situation of capitalist encirclement, we need not only a united party, not only a solid party, but a veritable party of steel, one capable of withstanding the assault of the enemies of the proletariat, capable of leading the workers to the final battle.[39]

Stalin delivered similar remarks a few months later at the thirteenth party congress in May, a gathering which proved a critical moment for the general secretary. With Lenin dead several months, the party finally decided to address his 'letter to the congress'. Trotsky pushed to publish the sensational document and he faced a barrage of criticism.[40] In this moment of personal vulnerability, therefore, Stalin chose to raise the political temperature, claiming once more how the opposition's behaviour endangered the Soviet Union, given its precarious international position and the enemies within their midst.

> The alignment of forces internationally is such that every attempt to weaken the authority of our Party and the stability of the dictatorship in our country will inevitably be seized upon by the enemies of the revolution as a definite gain for them, irrespective of whether such attempts are made by our opposition or by the Socialist-Revolutionaries and Mensheviks. Whoever fails to understand this, fails to grasp the logic of factional struggle within our Party, fails to realise that the outcome of this struggle depends not on personalities and desires, but on the results produced in the sum total of the struggle between the Soviet and anti-Soviet elements.[41]

Despite the dangers posed by Lenin's letter, Stalin survived the congress and was re-elected general secretary. But this high-tension political moment saw the perceived dangers from the outside world continue to feed into the party majority's attacks on Trotsky and his supporters. This is not to say this was the sole motive for the maintenance of a one-party dictatorship. The violent and brutal experience of the civil war, the personal ambition of men like Stalin, the way democratic practices were interpreted and then practised within Bolshevism played undeniable roles. Yet Bolsheviks on all sides – Lenin, Stalin, Trotsky, Kamenev, Zinoviev – characterized the outside world in more dangerous terms than was warranted and this understanding of international affairs in turn shaped attitudes towards whether freer democratic practices were permissible. A unified and disciplined party dictatorship was deemed critical for survival in a hostile world. Forming factions or other political groupings – the central accusation levelled against Trotsky and the opposition – was certainly ruled out. And while Trotsky rejected outright this characterization of his behaviour, his endorsements of the nature of foreign threats, in the same manner as accepted across the party, and his belief that unity was important when war threatened, boxed him into a corner.

The succession struggle moved to a new phase when Zinoviev and Kamenev began to break with Stalin from early 1925. Only months before, in the previous October, Trotsky lambasted the pair in a provocative essay *The Lessons of October* for resisting Lenin's push to seize power in 1917, drawing connections to the recent failure of revolution in Germany and to the conservatism and inertia he identified in the Bolshevik Party leadership. Yet from 1925, the three steadily found common causes. Not only had Zinoviev and Kamenev watched their political power weaken as Stalin widened the triumvirate into a looser body of seven, to include Bukharin, Rykov, Valerian Kuibyshev and Mikhail Tomskii (a move designed in part by the damage Trotsky had successfully wrought on the pair's reputation).[42] Rejecting the Stalinist political status quo and the market-orientated compromises inherent in NEP – typified by Bukharin's provocative call for Soviet peasants to 'enrich themselves' – Zinoviev and Kamenev moved towards Trotsky's economic position on the left of the party; a difficult transition considering the two had been, to a large degree, responsible for Trotsky's political isolation. Zinoviev had even pushed for his expulsion from the party (too far even for Stalin at that time). But now they were likewise troubled by Stalin's authoritarianism. In 1925, Zinoviev and Kamenev's supporters soon attracted the label 'the Leningrad Opposition', given the strength of the former's authority in the city stretching back several years. And as the political struggle deepened, by April 1926, under another new umbrella group, the United Opposition, Trotsky, Zinoviev, Kamenev and other leading oppositionists, more stridently championed rapid state-driven industrialization and criticized the growing bureaucracy and curtailment of freedom of expression in the party under Stalin.

Trotsky, however, remained the most frequent object of attack in major party forums and the international situation remained part of the backdrop to ongoing party controversies. A resolution from the January 1925 joint plenum of the central committee and central control commission, for instance, and before any other criticisms of Trotsky's activities were listed, noted that 'internationally, Trotsky's speeches against the party are regarded by the bourgeoisie and social democrats as a harbinger of a split in the RKP [Russian Communist Party] and the collapse of the proletarian dictatorship'. This, in turn, was shaping, to its detriment, how 'international imperialism' viewed the Soviet Union.[43] Facing rising pressure, Trotsky had little choice but to resign his post as head of the Red Army in late January and was replaced by Mikhail Frunze. The campaign against Trotsky continued across the year and the Soviet Union's international situation remained a core component. A secret central committee letter, for internal party consumption, produced for the April 1925 plenum of the central committee accused Trotsky's supporters of spreading 'monstrous' and 'exaggerated' rumours about division in the party. According to the letter, these were being picked up by the foreign and social-democratic presses, which in turn exaggerated rumours of damaged party unity.[44]

Heightened concerns about war against Piłsudski's Poland specifically and its capitalist backers piled more pressure on the political opposition in these years, generating new concerns about it undermining state defence. Dzerzhinskii, in particular, saw internal party disputes as highly dangerous. After Zinoviev and Kamenev's split with Stalin he warned of a potential 'new Kronstadt' in the party and a threat to its very existence.[45] But with Piłsudski back in power, the situation was even more fraught. Dzerzinskii claimed that Piłsudski would detect weakness in the Soviet state because of the activity of the opposition.[46] While Stalin was not as adamant as Dzerzhinskii about the imminence of war in 1926 as we know, he conveyed similar messages regarding the continuing dangers posed by factionalism. At the seventh enlarged plenum of the executive committee of the Communist International (ECCI) in December 1926, a forum Stalin used to outline his theory of Socialism in One Country in fuller terms, he also argued that a 'united party armed with iron discipline' was essential when imperialism was such a strong force in the world. In this context, attempts to undermine party unity or create a new parallel party had to be 'rooted out'.[47]

The 1927 war scare

1927 proved to be a dramatic year in the Soviet Union, a moment when anxiety about future military conflict reached yet another peak, but this time set off a war scare that rippled throughout party and society. This war scare should be understood in the context of the long-standing Soviet predictions of future war dating back to the end of the civil war era, then super-charged by Piłsudski's coup d'état in May 1926. In the months after, from the Bolsheviks' perspective, the European order was turning ever further to their disadvantage. Even so, the consensus in the party was that major war remained some years away. And this line ultimately held for most of the 1927 war scare, despite a fleeting moment in early summer when Stalin made claims to his allies about a British-inspired plot to spark war there and then. Outside this point, however, the Bolsheviks took what they saw as natural tensions between capitalist powers as still providing some break on imperialist ambitions (or at least that was the explanation for war not actually arriving). In the first six months of 1927, therefore, the war scare was more so a time when the ever-evolving perceived existential threat to the Soviet Union built to a fever-pitch, rather than a new and sudden fear of imminent conflict.

Public warnings about future war became noticeably louder in the Soviet Union in early 1927 and senior Bolsheviks delivered ominous speeches about threats arrayed against the country. 'They are preparing war', Bukharin claimed dramatically in the Moscow party conference. 'We do not know whether there will be a war or not in the near future, but we firmly know it is being prepared.'

According to him, and repeating a now-familiar conspiracy, the British government was orchestrating the coming conflict and 'very intensive' military preparations had been detected in Poland and Romania, the second dangerous proxy state, had received a large Italian loan for purchasing military materiel.[48] Reporting on the speeches at the Moscow party conference, for at least one British diplomat present, Bukharin's remarks seemed sincere and he described the Soviet people as in a 'state of nervousness'.[49] Other senior Bolsheviks delivered similar warnings elsewhere. Rykov, head of the government, and Voroshilov, head of the army, echoed Bukharin's dire predictions about looming conflict, though they likewise did not go as far as specifying when the war would come.[50] Adding a further detail, Voroshilov claimed not only that the British orchestrated Piłsudski's return to power but 'English imperialists' were responsible for the military coup in Lithuania in December 1926 (the coup brought the fascist government of Augustinas Voldemaras to power and Lithuanian communists were arrested *en masse* in the following turmoil).[51] Inside the Politburo, the party leadership discussed a new information campaign for Belorussia, to warn its people about a Polish attack, apparently one part of a wider British strategy to use 'fascist coups along the Soviet border' in preparation for an invasion into the Soviet Union.[52] Even the sometimes-measured deputy People's Commissar for Foreign Affairs, Maksim Litvinov, privately critical of the regime's messaging around the war scare during 1927, claimed to the British chargé d'affaires in February that Poland was 'making every preparation for aggression'.[53] Indicative of the heightened sense of threat, in January, the Society for the Assistance of Defence, Aircraft and Chemical Construction (Osoaviakhim) was formed, organized to train reservists for the Red Army and promote the militarization of society. With the domestic picture deteriorating at the same time in early 1927, and economic growth slowing, unemployment rising, food shortages, popular unrest and rising strike activity, this was undeniably a tense moment.[54]

Because of anxieties swirling in Moscow and rejuvenated fears about Britain compelling Poland into war, in mid-February the Soviet government pushed for negotiations for a non-aggression pact to be opened again, timed for Stanisław Patek's arrival as new Polish representative in Moscow.[55] Since the start of the year, the Poles had given fresh signals of their own about another effort to improve relations, but inside the NKID there were doubts that Piłsudski would ever meaningfully engage. Some suspected he would play for time, reserving a free hand for future aggressive action. On the ground in Warsaw, Voikov was certain that Piłsudski was dictating negotiating positions to Patek, and in any case, he saw worsening Anglo-Soviet antagonism as a disincentive for Poland to strike an agreement. Despite being more plugged into Polish politics and society, and indicative of the tensions in 1927, Voikov also more strongly entertained the prospect of war than he had done in the past. Due to stronger pressure from Germany for a new territorial settlement on Poland's western border, Voikov believed Piłsudski was swinging between two options: 'strengthen relations with us or prepare for war with us, during which the Polish rear would be defended by England, France and all of the League of Nations'. The military option was a way for Poland to gain territory in the east to compensate for what would be lost in the west to Germany through buying its neutrality. Voikov admitted he was presenting an extreme scenario and that Piłsudski would no doubt seesaw in the middle for some time. He also presented France differently to the evolving thinking in the NKID, which, after recent Franco-Soviet negotiations on outstanding Russian debts in 1926, had begun to see the country as a receding danger and even a restraining force on Piłsudski.[56]

Whatever danger France actually posed aside, although the NKID understood the difficulties for Poland in agreeing territorial concessions with Germany, this was not enough to dispel the hypothetical danger. Other institutions like Soviet military intelligence agreed, underlining in early 1927 how everything should be done to hinder reconciliation between Germany and Poland over Upper Silesia and Danzig (exchanges involving Lithuanian territory were also considered as plausible). Stopping the formation of a Polish-Baltic union – the Soviet Union's 'most probable adversary' – was a central priority as ever.[57] Despite the low chances of success, and the obvious risk that Rapallo-ally Germany would be further alienated by renewed Soviet-Polish contacts, the NKID therefore pushed for negotiations anyway. And that another Polish rejection of a bilateral non-aggression pact was seen as a good outcome underlined the pessimism surrounding these efforts and the low bar set for success. As Stomoniakov put it to Voikov, 'we need to demonstrate to the entire world that Piłsudski's politics are war not peace'. In spurning another Soviet offer, he would underline this very point, or so the thinking went. For now, this was the best the Bolsheviks could hope for.[58]

Renewed negotiations in spring were slow to start and gained little momentum in later months. Not long after his arrival in the Soviet Union, Patek, the new Polish representative, was under no illusions of the challenges ahead, writing to his superior, August Zaleski, that the Bolsheviks were 'difficult, highly sensitive and ready to exaggerate for propaganda purposes everything that can be turned to our detriment'.[59] Yet because he presented Polish red lines almost immediately, this only confirmed Stomoniakov's suspicion that Piłsudski was not serious. (Piłsudski later flippantly commented to N. D. S. Sokolov, a member of the Soviet diplomatic mission in Poland, that progress was slow because Polish diplomats were basing their position on the charter of the League of Nations, whereas the Bolsheviks were using '1000 pages of Marx'.)[60] The central and unchanged sticking point, however, clear to both sides from the beginning, was the disagreement about the type of pact to be negotiated. The Bolsheviks still refused to entertain a multilateral pact including the Baltic states and Finland; the Poles would only accept a multilateral arrangement. The negotiations were almost certainly doomed to fail. Indeed, Patek stuck fast to the Polish position that any new Soviet-Polish understanding could not risk violating agreements already made with other powers and League of Nations member states (an organization the Bolsheviks flatly refused to recognize and certainly not in a legal treaty). Patek, however, suggested maximum and minimum versions of a multilateral pact, the latter essentially the simultaneous ratifications of bilateral arrangements between the Soviet Union, Poland, Finland and the Baltic states. But the prospects of this were vanishing.

Not only were the Bolsheviks unenthusiastic about the Patek's proposal, but Soviet negotiations for non-aggression pacts with the Baltic states and Finland had not yet yielded results (pacts with Latvia and Estonia were signed later in July and August; negotiations with Finland were broken off). Soviet diplomats, moreover, continued to misjudge Piłsudski as obsessed with expansion at the Soviet Union's expense and believed he was prioritizing genuine negotiations with Germany to free his hands in the east.[61] Taken together, misapprehensions and irreconcilable positions meant both sides of the negotiating table were pessimistic and distrustful after early interactions in the spring.[62]

Conspiracies about future war spreading inside the Bolshevik Party were becoming more elaborate by the mid-to-late 1920s. In early 1927, for instance, the German press carried stories about a new Anglo-Polish military alliance which the Bolsheviks gave some credence, even if the Poles were quick to dismiss the reports as disinformation.[63] Some leading officials in the NKID now decided to push back. At a meeting of the foreign affairs commissariat in mid-January 1927, Litvinov broke ranks and argued it was a mistake to see malevolent British influence everywhere and that he did not accept the intelligence describing this picture. Litvinov saw Poland as a potential military threat for sure, but one much more in control of its destiny. Then in February, he suggested to Stalin that there was no reliable information about a forthcoming European war, nor that Britain was pushing Poland towards such a clash. Poland, Litvinov argued again, exercised control over its affairs and was not manipulated by the British. The Bolsheviks should, of course, strive to hinder Poland and the Baltic states becoming a bloc, but at the same time, Litvinov wanted to avoid unnecessarily worsening Anglo-Soviet relations. Like his boss Chicherin, who had raised similar points with Stalin before, Litvinov argued that the tone of the Soviet press and some Bolsheviks' public statements were the root causes of hostility with Poland. In this way, it is unlikely that Litvinov – or Chicherin – rejected the basic premise underlying the Bolsheviks' conspiratorial view of the world: that anti-Soviet coalitions were constantly in some stage of creation. He believed this before 1927 and would do again in the late 1920s and early 1930s. However, the starker tone of Soviet public commentary during the war scare was evidently a problem for Litvinov and it pushed him to try and draw down the rhetoric. However, efforts to correct the narrative stood little chance and Stalin's response was to outright reject Litvinov's criticism, raking him over the coals and expounding about the international conspiracy against the Soviet Union and the inevitability of war.[64] In the same month, and on Stalin's suggestion, the Politburo dedicated a session and convened a commission on Soviet defence. Indicative of how seriously a military threat was being taken, Stalin criticized formulations from Red Army head, Voroshilov, for saying too little about how the whole of Soviet industry and wider economy could be adapted to war, such was the predicted scale of the future conflict.[65] Still, as far as the leadership was concerned, time remained on their side. In a speech to a meeting of railway workers shortly after in March, Stalin could not have been clearer about the timeline to war. 'The majority of questions boil down to one: shall we have war this year, in the spring or autumn of this year? My reply is that we shall not have war this year, neither in the spring nor in the autumn.'[66]

It was at this moment, however, that a chain of events abroad from late spring to early summer suddenly accelerated the war scare. This not only cemented Stalin's vision of a credible prospect of war, but for the first time in several years truncated the perceived timeline to conflict. The first event in the chain was a raid by Chinese nationalist authorities on the Soviet embassy in Beijing on 6 April, seizing documents they said proved the embassy was working to undermine the Chinese government. Elsewhere, the nationalists' occupation of Shanghai, during which the small Chinese Communist Party and those on the political left fell victim to a massacre, sparked major political controversy in Moscow, which had been responsible for forcing the Chinese communists into an uneasy alliance with the anti-communist nationalists in the first place. The second shock came amid a worsening period of Anglo-Soviet relations in the first half of 1927. Already in February, and because of persisting Soviet propaganda in Britain, foreign secretary Austin Chamberlain delivered a warning about a break in diplomatic relations; and three months later, British police raided the building of the Soviet trade delegation and All-Russian Cooperative Society (ARCOS) in London on 12 May. Like in Beijing, the British authorities reported that the raid revealed evidence of Soviet subversion and espionage. Caught off guard, the Politburo planned a pushback against the British government, but Stanley Baldwin severed diplomatic relations and cancelled the Anglo-Soviet trade agreement.[67] This was a huge blow to Soviet foreign trade, where Britain had become the Soviet Union's largest partner despite increasingly acrimonious relations. There were consequences elsewhere too, and negotiations with France on security arrangements and trade ground to a halt.[68] The sluggish pact negotiations with Poland also became even harder work after the Polish government, in private, gave full backing to the British position and promised not to speed up the pact negotiations with the Bolsheviks, whom it believed would now push for a swift agreement. Yet with doubts gathering in the NKID, the more modest aim of increasing the volume of Soviet-Polish trade, rather than agree a pact, was emerging as a priority. 'Strong trade ties. It holds together better than cement and better than any pact', Voikov reiterated.[69] In any case, and true to form, the Bolsheviks saw the ARCOS raid as a symptom of the existential threat to the Soviet Union from the capitalist world. The raid in Beijing and persecution of communists in China were presented in similar terms, provoked also by 'foreign imperialist circles' and designed to push the Soviet Union into war.[70] Seemingly assailed from both sides, on 1 June, the central committee called in *Pravda* for the Soviet people to be ready for war at any moment.[71]

A third and final event in the chain over spring and summer then pulled Soviet-Polish relations to yet another low and crystalized fears about *imminent* war in Moscow. Dramatically, on 7 June, a Russian-Lithuanian monarchist émigré, a certain 19-year-old Boris Kowerda, shot and killed the Soviet plenipotentiary Voikov in Warsaw. Before his murder, Voikov knew about threats to his safety, some stemming from his involvement in the murder of Tsar Nicholas II and his family in the civil war in 1918. In the previous summer, he had flagged his concerns to the central NKID, reporting information about 'a certain officer who had decided to take revenge for Nicholas II [...] now they warn me that there is hope that scores will be settled on me for the murder of Petliura [it was widely assumed in Poland that the Bolsheviks were behind Petliura's death, PW]'.[72]

But with Voikov dead in June 1927, the minds of Stalin and other senior Bolsheviks focused more strongly on the military threat from Poland and Britain. The day after the murder, in a private letter to Molotov, for instance, Stalin wrote that he felt the 'hand of England' in Voikov's murder and speculated that the British government was seeking a proxy war with the Soviet Union. 'They want to provoke a conflict with Poland. They want to repeat Sarajevo.' The allusion to the assassination of Franz Ferdinand is more than suggestive of the danger Stalin saw in Piłsudski's Poland under British influence and the possibility of a new European-wide war. His claim that Voikov's assassination was staged to provoke war underlines also how he, at this moment, accepted a shorter timeline to major conflict than before. That a group of Russian émigrés managed to bomb a party club in central Leningrad in the hours before the Voikov murder only raised the temperature. In a kneejerk response, Stalin ordered that a group of White monarchists who had been held in Soviet captivity for some time be executed as a warning against future terrorist attacks. And the OGPU, with newly awarded emergency extra-judicial powers, was to carry out widespread searches for monarchist cells, reflective of the Bolsheviks' view of connections between Kowerda and the White émigré organizations.[73] Twenty White monarchists were executed a few days later and the OGPU unleashed a campaign of repression over the summer to also uncover supposed connections between domestic anti-Soviet networks and foreign intelligence services.[74] To take one example, it reported on British espionage in Leningrad, where it was said British and Polish agents were recruiting saboteurs to assist in a forthcoming invasion.[75]

Seemingly shocked by the Voikov murder, Stalin was operating chiefly with his instincts. His gut reaction that the British were to blame soon enough formed the basis of the official Soviet government response and was repeated elsewhere in the party hierarchy and to the public. Stalin's close ally Voroshilov, for instance, delivered a speech a few days after the murder, later printed in *Pravda*, where he expounded on the machinations of the British government, apparently trying to pull the Soviet Union into war. Britain was responsible for organizing Voikov's murder, Voroshilov claimed, and the 'next logical step' after the severing of Anglo-Soviet relations had been 'a military attack on us'. But by this point, it was clear to all that the 'next logical step' of war had not actually occurred. The British plot had seemingly failed, and expectations were being adjusted behind-the-scenes. In Voroshilov's account, the British government had 'miscalculated' and other countries – Germany, France, Italy, the Baltic states and Poland – had refused to join in a war. Even so, he was clear that the British would try again, and the Soviet people should expect war 'in a year or two'.[76]

The perceived military threat, in this sense, suddenly became heightened in early summer and Stalin, at least in the hours or days after Voikov's murder, saw a genuine outside attempt to engineer war. Showing the credibility the leadership attached to the wider security threat, the Politburo accepted Voroshilov's recommendation to create diversionary groups in enemy territories because of the deteriorating international situation. In his view, the Bolsheviks should draw on previous successes against anti-Soviet groups, such as those operating out of Poland in the early 1920s (and considering the role assigned to Britain in the crises of spring and summer, the Politburo discussed using Irish nationalists against the British government).[77] With the narrative that Britain was the chief enemy coordinating pliable border states set at the top, this echoed throughout the party in other highly conspiratorial formulations. On 17 June, in an example of a particularly complex picture of dangers, the first secretary of the Communist Party of Belorussia (a republic that would be directly threatened by another war with Poland) detailed in a secret report how the Voikov murder was evidence that 'England is putting together a bloc of anti-Soviet states, particularly states that border the USSR – Poland, Lithuania, Romania, Finland, and others, by organizing and supporting fascist, monarchist, and White guard organizations and enticing them to attack the USSR'.[78]

The increasingly sceptic Chicherin was in Germany, in Baden-Baden receiving medical treatment, when Kowerda murdered Voikov, and his immediate reaction departed from Stalin's vision once more. Speaking with the German minister of foreign affairs, Gustav Stresemann, Chicherin downplayed the murder as having 'no political significance' and he doubted that future British military intervention or major conflagration were likely. In fact, he was more concerned that Piłsudski might now take advantage of the febrile situation and, encouraged by the British, contrive a provocation on the borders to seize territory and try to blame the Bolsheviks. Chicherin repeated similar observations to the American journalist Louis Fischer.[79] Britain, then, was by no means an innocent party in Chicherin's analysis, and he was certain its government was pushing Poland in a hostile direction, but not necessarily and inexorably towards major war. Chicherin's comments were not only for a foreign audience. Following his return to Moscow, at a joint session of the Politburo and Soviet government in June, Chicherin told the assembled party members that the Soviet Union was not under threat of invasion from France, Germany, Poland, Lithuania or Finland. The chief dangers came instead from political isolation and economic blockade and the break with Britain was disastrous in this regard. He highlighted, moreover, the damage done to foreign relations by the provocative Comintern, and especially in the aftermath of the OGPU's execution of the twenty White émigré hostages, which had already stirred negative international responses.[80] So exercised by the Comintern's behaviour towards Germany, Chicherin tried to resign as People's Commissar for Foreign Affairs in protest.[81] However, Chicherin was an increasingly powerless voice by 1927. Even though respected in foreign affairs for much of the 1920s, he had always been outside the decision-making Politburo. And now, after successfully destroying his political rivals, Stalin wielded far more influence in shaping Soviet foreign policy to his liking. Dissenting viewpoints were easily side-lined, especially those that presented Britain and the capitalist conspiracy in a less threatening light (even if some reports still flowed in from Poland in support of the doubters).[82]

Official Soviet notes of protest about the Voikov murder, delivered to Poland in Litvinov's name, even though he almost certainly agreed with Chicherin, unsurprisingly followed Stalin's lead. The first note from 7 June claimed that Voikov's death was one in a series of hostile actions, including the ARCOS raid and the severing of Anglo-Soviet relations, designed to threaten peace. And a second more critical note sent days later on 11 June was especially scornful of the Polish government's assessment of the Voikov murder as an individual 'act of a madman' and something it could not therefore be held responsible. Indeed, reports of the emerging Polish position had come in quickly from Aleksandr Ul'ianov, an NKID official at the Soviet embassy in Poland, who gave Moscow the outlines of how news of the murder spread with 'lighting speed' in Warsaw but also how the Polish press immediately sought to distance the government from Kowerda.[83] This was in stark contrast to the Bolsheviks' elaborate account, which, as put to the Poles, characterized the murder as one act in a 'systematic and planned struggle against the Soviet Union', involving White Russian émigrés seeking war and the restoration of tsarism. For this reason, the second Soviet note was pointed in criticism of Polish accommodation and 'direct support' of anti-Soviet guerrilla organizations, and it dragged up past controversies, such as the arming of Stanislav Bułak-Bałakhovich in the early 1920s. As we have seen, Piłsudski renewed collaboration with the UNR in early 1927, but Kowerda was undoubtedly a lone gunman. Nevertheless, the Bolsheviks were convinced otherwise and demanded a rapid investigation, insisting as well on Soviet participation, and for several leading White émigrés and organizations to be expelled from Poland.[84]

While the initial Polish response to the Voikov murder expressed sympathy, the second more critical Soviet note sparked a backlash, and the Poles refused the Soviet demands. This had not been unexpected inside the NKID, but still, some officials were taken aback by the force of the reaction. Ul'ianov reported to Stomoniakov about a shift in the tone of the Polish press and how the second Soviet note was received 'extremely irritably and sharply' and viewed as an ultimatum and interference in Poland's domestic affairs. He drew attention to some Polish press articles now justifying 'Kowerda's heroic act' and in his view the roots of a 'Kowerda cult' were developing. Later, once the trial had been and gone, Kowerda was sentenced to imprisonment, not execution that the Bolsheviks had pushed for. In Ul'ianov's report, Kowerda's youth and 'deep patriotism' were used as mitigating factors. And because Stalin had ordered the twenty White émigrés executed in reprisal, the obvious point was made in the Polish press that the Bolsheviks had little grounds to criticize the nature of Polish justice. In fact, according to Ul'ianov, the execution of the twenty was being reported as reflective of Soviet weakness.[85] Before the sentencing, Patek had warned Polish foreign minister Zaleski against leniency, noting that the Bolsheviks, 'whose sensitivity has become so acute', saw the murder as 'one of the last links in the chain of larger and small disasters that befell the Soviet government'.[86] Unsurprisingly the non-aggression pact negotiations ground to a halt with this controversy. Provocative Soviet stipulations that Kowerda be shown 'no mercy' and that the Polish government expel thirty-seven White émigrés from a list drawn up by the Bolsheviks, in practice, meant there was little chance of them restarting.

On the one hand, Chicherin now worried about a total break in relations with Poland. 'Piłsudski himself, after a supposed period of peaceful politics has suddenly begun to speak in a belligerent tone', he wrote to Ul'ianov.[87] But on the other, while he was still sceptical about the Soviet Union facing invasion, Chicherin was convinced Kowerda was part of a foreign-backed White émigré conspiracy. Britain, he claimed, had a hand in Poland's hardening stance and refusal to allow Soviet participation in the murder investigation. Chicherin suspected also that Poland had come under wider international pressure at the Geneva naval disarmament conference in June. As he put it to Khristian Rakovskii and Nikolai Krestinskii, 'monarchist organizations dozed for a long time, but now, under the current international situation and with English support, they suddenly began to show extraordinary activity and their headquarters appeared in Poland [...] the Polish courts tried to throw a veil over Kowerda's connection with other émigrés, but this is absolutely certain'.[88] There was little room for common ground and a meeting with Patek about the Voikov case in late June went nowhere. Chicherin reported that the Polish envoy resisted the expulsion of the Bolsheviks' list of White émigrés on the grounds that this was impossible on the demands of a foreign power and without judicial review.

With no sign of tensions abating in the weeks after the Voikov murder, on 27 June the Politburo decreed that Rykov, head of the government, investigate what immediate preparations should be made 'to further strengthen the country's defence'.[89] Shortly afterwards, the so-called and union-wide Defence Week began on 10 July. Involving millions of Soviet workers and peasants and with military exercises scheduled in rural areas and political training for military units during what was framed as an unfolding international crisis, this was nothing less than a mass exercise in the mobilization of Soviet society.[90] The results, however, laid bare to a greater degree a widespread sense of defeatism, something already clear from various quarters, and especially so after the Voikov murder. OGPU reports on local opinion frequently reflected popular pessimism about future war, with some people making the same comparison as Stalin between Voikov and Franz Ferdinand.[91] The party's Polish Bureau reported on a similar sense of panic sparked by the murder and particularly among Polish populations in the border regions.[92] It called for stronger agitation to explain the current crisis, but the party leadership in Moscow had already started to see that its mobilization campaign was proving counterproductive, and only deepening popular anxieties. It was soon abandoned.[93]

Tension with Poland, nevertheless, had already begun to dissipate by this time, partly because the Bolsheviks lowered their demands, realizing that they had pushed for too much. If the Polish government expelled *some* leading White émigrés and if Kowerda did not receive a presidential pardon (he did not), the Bolsheviks made known they could move on.[94] In early July, while the final arrangements for Defence Week were underway, Ul'ianov reported that the Voikov dispute had 'completely disappeared from the [Polish] press' and that the Polish minister of foreign affairs, Zaleski, reportedly claimed there was no longer a conflict between the Soviet Union and Poland. Ul'ianov interpreted this as reflecting the Polish government's efforts to raise a stabilization loan in the United States to strengthen the złoty, which had been in trouble for two years. The project would be placed in jeopardy if Poland remained in a difficult dispute with the Soviet Union. As was often true in Soviet diplomatic reports, accurate information was mixed in with familiar conspiracies. Ul'ianov claimed the British government had also offered its own rival loan of 100 million dollars – exceeding the actual stabilization loan issued to Poland in late 1927 – in return for control over Polish foreign policy.[95] The NKID collegium, in any case, came to see a way through the crisis period. In reply to Ul'ianov, Stomoniakov expressed confidence that economic problems in Poland, combined with improving relations between Britain and Germany (which he suggested could lead to the latter being armed), would generate sufficient alarm in Poland to prompt a move towards improving relations with the Soviet Union. In his view, the Poles, and Patek in particular, were also now looking to settle over the Voikov murder and restart the stalled talks towards a non-aggression pact and trade agreement. Stomoniakov added that he was sure that Poland was 'still not prepared for war with us this year'.[96] The party leadership evidently saw a similar picture and, tellingly, on 4 July, the Politburo ordered the Soviet press to not exaggerate the military danger. This did not put a stop to the planned Defence Week, but pressure behind-the-scenes had evidently eased.[97] By late August, both sides found a way of settling the Voikov murder.[98] While the Poles still rejected the Soviet characterization of the incident, they agreed to expel some leading White émigrés. Negotiations for a pact resumed in the autumn but these remained as difficult as ever. Old arguments came quickly rushing back. The Polish demand for simultaneous treaties with Finland, Latvia and Estonia, while the Bolsheviks pursued a bilateral arrangement, fearful of Polish project to create a front from the White to the Black Seas, remained irreconcilable.[99]

As he did periodically, in July 1927, Stalin summarized the Soviet Union's international circumstances in the pages of *Pravda* after the crises of spring and summer. On the one hand, despite a dangerous British conspiracy to wage war, Stalin noted there was no imminent danger in 1927. This, of course, had proved true by the end of these high-tension months and it was hard to describe otherwise (Stalin also, no doubt, had an eye towards easing the noticeable anxiety among the Soviet public). Still, he was adamant that this did nothing to alter the likelihood of war in the future. Referring to his theory that the capitalist world was experiencing deep crisis with war as the only viable exit, Stalin remarked: 'It is not a matter of some vague and immaterial "danger" of a new war but of the real and actual *threat* of a new war in general, and of a war against the U.S.S.R. in particular.' Returning to well-worn conspiracies, Stalin blamed the British government for carrying out 'preparatory work for the formation of a "holy alliance" of large and small states'. The British had orchestrated the raids on the Soviet embassy in China and ARCOS in London; Voikov was murdered by 'agents of the Conservative Party'. The end goal, as ever, was to drag the Soviet Union into war with Poland. Yet Stalin claimed that the war had been forestalled for two reasons: the peaceful policies carried out by the Soviet Union and the reluctance of countries like Poland to 'serve as dumb tools of the (British) Conservatives to the detriment of their own interests'. Considering how Stalin had relayed much of this conspiracy to Molotov in private immediately after the Voikov murder, his public commentary should be taken seriously. Whether through accident or by design, he and other Bolsheviks believed the Soviet Union had dodged a bullet. For them, however, the capitalist powers would not back down and the immediate task facing the Soviet Union was improving economic and military power while 'cleansing the rear' of subversives.[100]

*

When Stalin spoke about cleansing the rear, he did not only have traditional targets in mind: various 'anti-Soviet elements' whether they were priests; rich peasants (in Bolshevik language 'kulaks'); assorted speculators, like the so-called Nepmen taking advantage of the opportunities of the economic changes in the 1920s; or people with connections to the White armies of the civil war. The political opposition, whose activity Stalin saw in the context of a deteriorating international climate was also at the centre of his thinking. As he put it in another letter to Molotov on 17 June 1927, in the short weeks after the Voikov murder, 'the course of terror, taken by agents of London, fundamentally changes the situation. It is open preparation for war. Concerning this, the central task is now to cleanse and strengthen the rear, for without a strong rear it will be impossible to organize defence [...] in order to strengthen the rear, we must restrain the opposition immediately'.[101] By this point, the forces of political opposition had coalesced around the United Opposition, bringing Zinoviev and Kamenev – both in political disgrace and removed from the Politburo – into alliance with Trotsky and other prominent oppositionists. And given the dramatic events of summer 1927, the political clashes in turn became louder. On 25 May, for example, and following the obvious failure of the party's strategy in China and the break of relations with Britain, the opposition's leaders wrote to the Politburo with a declaration, signed by another eighty-four critics of Soviet foreign relations, party affairs and economic policy. In response, at a plenum of the Comintern's executive committee a few days later, Stalin accused Trotsky of undermining the party at a dangerous moment:

> I must state, comrades, that Trotsky has chosen for his attacks [...] an all too inopportune moment. I have just received the news that the English Conservative government has resolved to break off relations with the USSR. There is no need to prove that what is intended is a wholesale crusade against communism. The crusade has already started. Some threaten the party with war and intervention; others with a split. There comes into being something like a united front from Chamberlain to Trotsky.[102]

As before, the opposition did not entirely disagree with everything Stalin had to say. Writing to the Politburo, Trotsky, Zinoviev, Ivar Smilga and Grigory Evdokimov underlined how, under conditions of 'life or death', genuine collective discussion inside the party was vital for the Bolsheviks to rise to the challenge of war. If this came, 'every worker, every farmhand, every pauper, on the one hand, and every kulak, bureaucrat, Nepman on the other, will ask the question point-blank: what is this war, whose name is it being waged, and how will it be fought?' For the opposition, avoiding open and frank discussion – covering up the serious mistakes made in China without meaningful debate – was, in effect, 'to close one's eyes and walk over the edge of the cliff'.[103] The debate about the merits of democratic practices in wartime continued to go around in circles.

Trotsky was also certain that Stalin was cynically using the military threat to crack down on the opposition. As he put it at a plenum of the central committee in June 1927, 'you are now exploiting the danger of war to harass the opposition and prepare for its defeat'.[104] Without question, Stalin was pushing more strongly for the opposition to be ostracized. He wrote to the Politburo also in June arguing against a decision that would have postponed doing something stronger about the opposition, without which, for him, it would be 'impossible to strengthen the rear'. Although not all in the party majority were in agreement, Stalin pushed harder and got his way. The Politburo voted to expel Trotsky and Zinoviev from the central committee on 20 June.[105]

Stalin kept little of this campaign against the opposition concealed and his *Pravda* article from July 1927, which in the main sketched out the status of the international order, contained another scathing political attack:

> What, after all this, should be said of our luckless opposition in connection with its latest attacks on our Party in face of the threat of a new war? What should be said of the fact that it, this opposition, has found the war threat an appropriate occasion to intensify its attacks on the Party? What is there creditable in the fact that, instead of rallying around the Party in face of the threat from without, it considers it appropriate to make use of the U.S.S.R.'s difficulties for new attacks on the Party? Can it be that the opposition is against the victory of the U.S.S.R. in the coming battles with imperialism, against increasing the defensive capacity of the Soviet Union, against strengthening our rear?[106]

The opposition pushed back against the pressure from Stalin and the party majority. One such moment was at a joint plenum of the central committee and central control commission, held between July and August, where as well as tackling varied controversies, including the disaster in China, the question of whether overt criticism of the party line was permissible in a dangerous international climate was subjected to lengthy debate. Here Zinoviev, speaking for the opposition's platform, took the opportunity to remind the assembled members that during the civil war, only years earlier, open criticism of the party line had been tolerated. Although Lenin started closing down opportunities for dissent in 1921, Zinoviev pointed to the freedom the Military Opposition enjoyed in the war years, a group that both Stalin and Voroshilov had at one time been associated. Kamenev made a similar point later in the plenum. After underling how war 'urgently requires criticisms of policies […] criticism of the Politburo', he noted that Stalin had not shied away from criticizing Lenin himself in 1918, 1919 and 1920. 'I repeat that good defence depends on good politics', he remarked.[107] Claiming the moral high ground, Zinoviev said that the opposition was not arguing for the sake of it; he simply did not accept that criticisms of the party should be silenced because of a military danger. That opposition supporters were also being discharged from the military – capable 'soldiers of the revolution' – for merely disagreeing with the party majority was only further damaging.[108]

Also on the opposition's platform, Khristian Rakovskii, then Soviet ambassador to France, like Zinoviev, saw nothing inherently wrong with disagreement in the party when war was on the horizon. Even the capitalist enemy, according to him, would not view this strangely. 'The bourgeoisie applies its own norms of political life to us [...] the bourgeoisie will not see anything unusual in these disagreements and arguments, any reason for the weakening of the party and the weakening of the Soviet Union.' Instead, Rakovskii claimed it was the high-profile expulsions of opposition leaders from the party – the 'attempt to politically eliminate the most important leaders of our revolution' – which damaged the Soviet Union's image overseas. The class enemy would not fail this see this as 'a sign of the weakening of the authority of the Central Committee of the party, a rapid destruction of the party itself, and finally, as a sign of a weakening of the country's defences'.[109] The opposition's key point, as ever, was that party unity was necessary in the face of the war threat, but the only way to achieve this was through more frank and open discussion. Otherwise, factions, born of rising frustrations, would inevitably begin to form.

Debate at the plenum continued to go along these lines, back and forth. Speaking for the party majority, Molotov described a 'significantly stronger' military threat in 1927 and lambasted Trotsky for choosing this moment to intensify political attacks on the party. Trotsky made it easy for Molotov in some respects, given his provocative comments in a letter to Stalin's ally, Sergo Ordzhonikide, just before the plenum. Here he had described how the opposition would position itself against the party majority even during an invasion, likening the situation to France in the early years of the First World War when Georges Clémenceau remained a vocal critic of the government even though the 'Germans were within eighty kilometers of Paris'.[110] With the line of attack generously gifted, Molotov put it to the plenum: 'comrade Trotsky finds nothing better to say than when an imperialist onslaught will be 80 kilometres from Moscow it is necessary to strike decisively against the party's policy'.[111] Molotov then accused the opposition of the cardinal sin: trying to split the party to form another. Elsewhere Rykov argued similarly that the opposition was distracting from vital discussion of the impending war, where party unity 'is of extreme, exceptional importance'. As he put it, 'we will organize the people and win only if not a single worker, not a single peasant, has doubts about the correctness of the party's politics, and there is no thought for a minute that its mistakes will put millions of workers and peasants under the bullets of Chamberlain and Piłsudski'. Rykov went on: 'isn't this a completely unacceptable disorganization of the rear?' he stated, when 'millions are threatened with death in war'.[112]

Stalin's speech to the plenum, like others, explicitly connected the internal and external threats to the Soviet Union in another scathing attack on Trotsky, pouncing on his clumsy reference to Clémenceau:

> This comic opera Clemenceau will first of all try to overthrow the present majority, precisely because the enemy will be eighty kilometres from the Kremlin, and only after that will he start defending [...] And in order to do this, he, Trotsky, i.e., Clemenceau, is first of all trying to "sweep away" the "garbage" "in the interests of the victory of the workers' state." And what is this "garbage"? It turns out that it is the majority in our Party, the majority in the Central Committee, the majority in the government [...] Comrades, we are faced by two dangers: the danger of war, which has become the threat of war; and the danger of the degeneration of some of the links of our Party. In setting out to prepare for defence we must create iron discipline in our Party. Without such discipline defence is impossible. We must strengthen Party discipline, we must curb all those who are disorganising our Party.[113]

Struggling to defend himself, Trotsky reiterated the core point in the opposition's case: freer discussion in the party, even during times of war, was essential. 'If our party has nothing to hide in the political sense from the working class during peace-time, then this is all the more true during war-time when the purity and clarity of the political line, the profundity of the ties with the masses are life-and-death questions.' Making another reference to French politics of the war era, Trotsky criticized any kind of '*Union sacree*' arrangement, a political truce between parties during wartime. The opposition's task, he argued, was to keep the party line in check, to ensure revolutionary unity and 'steer a firm revolutionary course, not out of fear, but from conviction'. Trotsky put his views plainly: 'the revolutionist gives his support, while criticizing, and the more undeniable is his right to criticize, all the greater is his devotion in struggling for the creation and strengthening of that in which he is a direct participant [...] What we need is not a hypocritical "*Union sacree*" but honest revolutionary unity.'[114] Only the opposition was capable of steering the country through tense international waters.

Because he had handed Stalin a straightforward line of attack, shortly after the plenum in September, Trotsky went on to clarify his comments about Clémenceau, rejecting the accusation that he and the opposition threatened to take power 'after the Clémenceau manner'. This was one part of a general softening of his positions following the attacks of the summer.[115] Yet at the same time, the core problem was how Trotsky still made one of his central arguments in similar terms as the party majority's, a major reason why the opposition's protests were easily brushed aside. Fundamentally both sides were calling for unity in 1927. As Trotsky put it, 'the dictatorship of the proletariat in a country which is surrounded by capitalist states does not allow either the existence of two parties or the factional splitting of a unified party'. And allowing freer discussion was still Trotsky's remedy for preventing such a split. 'It is a lie that the danger or even war itself excludes the self-action of the party, which discusses and decides all questions and which directs and checks all its organs from top to bottom.'[116]

In this way, Trotsky's position was undermined by the same problems apparent when he first became the party's chief internal critic. Trotsky did not dissent from the consensus that the Soviet Union would be endangered if the party split into factions and that unity was required in the face of cataclysmic war with the capitalist world. Trotsky had also been unequivocal about the existential danger in 1927, writing to the central committee at the height of the war scare that the threat of intervention was 'unquestionable'. Moreover, within the United Opposition's own political platform, in addition to stressing the common assumption that Britain could compel Poland into war, Trotsky argued:

> Another task of equal importance is to consolidate the ranks of our party, to put an end to the open speculation of the imperialist bourgeoisie and the leaders of Social Democracy on a split […] All the organs of the international bourgeoisie and the Social Democrats are now showing a quite unusual interest in our inner-party disputes. They are openly encouraging and spurring on the present majority of the Central Committee to exclude the Opposition from the leading organs of the party, and if possible from the party […] Moreover, we can buy ourselves off from a war, if that is possible – and conquer in the war, if we have to fight – only if we preserve complete unity; if we disappoint the hopes of the imperialists for a split or an amputation. Such a thing would benefit only the capitalists.[117]

But this was to make an argument in the same territory as the party majority; only mirror it with a different inflection. And during heated plenum debates it was easy enough for Stalin to dismiss the finer points about what unity entailed exactly when the Soviet Union's position in the world was viewed as increasingly precarious. As he sarcastically shot back at Trotsky during a September meeting of the Politburo and presidium of the central control commission:

> We cannot create the harmful illusion that the party here has turned into a discussion club, that the party is unstable, and so on. We cannot do this since, first, that does not correspond to reality, second, this contradicts our notion of the party, and third, we are surrounded by enemies. Otherwise, rejoice, please: the oppositionists have been visited by the fantasy of writing a major pamphlet – be sure to respond to this pamphlet so that this entire squabble becomes the property of foreign countries and creates the impression of weakness in our country.[118]

Trotsky failed to make inroads against these attacks when he accepted the core premise behind them. And even when the threat of war receded from its peak in May and June 1927, Stalin was still able to use the war danger to discredit the opposition with a new line of attack from the autumn, criticizing its exaggeration of the military threat, its 'repeated prophecies' and 'hysterics'.[119] In the party majority's presentation, Trotsky and his supporters not only failed to properly grasp the nature of the international climate, but also how the party should operate and respond to ensure Soviet security.

In the final months of 1927, pressure on the United Opposition was not just the product of heated plenum debates. Investigating opposition networks for some time, the OGPU relayed its findings on clandestine activities to the centre and began to arrest opposition sympathizers for conspiring against the state. Some connections were drawn between these supposed plots and the deteriorating international situation. In the middle of September, for instance, the OGPU arrested an opposition group running an underground printing press, and one member – a former White officer-turned-political informant – confessed, conveniently, to planning a coup inspired by Piłsudski.[120] In another echo of Polish affairs, during the discussion of this Trotskyist printing press inside the Politburo, the idea that some of the arrested oppositionists were connected to Red Army personnel and the prospect of a military coup was entertained.[121] Shortly after, the OGPU reported to the leadership that Trotsky and his supporters had indeed planned a coup d'état timed for the tenth anniversary of the 1917 revolution in November, but called this off at the last moment as not all preparations were in place. OGPU head, Viacheslav Menzhinskii, nevertheless, urged Stalin to take decisive action to 'eliminate' the leaders of the opposition, not least to correct the impression held by 'the statesmen of the great powers' of weakness in the party leadership.[122] Indeed, one element of the OGPU's scrutiny of the opposition was to record impressions abroad created by its activity. Reporting on Polish, German and Czechoslovak diplomatic opinion at the time of the supposedly aborted coup attempt, the OGPU summarized how Polish minister of foreign affairs, Zaleski, believed that domestic anti-communist forces would one day grow strong enough to overthrow Stalin. The Czechoslovak representative apparently expected the opposition's swift political defeat, but also that it would carry out a serious underground struggle following expulsion from the party. Only the Germans apparently dismissed the opposition's significance entirely.[123]

The OGPU's reports on the opposition helped seal its fate, but the writing had long been on the wall. The central committee and central control commission finally voted to expel Trotsky and Zinoviev from the party on 14 November 1927 as punishment for counterrevolutionary activities with the expulsions ratified one month later at the fifteenth party congress. Shortly after, Zinoviev, Kamenev and a number of others, chose the path of capitulation and humiliatingly renounced their opposition as the only way of returning to the party. Then in January 1928, the Politburo accused Trotskyists of supplying foreign journalists with falsehoods about the nature of the interparty conflict. Because of this, the Politburo claimed, more stringent countermeasures had to be taken, including exile of key opposition figures. While this was not the only reason for Trotsky's forced removal to Alma Ata soon after, the Politburo showed no sign of decoupling the opposition's activity from the perceived foreign threat.[124] According to one historian, at the end of the year, Stalin proposed to the Politburo that any person spreading oppositionist views should be regarded as working with both internal and external enemies, and sentenced accordingly by the security organs as a spy.[125]

*

As the party struggle reached its climax in winter 1927, Soviet-Polish relations remained a mixed picture. The Soviet line towards Poland had softened since the peak of the war scare in June and the compromise provisionally found to settle the Voikov murder helped to ease tensions. Nevertheless, the Bolsheviks pivoted again towards Germany to shore up their position. Iosif Unshlikht, deputy commissar for war, travelled to Berlin at the end of July to propose (unsuccessfully) an acceleration of the Soviet-German military collaboration. Given their own shifting international alignments, however, the Germans were not interested in expanding its scope.[126] The Poles then surprised nearly all shortly after when Zaleski proposed a universal non-aggression pact in September at a League of Nations meeting in Geneva. The French government had known something of the proposal beforehand, but it received immediate pushback from other European powers. Zaleski's proposal was dead before arrival and watered down to little more than a declaration. The official Soviet reaction was to adopt the usual line that the Poles were trying to put pressure on the Soviet Union. Yet behind closed doors, Chicherin understood that Zaleski's proposal was primarily directed against Germany, considering Poland's vulnerability following the Treaty of Locarno, and in his opinion, the Bolsheviks would have no choice but to agree if the League of Nations took it up. As he put it to Stalin, 'we cannot, on the one hand, declare that the promotion of universal peace is the basis of our politics, and on the other hand, refuse to join this formula'. More doubtful than others about a credible military threat to the Soviet Union, Chicherin was conscious of contradictions in the government's position being laid bare. 'It will be a very awkward situation if we say today that war is in preparation against the Soviet Union, and tomorrow, join with this [Polish proposal], which, in all likelihood, is inevitable.'[127]

Outside Zaleski's unexpected offer in Geneva, which contrary to Chicherin's prediction was roundly rejected, no progress was made in the renewed pact negotiations from the autumn. For NKID collegium members, Stomoniakov and Fedor Rotshtein, the Poles were playing for time once again and securing an American stabilization loan was at the forefront of their attentions. This was not totally off the mark, and Piłsudski was mindful not to encourage closer Franco-Soviet relations, a likely consequence of a Polish-Soviet pact.[128] Where the Baltic states and Finland fitted into any Soviet-Polish agreement was still no less a problem to resolve in the disagreement about a bilateral or multilateral pact. Resisting the latter, Chicherin delivered the same complaint to Zaleski in September about the prospect of Poland creating a 'closed front from the White to the Black sea'.[129] And although Chicherin and Litvinov had made their doubts clear about the nature of a military threat against the Soviet Union in party forums, the NKID collegium, on the whole, stayed closely to the party line, with the British government in the frame as urging Poland into war.[130] Indeed, in an assessment from October 1927, which Stomoniakov characterized as reflecting wider NKID opinion, the new Soviet plenipotentiary in Poland replacing Voikov, Aleksandr Bogomolov, stressed that the prospect of war would be the dominant issue in Soviet foreign policy for the coming two to three years, and repeated the assumption that 'war against the USSR in the west is unthinkable without Poland'. In tune with Stalin's theoretical pronouncements, Bogomolov explained how natural tensions and contradictions between capitalist powers were still hindering the formation of an extensive anti-Soviet bloc, meaning the 'inevitable collision' would be 'delayed for a rather long time'. Piłsudski was 'intensively preparing for war with us' and 'continues to dream of a "greater Federal Poland"', but for now, his immediate priorities were elsewhere. Piłsudski sought to delay war to give time to stabilize the Polish economy; improve relations with Germany; settle relations with Lithuania – by force or through voluntary union – and consolidate power at home. This was little different to how the Bolsheviks had presented Poland's aims since the end of the 1920 war. 'In general, one can summarize Piłsudski's policy towards the USSR as follows', Bogomolov detailed: 'strengthening military power and preparing for war against the USSR without setting a specific period, temporarily creating the appearance of normal relations with the USSR'.[131] Soviet policy towards Poland was effectively the mirror image. The NKID collegium believed that the pact negotiations were unlikely to succeed but continued with them regardless. In fact, opinion had swung back towards prioritizing a trading relationship with Poland as the potential damage to relations with Germany was deemed to outweigh the advantages of a Polish pact.[132] But the negotiations continued because these preserved the impression of stabilizing relations and were meant to ensure the Bolshevik side was not blamed for the predicted failure, when the anticipated war erupted. Just one year later, Stalin would throw all his efforts into rapidly strengthening Soviet military power preparing for this future certainty.

*

For the Soviet Union, there was no prospect of major war in 1927, in the year of the war scare. The Bolsheviks understood this, and outside of the crises of the spring and summer – and especially in the week following the Voikov murder when Stalin seemed to think that war was close at hand – the military threat was projected forwards to some unspecified time in the future. This did not alter the imperative of mobilizing the Soviet people around the inevitable war, and this was a core component of the war scare itself. Indeed, by the end of the year, at the fifteenth party congress in December, Stalin was going over familiar material and highlighting the inherent contradictions and competition between capitalist countries; increases in military spending abroad; the central role played by Britain in efforts to build an anti-Soviet alliance; and how the growing power of the Soviet Union made it more difficult to organize an attack.[133]

For Stalin's political rival, Trotsky, 1927 brought an end to his direct opposition to the party majority. But while Trotsky saw his and other oppositionists' expulsions from the party as endangering the Soviet Union, the party majority saw the exact opposite. Trotsky's conception of party unity meant 'above all maximum active participation by the entire mass of the party'.[134] The party majority saw this as unacceptable considering the international threats facing the Soviet Union. Even to allow more open discussion was viewed as potentially dangerous. Long-before his ascendancy to power, Stalin had in fact placed a higher premium on party unity than Lenin. Before the 1917 revolution, and for the sake of protecting the vulnerable foothold of Russian social democracy in the precarious conditions of late Imperial Russia, he had been willing to work with political opponents to avoid unnecessary division.[135] This changed, however, once the Bolsheviks were in power and found themselves in conditions of capitalist encirclement. In the 1920s, then, the nature of political participation in a dangerous international environment was the crux of the dispute and positions were irreconcilable. However, there was one crucial point of agreement. Trotsky fatally undermined his position by accepting the need for unity when war was on the horizon. In fact, the danger posed by the outside world had not been seriously disputed since 1917. The controversy was in how the party should respond and what exactly constituted 'unity'. And there was no chance that the party leadership would liberalize democratic practices when it judged the threat of war as acute. Trotsky did nothing to dispel this worldview.

A long-established interpretation of the 1927 war scare claims that Stalin did not believe in a military threat and was cynically manipulating a scare as a means of crushing the political opposition. The war scare was a useful tool for winning the succession struggle.[136] Other scholars have already questioned these assumptions, and as this book has shown so far, the Bolsheviks strongly believed in the prospect of future war and could even convince themselves of a shorter timeline.[137] The conclusion, therefore, should not be that the party majority used the war threat instrumentally to crush internal critics. That Stalin wanted Trotsky out of the way was no secret to anyone paying attention, but there was consensus in the party, opposition (and wider the population) that it would not be long until the Soviet Union was at war. If anything, Trotsky's unwavering endorsement of future war only further cemented an authoritarian response to the challenges posed the outside world and, with it, the maintenance of dictatorship.

Chapter 6

TRANSFORMATION, A PACT AND NEW ENEMY

In October 1928 Stalin launched the first five-year plan that would propel the rapid industrialization of the Soviet Union and shape the Soviet Union for decades to come. Even though the plan failed to meet its spiralling and utopian targets, when it was declared complete – ahead of schedule in 1932 – Soviet economic output had dramatically risen and especially in the sectors of heavy industry and defence. With subsequent plans set in motion in the 1930s, by 1940, industrial production had doubled from 1928 levels. Nearly the entire economy was brought under state control in the process.[1] The essential counterpart to industrialization was the collectivization of agriculture, formally begun in November 1929. This often-chaotic and brutal campaign ensured that grain deliveries to the cities and exports overseas were maintained, vital to sustaining levels of breakneck economic growth. Given justifiable resistance from the Soviet peasantry, the late 1920s saw the state once again rely on grain requisitions, but on a much wider scale, and these efforts soon encompassed the wholesale reorganization of agricultural lands under state control. Taken together, from 1928 Stalin forever transformed the Soviet Union and created the core components of the future Stalinist system, but not without sparking levels of popular unrest not seen since the years of the civil war.

There are several interrelated explanations for why Stalin turned to such a radical programme of industrial expansion in the late 1920s. First, a growing number of Bolsheviks, Stalin included, were quickly losing faith in the moderate New Economic Policy (NEP) and in its ability to deliver satisfactory levels of economic growth. Back in 1921 nearly all senior party members accepted Lenin's market-orientated economic programme, but under the surface the party never shed its fundamental ideological conviction that the building of socialism necessitated a large state-owned industry. Second, a series of poor harvests between 1927 and 1928 not only created immediate supply problems in the domestic market, risking supplies to the major cities, but it also sparked a collapse of grain exports vital for importing industrial goods and foreign technology. Further doubts about the viability of NEP grew, encouraging a mood in the party towards greater state control over the grain market to increase production. Third, the Bolsheviks judged the international situation as increasingly threatening in the late 1920s, providing a powerful motivation for expanding heavy and military industries.

The years of the supposed stabilization of capitalism were believed to be coming to an end, ushering in what the senior leadership anticipated as a fresh period of international crisis in the aftermath of the Wall Street Crash and amid the Great Depression. Rather than hindering the capitalist powers' ability to go to war, Stalin believed the economic downturn would only encourage conflicts over resources and territory.[2] Industrialization was his solution.

This chapter develops this final motivation to underline how the long-standing perceived military threat from Poland was a key force behind the crystalizing belief in Stalin's circle that industrialization and collectivization were essential to the survival of the Soviet Union in future war. As one scholar has pointed out, the significance of the 1927 war scare – during which possible war against Poland was a central concern – was in how this laid bare the Soviet Union's stark military and economic weaknesses, which would become more severe problems should the international situation suddenly worsen. This necessitated rapid improvements to economic and military power and a new relationship struck between the state and peasantry (which formed the bulk of the Red Army and, of course, produced essential food supplies). As a result, from 1928, the Stalinist regime led the country into a 'preparatory period for war'.[3] Moreover, as another scholar noted, while steps had been taken to improve Soviet defence capabilities before 1927, and Bolshevik priorities already turned towards creating a modern defence industry before that year, the war scare shaped the perception of future war from 'an ideological "inevitability" to looking like a "threatening reality"', even if the predicted cataclysmic conflict was projected still some way into the future.[4]

The 'Revolution from Above'

Before 1927 the Bolsheviks had no illusions about the serious deficiencies in Soviet industry and in their Red Army. The war scare, however, was a stark reminder of vulnerability at a time of international tension. At the height of the scare in May, the Politburo accepted a secret resolution on defence planning which highlighted significant weaknesses in technology and reserves, concluding that current resources were not sufficient for the defence of the country.[5] Such problems stretched into the following year, and between April and June 1928, a commission chaired by Voroshilov – whose mandate was to explore the future development of the Red Army – reported that the western theatre of war was looking increasingly unfavourable to the Soviet Union.[6] Meanwhile, according to military intelligence, the Soviet Union's enemies were, as ever, still coordinating in secret. Polish, Finnish, Estonian, Latvian and Romanian intelligence representatives were said to have gathered in Revel over the summer to agree joint actions against the Soviet Union and exchange intelligence.[7]

From the countries bordering the Soviet Union, Poland was still in prime position as the most significant danger, and Soviet-Polish relations remained in a poor state at the outset of 1928. Negotiations for a non-aggression pact were going nowhere because of persisting disagreements about its structure; Poland's responsibilities to the League of Nations were another stubborn point; and the Soviet Union's long-standing and dismissive attitude towards international arbitration did not help either. That the Bolsheviks, in Polish foreign minister Zaleski's words, 'always and in everything see the hand of the organizers of a fantastic international anti-Soviet conspiracy' was no less true in late 1920s.[8] NKID assessments of Soviet-Polish affairs in early 1928 displayed a strong sense of uncertainty about the future and characterized Poland as an unpredictable and increasingly militaristic power. For instance, amid Piłsudski's campaign for upcoming legislative elections, Stomoniakov believed he might order an assault on Lithuania as 'a major trump card' in order to renew his credentials as a strong leader (this was an NKID line of thinking going at least into 1930).[9] Soviet representative in Poland, Bogomolov, described similarly how Polish military preparations were progressing with high intensity but, in his view, revealed greater ambitions going beyond attacking Lithuania. Piłsudski, in Bogomolov's account, was like a 'temperamental child' playing games with soldiers and an unexpected attack on the Soviet Union was a real possibility. To lower the risk, Bogomolov advised maintaining the strategy that had re-emerged at the tail end of the war scare: namely to improve economic relations. Polish imports and exports made up little more than 2 per cent of wider Polish trade in each case. Unquestionably, this was a low base to build upon, but given the divides Bogomolov believed were emerging in Polish politics, between militarists around Piłsudski and business circles around August Zaleski, he hoped that stronger trade connections would encourage political stabilization.[10]

Bogomolov's suggestion for closer economic cooperation aligned with the mood in Moscow. As it turned out, improving trade unexpectedly became a rising priority in early 1928 because, in a measure chiefly directed at Germany, the Polish government from February planned to apply 100 per cent customs tariffs to countries where no trade agreements existed. While not the direct target, the Soviet Union faced the prospect of even worse trading conditions. NKID officials now found themselves thrown into preliminary talks with the Poles to arrange a framework for a new round of trade negotiations. Securing even an initial exchange of notes was enough to avoid the tariffs. The negotiations, however, were slow and halting, starting badly when the Polish delegation suddenly departed from Moscow following confusion about their location and terms (the Bolsheviks insisted on Moscow for the talks given their state monopoly on foreign trade). And the military collegium's sentencing of a Polish catholic priest, Teofil Skałki, to ten years' imprisonment on groundless charges of espionage at the same moment was unfortunately timed. Despite NKID denials, the Poles were certain that the trial had been purposely scheduled to embarrass them. What it also did was hand the Polish envoy, Patek, a means of slowing the pace further. Unlike his boss Zaleski, Patek was less committed to signing a trade agreement and was happy enough in using the negotiations as a way of pressuring Germany and for Poland to accrue benefit from a positive international reaction from simply entering them.[11] The talks failed to gain momentum going into 1929.

Inside the NKID, suspicions abounded from the beginning that the Polish government had more of an eye towards using the trade negotiations to benefit its domestic election campaign. With justification, some Soviet officials were quick to blame Patek for the slow progress, and when information then came through in March, suggesting that Piłsudski was considering replacing Zaleski with Patek as head of the foreign ministry, this was interpreted as likely only worsening the marshal's impulsive instincts. The NKID saw Zaleski as a restraining force whereas Patek's mooted promotion was interpreted as evidence of a rising military danger (that Patek stressed to Soviet officials that a Polish attack was out of the question made no difference).[12] Working in the other direction and in line with often-mixed assessments of Poland as a security threat, the NKID at the same time saw Piłsudski's increasingly poor health, which had forced him to step away from government and later resign as prime minster in June, to their advantage.[13] Intelligence that the Polish government was seeking another larger American loan also suggested that it might try to stabilize relations to achieve this end. Despite these glimmers of hope, however, the dominant picture held by the party elite in 1928 remained Poland as a credible military threat and it had been discussed this way in the Politburo in April.[14] Relations then soured again one month later in May when an attempt was made on the life of the Soviet trade official in Poland, A. S. Lizarev. The bitter arguments of 1927 following the Voikov murder came rushing back. The NKID accused the Polish government of showing weak commitment to stamping out White émigré terrorism (the culprit, a certain Iurii Voitsekhovskii, was said to belong to émigré monarchist organizations).[15] For much of this time, the Bolsheviks saw little scope of agreeing a trade agreement, let alone a non-aggression pact.

None of this meant, however, that the regime saw poor relations developing into war any time soon. By the turn of 1928, it was several months gone since the height of the war scare. And even during that year, Stalin worried about an imminent invasion only fleetingly. One year on, Soviet military intelligence expressed some confidence that, despite the forces assembled against the Soviet Union, the combined military strength of Poland, Romania and the Baltic states, even with British and French support, would not necessarily guarantee victory. War was a risk for their enemies and superiority over the Red Army was, at this stage, uncertain.[16] Likewise in his 1928 major strategic study, *Future War*, Tukhachevskii highlighted the high costs of an attack on the Soviet Union, for both Poland and backers in the west (though war was not explicitly ruled out here).[17] In this climate, therefore, exaggerated predictions of imminent war were typically rejected, as they had been when Stalin was finishing off the United Opposition just months before. When Bogomolov wrote to the NKID collegium to warn that a possible Polish and Romanian attack might come in the autumn, for instance, Stomoniakov expressed doubts immediately.[18] For him, Poland faced challenging international pressures and growing German influence with the western powers, but this did not mean it would choose war as a way out. In fact, Stomoniakov pointed out that when Poland had faced deteriorating relations with the west before, this had prompted its government to seek better relations with the Soviet Union. Still, he conceded that the international situation looked different in 1928 and rumours of capital flight from Poland suggested the Polish middle classes at least potentially anticipated something.[19]

In a similar vein, the Bolsheviks were as convinced in 1928 as they had been in 1920 that Poland would not go to war independently. A Polish attack on the Soviet Union was still deemed almost inconceivable without the backing and direction of a powerful western capitalist ally. And in the Bolsheviks' hierarchy of international dangers, Britain was no less in the frame in 1928 as the anti-Soviet force standing behind Poland. For this reason, Bogomolov's other suggestion to the collegium that France was trying to engineer war between Poland and the Soviet Union was met with immediate pushback as 'completely unfounded'. Bogomolov claimed to see rising French support for military action due to uncertain outcomes of upcoming elections and the strengthening French workers' movement. In other potentially worrying signs, French Marshal Louis Franchet d'Esperey visited Poland in November 1927 and met with Piłsudski, presenting him with the high military honour, the *Medaille Militaire*. In Bogomolov's opinion, secret preparations for a new military union were taking place. He also attached importance to reports of a banquet held in the French embassy where the French ambassador to Poland, Jules Laroche, gave a toast to Piłsudski as 'the victorious leader of the 1920 war'. The toast aside, the reality of France's position was almost the total opposite. Franchet d'Esperey travelled to Poland not to strengthen military ties, but to weaken French obligations from the 1921 Franco-Polish alliance.[20]

At another time, Bogomolov's reports about French hostility would have sent alarms bells ringing throughout the NKID. But in a testament to how France was now established as a lower order danger in early 1928, Stomoniakov saw little cause for concern. As he explained in reply, even if French politics moved further to the right, orchestrating war would be prohibitively expensive for the French government and risked damaging its relations with Germany. 'Over the past two years we have had a lot of evidence of the peaceful influence of France on Poland in relation to us, and not for war with us.'[21] Since 1927, the NKID had attempted to improve relations with France by offering to find a settlement to outstanding tsarist debts and agree a non-aggression pact. Little was achieved, and the mood worsened noticeably when the Soviet ambassador to France, Kristian Rakovskii, was declared *persona non grata* in October 1927 (Rakovskii had faced mounting pressure from a French press campaign centred on his signature of a Trotskyist document calling for the working classes of capitalist countries to overthrow their governments in wartime).[22] Even so, it was Britain, not France, that was believed to be the pre eminent danger in 1928, and one with a powerful hold over Poland. As Chicherin put it in conversation with the King of Afghanistan, Amānullāh Khān, in early May: 'whether England is preparing a war for us, we shall see later. England is always striving to push others instead of itself into military actions against us. She could push Poland against us.'[23]

As to where the future war would come, Soviet Ukraine was once more creeping up the security agenda. Taking cues from a vocal campaign in the Polish press, in May 1928 the NKID suggested that the Polish government was working towards declaring western Ukraine an independent republic to incorporate in federation with Poland in the future. Apparently, this would be the first stage in advance of war, a plan with influential supporters like the arch-imperialist Winston Churchill. According to the NKID, only Piłsudski's ill-heath cast doubt on the strategy coming to fruition.[24] Still, the danger to Ukraine resonated in Bolshevik circles over the summer. One month later, Bogomolov noted: 'If Poland decides on military adventure against us, it will be carried out under the slogan of "freedom" for Ukraine, and for this, she must first create and strengthen her Ukrainian rear in western Ukraine.'[25] Other institutions, like the OGPU, shared these concerns and in a report sent to the senior party leadership in August, its foreign department described how Piłsudski's was seeking to seize Ukraine and that an attack on its Right-bank was in preparation. To avoid repeating their errors of the 1920 war when the Red Army managed to regroup and launch a successful counterattack in early summer, the new Polish strategy apparently sought to maintain pressure by deploying the Romanian Army towards Odessa; a UNR uprising, funded by the British, who the OGPU claimed had given Piłsudski £100,000 in 1927 for these purposes, would be another point of pressure. Apparently, the plan might be set into action in early 1929.[26] This, of course, was nothing but fantasy, and information about Piłsudski's deteriorating health or his priorities in domestic consolidation and handling yet another political crisis did little to dent it. A few months later in October, the OGPU reported again that Ukrainian nationalists, former supporters of Petliura in particular, planned to turn Soviet Ukraine into a bridgehead for a 'future imperialist campaign'.[27] As had been true in 1920, Ukraine was judged the vulnerable point on the Soviet Union's western border.

The picture so far described was the context in which Stalin's mind turned towards significantly building up the Soviet Union's military power and reserves as quickly as possible. In a speech to the July 1928 plenum of the central committee, a time when discussions of the upcoming war were commonplace, Stalin delivered a stark warning against complacency. The Soviet economy would struggle to supply the Red Army in a major conflict. He argued that without guaranteed grain reserves, the country faced war not only from without, but also from within, due to likely widespread disorder and resistance from the Soviet peasantry as the state sought to secure its supply once war began:

> First, we are not guaranteed against military attack. Do you think it is possible to defend the country, not having any reserves of bread for the army? [...] Can we, in the event of an attack by our enemies, carry out a war with the Poles at the front and with men in the rear for the sake of getting an emergency supply of bread for the army? No, we cannot and should not. To defend the country, we must have known reserves to supply the army, at least for the first six months.[28]

This was not the first time a member of the party elite had warned about self-sufficiency. Months earlier in March, Voroshilov described to a military audience how hostile powers were deploying new methods to pressure the Soviet Union, including economic blockade. And as the 1928 harvest proved to be poor yet again, it is hardly surprising that the leadership started to think more seriously about grain resources.[29] At this same time, in early 1928, Stalin spent two weeks in Siberia to see first-hand the circumstances on the ground in grain-growing regions. He came away convinced that kulaks, the supposedly richer peasants, were deliberately withholding grain from the market and should be blamed for the crisis. Over the first six months of 1928, therefore, the interlinked dangers of future war – primarily foreseen against Poland backed by Britain – and declining agricultural yields made worse through 'kulak sabotage', concentrated the minds of Stalin and other senior Bolsheviks towards pushing through grain requisitions that would eventually lead to the wholesale collectivization and state control of the grain supply. Bread rationing and a dramatic ratcheting up of persecution and arrest of any person accused of hoarding soon followed. Just a few years later, millions had suffered intense hardship, mass starvation and imprisonment in a newly formed mass prison camp network. Yet Stalin was convinced that without tight state control of agriculture, whatever the consequences for the Soviet people, the ambitions of the first five-year plan would fall dangerously short. Heavy and defence industries would not be adequately prepared for the inevitable future war. Industrialization was widely accepted as vital for creating the basis of socialist society, but the defence imperative ran throughout. Later in April 1929, for instance, on the cusp of the roll-out of collectivization, the Defence Sector of Gosplan (the State Planning Committee) affirmed one of its key priorities: that the socialization of agriculture was a 'major factor of importance for defence'. State control, it said, was 'especially important' in wartime and so were 'the existence of large production units, which are more easily subject to planned influence than many millions of small, scattered farms'.[30] To the central committee in November 1929, Molotov, then, once more, underlined the close connection to future military invasion: 'We still have November, December, January, February, and March, four and a half months in which, if the imperialists do not attack us head-on, we can make a decisive breakthrough in the economy and in collectivization.'[31] Stalin was forging ahead with his forced solution to the Soviet Union's perceived security dilemma, proving disastrous for swathes of the Soviet population.

Political resistance to Stalin's transformative policies went nowhere, with the dictator's power increasingly assured by the late 1920s. The only real challenge came from a loose political grouping which Stalin labelled the 'Right Deviation', of Nikolai Bukharin, Aleksei Rykov and Mikhail Tomskii, who argued for a gradual economic transformation staying within NEP limits. NEP had rejuvenated some economic growth by 1928, nearly reaching levels seen before the First World War, but for Stalin this was nowhere near enough. Under pressure, the Right Deviation was easily quashed, and all three men removed from the Politburo. Bukharin and Tomskii were demoted in 1929, losing positions as editor of *Pravda* and leader of the trades union movement, respectively (Rykov clung on as head of the Soviet government). Like others who positioned themselves against the party line, the three later recanted their political 'errors' as a route back into the party fold, though each later lost their lives in the Great Terror.

As was true when Trotsky was in opposition, the atmosphere of the late 1920s left little room for dissent. Stalin, for sure, was forever tightening the screws on dissenters but the widely accepted threat of inevitable war hardly created an environment receptive to a gradual path to industrialization and socialism, even if some uncertainty lingered in Stalin's own circle about the sudden shift from NEP.[32] At the outset of the five-year plan, the very same military threats were being analysed. Inside the NKID in October 1928, for example, Stomoniakov stressed to Bogomolov the importance of exposing Poland's hostile designs and that intelligence showed the country was 'systematically preparing for war, both technically and politically'.[33] Bogomolov, however, evidently having travelled the same road as Chicherin and Litvinov, had now swung in the other direction and he was convinced (rightly) that the Polish government saw internal affairs as the priority and that it was seeking further foreign financial assistance, both keeping militarism in check.[34] But for Stomoniakov, this was the height of naivety. 'The Piłudskiites staging a "thaw" in Polish-Soviet relations are not only trying to fool us', he replied, 'but they want to encourage us to take the initiative in the staged "improvement" of these relations, designed to calm the creditors of Poland abroad and for the strengthening of its international situation'.[35] Similar heightened suspicion was on display in these months. When Piłsudski visited Romania for six weeks in September and October, Soviet military intelligence claimed this was for the inspection of the country's armed forces for widening the scope of the Polish-Romania military convention and included discussion of a united command in the event of war. The NKID did not disagree. Yet the simpler explanation was more likely: rather than conspiring with Romania, Piłsudski travelled to its warmer climate to recuperate following a minor stroke earlier in the year, a trip he would repeat in the future as his health declined.[36]

In the weeks after the launch of the five-year plan, another noticeable trend in Soviet assessments of the ever-changing global conspiracy was the framing of France as a dangerous supporter of a future Polish offensive. As we have seen, there had been doubts in the NKID collegium about whether the country represented much of a danger any longer, but this attitude clearly did not extend to other influential Soviet officials. At a plenum of the central committee in November 1928, Iosif Unshlikht, Deputy Commissar of Military and Naval Affairs (who had a long history in intelligence), spoke in detail about rising French aggression. He remarked on visits by French generals to Poland, Romania and the Baltic states, and Unshlikht claimed the purpose here was to unite 'separate states against the USSR, distributing functions between them, achieving unity of operational actions of the Polish and Romania armies under direct supervision and leadership of the French general staff'. The truth was, however, that ties between France and Poland were weakening at this very moment, not becoming stronger. The shifting French position towards Germany after the Treaty of Locarno only weakened the 1921 alliance.[37]

Unshlikht made the danger from Britain equally clear at the plenum. Reflecting the heightened security concerns about the western borders and drawing on long-standing assumptions, he claimed that the British chargé d'affaires in Poland, Rex Leeper, advocated for a federation of Ukraine and Poland. The British ambassador in Finland, Ernest Rennie apparently wanted the same. New anti-

Soviet formations were said to be appearing in Ukraine, funded by the British. Yet in contrast to some opinion coming out of the military and intelligence earlier in the year, Unshlikht assessed the Soviet Union's likely foes to have potentially stronger combined military power. This perhaps reflected the fact that the five-year plan was now in operation and there was a greater imperative to justify the radical shift in policy – and future sacrifices – to the party.[38] However, the same shifting power dynamic between the Soviet Union and its opponents was reported in intelligence in private. Outside the public eye, the counterintelligence department of the OGPU estimated one month later that a combination of Polish, Romanian and Ukrainian troops would reach around 2 million soldiers. This was not judged enough to topple Soviet power, but a simultaneous attack from Japan in the east would create serious problems for the supply of the Red Army.[39] And as the 1920s turned into the 1930s, the prospect of future war, but on two fronts, looked ever likely.

Towards a non-aggression pact

While Stalin and the party elite scrutinized worsening forecasts about future war and prepared the ground for the launch of the first five-year plan, political leaders from France, Germany and the United States gathered in Paris in August 1928 for an initiative of an entirely different kind. On 27 August 1928, the Kellogg-Briand pact was signed, named after United States secretary of state, Frank Kellogg, and French foreign minister, Aristide Briand. Designed to outlaw war as a tool of foreign policy, the treaty gathered more signatories in coming months, such was initial optimism behind this new peace initiative, even though it lacked mechanisms for punishing aggressor states. The Soviet Union acceded to the treaty in September in a departure from its traditional position of shunning multilateral agreements, but the Bolsheviks were cautious of the pact from the beginning, suspecting it would provide cover for foreign aggression.

Still, the Bolsheviks signed the Kellogg-Briand pact because it offered certain opportunities. First, even though a multilateral pact, its aspiration to guarantee international peace aligned with their priority of delaying war in the short term. The NKID latched on to weak points in the pact for sure, such as the missing provision for complete disarmament (and the Bolsheviks took offense at not being one of the original signatories), but there was plenty of scope for their own peace propaganda around the pact.[40] Second, and more importantly, Soviet diplomats took advantage of the long delay to ratification of the Kellogg-Briand pact to pressure Poland to sign a non-aggression pact by other means. At the end of December 1928, they presented Poland with the so-called Litvinov protocol, which would put the Kellogg-Briand pact immediately into effect between the Soviet Union, Poland and Lithuania, simultaneously undermining the long-standing Polish position of negotiating collectively.[41] This was, in short, an attempt to bounce Poland into something resembling a non-aggression agreement of Soviet design. Because if the Polish government refused, it risked being seen as spurning the chance of a peace settlement and one in line with the international mood gathering behind the Kellogg-Briand pact (which Poland had signed). The Poles knew that the Bolsheviks, who hardly kept their intentions secret, were exploiting the situation.[42] Speaking in Moscow, Voroshilov remarked that the Kellogg-Briand pact provided opportunity not only to combat foreign anti-Soviet propaganda but to pressure 'our aggressive neighbour – Poland – to ratify it immediately'. With Poland 'forced' to sign the pact, the Soviet Union would apparently be safe from war for another year.[43]

Given that other major powers were signing up to the Kellogg-Briand pact, as the Bolsheviks anticipated, the Polish government did not dismiss the Litvinov protocol outright; but after several weeks of silence, in January 1929, it sought to widen its scope and bring Latvia, Estonia and Romania on board as other signatory powers (something also anticipated in the NKID).[44] In doing so, the Poles believed they could use the Litvinov protocol for their own ends to pressure Germany and fulfil the strategic ambition of creating a collective security agreement, something resembling an 'Eastern Locarno', by other means. Like the Bolsheviks, the Polish government, and Piłsudski included, doubted the Kellogg-Briand pact would forestall a future Soviet-Polish conflict in the long run, and therefore trying to bend the Litvinov protocol to their advantage was an obvious strategy. And boxed in by their offer of the Litvinov protocol in the first place but determined to secure an agreement of some kind, the Bolsheviks accepted the proposal and the inclusion of Romania, Latvia and Estonia as other signatories.[45] This compromise was another shift away from earlier refusals to entertain a multilateral non-aggression pact and an instinctive distrust of international treaties. The Litvinov protocol was then signed on 9 February 1929 in Moscow, with Lithuania, Persia and Turkey also joining separately in April. This was first substantive international agreement signed between Poland and the Soviet Union.[46]

Agreeing to the Polish amendments to the Litvinov protocol, in part, reflected a certain urgency in Moscow towards doing more to support and improve the Soviet Union's security situation, but this was far from tangible progress. Being able to exploit a public image of the Soviet Union as a peace-making power was really the core benefit. Indeed, both sides privately doubted the long-term effectiveness of their new agreement. Certainly, in Moscow, there were immediate questions about its implications. This was not the bilateral non-aggression pact with Poland the NKID had sought; effectively it had put in place an international agreement of the type the Bolsheviks openly criticized. Tellingly, in March, Stalin asked Chicherin for his opinion of the 'pros (and cons)' of the protocol. With his health deteriorating and often absent from the NKID, by this point Chicherin had *de facto* been replaced as head of the foreign ministry by his rival Litvinov, personal relations with whom he described elsewhere to Voroshilov as 'white-hot'. Knowing he was on the way out, Chicherin made his misgivings to Stalin clear and told him the NKID had gone too far with the Litvinov protocol. It should have been used simply as a 'pacifist demonstration' to counterbalance the rumours of Soviet military plans, he argued. The NKID had done the very thing it had sought to avoid for years. 'We created and recognized the Polish-Baltic united front, Polish hegemony in the Baltics with our own hands.'[47]

Chicherin was right to question where exactly signing the Litvinov protocol and Kellogg-Briand pact left the Soviet Union. Even though Poland was also a signatory to both, Soviet assessments of future war were not noticeably scaled back (suggesting again that short-term gains in propaganda was the priority). In the NKID, Stomoniakov made his lack of confidence plain in a message to Bogomolov in March 1929. As well as criticizing the latter's belief in the transformative power of trade negotiations, Stomoniakov noted:

> [W]e have said many times that neither the Kellogg pact nor any aggression pact can prevent a state from launching war if it wants to. If the Kellogg pact will not stop Poland from going to war against us, do you really think that it will be stopped by your proposal to begin negotiations on a trade agreement or even by negotiations already begun?[48]

According to Soviet military intelligence, in a report drawn up the same month the Litvinov protocol was agreed, the British were collaborating with countries on the Soviet western border and Poland still harboured ambitions for Ukraine to be brought into a Polish protectorate. Following the usual line, because the necessary anti-Soviet bloc had apparently not yet formed, a large-scale war was still some time away (though military intelligence suggested that Britain might claim a Bolshevik infringement of the Kellogg-Briand pact as a pretext for declaring war). When the war did arrive, however, military intelligence predicted this would be even more extensive than both the 1920 Soviet-Polish war and Russia's engagement in the First World War.[49] Similar analysis was drawn up inside the foreign department of the OGPU, which spoke about the new peace agreements in terms of their future failure. In its opinion, the Kellogg-Briand pact and Litvinov protocol were convenient pretexts for allowing Poland and Romania to reactivate 'in a new form the old Polish plan' of creating an anti-Soviet bloc in the Baltic region. When the pact and protocol failed to maintain peace, and if the Soviet Union was deemed responsible, a ready-made alliance would exist, operating on the principle of collective security.[50] This was a worrying outcome for the balance of power. Later in May 1929, and in starker comments than most, the OGPU's foreign department assessed Poland as having more freedom of action against the Soviet Union in the east than against Germany in the west, creating a greater degree of unpredictability for war.[51]

*

What changed Soviet calculations about the future war more than the Kellogg-Briand pact or Litvinov protocol, at least temporarily from the second half of 1929, was the election of a minority British Labour government in May, with Ramsey Macdonald returned to power. Although the government proved short-lived, falling in August 1931 on the formation of the First National Government, as had been true back in 1924, Soviet officials saw scope for the improvement of the Soviet Union's international circumstances. Diplomatic relations between the Soviet Union and Britain were restored at the end of 1929, including full ambassadorial representation; a trade agreement followed in 1930. Even so, sponsorship of revolutionary activity in the east of the British empire continued to stoke controversy.[52] But the NKID placed most significance on the barriers now hindering military action. Considering how deeply connected Britain and Poland were believed to be, inside the NKID, Bogomolov predicted that the election of the new Labour government would make Polish military action 'extraordinarily risky'. As he put it: 'with a coming to power of a workers' party in England, the value of Poland as an anti-Soviet factor (of course, only in the short term) has significantly lessened [...] [Poland] cannot allow itself the luxury of any kind of serious conflict with us'.[53] The NKID collegium had openly disagreed with Bogomolov on several points in past years, from the importance of trade negotiations to the imminence of war, but it agreed with this assessment. Due to shifts in the international balance of power and the fall of the British Conservative government, the NKID saw scope to ease the tense atmosphere and called for restrained tones towards Poland.[54]

The election of a British Labour government did nothing, however, to alter the momentum behind the first five-year plan (in fact, as one historian points out, it seemed like a stamp of approval).[55] Given how transitory gains in the west tended to be, increasing the defence capabilities of the Soviet Union remained no less a priority. Indeed, with the plan forging ahead, in mid-July 1929, the Politburo adopted a new decree on Soviet defence that underlined the still-weak state of Soviet armed forces. Lagging behind other foreign powers, the Red Army lacked sufficient provision for mobilization and reserves. Military industry – but also wider Soviet industry – was not up to the challenge of meeting the needs of an armed front either. The state of the Red Army's artillery was woeful and little better than before the First World War. The Politburo called for a significant qualitative and quantitative increase in defence capability.[56] While building such capacity takes time, by the end of the year, criticisms were still being aired. In December 1929, Valerian Kuibyshev, Chairman of the Supreme Council of the National Economy, delivered another reminder about the poor state of Soviet defences and pointed to inadequate mobilization plans. Later in the month, the Politburo approved a reorganization of war industries and replenishment of them with fresh expertise. It pointed to other weaknesses in the production of guns and artillery in early 1930.[57]

Following the established yearly pattern, at the end of 1929 predictions about the outbreak of war in the coming spring featured again in Soviet intelligence. The election of a British Labour government had certainly softened the broader picture for some, but this was chiefly true in the NKID rather than in military intelligence or the OGPU. Notably, reports that 'fascists' in Poland were seeking war against the Soviet Union were printed in the Soviet press, in *Izvestiia*, at the end of 1929.[58] Other trends, to an extent, counteracted the gains made in Britain. The Soviet dumping of grain in international markets to fuel industrialization at home, driving down already depressed world grain prices in the wake of the Wall Street Crash, worsened relations with France, which now put trade restrictions in place.[59] Neither Soviet intelligence nor the OGPU's foreign department was convinced the international situation was improving, and they sketched out a familiar picture of threat as the year ended. In October 1929, for instance, from its sources in Turkey, military intelligence described how the country's general staff apparently believed war between the Soviet Union and Poland would erupt at the beginning of 1930. According to this information, Poland was 'seriously preparing for war' and was lobbying Germany to allow the passage of French war materiel and troops (the OGPU also pinpointed transit through Germany as crucial for war, but noted this required unpopular territorial concessions from Poland).[60] Britain, despite its more amendable minority Labour government, according to the Turkish general staff report, was trying to obtain Turkey's neutrality and a free passage for the Royal Navy through the Dardanelles, or Turkish action in the war itself in exchange for new territories. When Stalin read this frankly outlandish report, he seems to have taken some elements seriously, underlining the following with his red pencil: 'Poland is seriously preparing for war […] among the military attaches in Moscow rumours are circulating about a coming war.'[61]

With reports of future war coming through to the leadership and the impact of the Litvinov protocol difficult to detect, on 18 March 1930 the Soviet government restated its goal of signing a bilateral Soviet-Polish non-aggression pact in the pages of *Izvestiia*. The atmosphere was not exactly conducive to new negotiations, however, with parts of the Polish press carrying articles calling for preventative war against the Soviet Union. This sparked sufficient alarm in Moscow that Zaleski eventually issued public denial that Poland was planning such a step.[62] It did not help either that the NKID was convinced that the government of new Polish prime minister, Walery Sławek, was the 'most dangerous of all the governments that have ruled Poland over the last four years of the Piłsudski regime'. Still, the NKID was evidently serious about striking a pact but as Stomoniakov stressed to the newly installed Soviet representative in Warsaw, Vladimir Antonov-Ovseenko, it was important not to give the Poles the impression that this was prompted by alarm in Moscow.[63] What the NKID underestimated, however, was that Piłsudski, doubtful of the reliability of French support in the future and concerned about a confident revisionist Germany, was in fact entertaining a Soviet-Polish pact more than ever before.[64]

In a clear signal that concerns about war were significantly building at the top echelon of the party in 1930, at the outset of the year Stalin ordered Tukhachevskii, then commander of the Leningrad military district, to draft a plan for a future war against Poland.[65] And in a sign of growing caution, the Politburo ordered that relations with Poland should not be needlessly worsened, despite the hostility of some sections of the Polish press.[66] It also ordered the OGPU's foreign department to concentrate intelligence gathering on Britain, France, Germany, Poland, Romania, other states on the borders and Japan to uncover more intelligence about 'interventionist plans'. It is noteworthy that despite French support of Poland's security steadily evaporating, the country remained in the frame in this list of opponents as a key force behind an anti-Soviet campaign.[67]

In this febrile atmosphere, the Polish general staff began to plan for war on the basis that the Soviet Union was a more imminent threat than Germany.[68] Still, Polish-German relations remained tense in early 1930, nevertheless. A new commercial agreement from March ended the long-running tariff war, yet the Reichstag failed to ratify it until the following year after pressure from German domestic agrarian interests.[69] In the context of the rising popularity of the National Socialist German Workers' Party, moreover, German politicians from various political wings now called more stridently in the second half of 1930 for the revision of Poland's territory to German advantage, amid growing anti-Polish sentiment and backlash against the treatment of German minorities in disputed territories like Polish Silesia.[70]

The Bolsheviks continued to scrutinize this ebb and flow of Polish-German relations for strategic advantage, but the weakening of their ties with Germany and its continued *rapprochement* with the west remained troubling in Moscow. There were some signs of improvement in Soviet-German ties, for sure. January 1929 saw a Soviet-German conciliation treaty and new German government-backed credits were extended to the Soviet Union one year later.[71] This was economic collaboration, however, while the Rapallo alliance faded away.[72] By the late 1920s German foreign minister Stresemann already believed negotiations with the west was the best path towards securing a border revision with Poland. His death in October 1929, nevertheless, was still a blow to Rapallo. Count Brockdorff-Rantzau, long-time advocate of a strong Soviet-German partnership, had died the year before in September. And once Poland and the Soviet Union signed the Litvinov protocol, Soviet-German relations further soured, despite Litvinov's reassurances that the Bolsheviks had not given Poland concrete territorial guarantees. Then in the same year, another American-brokered process agreed a new settlement for German reparation payments. The so-called Young Plan, which Germany accepted in exchange for the Allied evacuation of the Rhineland (further evidence of its inexorable drift to the west) put Franco-German relations on surer footing. As Litvinov, officially Chicherin's successor from July 1930, told the new German ambassador to the Soviet Union Herbert von Dirksen in February 1931, 'the end of Rapallo' had been reached.[73] It was true that April 1931 saw a new Soviet-German trade agreement that increased imports of German goods and the Treaty of Berlin was extended in June (though on a more limited basis). But this merely slowed the ongoing weakening Soviet-German partnership, itself further damaged by the political polarization in Germany of the early 1930s.[74] As ever, all this had implications for the Soviet perception of the Polish threat. Germany had lost even more value as a counterweight and Soviet officials in NKID and Soviet military intelligence, as we know, had been speculating for some time about the prospect of French troops transiting through Germany in future Soviet-Polish war.

In another familiar trend, unexpected events like the Voikov murder of 1927 intervened at the worst possible moments. On 26 April 1930, a bomb was discovered in the chimney of the Soviet Legation in Warsaw, sparking another controversy. Although the device had little power, in the tense climate of 1930 and just weeks after the peak of a major crisis in the collectivization drive, the Bolsheviks were even less inclined to accept that the Poles had peaceful intentions. The NKID pointed to White émigré terrorists as having left the device, but Stomoniakov suspected participation from Piłsudski's circle. In a message to Stalin he claimed the incident had been designed to aggravate relations to the point of war (to

Antonov-Ovseenko in Warsaw he labelled it a 'satanic plan' and highlighted once more a need to draw attention to Piłsudski's 'systematic preparations for war').[75] The Politburo followed this line and framed the incident as evidence of a growing anti-Soviet campaign in Poland, another link in the chain of hostile actions going back to the Voikov murder, designed for 'provoking conflict between the Soviet Union and Poland'.[76] The Soviet note delivered to the Polish government, underlined these same claims, although it did not repeat old calls for the expulsion of White émigrés. Stomoniakov had learnt his lesson, noting to others that this was a pointless demand bringing only long negotiations and complications. He wanted the Bolsheviks' complaints channelled to the wider public instead, to demonstrate that Polish provocations were a threat to world peace.[77] When one month passed by without a response from the Polish government to the attempted bombing, Stomoniakov wrote again to Stalin to complain that the Poles were not taking an investigation seriously and that Piłsudski, who claimed the bomb in the legation was planted by the OGPU, was likely preparing yet another provocation. The NKID resolved to send a further note pointing to 'unacceptable attacks' in its press and the 'silence from Polish authorities' following the legation incident. The perpetrators, who 'sought to provoke conflict between Poland and the Soviet Union' had to be identified.[78]

Away from the NKID collegium, in Warsaw Antonov-Ovseenko reported a picture going against the grain. In messages to Moscow, he described that the Sławek government was not in fact looking to aggravate relations and was open to negotiating a non-aggression pact and trade agreement. The Bolsheviks should, he said, seize the initiative.[79] In a typical exchange, Stomoniakov rejected Antonov-Ovseenko's optimism as 'completely paradoxical' considering recent events. Poland's political system was fundamentally anti-Soviet with 'economic roots of aggression in Polish heavy industry and financial capital', still supportive of Piłsudski's federalist programme. With views indicative of the wider collegium, Stomoniakov was entirely dismissive of Polish goodwill towards any kind of pact or agreement and continued to speculate that the culprits behind the attempted bombing of the Soviet legation exercised influence on the Polish government. He even saw scope for a potential 'revolutionary situation' in Poland given the tensions he perceived within the Piłsudski camp when combined with the country's substantial economic woes during the Great Depression.[80] Nevertheless, Antonov-Ovseenko continued to push for diplomacy, and particularly following the Polish elections later in the year in November that saw Piłsudski increase his control over the Sejm. He was keen to stress that the Polish government was prioritizing combatting new German revisionism which created some space for Soviet-Polish *rapprochement*. Antonov-Ovseenko had gained a reputation as an optimist, no doubt, but by the end of 1930, even Stomoniakov was coming around to supporting trade negotiations that he had earlier been so scornful. The mounting dual crisis of 1930 was most likely the galvanizing factor. As he now put it, motivating influential Polish business circles to support a trade agreement was a way to 'seriously oppose the well-known interventionist plans' of the Sławek government.[81]

While the NKID collegium debated how to handle Poland, wider Soviet security concerns about the consolidation of an anti-Soviet alliance remained acute as ever. In a letter to Molotov from September 1930, Stalin again revealed the extent of his worries about coalitions building against the Soviet Union. Soviet intelligence reported already in early summer about discussions between France and Poland held in Warsaw on mobilization measures, with Romanian involvement.[82] And to Molotov a few months later, Stalin detailed the widespread Soviet theory that Poland was putting together an alliance with the Baltic states, and this threatened Leningrad and Right-bank Ukraine. In response, Soviet military reserves had to be increased by another '40-50 divisions', Stalin argued, and 'considerable funds' set aside to ensure victory (he suggested such funds could be found in increased vodka production).[83]

One month later, in October 1930, and referring to interrogation transcripts from an investigation into the so-called Industrial Party – a group of Soviet industry specialists unjustly accused of carrying out espionage and sabotage – Stalin questioned OGPU head, Viacheslav Menzhinskii, about why the much-anticipated foreign intervention had not yet occurred. Indeed, the timing of such an intervention had featured in the very testimony of one engineer from the Industrial Party investigation, a certain Professor Leonid Ramzin (whose confession was undoubtedly forced). Stalin demanded that this be elaborated into a line of questioning in future interrogations to find out why intervention in 1930 had been postponed. He had his own ideas already and speculated that neither Poland nor Romania was ready to attack. But with more information from the Industrial Party investigation, Stalin believed a propaganda campaign run through the Comintern could 'head off the interventionists for one to two years'.[84] As had been true before, Stalin's strategy was to play for time. The threat of foreign intervention subsequently held a prominent place in the Industrial Party trial at the end of 1930, and the defendants – who each received lengthy prison sentences – described how forces from the usual suspects, Poland, Romania, France, Britain and the White émigré organizations, were planning to invade. Outside the trial verdicts, the Politburo resolved to launch a press campaign to highlight these dangers to the Soviet people.[85] But this episode, and the pressure Stalin placed on Menzhinskii and the channelling of the Industrial Party investigation to incorporate the foreign military threat, unmistakably reveals his sensitivities about a coming war. That Stalin was also thinking seriously about expanding the size of the Red Army, in contrast to earlier in the year when he rejected calls for higher military spending, suggests priorities had shifted and that he saw war as something more likely in the shorter term.[86]

*

With typical asymmetry, at the moment when Stalin was most focused on the prospect of war with Poland in summer 1930, the latter's government was beginning to signal more strongly its intentions towards improving relations. Spurred on by collapsing Franco-Polish ties and the rising popularity of the National Socialist Party in Germany, whose ambitions for retrieving territory lost to Poland had gained influential supporters in the west, Zaleski proposed to Antonov-Ovseenko in August that something radical be done to improve Soviet-Polish relations. Shortly after, though less ambitiously, Patek spoke with Litvinov about concluding a series of conventions, for instance on aviation and borders.[87] Yet Zaleski came through in December when he communicated Piłsudski's position that a non-aggression pact was now in the realms of possibility. This had already been aired a couple of weeks earlier between the Soviet and Polish ambassadors in Turkey, who informally discussed the same thing. As one scholar has pointed out, Stalin in fact encouraged this very conversation in Turkey to test the ground, on the understanding that the Polish government was more serious about a non-aggression pact. However, this now became the first sign of a division between Stalin and the NKID collegium, which was still sceptical about the prospect of a pact and wanted to avoid needlessly worsening fragile Soviet-German ties.[88] In Litvinov's view, there was no evidence that Poland's attitude towards the Soviet Union had changed. 'Patek loves to speak about Polish-Soviet relations in a rose-coloured light', he noted to Antonov-Ovseenko, and stressed that 'maintaining loyal and friendly relations with Germany should remain the core of our politics'. Germany, he went on, was 'almost the only link that is missing from the closing of the anti-Soviet chain about which [Henri] Deterding, Churchill and the White émigrés, and so on, dream'. In the meantime, the NKID should concentrate on improving relations with Poland with 'temporary agreements, especially of economic character'.[89]

Despite this new momentum on both sides towards a pact, disagreements about what form this would take remained the central barrier to progress in winter 1930 to 1931. As Patek reminded Krestinskii, the League of Nations forbade Poland from accepting unconditional neutrality (a central Soviet demand); the Bolsheviks, in turn, still refused to agree a multilateral non-aggression pact or recognize international arbitration procedures (the view in the NKID was that because Poland had signed the Kellogg-Briand pact and Litvinov protocol, neither of which said anything about arbitration or the League of Nations, it was inconsistent to insist on these now).[90] The pace of these new talks therefore dipped. With neither side wanting to make the first move or reveal their hand, formal negotiations were suspended from January 1931 until the summer.[91] The Poles, as the NKID suspected, prioritized renewing their treaty of alliance with Romanian first.[92] Even so, a Soviet-Polish pact would be agreed in less than two years.

Soviet defence spending continued apace in the meantime. At the close 1930, and corresponding with Stalin's openness to higher spending, the Politburo approved a new tank construction programme and increases in artillery and the air force. Later in August 1931, the Council of Labour and Defence sanctioned a further significant increase in tank production.[93] In other clear signs that the regime was intent on propelling its military build-up, in June 1931, Tukhachevskii, one of the most ambitious proponents of military expansion, was given the position of director of armaments. Even though he was disliked by Stalin's allies in the rivalrous high command, and still subjected to attacks for the failure of the 1920 campaign on Warsaw, Tukhachevskii's promotion was highly indicative of the Soviet Union's direction of travel, something plain to see for anyone paying attention.[94] Earlier in February and harking back to Imperial Russia's defeats to various foes in past centuries, Stalin declared in one of his most famous speeches: 'To restrain tempos is to fall behind. And those who fall behind are beaten.' In the following month, at the congress of soviets, Molotov likewise took the opportunity to sketch out once more the dangers inherent to the outside world. Closely reflecting recently received Soviet intelligence, Molotov repeated a warning that France was encouraging and supporting Poland, Romania and the White émigrés into war.[95] Claims about France, however, would again be soon belied by events. Not long after in April and responding to the German naval programme and news of a planned customs union between Germany and Austria, the French reached out to the Soviet Union for negotiations on a non-aggression pact. Talks proceeded quickly and a pact was initialled on 10 August 1931. Both sides agreed to lift trade restrictions put in place in the previous year. However, because of a domestic backlash, the French government slowed the pace and declared that the Franco-Soviet pact could not be definitive unless a Soviet-Polish pact was also agreed.[96] Litvinov suspected, rightly, that France was seeking to draw down its commitments to Poland.[97]

Regardless of French motives, what this meant in practice was renewed scope for a Soviet-Polish non-aggression pact. Spooked by the talks between France and the Soviet Union, on 4 August 1931 Patek informed the NKID of the Polish government's intention to submit a draft non-aggression pact. Shortly after on 23 August Patek then delivered a note to Litvinov suggesting, indirectly, that negotiations could be resumed.[98] Yet this offer was to use the negotiations from the 1926 draft non-aggression pact as a baseline, and with it, many of the same stubborn sticking points, including Poland's demand for collective negotiations with other powers.[99] Litvinov and Karakhan questioned whether Patek was serious (there was something to this, as Patek believed that the Litvinov protocol bolstered with a conciliation convention would be as good a non-aggression pact). More generally, the NKID judged the Polish offer as an attempt to spread rumours about negotiations in order to reap benefits abroad and it was unhappy with reports appearing in the Polish press.[100] With his usual eye towards stabilizing relations with Germany, Litvinov, in the country at the time, denied that any negotiations with Poland were ongoing (though soon after, to keep other parties happy, he communicated to the French the Bolsheviks' willingness to potentially sign a Soviet-Polish pact).[101] Antonov-Ovseenko was the notable exception in the NKID. He believed the Poles were serious about a non-aggression pact and that Patek's proposal most likely had French backing. In the end, however, it was the form of the offer that remained the overriding problem. The NKID officially rebuffed Patek's proposal in a communique on 27 August as it was based on already rejected proposals.[102] The year 1931 also presented a changed environment to the crisis year of 1930. Having initialled a pact with France and renewed the Treaty of Berlin with Germany in early summer 1931, the NKID felt more confident in pushing for its preferred terms in a Soviet-Polish agreement.

The NKID's rejection of Patek's offer, however, brought the divisions between it and party leadership to the surface in a stronger form. The point of controversy in summer 1931 was that neither Stalin nor the Politburo had given the go ahead to reject Patek's proposal. At the end of August, Krestinskii defended the NKID's actions, writing to Lazar Kaganovich to justify how the rumours spread by Poland about renewed Soviet-Polish negotiations had been designed to spook Germany, compelling the NKID to give a public denial in the press, first in January, and then definitively in the August formal rebuff. Krestinskii described the NKID rejection of Patek's offer as covering the same ground as past objections, meaning nothing was included not already agreed by the leadership.[103] By 1931, however, Stalin was coming around to making a deal with Poland, even if this alienated Germany, and was unhappy with the NKID. He was less wedded than Litvinov, and Chicherin before him, in maintaining Germany's position as a barrier to the formation of an anti-Soviet bloc and believed the Bolsheviks should be cautious about its growing power in Europe.[104] In this context, a non-aggression pact with Poland looked increasingly advantageous. Away in Sochi for summer 1931, a few days after the NKID's formal rejection of Patek's proposal, Stalin wrote to Kaganovich to find out more:

> This is a very important matter, which almost determines the issue of peace (for the next two or three years), and I am afraid that Litvinov will yield to so-called 'public opinion' and will dismiss it as a trifle. Give serious attention to this matter and let the Politburo place it under special supervision and try to carry it to a conclusion by every means. It would be laughable if we surrendered in this matter to the common, narrow-minded mania of 'anti-Polandism' while forgetting, even for a minute, about the fundamental interests of the revolution and socialist construction.[105]

Kaganovich wrote several times to Stalin on this issue, agreeing with the general secretary that the NKID had acted incorrectly in rebuffing Patek's offer before this was put to the Politburo, labelling this a 'grave mistake' (there was concern too in the Politburo about what would come of the pact with France should negotiations with Poland go nowhere).[106] Even so, Stalin did not press for negotiations just yet. For now, the Politburo ordered the NKID to draw up a report on whether Poland was serious or not about a non-aggression pact.[107]

Litvinov continued to make the case that relations with Germany should not be needlessly damaged. As he put it to Kaganovich, efforts to create 'a united capitalist front' had unravelled because of the Soviet Union's stable relations with Germany. Like others in the NKID, he was convinced that the Poles, unserious about signing a pact, were in truth spreading stories about improving Soviet-Polish relations to spook Germany, drive it into the arms of France and in doing so bring about the failure of the proposed customs union with Austria. The other motivation Litvinov highlighted was heard time and again: to bring the countries bordering the Soviet Union under Polish influence. 'Poland insists on the creation of a bloc against us with all our neighbouring states', Litvinov argued.

It was only Lithuania – which still resisted entering such a coalition – that was causing the plan to fail. Yet according to him, if ties between the Soviet Union and Germany weakened, which Lithuania saw as a counterweight to Polish influence in Europe, then the country might finally give in to Polish designs. On the still-initialled Franco-Soviet pact, Litvinov doubted the Bolsheviks would be able to support France in the international arena given their ideological differences and the French attachment to the Treaty of Versailles system. Like others, he did not believe the French would see through the process to the end and their priority, like Poland, was to pressure Germany into making concessions.[108] In short, in autumn 1931, Litvinov saw little good coming from a pact with Poland. 'Any plus from the pact with Poland would be opposed by the negative consequences of such a pact.' He reported being 'amazed' and 'dejected', moreover, that his efforts to publicly deny negotiations with Poland were taking place, to ease anxieties in Germany and Lithuania, had been so badly received in Moscow.[109] Kaganovich wrote to Stalin again, complaining about Litvinov and his 'overly vain' conduct. 'I must tell you that I came away from a discussion with Litvinov even more convinced that he is a kind of "Germanophile," since there is nothing happening so far with the French. He does not understand that we cannot subordinate our diplomacy just to relations with Germany.'[110] On 20 September, going against Litvinov's advice, the Politburo ordered the NKID to report, within ten days, on the necessary measures to achieve a non-aggression pact with Poland.[111]

An important catalyst behind the agreement of a pact came from unexpected quarters: Japan's invasion of Manchuria on 18 September 1931. The rapid advance of the Japanese Army across northeast China threw Soviet vulnerabilities in the east into sharp relief. Soviet military numbers and the civilian presence on the eastern border were small and precarious. In the weeks after, Stalin anticipated Japan's ambitions for control over the wider Far East (and he suggested to Voroshilov in November that Japan might attack the Soviet Union in 1932, something which the former repeated to his colleague, Ian Gamarnik).[112] The invasion of Manchuria, in this way, was another sign that Poland would soon be eclipsed by more pressing dangers. Indeed, the war danger, as it was consistently framed later in the 1930s, was now presented in Soviet intelligence as a war on two fronts. A few years later, Hitler's Germany occupied the prominent position, but for now Soviet intelligence pointed to a possible simultaneous struggle against Japan in the east and Poland in the west. Vsevolod Baltskii from the OGPU, for instance, sent Stalin intelligence describing how the Japanese military attaché in Moscow had claimed the Japanese general staff were advocating for war against the Soviet Union sooner than later, and ideally with concurrent Polish and Romanian attacks. Soviet military spending was immediately responsive, rising significantly from 1932.[113] In addition to scrambled and fruitless NKID efforts to secure a non-aggression pact with Japan to bolster the Soviet Union's international position, the invasion of Manchuria finally cemented the direction of travel towards a pact with Poland and other countries on the western border. On 20 November, the Politburo ordered that the NKID begin formal negotiations, the news of which was published two days later. 'Negotiations are underway', Stalin wrote to Voroshilov, 'although it is difficult to say how they will end, but even the simple fact of negotiations with Poland gives us considerable advantage in view of events in the Far East'.[114] The negotiations proceeded more smoothly than past efforts, reflecting Stalin's growing preference for a pact and Poland's fears of isolation. Importantly, the Poles dropped the long-standing demand for a collective agreement and the Bolsheviks, in turn, proved open to carrying out parallel bilateral discussions with Finland, Latvia and Romania. The Bolsheviks also dropped objections over Polish obligations to the League of Nations, while the Poles no longer saw an arbitration clause as essential.[115] Despite the consequences for relations with Germany, Stalin had decided to lean towards Poland. He and his allies tried to calm German apprehensions along the way. While Voroshilov used his contacts in the German military to underline the Bolsheviks' unbroken opposition to the Treaty of Versailles, Stalin, in an interview with the author Emil Ludwig, published in December 1931, assured that a Soviet-Polish pact would not mean guaranteeing Poland's western frontiers, though this failed to ease German concerns.[116]

The remaining barriers to signing a pact with Poland quickly fell away after Stalin had given the signal. The NKID, for instance, compromised on the remaining, and most contentious, point of disagreement in the negotiations. Wanting to preserve their freedom of action, the Poles argued that each side should not be prohibited from entering agreements with other parties – either political or economic – harmful to the other, or in conflict with the non-aggression pact.[117] Backing down and indicative of the gathering mood for a pact in Moscow, Litvinov accepted a vaguer amended formulation of this article if Poland agreed to sign the pact immediately. Elsewhere, a Soviet-Finnish pact agreed on 21 January 1932, and progress made so far with Latvia, had begun to put parallel pacts in place. This had been one of the Polish suggestions for moving the negotiations forwards, and with progress underway it weakened the case for multilateral talks almost entirely. On 25 January 1932, a Soviet-Polish non-aggression pact was initialled.[118]

Long-lasting suspicions about Polish intentions were never going to disappear entirely even now, and these lingered on. When Zaleski informed Litvinov that the Polish government was ready to sign the non-aggression pact, although only when a Soviet-Romanian accord was also agreed, Stomoniakov saw this delay as proof that Poland did not want a pact after all, and had been coerced under French pressure.[119] He had already written to Antonov-Ovseenko describing how Piłsudski was biding his time, waiting to see how the state of political leadership in Germany and France turned out, and was tracking how military events unfolded in the east. The NKID kept on eye on Piłsudski's negotiations in Romania, analysing these in the context of a possible Soviet-Polish war triggered by Japan's operation in the east (in truth, Piłsudski was most likely seeking the agreement of Romania to enter a non-aggression pact with the Soviet Union).[120]

Alarming intelligence also continued to make its way to the Kremlin from early 1932 once the pact had been initialled. At the end of February 1932, Stalin received more intelligence with materials written by the same Japanese military attaché, who called again for a pre-emptive war on the Soviet Union and speculated as before about Poland's and Romania's involvement.[121] In a similar vein, in mid-March,

Balitskii and Artuzov wrote to Stalin with intelligence about the French general staff's supposed schemes for war against the Soviet Union, something 'categorically confirmed' by the Polish chief of staff. The French were apparently in negotiations with the British to bring them on board, or so the pair claimed. The danger posed in a future war remained unchanged: Japan would attack in the east and Poland's role was to draw the Soviet forces west at this very moment. Piłsudski, apparently, had a small group of officers working on the execution of such a plan.[122] It is also worth noting that Tukhachevskii had been examining a Soviet plan for war against Poland and Romania, which would involve the pre-emptive bombing of Warsaw.[123]

The Soviet-Polish pact was signed, finally, on 25 July 1932. Limited to three years, both sides committed to non-aggression and to not supporting third party powers in future conflicts. Ratification came in late November, and the pact with France swiftly followed.[124] While relations between the Soviet Union and Poland were now on a surer footing, something valuable in a difficult and unpredictable international climate, given the Bolsheviks' long-standing distrust of pacts, mutual suspicion was hardly eliminated. And all of this came at a cost. The pact's first clause, noting the 'integrity and inviolability' of each parties' territory – in effect recognition of Poland's borders – meant for Germany nothing less than an indirect guarantee. This brought a definitive end to the Rapallo era, a price Stalin believed was worth paying.[125]

The enemy within

As the perceived threat of future war propelled forward the industrialization of the Soviet Union – and in doing so, cemented the outlines of the future Stalinist system – the party leadership's attentions were at the same time turning inwards, and state violence, coercion and persecution deployed against supposed internal enemies reached new heights. As we have seen already, the drive to collectivize agriculture to fuel breakneck industrialization created enormous suffering and turmoil in the lives of the Soviet peasantry. Cracking down on growing popular resistance to Stalin's revolution with full force, widespread arrests and mass deportations to far flung regions of the Soviet Union came to characterize state power for ordinary people in rural areas in these hinge years. Far worse still, in Soviet Ukraine millions died because of a man-made famine that took hold from 1932. This was a direct consequence of unsustainable grain requisitions that Stalin did nothing to alleviate.

During this period of brutality, the regime expressed stronger concerns than before about Polish subversion which acted to magnify its use of violence. This was notably the case in Soviet Ukraine, where the perceived danger of war from without coincided with mass turmoil from within. In a republic long judged to be vulnerable to Polish attack and subversion, over one half of acts of peasant resistance against collectivization were recorded in the border regions with Poland, where rumours of war were widespread. Yet the impact of real acts of popular resistance was combined, as usual, with deeply conspiratorial thinking in Moscow. At the end of 1933, for instance, Litvinov claimed to Kaganovich that Poland was exploiting the 'imaginary famine' in Ukraine to build an anti-Soviet campaign across the republic, something also apparently involving German and White émigré groups.[126] It is important to stress that Stalin's so-called revolution from above generated pressure on 'internal enemies' across the Soviet apparatus. Notoriously in urban areas, 'class enemies' and pre-revolutionary industrial specialists came under intense pressure and persecution for doubting the spiralling and unachievable targets of the five-year plan. Poles, therefore, were by no means the only group, or national minority, subjected to heightened suspicion and violence in these years.[127] But the specific Polish military and subversive threat to Soviet Ukraine, as it was understood from Moscow, cannot be ignored as a factor making circumstances on the ground materially worse for its people.

One of the first signs of the period of state violence that came to underpin the revolution from above was when sensational news broke across the Soviet Union on 10 March 1928 about the OGPU's unearthing of what it claimed was a counterrevolutionary sabotage organization of engineers and foreign 'bourgeois' specialists operating in the Shakhty coal mines Don Basin coal administration. The case became central to the state's efforts to mobilize the Soviet people behind the soon-to-launch first five-year plan. It helped draw a stark dividing line between the doubting, and supposedly unreliable, pre-revolutionary experts who favoured slower tempos of industrial growth, and the more radical loyal younger generation of newer party members. The Shakhty case played into Stalin's hands in other ways, principally by dividing the forces of the political right of the party. Aleksei Rykov, still an influential figure as head of the Soviet government, emerged as one of the specialists' most vocal defenders. However, Bukharin and Tomskii, his allies in the 'Right Deviation', who positioned themselves as much against the five-year plan, seem to have accepted the charges of the Shakhty case. This was telling of how pervasive fears of economic sabotage on the orders of enemy foreign powers were becoming.[128]

The Shakhty case culminated in a notorious and highly publicized show trial in Moscow of fifty-three defendants opening in late May which laid bare the connections the party leadership drew between the outside military threat and internal subversion. As the Shakhty case was designed to demonstrate, foreign intelligence agents were apparently central to plots to disorganize not only the coal industry but the wider economy. This had been a central theme from the outset of the investigation. Iagoda, *de facto* OGPU head while Menzhinskii was in poor health, reported to Stalin at the very beginning to describe how conspirators operating in the Don Basin coal administration had organizational centres in Poland and Germany, with subversive activities tied to a future military intervention. Stalin agreed entirely.[129] The Shakhty conspiracy soon widened as the investigation rolled on to encompass other major industrial centres in Soviet Ukraine and further afield. Kaganovich confirmed to Stalin in late April, for instance, that 'the investigation has established that this kind of organization existed on an all-union scale in Moscow'. The conspiracy, apparently, extended to Polish and French diplomatic representatives in the Soviet Union. 'The Poles played the most immediate part in the very creation of the organization, generously subsidizing it and using it broadly for spying and subversive work', Kaganovich claimed. The existence of the organization, Kaganovich also noted, supported Stalin's already-publicized analysis 'about new forms of counterrevolutionary work, and about preparations for interventions on the part of world imperialism'.[130] Before long, this framing was detailed to a wider party audience at a plenum of the central committee, where it was the doubter Rykov, who, probably overwhelmed by the pressure he was coming under from cautioning against 'specialist baiting', confirmed a link between the Shakhty case and Polish intelligence. 'There is no doubt that the Poles had the possibility to prepare for war with us not only through organizing their armed forces but by disorganizing our economy.'[131] Abroad the Shakhty trial created significant discord with Germany, given that a small number of the sentenced men were German engineers. Litvinov worried about the consequences, though Stalin refused to back down. The German government broke off only recently cemented trade relations, but for Stalin, this was nothing more than collateral damage. Not only was he convinced that foreign specialists could easily become saboteurs, but the Shakhty case proved a valuable tool to engineer class warfare on the one hand and cement his political consolidation of power on the other, by forcing the party into line.[132]

The Shakhty trial was not the only device for popular mobilization and other cases soon followed. In 1929, the OGPU began an investigation into the so-called Union for the Liberation of Ukraine (SVU) over March and April, an organization it said was closely linked to nationalist and Petliurite groups plotting the overthrow of Soviet power. This apparently involved planning uprisings to assist a Polish intervention using a network embedded across Ukraine. A show trial of mostly Ukrainian intellectuals was staged in spring 1930. This was another opportunity for the regime to broadcast the danger of subversives in the pay of foreign powers, but in this case, it also formed a line of attack against Ukrainian intellectuals more generally as the Stalinist regime turned increasing towards a Russified and harder line national policy as a means of breaking the influence of cultural elites.[133] Away from the public eye, the security organs delivered increasingly stark warnings to the party leadership about the vulnerability of Soviet Ukraine as a hub of internal counterrevolution. The threat of intervention, as ever, was a prominent theme.[134] Indeed, shortly after the Shakhty trial, in July 1928, head of the Ukrainian GPU, Vsevolod Balitskii sent a memorandum to Kaganovich that claimed that nationalist counterrevolutionary activity, aimed at securing Ukrainian independence, was on the rise and that this corresponded 'directly to the complexity and acuteness of the USSR's international status'.[135] The activity of Polish intelligence, unsurprisingly, became a chief object of concern. As it had done repeatedly in the past, the Ukrainian GPU targeted the consulate in Kiev and eleven Polish officials were arrested in the first half of 1929.[136] Further cases of Polish espionage followed. As before, there was an element of truth in these arrests. Some clandestine Polish circles, coordinated by Piłsudski's ally Henryk Jozewski, the head of the Volhynia province from September 1928, were busy reviving a Promethean movement to undermine Soviet control across the border and, as a long-term goal, achieve long-coveted Ukrainian independence. Numerous espionage missions into Soviet Ukraine had been set into motion.[137] In early 1929, Ukrainian nationalist counterintelligence officers, coordinated from Poland, also made plans to infiltrate Soviet institutions.[138] Nevertheless, Polish initiatives to undermine Soviet power in Ukraine of this type were still nowhere near the scale as presented inside the OGPU and the state's response revealed a gulf in perception. In 1930, the year that Stalin's mind was most fixed on a possible war against Poland and a coalition of border states, the OGPU carried out widespread searches and arrests in the border regions of Soviet Ukraine and Belorussia of supposed spies, kulaks and counterrevolutionaries. Individuals with some connection to Poland were at a higher risk. In all, the OGPU arrested approximately 12,000 people, accused of belonging to 'counterrevolutionary groups' and preparing for 'armed revolution'.[139]

A central reason behind this escalating state repression, including the targeting of Polish nationals, was the widespread disorder on the ground sparked by the collectivization of agriculture. This was true also of the resistance to so-called dekulakization, the state's effort to 'liquidate' the kulaks as a class, an aspiration Stalin notoriously proclaimed in late 1929. The dekulakization campaign grew organically from local party organizations before being brought under firmer regime control in the early months of 1930; its grim results were the execution or internment of hundreds of thousands of people and the exile of millions of others, with fates defined by the regime's crude classification of the severity of their perceived dangers.[140] Both collectivization and dekulakization were met with fierce and widespread popular resistance from the beginning. Communist Party officials were frequently murdered, and thousands of peasant uprisings shook targeted regions with most resistance taking place in Ukraine, already identified as a potential bridgehead for enemy forces. The regime blamed kulaks for encouraging the revolts, but the leadership and security organs, nevertheless, worried about the consequences for wider security. The Ukrainian GPU arrested what it claimed were subversives working for Poland and various counterrevolutionary kulak groups, giving further backing to a picture of internal and external threats intertwined.[141] (It was certainly true that Polish intelligence managed to recruit some new Ukrainian agents from the large number of peasants fleeing across the border.)[142] Amid the turmoil, there were also rising numbers of attempted border crossings as ordinary people sought refuge from collectivization.[143] In some cases, entire villages attempted to flee, and this created the potential for flashpoints at the border. As in past years of high tension, the OGPU recorded more rumours spreading about an upcoming war.[144]

The chaotic situation in early 1930 alarmed some in the party elite. In February, Litvinov worried about a diplomatic incident with Germany, but more pointedly warned Stalin that the numbers illegally crossing the border and the levels of anti-Soviet agitation on the ground might provoke Poland to intervene.[145] The OGPU reported that counterrevolutionary kulak groups were seeking this very end and the separation of Ukraine from the Soviet Union as a result. Not long after Litvinov gave his warning to Stalin in mid-March, the OGPU pointed to an increase in the activity of counterrevolutionary groups on the ground, supposedly planning uprisings later in summer 1930. It said weapons were stockpiled waiting for the right moment.[146] These groups also apparently sought to establish links to the Red Army, which, with its large majority of peasant soldiers had already suffered an immediate and dangerous drop in morale from the beginning of grain requisitions in 1928.[147] This was the context in which Stalin decided to temporarily scale back the pace of collectivization with his well-known intervention in *Pravda*, 'Dizzy with Success', published on 2 March 1930. Here he self-servingly blamed overenthusiastic officials for the chaos, but at the same time, the leadership had been conscious of the coming together of the domestic and external dangers, a long-running theme in predictions of future war. The disorder had to be brought under control. The Red Army's reliability, evidently, posed a pressing problem for the high command which was still pouring over signs of future war. Writing to Ian Gamarnik, the head of the Political Administration of the Red Army, Voroshilov elaborated on the deteriorating international situation for the Soviet Union in the spring, describing how 'lies published in the foreign press' about collectivization and religious persecution in Soviet territory were strengthening militarism abroad. With Poland and Romania in economic crisis and considering 'the general political uncertainty which exists in most of the capitalist countries', Voroshilov suggested that a climate was emerging in the outside world 'favourable to a decision to undertake military adventures'.[148] Shortly after Stalin's article in *Pravda* was published, the Revolutionary Military Council of the Republic met to discuss bolstering the country's defences and, despite the morale problems that had spread through its ranks, Red Army units in the west were put on war footing for a possible Polish attack.[149] In truth, the Polish government went on to rebuff a proposal from the army of the UNR in June 1930 to go to war against the Soviet Union and the country was steadily moving towards signing a non-aggression pact. As one scholar points out, Piłsudski perhaps entertained an attack at the height of the famine in Ukraine, something akin to a war of liberation. However, facing cuts in Polish military spending in the early 1930s at the same time as this was rising in the Soviet Union – and aware that the OGPU's methods were steadily breaking popular resistance on the ground – Piłsudski gave up on the idea of intervention, choosing to still pursue better relations.[150]

The chaos of spring 1930 died down once Stalin eased the pace of collectivization, though the plots described in OGPU reports remained of the same character with the same threats recycled. In June, for instance, the Ukrainian GPU claimed it had unearthed a counterrevolutionary group in Khar'kov that was planning the overthrow of Soviet power in Ukraine and the transfer of the republic to Poland. The Polish second department, one of the common villains, was said to be carrying out constant intelligence in the republic in preparation of war.[151] (In the lengthy internal reports on such investigations, Ukrainian counterrevolutionary groups were given long histories going back to the early 1920s with their very formation under Polish intelligence.)[152] And as the collectivization drive pushed on in earnest one year later in 1931, with the chief grain-growing regions reaching full state control by the end of 1932, ongoing peasant unrest and tensions along the Soviet-Polish border kept alive the spectre of war in Moscow (something akin to 'almost pre-war conditions', as Antonov-Ovseenko put it).[153] Conspiracies about the invasion of Soviet Ukraine continued to swirl, sustained by the GPU's almost continual investigations. One of the more extensive examples, 'operation vesna', came in spring 1931 when the central OGPU was busy uncovering what it said was a major military plot in the Red Army, apparently coordinated by officers with pre-revolutionary experience – the so-called military specialists. Thousands of officers were arrested over 1930 to 1931, almost including Tukhachevskii who was smeared, unsuccessfully in the end, as a counterrevolutionary.[154] Yet the OGPU claimed it had uncovered close connections between Poland and the conspiracy. It had already reported that the British government supposedly paid Piłsudski £100,000 in 1927 to organize uprisings in Ukraine, deploying nationalists and traitorous Red Army soldiers. Piłsudski's ill-health was said to be the reason the plan was delayed, but its outlines featured strongly in the OGPU's future investigations. This played a key role in providing the spark for operation vesna itself, once the OGPU discovered new 'evidence' that Piłsudski's British-backed plot in Ukraine was back on.[155] During the operation against the Red Army officers, moreover, interrogation testimony revealed the long-time preoccupation with Poland. Almost certainly under brutal questioning, one arrested military specialist, General Vladimir Ol'derogge, described how Polish organizations were operating in Kiev, Khar'kov, Moscow and elsewhere in Belorussia. Echoing dangers reiterated time and time again, the chief task of these groups was to prepare the local Polish populations for coming war and to carry out espionage. A central goal was, once again, the seizure of Ukraine and Belorussia.[156]

Despite the regime's progress in collectivizing peasant farms and holdings, the emerging system of state-controlled agriculture was not producing sufficient grain, for export or consumption, by 1932. The harvest of that year was worse than 1931 and the signs of famine in Ukraine were becoming unavoidable. Still, Moscow refused to lower grain quotas despite pleas from Ukrainian party leaders.[157] During one moment in July Stalin suggested to Kaganovich that the grain collections could be reduced for 'particularly affected areas of Ukraine'. Among his reasons, alongside avoiding 'suffering' and 'demoralization' was 'the special situation of Ukraine, the common border with Poland'.[158] Yet the decrease never took place, and Stalin switched back to a hard-line position, prompted by OGPU reports of rising cases of grain theft, driven by desperation and hunger. Stalin, moreover, received other reports from the OGPU about the resistance by Ukrainian communists themselves. Taken together, and considering his long-standing fixation with the threat of war and conspiracies, Stalin expressed rejuvenated fears of losing Ukraine to Poland entirely.[159] On 11 August, he fired off a telegram to Kaganovich warning of this very risk. Highly critical of the Ukrainian Communist Party leadership, Stalin claimed that Polish subversives had infiltrated the party's ranks and were taking advantage of ground-level discontents caused by the ongoing collectivization drive. Stalin cautioned Kaganovich to 'bear in mind that Piłsudski is not daydreaming, and his agents in Ukraine are many times stronger' than assumed by the Ukrainian party leaders. Because the Ukrainian Communist Party had apparently been infiltrated by enemies (including 'direct agents of

Piłsudski') he wanted new officials brought into leadership positions. The risk was the Poles might open 'a front inside (and outside) the party, against the party' if the situation on the ground went from bad to worse.[160] The landmark non-aggression pact with Poland had been signed one the month before, but Stalin's tendency to see Polish-inspired conspiracies was evidently not diminished. It is possible, as one scholar suggests, that Stalin was simply exploiting the situation, and purposely using the still-resonant Polish threat to further consolidate his position and crack down on resistance to collectivization.[161] However, the simpler explanation is more likely. Given his suspicions about the international order, Stalin did not believe non-aggression pacts were particularly strong guarantees against war; something especially true for him when OGPU materials crossed his desk, describing Polish subversion intertwining with popular resistance in Ukraine.

To continue the unremitting pressure for grain and root out 'enemies' on the ground, therefore, further cleansing operations in the western borders followed in March 1933. This time, counterrevolutionary groups organized by the Polish and Finnish general staffs were apparently exposed, some operating in strategic positions, such as railroad junctions and defence installations.[162] In spring 1933, the OGPU's foreign department claimed that a high percentage of Poles belonged to such conspiracies.[163] As was often true, Stalin put his faith in hard-liners, like the OGPU deputy leader Vsevolod Balitskii, to combat internal enemies. Not long in his position in Moscow, he was brought back to head the Ukrainian GPU.[164] Balitskii was convinced about the reality of Polish conspiracies in Ukraine and his reports to the centre describing a range of imaginary plots only reinforced suspicions there. At the end of 1932, he wrote to Stalin about the existence of a 'widespread Polish-Petliurite insurgent underground' in Ukraine, apparently discovered in sixty-seven counties, which Stalin then had circulated among the party leadership.[165] The activities of the Polish Military Organization (POV), in truth long-defunct from 1921, appeared frequently in Balitskii's investigations. The phantom organization was apparently running numerous campaigns, all aligning neatly with the Bolsheviks' long-running security worries. These included efforts to turn Soviet Ukrainians against the regime; the infiltration of the Red Army; and the separation of Ukraine and Belorussia from the Soviet Union. The POV was also, the GPU claimed, interested in the party 'mood' and interparty situation and had apparently supported Trotsky's opposition years before (one report said the organization had seized control of the party leadership in the Marchlevsk Polish Autonomous Region, later described as 'saturated by anti-Soviet and counterrevolutionary elements').[166]

While much of this was therefore familiar, GPU reports of this type were also evolving after the electoral victory of the National Socialist Party and Germany was framed as an increasingly prominent security danger. Alongside Balitskii's reports about the POV appeared information about the Ukrainian Military Organization (UOV), said to be partly in the hands of Polish intelligence but also with a wing operating under 'Anglo-German' control, with organizations active in Moscow, and across Ukraine and Belorussia.[167] With fresh concerns now about possible rapprochement between Germany and Poland, plain to see in the pages of the Soviet press, old security priorities about the vulnerability of Ukraine were refashioned in a new guise. The NKID collegium ordered Antonov-Ovseenko to find out more about whether Piłsudski's circle was formulating war plans with Germany, should Japan launch a strike at the Soviet Union.[168] At the twelfth congress of the Communist Party of Ukraine, later in 1934, and trumpeting his successes, Balitskii, bringing several dangers together, proclaimed that a dangerous bloc of Ukrainian nationalists backed by German and Polish fascism had apparently been crushed.[169]

Despite the surge in state violence and mass deportations of the early 1930s to strengthen the regime's hold over Ukraine, its status as a vulnerable republic nevertheless remained intact in the years after. This was because the perceived danger was understood not only from peasants resisting collectivization and dekulakization. The sudden and widespread backlash against grain requisitions caught the regime off guard, but the perception of sustained Polish subversive and military threats to Soviet Ukraine, which stretched back over ten years to the Soviet loss of the 1920 war, added fuel to the fire. Stalin's responses, or lack of, were shaped by both domestic and external priorities, coming together to create deadly circumstances for so many. The threat of future war, as we have seen, became even louder throughout the revolution from above and a Polish subversive threat to the Soviet Union's western border was an accepted fact, as always. Stalin was no less convinced that war against the capitalist world was inevitable, but for another fleeting moment, saw this in the imminent future, as he described in 1930. Poland was also no less framed as a direct military threat, but one now joined by other enemy powers as the Soviet Union's international situation became increasingly complicated and difficult. By the mid-1930s, war against Poland, Japan and Germany was deemed a real possibility. This not only required the Soviet Union to continue to build its grain reserves but also its military power, giving further weight to the decision to abandon NEP and launch breakneck industrialization. At the same time, perceived subversive threats to the western border regions encouraged the OGPU to dramatically escalate its operations, opening the way for the use of mass deportations, methods that would be deployed again more lethally in the late 1930s.

CONCLUSION

Labelled the 'Congress of Victors', the seventeenth party congress held between January and February 1934 was characterized by delegates stormily celebrating the dual successes of the first five-year plan and the collectivization of agriculture. The human costs throughout had been significant, in some places staggering; yet what mattered for the party were the gains in Soviet military and industrial power, even if these fell short of the utopian ambitions at the outset of the plan. Stalin's main report to the congress went through trends in industrial development in great detail, but among other talking points, he chose to hail the successes of the diplomatic campaign waged to conclude non-aggression pacts with countries across Europe and beyond, including the United States in November 1933. These were undeniable signs of warming relations with other powers, some of whom had been judged as unremittingly hostile in recent years, even if the Bolsheviks were still overwhelmingly distrusted. It also marked – as this book has shown several times – another easing of tensions in a regular cycle of rising and falling perceived international threats. At the Congress of Victors, Stalin claimed that respect was finally being shown to the Soviet Union, thanks to its growing military and industrial power. At the same time, however, he made clear to his audience that non-aggression pacts could never truly guarantee peace and singled out Poland as a country where 'anti-Soviet sentiments' were still strong and 'surprises and zigzags in policy' could not be discounted. Germany's foreign policy too, Stalin noted, was returning to that of Kaiser Wilhelm's, 'who at one time occupied the Ukraine and marched against Leningrad'.[1] None of this was a revelation for the wider party in 1934. The final demise of the Treaty of Rapallo, cemented by the pact with Poland in 1932, and Hitler's steady takeover of political power in Germany, although not viewed with as much alarm as in years ahead, gave fresh momentum to new Soviet security priorities.

While the outward features of the Bolsheviks' international security concerns continued to shift over time in this way, with Germany to supplant all others by the late 1930s, this book has shown how one constant danger underpinned them for over a decade: the threat of invasion by an anti-Soviet coalition. At the time of the seventeenth party congress, the Soviet leadership, security organs, intelligence services and NKID still conceived of multiple enemies secretly acting in concert. Associated doubts about Poland's intentions ran deep as ever, a few years after the non-aggression pact of 1932. The prevailing view in the NKID was that Piłsudski signed the pact 'only reluctantly', something, in Stomoniakov's words, which cast 'a very serious shadow on the position of Poland towards the USSR'. Despite barely any evidence surfacing for over a decade, the NKID, like other Soviet institutions, could not let go of the decade-long suspicion that Piłsudski still clung to his old federal programme for the east and believed he might seek, or already be involved in, close collaboration with Germany.[2] This was not a minority view in Soviet circles, where the twin dangers of rising anti-communism and nationalism under Hitler sparked worries about a potentially more dangerous anti-Soviet alliance involving both Poland and Germany, something the Treaty of Rapallo had been designed to avoid.[3]

To forestall the emergence of this new and more dangerous anti-Soviet alliance, in 1933, Stalin moved to shore-up relations with Poland, even if doubts still lingered about Piłsudski's intentions. The NKID was to forge closer contacts in the realms of politics, trade, culture and military affairs.[4] But collaboration between Poland and Germany proved impossible to prevent in practice. With Hitler's Germany on one side and Stalin's Soviet Union on the other, Poland faced pressures of its own to find a new security arrangement. And Germany, for geopolitical advantage, sought to break apart the Franco-Polish alliance. For these reasons, Polish and German officials engaged in secret negotiations for a non-aggression pact, later signed on 26 January 1934.[5] This undermined the gains of the 1932 Soviet-Polish pact for sure, but it was some distance away from a military alliance which the Bolsheviks, true to form, suspected to be the reality. Inside the NKID and OGPU, officials were convinced that secret protocols in the pact allowed for joint military action against the Soviet Union. Stalin received intelligence to the same effect, describing how Piłsudski was encouraging the French to join a Polish-German military alliance against the Soviet Union, something apparently with British approval and the promise of support. This was yet another variation of the same conspiracies about the international order the Soviet elite had poured over for more than a decade. And the impact was tangible. Red Army strategy was now reshaped to account for war against Poland and Germany.[6] In another indication of the regime's low confidence in treaties, the later renewal of the Soviet-Polish non-aggression pact on 5 May 1934 made little difference to the Politburo's placement of Poland as a priority for Soviet military intelligence, alongside Germany and Britain in Europe, and Japan in Asia. The country was evaluated as a prominent danger in the years after 1932 and Stalin often received pieces of intelligence about the credible prospect of war against Poland, Germany and Japan supposedly working towards invasion in 1935, and working in collaboration.[7]

Stalin and his senior officials' misperception of international security dangers and framing these as complex anti-Soviet conspiracies was not simply the result of poor intelligence or inaccurate analysis. This book argues that to a greater degree this was a direct legacy of the war fought against Poland in 1920. Lenin and other Bolsheviks misperceived the very nature of the 1920 war from the beginning, attributing outsized roles to Britain and France as the chief coordinators and financiers of the Polish armed forces. This was not something unique to the Soviet-

Polish war. Throughout the wider civil war from 1918, of which the war against Poland was one of the final acts, the Bolsheviks likewise exaggerated British and French participation and influence. They overestimated the unity and common purpose among the Allied Powers behind toppling the revolution. As an article of faith, Lenin expected that if world revolution failed to ignite, the capitalist powers would seek to destroy their new revolutionary state.

These instincts, however, deepened and became entrenched after the Soviet-Polish war. The nature of the Red Army's defeat in summer 1920 ensured that Poland was at the centre of Soviet attentions in subsequent years as the leading danger, long before Hitler's rise to power. The Bolsheviks' interpretation of this war also ensured that a perceived threat from anti-Soviet coalitions assumed a permanent component of future security assessments. Despite winning the wider civil war (at huge costs), the regime took various lessons from the defeat to Poland. The military scrutinized Red Army power, strategy and logistics; the Bolsheviks' popularity outside Soviet Russia was a cause for concern after the failure to attract the Polish people to their cause. Yet the most significant lesson was that the Red Army's gains in early summer – to the point of nearly achieving the sovietization of Poland (at least in the Lenin's view) – had been cruelly crushed by the Allied Powers. For the party, this was a real-world example of one of their deepest convictions about the unwavering hostility of the capitalist world towards the revolution, armed with seemingly pliable proxy states. It was no accident that the dominant security threat, as understood in Moscow in the decade after, was Poland, financed and influenced (in some cases portrayed as directly coordinated) by capitalist powers. Although the perceived level of threat waxed and waned in the 1920s, easing in the middle of the decade to worsen once more when Piłsudski returned to power in 1926, the danger of war never fully receded and neither did related dangers of subversion in the border regions (deemed war by other means). In the Bolsheviks' impressions of their vulnerability on the western border – the higher priority until the Japanese invasion of Manchuria – it was Poland that sat as a central cog in a dangerous anti-Soviet coalition. This was a shared understanding going beyond the leadership, or Stalin's sole imagination. It was difficult to avoid being led by Stalin's instincts once he was consolidating power following Lenin's death, but the NKID, GPU/OGPU and Soviet intelligence had years before each accepted the core outlines of a conspiratorial picture of the international order, even if prominent doubters and dissenters, people like Chicherin, emerged from time-to-time. Lenin, therefore, did the most to originate the very idea that Britain and France manipulated Poland at will. The Soviet-Polish war, in this way, came to shape and define the Bolsheviks' understanding of the outside world in the decade after 1917. The defeat fuelled a sense of threat that did not exist, and near-yearly projections about inevitable war that did not arrive until 1941, and then in an unexpected form.

The Bolsheviks' misperception of international security threats not only mattered in elevating Poland to a status in the 1920s that, for them, nearly matched that of Germany in the 1930s, but the trajectory and development of the Soviet Union was pushed in a particular direction as a result, and more quickly towards authoritarianism and the emergence of the Stalinist dictatorship. None of this is to say that Stalin's rise to power, the transformation of the Soviet Union during the 'revolution from above', or the widespread use of state violence or limits on democracy were prompted solely by the Bolsheviks' perceptions of the outside world. Most of these trends were already underway from 1917, and some before, detectable in Bolshevik ideology and accelerated by the widespread brutality of the civil war.[8] Lenin and the Bolsheviks had for a long time held an exclusionary attitude towards democratic practices; industrialization was broadly accepted as the essential method of reaching a true communist society; one of the most notorious events of the civil war era, the Red Terror, from summer 1918 starkly revealed the Bolsheviks' propensity towards extreme violence at an early stage. However, the prominence that the Bolsheviks gave to the threat of an international anti-Soviet coalition during and after the Soviet-Polish war, with Poland framed as a most pressing danger to their state, created a raft of security anxieties that only magnified these trends and behaviours. As we have seen, while most Bolsheviks believed industrialization was central to the Soviet Union's survival and future power, it was the perceived danger of future war against the capitalist world, sharpening suddenly in the mid-to-late 1920s with Piłsudski's Poland deemed the likely instrument, which set the five-year plan in motion from 1928. The state violence and mass coercion of the collectivization drive followed soon after, without which the radicalism of Stalin's plan was impossible in such short order. While the people of Ukraine faced incredible hardships Stalin refused to alleviate, he and his allies obsessed instead with conspiracies about subversion and war. This book has shown, too, how the perceived threat of invasion – again with Poland imagined at the centre of an anti-Soviet coalition – contributed to the downfall of Trotsky and the crushing of political opposition in the Bolshevik Party; opportunities for dissent were removed and intra-party democracy fatally weakened. While Stalin's rise to power should not, and cannot, be explained by a single cause, the ever-evolving perceived wartime emergency left little space for political competition. Stalin and his allies truly believed in the certainty of future war; this was not simply a useful excuse for cracking down on political rivals.

The legacy of the Soviet-Polish war had echoes and ramifications beyond the scope of the material examined in this book. Considering the long-standing danger that the Bolsheviks attributed to Poland and, in turn, the Polish minority in the Soviet Union (some of the first to come under pressure and scrutiny in the international crises of the 1920s), it is hardly surprising that the latter remained at high risk of false accusations, arrests and deportations in the 1930s. Reflecting the Soviet security priorities of the mid-1930s described above, when the regime expressed starker concerns about a Polish-German military alliance, tens of thousands of Polish and German nationals were soon deported from the western border regions of the Soviet Union to republics in Central Asia. The OGPU pursued investigations into Polish counterrevolutionary organizations with no less zeal, frequently sending reports to Stalin detailing harmful acts by Polish subversives, their infiltration into Soviet institutions and major cities and extensive Polish intelligence operations.[9] The political violence against Polish citizens in the Soviet Union reached a crescendo two years later in summer 1937, at the height of the Great Terror. Historians increasingly attribute the regime's perception of the foreign threat and the fear of war as the overriding cause behind this explosion of political violence across state and society. It is hard not to see the linkages when, in summer 1937, Stalin sanctioned a series of so-called mass operations, extensive campaigns of state repression targeted at entire population cohorts, whether on a class or national basis (kulaks, priests, former White officers, Germans, Poles, Koreans and so on). Designed at neutralizing a potential 'fifth column' of enemies, whom Stalin believed might sabotage the Soviet war effort in the event of invasion, the mass operation based on the NKVD's operational order 00485, targeting Poles in the Soviet Union, was the most extensive of those aimed at national minorities. Poles suffered more than any other national minority during the years of the Great Terror: 111,091 Polish nationals were murdered.[10] Three years later, in the Katyn Forest near Smolensk, on Stalin's orders the NKVD executed nearly 22,000 Polish officers and prisoners of war captured during the Soviet invasion of Poland in 1939. The Katyn massacre is a notorious moment in the history of the twentieth century and was another episode in a long history of Soviet state violence against Poles. The question is whether the Stalinist regime would have engaged in such violence without its long-standing distrust of Poland and Poles, which stretched back to the early 1920s? Without doubt, Stalin frequently sanctioned mass violence against a wide range of Soviet citizens, and the same was true of his closest allies and changing political police chiefs. But the permanent war scare of the 1920s not only locked in a tendency towards authoritarianism and growing state power more broadly, it put the Polish minority at high risk of persecution. Erroneously presenting Poland for so long as the Soviet Union's most immediate opponent had deadly consequences.

Taken together, the way that the Bolsheviks perceived and assessed the outside world in the transformative decade of the 1920s contributed to the closing down of other potential paths of development for the Soviet Union, whether this was accepting a slower pace of industrialization; a more lenient approach towards the peasantry; or the maintenance of some democratic norms in the party, detectable, at least, in the early post-revolutionary years. It is impossible to say if any of these options would have proved acceptable to the party leadership in practice as strategies for state building, but there were diminishing opportunities to find out, given how quickly these were closed off in an environment of consecutive war scares. Furthermore, while there is a temptation to think, as some historians have done, that the Bolsheviks' defeat to Poland in the Soviet-Polish war of 1920 encouraged the Soviet regime towards moderation, in terms of discouraging future efforts to spread revolution overseas by armed force and considering the launch of the New Economic Policy almost immediately after, the reality was that trends in the other direction, examined in this book, were stronger. Lenin's risky campaign into Poland, his foolhardy decision to manufacture revolution in the heart of Europe, was a failed gamble. The consequences, however, were not just a near-term humiliation of the Bolsheviks and the temporary laying bare of weaknesses in the Red Army. What Lenin did not live to witness was how his defeat in 1920 accelerated the emergence of Stalinism.

NOTES

Introduction

1 Edgar Vincent D'Abernon, *The Eighteenth Decisive Battle of the World* (London, 1931), 11–12.
2 For an explicitly counterfactual academic analysis of the Battle of Warsaw, see Ian Ona Johnson, 'The Fire of Revolution: A Counterfactual Analysis of the Polish-Bolshevik War, 1919 to 1920', *The Journal of Slavic Military Studies* 28/1 (2015), 156–85. Many public-facing articles were published during the centenary of the Battle of Warsaw, such as by the Polish Institute of National Remembrance. See 'The Battle of Warsaw, 1920' in which the author claims the battle was one of the most decisive in the world for stopping the march of communism in Europe. https://ipn.gov.pl/en/digital-resources/articles/4397,Battle-of-Warsaw-1920.html [accessed August, 2022]. A recent major biography of Jozef Piłsudski is sympathetic to this view, see Joshua D. Zimmerman, *Jozef Pilsudski: Founding Father of Modern Poland* (Cambridge, MA, 2022), 368–9.
3 Vladimir Brovkin, 'Workers' Unrest and the Bolsheviks' Response in 1919', *Slavic Review* 49/3 (1990): 350–73.
4 That Lenin aimed to use the war to spread revolution is broadly accepted, however, there have been some unconvincing arguments to the contrary. See Thomas C. Fiddick, *Russia's Retreat from Poland 1920. From Permanent Revolution to Peaceful Coexistence* (New York, 1990).
5 For the best recent articulation of the nature of the civil war, see Jonathan D. Smele, *The 'Russian' Civil Wars 19190–1926. Ten Years That Shook the World* (London, 2015).
6 These details, and far more, are covered extensively in books on the wider civil war. See Bruce W. Lincoln, *Red Victory: A History of the Russian Civil War* (New York, 1989); Evan Mawdsley, *The Russian Civil War* (New York, 2007); Smele, *The 'Russian' Civil Wars*; Laura Engelstein, *Russia in Flames: War, Revolution, Civil War, 1914–1921* (Oxford, 2017).
7 Although not strictly a 'revisionist' account, for cogent discussion of this argument, see Sheila Fitzpatrick, 'The Legacy of the Civil War', in Diane Koenker, William G. Rosenberg, and Ronald G. Suny (eds), *Party, State and Society in the Russian Civil War* (Bloomington, 1989), 385–98; Fitzpatrick, 'The Civil War as a Formative Experience' in Abbott Gleason, Peter Kenez, and Richard Stites (eds), *Bolshevik Culture: Experiment and Order in the Russian Revolution* (Bloomington, 1985), 57–76. In qualification, however, Fitzpatrick points out that the Bolsheviks were naturally receptive to civil war emergency measures, using violence and social polarization as a means of consolidating their power and defeating opponents. See 74.
8 For example, see Smele, *The 'Russian' Civil Wars*, 242–4.
9 A few historians have looked at the impact of the Soviet-Polish war after 1920 on the Soviet Union, but only in bookended ways. In the epilogue of his study of the Treaty of Riga, the 1921 peace settlement which officially brought the war to a close, Jerzy

Borzęcki argues that this established stability on the Soviet western border – and for eastern Europe on the whole – until 1939 and gave Lenin little choice but to give up on the prospect of European revolution; the Bolsheviks, under Stalin, instead turned towards Socialism in One Country. See *The Soviet–Polish Peace of 1921 and the Creation of Interwar Europe* (New Haven, 2008), 275–82. This degree of stability has been questioned, however: see David R. Stone's review of Borzęcki's book in *The Journal of Modern History* 82/1 (2010): 171–3. For the Bolsheviks' enthusiasm for revolution abroad after 1921, see also David R. Stone, 'The Prospect of War?' Lev Trotskii, the Soviet Army, and the German Revolution in 1923', *The International History Review* 25/4 (2003). In his well-known account of the Soviet-Polish war, and careful not to exaggerate, Norman Davies suggests in short form in a final chapter that the Soviet defeat was a factor behind forcing the Bolsheviks to adapt to their international isolation, diminishing enthusiasm for world revolution and encouraging an alliance with Germany. For Davies, the defeat also had a moderating effect on the regime, contributing to the introduction of the market-orientated New Economic Policy in 1921. See *White Eagle, Red Star: The Polish-Soviet War 1919–20 and 'the miracle on the Vistula'* (London, 2003), 264–78.

10 Davies, *White Eagle, Red Star*; Piotr S. Wandycz, *Soviet–Polish Relations, 1917–1921* (Cambridge, MA, 1969); Adam Zamoyski, *The Battle for the Marchlands* (New York, 1981); Irina Mikhutina, *Pol'sko-sovetskaia voina, 1919–1920 gg.* (Moscow, 1994).
11 Smele, *The 'Russian' Civil Wars*; Engelstein, *Russia in Flames*.
12 The centrality of Poland in Soviet military and industrial planning in the late 1920s was a focus of some of Oleg Ken's work. See the early chapters of *Collective Security of Isolation? Soviet Policy and Poland, 1930–35* (St. Petersburg, 1996) and *Mobilizatsionnoe planirovanie i politicheskie resheniia. Konets 20-x-seredina 30-x gg.* (St. Petersburg, 2002). For a recent Russian-language account focused on Soviet counterintelligence against Poland in the 1920s, see Aleksandr Zdanovich, *Pol'skii krest sovetskoi kontrrazvedki: pol'skaia liniia v rabote VChK-NKVD 1918–1938* (Moscow, 2017). Other recent work has emphasized the centrality of the countries on the Soviet western border to Stalin's wider security policies, see Alfred J. Rieber, *Stalin and the Struggle for Supremacy in Eurasia* (Cambridge, 2015). In terms of work on Soviet foreign relations, a recent study of the 1920s notes Poland only as a background issue. See Michael Jabara Carley, *Silent Conflict: A Hidden History of Early Soviet-Western Relations* (Lanham, MD, 2014).
13 See, in particular, Olga Velikanova, *Popular Perceptions of Soviet Politics in the 1920s. Disenchantment of the Dreamers* (Basingstoke, 2013); Sarah Davies and James Harris, *Stalin's World: Dictating the Soviet Order* (New Haven, 2014).
14 For a good survey of intelligence in the period and its study, see John Ferris, 'Intelligence' in Robert Boyce and Joseph A. Maiolo (eds), *The Origins of World War Two. The Debate Continues* (Basingstoke, 2003), 308–29.
15 The connection between the worsening international climate and the launch of industrialization has previously been drawn by scholars, however, not specifically highlighting the centrality of the perceived Polish military threat to the Soviet Union. See for instance, R. W. Davies, *The Socialist Offensive: The Collectivisation of Soviet Agriculture, 1929–30* (Basingstoke, 1980), 37. See also David R. Stone, *Hammer and Rifle: The Militarization of the Soviet Union, 1926–1933* (Kansas, 2000); Lennart Samuelson, *Plans for Stalin's War Machine: Tukhachevskii and Military-Economic Planning, 1925–1941* (Basingstoke, 2000).

16 Clear intersections of the perceived foreign threat and Soviet political violence appear in Oleg V. Khlevniuk, *The Master of the House: Stalin and His Inner Circle* (New Haven, 2009); Peter Whitewood, *The Red Army and the Great Terror: Stalin's Purge of the Soviet Military* (Kansas, 2015); James Harris, *The Great Fear. Stalin's Terror of the 1930s* (Oxford, 2016); Lynne Viola, *Stalinist Perpetrators on Trial: Scenes from the Great Terror in Soviet Ukraine* (Oxford, 2017); David Shearer, 'Stalin at War, 1918–1953: Patterns of Violence and Foreign Threat', *Jahrbücher für Geschichte Osteuropas* 66/2 (2018): 188–217.
17 Hiroaki Kuromiya, 'Stalin in the Light of the Politburo Transcripts', in Paul R. Gregory and Norman Naimark (eds), *The Lost Politburo Transcripts: From Collective Rule to Stalin's Dictatorship* (New Haven, 2008), 49–50.

Chapter 1

1 On the 'wars after the war', see Robert Gerwarth and John Horne, 'Vectors of Violence: Paramilitarism in Europe after the Great War, 1917–1923', *The Journal of Modern History* 83/3 (2011): 489–512; Gerwarth, *The Vanquished: Why the First World War Failed to End, 1917–1923* (London, 2016).
2 Davies, *White Eagle, Red Star*, 23; 44–5; Wandycz, *Soviet–Polish Relations*, 90; Richard K. Debo, *Survival and Consolidation: The Foreign Policy of Soviet Russia, 1918–1921* (Montreal, 1992), 58. Jerzy Borzęcki, 'The Outbreak of the Polish-Soviet War: A Polish Perspective', *The Journal of Slavic Military Studies* 29/4 (2016): 658–80.
3 Ibid., 659.
4 John Erickson, *The Soviet High Command: A Military–Political History, 1918–1941* (London; Portland, OR, 2001), 85; Adam Zamoyski, *Warsaw 1920: Lenin's Failed Conquest of Europe* (London, 2008), 9; Borzęcki, *The Soviet–Polish Peace*, 26–7.
5 Debo, *Survival and Consolidation*, 191.
6 For Denikin's account, see A.I. Denikin, *Tragediia Beloi Armii: Kto spas sovetskuiu vlast' ot gibeli* (Moscow, 1991). See also Anatol Shmelev, *In the Wake of Empire: Anti-Bolshevik Russia in International Affairs, 1917–1920* (Stanford, California, 2021), 500.
7 Zimmerman, *Jozef Pilsudski*, 339.
8 Borzęcki, *The Soviet–Polish Peace*, 29.
9 Debo, *Survival and Consolidation*, 57–9.
10 E.L. Woodward and Rohan Butler (eds), *Documents on British Foreign Policy, 1919–1939. First series, Vol. I, 1919* [hereafter DBFP] (London, 1947), 689.
11 Michael Jabara Carley, 'The Politics of Anti-Bolshevism: The French Government and the Russo-Polish War, December 1919 to May 1920', *The Historical Journal* 19/1 (1976): 168–9; Debo, *Survival and Consolidation*, 194.
12 For Markhlevskii's account, see *Voina i Mir mezhdu Burzhuaznoi Pol'shei i Proletarskii Rossiei* (Moscow, 1921), 12–15.
13 Borzęcki, *The Soviet–Polish Peace*, 44–5. Zimmerman, *Jozef Pilsudski*, 348.
14 Davies, *White Eagle, Red Star*, 84.
15 Ibid., 84–5, 92. For Churchill's support of the Poles in late 1919, see for instance, The Churchill Archive, Chartwell Papers [hereafter CHAR], 16/18A-B/29.
16 In Piłsudski's mind, incorporating eastern Galicia into Poland would create a border with Romania, a valuable link in a future Polish-Germany war. Zimmerman, *Jozef Pilsudski*, 337. See also 350.

17 Debo, *Survival and Consolidation*, 194.
18 Richard Pipes, 'New Materials on the Polish-Soviet War of 1920' in Robert Conquest and Dusan J. Djordjevich (eds), *Political and Ideological Confrontations in Twentieth-century Europe: Essays in Honor of Milorad M. Drachkovitch* (New York, 1996), 72.
19 *Dokumenty vneshnei politiki SSSR* [hereafter DVP], tom II (Moscow, 1958), 312–13. This is Borzęcki's interpretation of this episode, see *The Soviet–Polish Peace*, 47. See also Wandycz, *Soviet–Polish Relations*, 152, 175–6.
20 Rossiiskii gosudarstvennyi arkhiv sotsial'no-politicheskoi istorii [hereafter RGASPI], f. 17, op. 109, d. 74, ll. 1–1a.
21 Jan M. Meijer (ed.), *The Trotsky Papers, 1917–1922. Vol. 1, 1917–1919* (The Hague, 1964), 800–1.
22 Arkhiv vneshnei politiki Rossiiskoi Federatsii [hereafter AVPRF], f. 4, op. 52, p. 340, d. 55240, l. 3.
23 Davies, *White Eagle, Red Star*, 83, 87.
24 RGASPI, f. 17, op. 109, d. 74, l. 2.
25 Davies, *White Eagle, Red Star*, 69; Carley, 'The Politics of Anti-Bolshevism', 167–8.
26 DVP, tom II (Moscow, 1958), 331–3.
27 Kirsteen Davina Croll, 'Soviet-Polish relations, 1919–1921' (unpublished PhD thesis, University of Glasgow, 2009), 109.
28 On numerous occasions Piłsudski made it known he would not make peace with the Bolsheviks, see to British ambassador to Poland, Sir Horace Rumbold, in December 1919, CHAR 16/32/13; to Russian émigré, Boris Savinkov in February 1920, suggesting 'the idea revolts him', CHAR 16/65/128, 113. For similar, see Borzęcki, *The Soviet–Polish Peace*, 37, 42. In January 1920, however, Piłsudski did hold out the possibility of agreeing to peace in discussion with the American minister to Poland. Even though a 'gambler's chance', peace was better than being overrun by the Red Army. Joseph V. Fuller (ed.), *Foreign Relations of the United States* [hereafter FRUS], *1920*, Vol. III (Washington, 1936), document 433.
29 RGASPI, f. 558, op. 1, d. 727, ll. 1–2.
30 For Chicherin's comments to the central committee from 9 January on the Allied Powers' incitement of Poland into war, see AVPRF, f. 4, op. 52, d. 55238, p. 340, l. 9.
31 Wandycz, 'France and the Polish-Soviet War 1919–1920', *The Polish Review* 62/3 (2017): 7.
32 Ibid., 9–10; Carley, 'The Politics of Anti-Bolshevism', 167.
33 For Lloyd George's comments on the failings of the intervention, see Woodward and Butler (eds), DBFP, First series, vol. II, 745.
34 HC Deb. Vol. 125, cols. 41 10 February 1920. Available at https://hansard.parliament.uk/Commons/1920-02-10/debates/35bec712-e37a-4395-ab9c-cf5169dfe447/DebateOnTheAddress [accessed March 2021].
35 Lloyd George's ignorance of Bolshevism was plain to see on many occasions. He once surprised the Russian émigré Boris Savinkov by asking him to explain what the dictatorship of the proletariat actually was; in a speech elsewhere he referred to a 'General Kharkoff', mistaking the city for an imaginary White general. On Savinkov, see CHAR 16/65/5; for the supposed General Kharkoff, see Richard H. Ullman, *Anglo-Soviet Relations, 1917–1921, Vol. 2: Britain and the Russian Civil War: November 1918–February 1920* (Princeton, 1961), 155. According to Churchill, in another conversation with Savinkov at Chequers, Lloyd George remarked that 'revolutions like diseases run a regular course' and once the Bolsheviks were 'confronted with the responsibility of actual government', they would 'quit their

communist theories' or 'quarrel among themselves and fall like Robespierre and St. Just'. Savinkov's retort was to say, 'after the fall of the Roman Empire there ensued The Dark Ages'. Winston Churchill, *Great Contemporaries* (Chicago, 1974), 132.
36 Richard H. Ullman, *Anglo-Soviet Relations, 1917–1921, Vol. 3: The Anglo-Soviet Accord* (Princeton, 1968), 27; CHAR 16/32/7–8.
37 Woodward and Butler (eds), DBFP, First series, vol. III, p. 803; CHAR 16/63/72.
38 Cabinet Papers [hereafter CAB] 23/20. 27 January 1920.
39 Ullman, *Anglo-Soviet Relations*, vol. 3, 31.
40 Norman Davies, 'Lloyd George and Poland, 1919–20', *Journal of Contemporary History* 6/3 (1971): 142–3. See also Wandycz, *Soviet–Polish Relations*, 161.
41 S. Bron'skii, V. Gostyn'skaia, A. Zatorskii, T. Kuz'min'skii, and A. Leinvand (eds), *Dokumenty i materialy po istorii sovetsko-pol'skikh otnoshenii* [hereafter DiM] tom II (Moscow, 1964), 517–18; Carley, 'The Politics of Anti-Bolshevism', 170–5. Piotr Wandycz, *France and her Eastern Allies, 1919–1925: French-Czechoslovak-Polish Relations from the Paris Peace Conference in Locarno* (Minneapolis, 1962), 140–1.
42 Ibid., 141.
43 RGASPI, f. 17, op. 109, d. 74, ll. 12–15.
44 AVPRF, f. 4, op. 52, p. 340, d. 55230, l. 3.
45 V.I. Lenin, *Polnoe sobranie sochinenii* [hereafter PSS], tom 40 (Moscow, 1974), 69.
46 Ibid., 96.
47 DVP, tom III, 363–4.
48 C. Bron'skii, V. Gostyn'skaia, A. Zatorskii, T. Kyz'min'skii, and A. Leinvand (eds), DiM, tom II, 502; Ullman, *Anglo-Soviet Relations*, vol. II, 137.
49 AVPRF, f. 4, op. 52, p. 340, d. 55240, l. 4.
50 Jan M. Meijer (ed.), *The Trotsky Papers, 1917–1922. Vol. 2, 1920–1922* (The Hague, 1974), 20–1.
51 For Lenin's comments about Churchill at the eighth all-Russian conference of the Bolshevik Party in December 1919, see DiM, tom II, 411.
52 For Churchill's memorandum to cabinet, from November 1919, see CAB 24/94/40; Ullman, *Anglo-Soviet Relations*, vol. 3, 6.
53 CHAR 2/110/1–2. Churchill's colleague, general Sir Edward Spears, also argued for a 'common policy of the border states united against the Bolsheviks.' CHAR 16/63/38–39. Curzon entertained the idea of an anti-Soviet coalition of border countries, at least in December 1919, but he was more focused on disrupting Bolshevik influence in Asia and the Middle East. FRUS, 1920, Vol. III, document 538.
54 For Churchill's suggestion of Foch, see CHAR/2/110/13–14. On Patek's suggestion, see CHAR 16/63/58. For Piłsudski's comment to Rumbold, see Woodward and Butler (eds), DBFP, First series, Vol. III, 800–1.
55 AVPRF, f. 4, op. 52, p. 340, d. 55240, ll. 3–4.
56 AVPRF, f. 4, op. 52, p. 340, d. 55246, l. 3.
57 RGASPI, f. 17, op. 86, d. 208, l. 2.
58 Meijer, *The Trotsky Papers*, vol. II, 80–1.
59 Borzęcki, *The Soviet–Polish Peace*, 51; See also Pipes, 'New Materials on the Polish-Soviet War of 1920', 73.
60 Borzęcki, *The Soviet–Polish Peace*, 64; RGASPI, f. 17, op. 109, d. 74, ll. 9–9a.
61 RGASPI, f. 17, op. 109, d. 74, ll. 12–15.
62 DiM, tom II, 347.
63 Stephen Brown, 'Lenin, Stalin and the Failure of the Red Army in the Soviet-Polish War of 1920', *War & Society* 14/2 (1996): 41.

64 RGASPI, f. 558, op. 1, d. 1522, ll. 1–5.
65 AVPRF, f. 4, op. 52, p. 341, d. 55292, l. 6; p. 340, d. 55240, l. 5; Borzęcki, *The Soviet–Polish Peace*, 61–3.
66 RGASPI, f. 17, op. 86, d. 208, l. 4.
67 Wandycz, *Soviet–Polish Relations*, 168, 179.
68 RGASPI, f. 17, op. 86, d. 209, l. 12.
69 Meijer, *The Trotsky Papers*, vol. II, 117.
70 DVP, tom II, 397–402.
71 Meijer, *The Trotsky Papers*, vol. II, 123.
72 Butler, Bury, and Lambert (eds), DBFP, First series, Vol. XI, 245–6.
73 Wandycz, *Soviet–Polish Relations*, 182. The same comparison with the Treaty of Versailles was also made in the British Foreign Office. Ullman, *Anglo-Soviet Relations*, vol. 3, 34.
74 Lenin, PSS, tom 51 (Moscow, 1974), 146.
75 AVPRF, f. 4, op. 52, p. 340, d. 55240, l. 10.
76 Ibid.; I.I. Kostiushko, M.N. Chernykh and V.N. Savchenko (eds), *Pol'sko-sovetskaia voina 1919–1920. Ranee ne opublikovannye dokumenty i materialy* [hereafter PSV], ch. 1 (Moscow, 1994), 53–4.
77 Meijer, *The Trotsky Papers*, vol. II, 133–4.
78 Gosudarstvennyi Arkhiv Rossiiskoi Federatsii [hereafter GARF], f. r-393, op. 19, d. 4, l. 105; Borzęcki, *The Soviet–Polish Peace*, 51, fn. 35.
79 Norman Davies, 'The Missing Revolutionary War: The Polish Campaigns and the Retreat from Revolution in Soviet Russia, 1919–21', *Soviet Studies* 27/2 (1975): 182.
80 Lenin, PSS, tom 51, 158.
81 RGASPI, f. 5, op. 1, d. 2528, l. 28.
82 Lenin, PSS, tom 51, 158. For Chicherin's report, see AVPRF, f. 4, op. 52, p. 340, d. 55246, l. 7.
83 Wandycz, *Soviet–Polish Relations*, 180; Debo, *Survival and Consolidation*, 203.
84 Lenin, PSS, tom 51, 159.
85 RGASPI, f. 17, op. 3, d. 70, l. 1; op. 109, d. 79, l. 19.
86 Richard Pipes (ed.), *The Unknown Lenin: From the Secret Archive* (New Haven, 1996), 78–9.
87 V.I Lenin, Speech at the Ninth Congress of the RKP(b). Available at https://www.marxists.org/archive/lenin/works/1920/mar/29.htm [accessed March 2021].
88 RGASPI, f. 17, op. 86, d. 209, l. 2.
89 N.M. V'iunova, N.I. Deeva and T.F. Kariaeva (eds), *Direktivy glavnogo komandovaniia krasnoi armii (1917–1920). Sbornik dokumentov* (Moscow, 1969) [hereafter DGKKA], 629–30.
90 DiM, tom II, 634.
91 Wandycz, *Soviet–Polish Relations*, 180–2.
92 Josef Korbel, *Poland between East and West. Soviet and German Diplomacy towards Poland, 1919–1933* (Princeton, 1963), 37.
93 DiM, tom II, 634.
94 PSV, ch. 1, 61; RGASPI, f. 159, op. 2, d. 37, ll. 3–3ob.
95 DiM, tom II, 637.
96 DVP, tom II, 436–7, 448; Wandycz, *Soviet–Polish Relations*, 184–7.
97 RGASPI, f. 2, op. 1, d. 13455, l. 1.
98 AVPRF, f. 4, op. 52, p. 340, d. 55240, l. 15.
99 S. Broński, V. Gostyn'skaia, A. Zatorskii, A. Leinvand, and I.S. Iazhborovskaia (eds), DiM, tom III (Moscow, 1965), 29.

100 I.V. Stalin, 'The Entente's new campaign against Russia' (25–26 May 1920). Available at https://www.marxists.org/reference/archive/stalin/works/1920/05/25.htm [accessed March 2021].
101 AVPRF, f. 4, d. 52, p. 340, d. 55240, l. 13.
102 Dov B. Lungu, 'Soviet-Romanian Relations and the Bessarabian Question in the Early 1920s', *Southeastern Europe* 6/1 (1979): 35.
103 Debo, *Survival and Consolidation*, 204, 206; AVPRF, f. 4, op. 52, p. 340, d. 55238, l. 24; RGASPI, f. 17, op. 109, d. 79, l. 80. For the Latvian general staff's view from June about the benefits of good relations with Poland to defend against a Bolshevik attack, see f. 2, op. 1, d. 14561, l. 2; Meijer, *The Trotsky Papers*, vol. II, 189.
104 Davies, *White Eagle, Red Star*, 75.
105 DiM, tom II, 656–8, 600–3.
106 Jan Karski, *The Great Powers and Poland: From Versailles to Yalta* (Plymouth, 2014), 46. Writing to Litvinov, Chicherin later referred to Piłsudski and Petliura's collaboration as one of 'former German-and-Austrophiles' who had 'in a strange way' become 'darlings of the Entente'. AVPRF, f. 059, op. 1, p. 4, d. 35, l. 266.
107 Matthew D. Pauly, 'Soviet Polonophobia and the Formulation of Nationalities Policy in the Ukrainian SSR, 1927–1934' in David L. Ransel and Bozena Shallcross (eds), *Polish Encounters, Russian Identity* (Bloomington and Indianapolis, 2005), 174.
108 Davies, *White Eagle, Red Star*, 86.
109 CAB 23/20/63.
110 CAB 24/97/12/45. Zimmerman, *Jozef Pilsudski*, 349.
111 Pipes 'New Materials on the Polish-Soviet War of 1920', 73; Wandycz, *Soviet–Polish Relations*, 194; Debo, *Survival and Consolidation*, 213; Zamoyski, *Warsaw 1920*, 33.
112 Borzęcki, *The Soviet–Polish Peace*, 65.
113 Wandycz, *Soviet–Polish Relations*, 194; Debo, *Survival and Consolidation*, 213; RGASPI, f. 17, op. 109, d. 84, ll. 13–13ob.
114 RGASPI, f. 17, op. 86, d. 209, l. 11; Davies, *White Eagle, Red Star*, 116.
115 RGASPI, f. 17, op. 109, d. 84, l. 14; f. 325, op. 1, d. 487, l. 102.
116 Borzęcki, *The Soviet–Polish Peace*, 65, 68.
117 Ibid., 66. On reinforcements, see N.E. Kakurin and V.A. Melikov, *Voina s velopoliakami 1920 g.* (Moscow, 1925), 438–9.
118 Norman Davies, 'The Genesis of the Polish-Soviet War, 1919–20', *European History Quarterly* 5/1 (1975): 62.
119 Zamoyski, *Warsaw 1920*, p. 36.
120 Wandycz, 'France and the Polish-Soviet War 1919–1920', 11.
121 RGASPI, f. 63, op. 1, d. 5, ll. 2–21.
122 Davies, *White Eagle, Red Star*, 114; Ullman, *Anglo-Soviet Relations*, vol. 3, 77–8; DVP, tom II, 490–1.
123 Erickson, *The Soviet High Command*, 87–8; Borzęcki, *The Soviet–Polish Peace*, 52; Robert M. Ponichtera and David R. Stone, 'The Russo-Polish War' in Robin Higham and Frederick W. Hagen (eds), *The Military History and the Soviet Union* (New York, 2002), 40.
124 RGASPI, f. 17, op. 3, d. 73, l. 1.
125 V'iunova, Deeva and Kariaeva (eds), DGKKA, 678–9.
126 RGASPI, f. 17, op. 163, d. 63, l. 3; op. 3, d. 76, l. 2.
127 V.I Lenin, *Collected Works*, vol. 31 (Moscow, 1965), 120–1, 131.
128 L.D. Trotsky, 'The Polish Front and Our Tasks' (30 April 1920). Available at https://www.marxists.org/archive/trotsky/1920/military/ch20.htm [accessed March 2021].

129 Trotsky 'In a State of Intoxication' (13 May 1920). Available at https://www.marxists.org/archive/trotsky/1920/military/ch34.htm [accessed March 2021].
130 RGASPI, f. 558, op. 1, d. 1630, ll. 1–2.
131 AVPRF, f. 4, op. 52, p. 340, d. 55240, l. 16.
132 AVPRF, f. 4, op. 32, p. 204, d. 52423, l. 85.
133 Debo, *Survival and Consolidation*, 215.
134 Ibid., 215, citing *Lord Riddell's Intimate Diary of the Peace Conference and After* (New York, 1934), 191.
135 CHAR 16/67/20.
136 DiM, tom III, 64; Ullman, *Anglo-Soviet Relations*, vol. 3, 49.
137 AVPRF, f. 059, op. 1, p. 4, d. 34, l. 41.
138 CAB 20/23/63.
139 Wandycz, *Soviet–Polish Relations*, 165.
140 Debo, *Survival and Consolidation*, 216; Zimmerman, *Jozef Pilsudski*, 355.
141 Erickson, *The Soviet High Command*, 89.
142 Quoted in ibid.
143 Earl F. Ziemke, *The Red Army, 1918–1941: From Vanguard of World Revolution to America's Ally* (London, 2006), 122.
144 Robert Service, *Trotsky: A Biography* (CA, Massachusetts, 2009), 271.
145 Meijer (ed.), *The Trotsky Papers*, vol. II, 159, 168.
146 PSV, ch. 1, 93–108.
147 RGASPI, f. 17, op. 109, d. 84, l. 25.
148 Ibid., l. 28.
149 RGASPI, f. 558, op. 1, d. 5464, l. 1; Davies, *White Eagle, Red Star*, 139.
150 RGASPI, f. 17, op. 109, d. 84, l. 30.
151 Davies, *White Eagle, Red Star*, 125.
152 Zamoyski, *Warsaw 1920*, 43–9; Erickson, *The Soviet High Command*, 90.
153 AVPRF, f. 4, op. 52, p. 340, d. 55240, l. 18.
154 AVPRF, f. 4, op. 54, p. 351, d. 7, ll. 3–4; DiM, t. III, 78.
155 RGASPI, f. 17, op. 86, d. 210, ll. 60–1.
156 RGASPI, f. 17, op. 86, d. 209, l. 40.
157 Ibid., l. 18.
158 RGASPI, f. 17, op. 109, d. 74, l. 28; Trotsky, Telegram to Lenin, Chicherin, Karakhan, Krestinskii and Radek (12 June 1920). Available at https://www.marxists.org/archive/trotsky/1920/military/ch39.htm [accessed March 2021].
159 RGASPI, f. 17, op. 3, d. 84, l. 1; AVPRF, f. 059, op. 1, p. 4, d. 36, l. 74.
160 RGASPI, f. 17, op. 109, d. 84, l. 34.
161 Stalin, 'The Entente's new campaign against Russia' (25–26 May 1920). Available at https://www.marxists.org/reference/archive/stalin/works/1920/05/25.htm [accessed March 2021].
162 Meijer (ed.), *The Trotsky Papers*, vol. II, 211–13; RGASPI, f. 558, op. 1, d. 4693, ll. 2ob.
163 RGASPI, f. 558, op. 1, d. 1737, ll. 1–2.
164 AVPRF, f. 4, op. 54, p. 351, d. 7, l. 18; Meijer (ed.), *The Trotsky Papers*, vol. II, 167.
165 Meijer (ed.), *The Trotsky Papers*, vol. II, 217; Isaac Deutscher, *The Prophet Armed: Trotsky 1879–1921* (Oxford, 1954), 462–3.
166 M.M. Narinskogo and A.V. Mal'gina (eds), *Sovetsko-pol'skie otnosheniia v 1918–1945 gg.: Sbornik dokumentov v chetyrekh tomakh. Tom 1 1918–1926* [hereafter SPO] (Moscow 2017), 86–9; Ullman, *Anglo-Soviet Relations*, vol. 3, 98.
167 Fiddick, *Russia's Retreat*, 44, 45.

168 SPO, tom 1, 90–1.
169 RGASPI, f. 558, op. 1, d. 3480, l. 1; Fiddick, *Russia's Retreat*, 92.
170 Lenin, PSS, tom 51, 215.
171 RGASPI, f. 558, op. 1 d. 1684, l. 1.
172 AVPRF, f. 059, op. 1, p. 4, d. 36, l. 65.
173 DVP, tom II, 567–8; AVPRF, f. 4, op. 52, p. 340, d. 55231, l. 11; Shmelev, *In the Wake of Empire*, 551, 583.
174 Ullman, *Anglo-Soviet Relations*, vol. 3, 118.
175 AVPRF, f. 4, op. 32, p. 205, d. 52427, ll. 6–7.
176 SPO, tom 1, 92–3.
177 Ullman, *Anglo-Soviet Relations*, vol. 3, 127.
178 SPO, tom 1, 92–3.
179 AVPRF, f. 4, op. 54, p. 351, d. 8, l. 34.
180 H.J. Elcock, 'Britain and the Russo-Polish Fronter', *The Historical Journal* 12/1 (1969): 146.
181 RGASPI, f. 558, op. 1, d. 1777, l. 1.
182 RGASPI, f. 17, op. 86, d. 209, l. 19; op. 109, d. 21, l. 210.
183 A.A Avdeev and M.-R. Ungurianu, *Sovetsko-rumynskie otnosheniia: dokumenty i materialy*, t. 1. 1917–1934 (Moscow, 2000), 52.
184 RGASPI, f. 2, op. 1, d. 14557, l. 1; Meijer (ed.), *The Trotsky Papers*, vol. II, 223.
185 RGASPI, f. 17, op. 86, d. 208, l. 5.
186 Stalin 'The situation on the South-Western Front' (24 June 1920). Available at https://www.marxists.org/reference/archive/stalin/works/1920/06/24.htm [accessed March 2021].
187 Debo, *Survival and Consolidation*, 238.
188 John Wheeler-Bennett, *The Nemesis of Power: The German Army in Politics, 1918–1945* (London, 2005), 122–5; Debo, *Survival and Consolidation*, p. 66; Ian Ona Johnson, *Faustian Bargain: The Soviet-German Partnership and the Origins of the Second World War* (Oxford, 2021), 35–40.
189 CHAR 16/63/69,84,108; CAB/24/106/34.
190 CHAR 16/63/123–7.
191 CHAR 16/63/140-4; 16/64/1–2,6,22–4,89.
192 Shmelev, *In the Wake of Empire*, 547; DiM, tom II, 502, fn.3; *The Daily Herald*, 16 Feb 1920, 3.
193 CHAR 16/63/58.
194 CHAR 16/67/124.

Chapter 2

1 Zamoyski, *The Battle for the Marchlands*, 84.
2 *Dekrety sovetskoi vlast*, tom III (Moscow, 1964), 259.
3 Davies, *White Eagle, Red Star*, 145.
4 RGASPI, f. 17, op. 109, d. 222, l. 29.
5 RGASPI, f. 17, op. 109, d. 215, ll. 50–1; Brown, 'Lenin, Stalin and the Failure of the Red Army in the Soviet-Polish War of 1920', 43; Pontichera and Stone, 'The Russo-Polish War', 41.
6 Erickson, *The Soviet High Command*, 91.

7 A.V. Kashonkin, O.V. Khlevniuk, L.P. Kosheleva and L.A. Rogovaia (eds), *Bol'shevistskoe rukovodstvo perepiska 1912–1927* [hereafter BRP] (Moscow, 1996), 140.
8 For Stalin's telegram to Lenin from 11 July, see *Leninskii sbornik*, XXXVI (Moscow, 1959), 110–11. For Stalin's *Pravda* article, see https://www.marxists.org/reference/archive/stalin/works/1920/07/11.htm [accessed July 2021].
9 See efforts by Petr Struve, Wrangel's foreign minister, to reach accommodation with the Polish government in April 1920, DiM, tom II, 647. For further efforts brokered by Savinkov from June 1920, see DiM, tom III, 89.
10 AVPRF, f. 4, op. 54, p. 351, d. 7, l. 9.
11 Borzęcki, *The Soviet–Polish Peace*, 77; Wandycz, *Soviet–Polish Relations*, 211, 213; Karski, *The Great Powers and Poland*, 47–8.
12 CAB 23/22/3.
13 Davies, 'Lloyd George and Poland', 144.
14 Borzęcki, *The Soviet–Polish Peace*, 78.
15 Evan Mawdsley, *The Russian Civil War* (New York, 2007), 254.
16 DiM, tom III, 150, 171–2.
17 Butler and Bury (eds), DBFP, First series, vol. VIII, pp. 368–9; Ullman, *Anglo-Soviet Relations*, vol. 3, 210–11; Elcock, 'Britain and the Russo-Polish Frontier', 147; Peter Jackson, *Beyond the Balance of Power: France and the Politics of National Security in the Era of the First World War* (Cambridge, 2013), 337; Michael Jabara Carley, 'Anti-Bolshevism in French Foreign Policy: The Crisis in Poland in 1920', *The International History Review* 2/3 (1980): 413–14.
18 DVP, tom II, 699–700.
19 Lenin, PSS, tom 51, 238.
20 G.V. Chicherin, *Stati i rechi po voprosam mezhdunarodnoi politiki* (Moscow, 1961), 283. Lenin articulated his views on the nature of the civil war in September 1920. Pipes (ed.), *The Unknown Lenin*, 98. Klyshko wrote to Moscow on 13 July, noting that the British 'cannot send one soldier, one weapon'. RGASPI, f. 2, op. 1, d. 14672, l. 1.
21 RGASPI, f. 558, op. 1, d. 1815, l. 1. In a follow-up telegram to Lenin, Stalin argued that to hold a peace conference in London would give the British undue influence and that negotiations should instead take place in Soviet Russia. RGASPI, f. 558, op. 1, d. 1818, l. 1.
22 RGASPI, f. 2, op. 1, d. 14673, ll. 1–1ob; Deutscher, *The Prophet Armed*, 463.
23 Meijer, *The Trotsky Papers*, II, 229–31.
24 Ibid., 233.
25 Chicherin, *Stati i rechi*, 283.
26 PSV, tom 1, 130–2.
27 Ibid., 137–40; Borzęcki, *The Soviet-Polish Peace*, 81. In late June, Chicherin expressed greater concerns about France, although partly also about Britain, pushing Romania into war, but he was sceptical that Britain alone would exert such influence on Finland or Latvia. AVPRF, f. 4, op. 54, p. 351, d. 8, l. 28. For similar see, f. 4, op. 59, p. 390. d. 56378, l. 7.
28 AVPRF, f. 059, op. 1, p. 4, d. 36, l. 149; d. 34, l. 217; SPO, tom 1, 102.
29 AVPRF, f. 4, op. 32, p. 205, d. 52427, ll. 30–1; Brown, 'Lenin, Stalin and the Failure of the Red Army in the Soviet-Polish War of 1920', 40.
30 Quoted in ibid.
31 DGKKA, 611–12; Erickson, *The Soviet High Command*, 92.

32 Rossiskii gosudarstvennyi voennyi arkhiv [hereafter RGVA], f. 6, op. 4, d. 468, ll. 175; RGASPI, f. 17, op. 109, d. 115, l. 1; Lungu, 'Soviet-Romanian Relations', 35; Shmelev, *In the Wake of Empire*, 545–6.
33 PSV, ch. I, 142–3. Borzecki presents a similar account of the debate on the Curzon note, see *The Soviet-Polish Peace*, 79–82.
34 RGASPI, f. 5, op. 1, d. 2933, ll. 14–14ob.
35 Pipes (ed.), *The Unknown Lenin*, 88; Stephen Kotkin, *Stalin. Vol. 1: Paradoxes of Power 1878–1928* (London, 2014), 360, fn. 94. For Unshlikht's view, see Kashonkin, Khlevniuk, Kosheleva and Rogovaia (eds), BRP, 144.
36 Service, *Trotsky*, 271–2.
37 Stalin, 'The Entente's new campaign against Russia' (25–26 May 1920). Available at https://www.marxists.org/reference/archive/stalin/works/1920/05/25.htm [accessed July 2021]. On Stalin as Lenin's authority on nationalism, see Ronald Grigor Suny, *Stalin: Passage to Revolution* (Princeton, 2020), 519–36.
38 SPO, tom 1, 103–5; for Lenin's reaction to Radek see, Klara Zetkin, *Reminiscences of Lenin* (London, 1929), 20.
39 DVP, tom III, 61–2.
40 Ibid., 47–53; Borzęcki, *The Soviet-Polish Peace*, 82.
41 RGASPI, f. 558, op. 1, d. 1841, ll. 1–12.
42 DiM, tom III, 190; Wandycz, *Soviet–Polish Relations*, 222–3.
43 Ullman, *Anglo-Soviet Relations*, vol. 3, 172–3.
44 DGKKA, 643–5.
45 Kakurin and Melikov, *Voina s velopoliakami 1920*, 475.
46 RGASPI, f. 17, op. 109, d. 21, l. 123–4; Meijer, *The Trotsky Papers*, vol. II, 223.
47 AVPRF, f. 059, op. 1, p. 4, d. 34, ll. 134, 207.
48 PSV, ch. I, 144–5; RGASPI, f. 63, op. 1, d. 271, l. 34.
49 *Izvestiia, TsK KPSS* 2 (1991), 115.
50 Fiddick, *Russia's Retreat*, 114.
51 Lenin's confidence in exporting revolution was evident two weeks before when he, along with other Bolsheviks, considered sovietizing Lithuania even though a peace treaty was about to be signed. 'We must occupy and sovietize. Judge, and judge only from this point of view […] Occupy and organize a revolution in Lithuania.' Pipes (ed.), *The Unknown Lenin*, 85–8; 90–2; 99; Croll, 'Soviet-Polish relations, 1919–1921', 58.
52 Kashonkin, Khlevniuk, Kosheleva and Rogovaia (eds), BRP, 148.
53 Brown, 'Lenin, Stalin and the Failure of the Red Army in the Soviet-Polish War of 1920', 42; Mawdsley, *The Russian Civil War*, 258; see also DGKKA, 643–4, 704–5. On the potential Romanian intervention, see Kotkin *Stalin. Vol. 1*, 360.
54 Davies, *White Eagle, Red Star*, 148.
55 Borzęcki notes this in *The Soviet-Polish Peace*, 89.
56 DiM, tom III, 193.
57 RGASPI, f. 558, op. 1, d. 5519, l. 3.
58 RGASPI, f. 558, op. 1, d. 5518, l. 2.
59 AVPRF, f. 4, op. 52, p. 340, d. 55240, l. 29; see also Borzęcki, *The Soviet–Polish Peace*, 91, 104.
60 RGASPI, f. 558, op. 1, d. 5523, l. 3.
61 RGASPI, f. 17, op. 86, d. 209, l. 21.
62 Borzęcki, *The Soviet–Polish Peace*, 103.
63 Debo, *Survival and Consolidation*, 232.

64 AVPRF, f. 059, op. 1, p. 4, d. 36, ll. 190–1.
65 DiM, tom III, 262. For the claim that 'atmospheric conditions' hindered the radio broadcast, see the message to the British government, AVPRF, f. 4, op. 4, p. 17, d. 248, l. 7. On Trotsky's accusation of Polish delays, see his message on 11 August. Available at https://www.marxists.org/archive/trotsky/1920/military/ch46.htm [accessed July 2021].
66 DBFP, First series, vol. XI, 422.
67 Borzęcki, *The Soviet–Polish Peace*, 90–3; AVPRF, f. 4, op. 52, p. 340, d. 55240, l. 29.
68 Kashonkin, Khlevniuk, Kosheleva and Rogovaia (eds), BRP, 150.
69 Ibid., 151–2.
70 Lenin, *Collected Works*, vol. 31, 264; RGASPI, f. 558, op. 1, d. 5527, l. 3.
71 Wandycz, *Soviet–Polish Relations*, 233 citing N. F. Kuzmin, *Krushenie poslednego pokhoda Antanty* (Moscow, 1958), 256–7; Borzęcki, *The Soviet–Polish Peace*, 92; Meijer, *The Trotsky Papers*, vol. II, 241.
72 Borzęcki, *The Soviet–Polish Peace*, 86.
73 Davies, *White Eagle, Red Star*, 186.
74 RGASPI, f. 63, op. 1, d. 271, l. 34; f. 17, op. 3, d. 96, l. 1; Wandycz, *Soviet–Polish Relations*, 208, 225–6, 232; Davies, *White Eagle, Red Star*, 158.
75 A.A. Plekhanov and A.M. Plekhanov (eds), *F. E. Dzerzhinskii – predsedatel' VChK-OGPU 1917–1926* (Moscow, 2007), 202–3.
76 RGASPI, f. 17, op. 86, d. 209, l. 24; Trotsky Papers, II, 235, 243.
77 RGASPI, f. 17, op. 86, d. 210, l. 19; Davies, *White Eagle, Red Star*, 156.
78 RGASPI, f. 558, op. 1, d. 5534, l. 2.
79 RGASPI, f. 17, op. 86, d. 209, l. 30; PSV, ch. I, 193; Korbel, *Poland between East and West*, 64.
80 Ullman, *Anglo-Soviet Relations*, vol. 3, 195–7.
81 DiM, tom III, 261.
82 DVP, tom III, 83–6; Ullman, *Anglo-Soviet Relations*, vol. 3, 196.
83 For the proposed truce, see AVPRF, f. 4, op. 4, p. 17, d. 248, l. 80.
84 CAB 24/110/52/268; Ullman, *Anglo-Soviet Relations*, vol. 3, 206.
85 AVPRF, f. 059, op. 1, p. 5, d. 37, l. 204.
86 Quoted in Debo, *Survival and Consolidation*, 234; CAB 23/22/89; AVPRF, f. 059, op. 1, p. 5, d. 37, l. 192.
87 Lenin, PSS, tom 51, 250.
88 Ibid.
89 RGASPI, f. 558, op. 1, d. 1, d. 4442, l. 1.
90 PSV, ch. I, 171.
91 DGKKA, 806–7, fn. 117.
92 Debo, *Survival and Consolidation*, 234.
93 Hansard, vol. 133, col. 264 (10 August 1920). Available at https://hansard.parliament.uk/Commons/1920-08-10/debates/4f20d00b-4755-48cc-a929-c7764befa91f/RussiaAndPoland [accessed July 2021[.
94 For the report from London, see AVPRF, f. 059, op. 1, p. 5, d. 37, l. 205.
95 AVPRF, f. 059, op. 1, p. 4, d. 34, ll. 231, 243; Ullman, *Anglo-Soviet Relations*, vol. 3, 208–9.
96 Kashonkin, Khlevniuk, Kosheleva and Rogovaia (eds), BRP, 153–4; RGASPI, f. 558, op. 1, d. 5530, l. 2. RGASPI, f. 558, op. 1, d. 5533, l. 3.
97 Wandycz, *Soviet–Polish Relations*, 238.
98 CAB/23/22/135; DBFP, First series, vol. XI, pp. 455–6.

99 Carley, 'Anti-Bolshevism in French Foreign Policy', 422.
100 DBFP, First series, vol. XI, 475–6.
101 Debo, *Survival and Consolidation*, 235.
102 AVPRF, f. 059, op. 1, p. 5, d. 37, l. 192.
103 Debo, *Survival and Consolidation*, 237; for Chicherin's message to Lenin about the differences in Kamenev's terms to the British government, see AVPRF, f. 4, op. 4, p. 17, d. 248, l. 113.
104 AVPRF, f. 059, op. 1, p. 5, d. 37, ll. 223, 227; Ullman, *Anglo-Soviet Relations*, vol. 3, 257.
105 RGASPI, f. 17, op. 163, d. 85, l. 63.
106 Jonathan Haslam, *The Spectre of War: International Communism and the Origins of World War II* (Princeton, 2021), 32–3.
107 AVPRF, f. 4, op. 52, p. 340, d. 55240, l. 37. Chicherin was not against the idea of using German communists on the western front, but he did not want them organized in such an obvious manner. For Poland as the revolutionary bridge, see Radek's comments from July in Korbel, *Poland between East and West*, 45. For Chicherin's assurances, see 87.
108 Zamoyski, *Warsaw 1920*, 111.
109 RGVA, f. 6, op. 4, d. 500, l. 8.
110 Korbel, *Poland between East and West*, 46.
111 Richard Pipes, *Russia under the Bolshevik Regime* (New York, 1993), 190. Pipes noted a telegram from Viktor Kopp to Lenin from 19 August that made this aspiration clear.
112 RGASPI, f. 17, op. 109, d. 215, l. 61.
113 Brown, 'Lenin, Stalin and the Failure of the Red Army in the Soviet-Polish War of 1920', 45. Brown notes that on 12 August, Stalin and Egorov had suggested redeploying the 1st Cavalry Army to Proskurov, which undermines the case it could not be removed from Lwów.
114 Brown, 'Lenin, Stalin and the Failure of the Red Army in the Soviet-Polish War of 1920', 44; Erickson, *The Soviet High Command*, 97; RGASPI, f. 558, op. 1, d. 5537, l. 2.
115 Lenin, PSS, tom 51, 254–5. For this interpretation, see Brown, 'Lenin, Stalin and the Failure of the Red Army in the Soviet-Polish War of 1920', 45.
116 Kashonkin, Khlevniuk, Kosheleva and Rogovaia (eds), BRP, 155.
117 Mawdsley, *The Russian Civil War*, 259; Meijer, *The Trotsky Papers*, vol. II, 249.
118 AVPRF, f. 4, op. 32, p. 209, d. 52482, l. 137.
119 RGASPI, f. 5, op. 1, d. 2429, l. 51.
120 Fiddick, *Russia's Retreat*, 214–15; DGKKA, 652–3; Erickson, *The Soviet High Command*, 98; Zamoyski, *Warsaw 1920*, 91; Davies, *White Eagle, Red Star*, 201.
121 RGASPI, f. 17, op. 109, d. 215, l. 63.
122 Erickson, *The Soviet High Command*, 97; RGASPI, f. 558, op. 1, d. 1945, l. 3.
123 AVPRF, f. 059, op. 1, p. 5, d. 39, l. 140.
124 Mawdsley, *The Russian Civil War*, 255.
125 Erickson, *The Soviet High Command*, 97; Davies, *White Eagle, Red Star*, 186.
126 Pontichera and Stone, 'The Russo-Polish war', 45.
127 RGASPI, f. 17, op. 109, d. 216, l. 68.
128 Mawdsley, *The Russian Civil War*, 255.
129 AVPRF, f. 4, op. 32, p. 209, d. 52482, l. 136; CAB 23/22/91; Carley, 'Anti-Bolshevism in French Foreign Policy', 412; Zimmerman, *Jozef Pilsudski*, 360.
130 RGASPI, f. 17, op. 86, d. 210, l. 25; f. 2, op. 1, d. 15088, l. 2.

131 DGKKA, 654; Meijer, *The Trotsky Papers*, vol. II, 253–5.
132 Lenin, PSS, tom 51, 264; Debo, *Survival and Consolidation*, 241; Meijer, *The Trotsky Papers*, vol. II, 261.
133 RGASPI, f. 5, op. 1, d. 2429, l. 52; AVPRF, f. 059, op. 1, p. 4, d. 36, l. 224ob.
134 Quoted in Ullman, *Anglo-Soviet Relations*, vol. 3, 269; Lenin, PSS, tom 51, 266.
135 RGASPI, f. 17, op. 109, d. 74, l 30.
136 Lenin, PSS, tom 51, 259–60.
137 Borzęcki, *The Soviet–Polish Peace*, 97.
138 For the British comparison of the terms, see CHAR 16/32/8. For the British response, see AVPRF, f. 69, op. 5, p. 6, d. 7, ll. 23–5.
139 RGASPI, f. 17, op. 86, d. 210, l. 26; AVPRF, f. 059, op. 1, p. 5, d. 39, l. 148.
140 RGASPI, f. 17, op. 3, d. 103, l. 1.
141 Pontichera and Stone, 'The Russo-Polish war', 46–7; Mawdsley, *The Russian Civil War*, 256.
142 RGASPI, f. 17, op. 109, d. 84, l. 95; f. 17, op. 86, d. 209, l. 38.
143 RGASPI, f. 5, op. 1, d. 2055, l. 8.
144 AVPRF, f. 059, op. 1, p. 4, d. 34, l. 269.
145 CAB 24/110/64/341. Polish losses have been estimated at 4,500 by contrast. Zimmerman, *Jozef Pilsudski*, 363.
146 Mawdsley, *The Russian Civil War*, 257.
147 Quoted in Debo, *Survival and Consolidation*, 243.
148 Pipes (ed.), *The Unknown Lenin*, 95–115.
149 Zetkin, *Reminiscences of Lenin*, 20–2.
150 Lenin, 'Speech Delivered at a Congress of Leather Industry Workers' (9–10 October 1920). Available at https://www.marxists.org/archive/lenin/works/1920/oct/02b.htm [accessed July 2021].
151 RGASPI, f. 558, op. 1, d. 5210, l. 2.
152 Kotkin *Stalin. Vol. 1*, 365; on Stalin's weak position, see Robert Service, *Stalin: A Biography* (London, 2010), 184.
153 RGASPI, f. 558, op. 1, d. 5541, l. 2; Kashonkin, Khlevniuk, Kosheleva and Rogovaia (eds), BRP, 160, fn. 2.
154 RGASPI, f. 558, op. 11, d. 1101, ll. 63; Erickson, *The Soviet High Command*, 99–102.
155 RGASPI, f. 558, op. 1, d. 2032, ll. 1–2.
156 Kashonkin, Khlevniuk, Kosheleva and Rogovaia (eds), BRP, fn. 2; Service, *Trotsky*, 277. Elsewhere in messages to the revolutionary military council of the western front and to the Polish Bureau, Trotsky suggested that revolution might have taken hold had the Bolsheviks been better prepared and criticized insufficient work undertaken to win over the Polish masses. RGASPI, f. 17, op. 86, d. 209, l. 34.
157 L.D. Trotsky, 'The War with Poland: Is a Second Lesson Needed?' (8 September 1920), *The Military Writings of Leon Trotsky. Volume 3: 1920*. Available at https://www.marxists.org/archive/trotsky/1920/military/ch51.htm [accessed July 2021].
158 Carley, 'Anti-Bolshevism in French Foreign Policy', 423–4.
159 AVPRF, f. 059, op. 1, p. 4, d. 36, ll. 224–ob.
160 Kashonkin, Khlevniuk, Kosheleva and Rogovaia (eds), BRP, 156–7.
161 PSV, ch. II, 39–40.
162 Pipes (ed.), *The Unknown Lenin*, 109–10.

Chapter 3

1. Zygmunt J. Gąsiorowski, 'Poland's Policy towards Soviet Russia, 1921–1922', *The Slavonic and East European Review* 53/151 (1975): 233.
2. Plekhanov and Plekhanov (eds), *Dzerzhinskii*, 210.
3. S.A. Kokin, R.Iu. Podkur and O.S. Rubl'ov (eds), *Sprava 'Pol's'koi Organizatsii Viis'kovoi' v Ukraini. 1920–1938 rr.: Zbirnykh dokumentiv ta materialiv* (Kyiv, 2011), 37–42.
4. See investigation of the POV in Khar'kov in March 1921, ibid., 59.
5. PSV, ch. II, p. 11; AVPRF, 4, op. 32, p. 210, d. 52514, ll. 36–7, 43.
6. Borzęcki, *The Soviet-Polish Peace*, 155; DiM, III, 430.
7. Nataliia Rubl'ova and Oleksandr Rubl'ov (eds), *Ukraïna – Pol'shcha 1920–1939 rr.: Z istoriï dyplomatychnykh vidnosyn USSR z Druhoiu Richchiu Pospolytoiu: Dokumenty i materialy* (Kyiv, 2012), 73–6; Jan Jacek Bruski, *Between Prometheism and Realpolitik: Poland and Soviet Ukraine, 1921–1926* (Krakow, 2016), 200.
8. DVP, tom IV, 312; Gąsiorowski, 'Poland's Policy towards Soviet Russia', 241; AVPRF, f. 4, op. 1, p. 489, d. 77, l. 5.
9. PSV, ch. II, 97–105; Borzęcki, *The Soviet-Polish Peace*, 151–2.
10. Ibid., 156.
11. PSV, ch. II, 117; GARF, r-393, op. 1A, d. 13, ll. 119–20, 139.
12. AVPRF, f. 4, op. 32, p. 207, d. 52462, ll. 27–9.
13. Meijer, *The Trotsky Papers*, vol. II, 347.
14. Bruski, *Between Prometheism and Realpolitik*, 120; SPO, tom 1, 432.
15. Borzęcki, *The Soviet-Polish Peace*, 166, 171.
16. PSV, ch. II, 100.
17. AVPRF, f. 4, op. 32, p. 207, d. 52460, l. 115. On the retreats and internments, see Borzęcki, *The Soviet-Polish Peace*, 157.
18. Ibid., 240; SPO, tom 1, 362; Bruski, *Between Prometheism and Realpolitik*, 119.
19. Zimmerman, *Jozef Pilsudski*, 364.
20. Karski, *The Great Powers and Poland*, 56.
21. SPO, tom 1, 380–1.
22. AVPRF, f. 4, op. 32, p. 210, d. 52499, l. 1.
23. Among many examples, see DVP, tom IV, 70–2, 96–8, 203–308, 340–6; Tsentral'nyi derzhavnyi arkhiv vyshchykh orhaniv vlady ta upravlinnia Ukraïny [hereafter TsDAVO], f. 4, op. 1, d. 29, l. 26; d. 631, l. 19.
24. DVP, tom IV, 70; TsDAVO, f. 4, op. 1c, d. 31, l. 3.
25. Bruski, *Between Prometheism and Realpolitik*, 43.
26. V. Gostyn'skaia, A Deruga, A. Zatorskii, G.V. Makarova, P.N. Ol'shanskii and Ia. Iurkevich (eds), DiM, IV, 22–6.
27. AVPRF, f. 4, op. 1, p. 490, d. 90, ll. 7, 11–12, 39; Bruski, *Between Prometheism and Realpolitik*, 120.
28. AVPRF, f. 4, op. 1, p. 490, d. 90, l. 48.
29. AVPRF, f. 4, op. 32, p. 210, d. 52499, l. 2.
30. SPO, tom 1, 410, 412, 422, 442–3.
31. Bruski, *Between Prometheism and Realpolitik*, 124.
32. SPO, tom 1, 426.
33. AVPRF, f. 4, op. 32, p. 211, d. 52523, l. 10.
34. DVP, tom IV, 366–9.

35 SPO, tom 1, 445; AVPRF, f. 4, op. 32, p. 211, d. 52524, ll. 9, 28; DiM, IV, 61.
36 SPO, tom 1, 451; DiM, IV, 67-9.
37 Bruski, *Between Prometheism and Realpolitik*, 127-8.
38 DVP, tom IV, 430.
39 SPO, tom 1, 473, 476.
40 On Petliura, see Borzęcki, *The Soviet-Polish Peace*, 238.
41 SPO, tom 1, 477, 481.
42 AVPRF, f. 4, op. 32, p. 209, d. 52491, l. 58.
43 TsDAVO, f. 4, op. 1c, d. 31, l. 3; DVP, tom IV, 518, 529; 128-129; DiM, IV, 106-8.
44 GARF, r-393, op. 23A, d. 173, ll. 1-16, 18, 55.
45 Bruski, *Between Prometheism and Realpolitik*, 103; SPO, tom 1, 489.
46 G.N. Sevost'ianov et al. (eds), *'Sovershenno Sekretno': Lubianka Stalinu o polozhenii v strane (1922-1934 gg.)* tom 1, ch. 1 (Moscow, 2001), 163, 302, 358, 372; ibid., tom 1. ch. 2, 788, 928, 947; ibid., tom 2, ch, 1, 69; ibid., tom 3, 247.
47 RGASPI, f, 17, op. 87, d. 177, ll. 89-129, 195.
48 Andrzej Pepłoński, *Wywiad Polski na ZSRR 1921-1939* (Warsaw, 1999), 81; Rubl'ova and Rubl'ov (eds), *Ukraïna – Pol'shcha*, 136-7.
49 David Shearer, *Policing Stalin's Socialism: Repression and Social Order in the Soviet Union, 1924-1953* (New Havenm, 2009), 96; Bruski, *Between Prometheism and Realpolitik*, 104, 108, 155.
50 Plekhanov and Plekhanov (eds), *F.E. Dzerzhinskii*, 344-5. Not as strongly, or consistently, Soviet military intelligence sometimes raised the spectre of war when reporting on Savinkov, Petliura and Bułak-Bałakhovich. GARF, r-393, op. 23A, d. 173, ll. 7, 31.
51 AVPRF, f. 4, op. 32, p. 207, d. 52460, l. 90.
52 AVPRF, f. 4, op. 32, p. 207, d. 52461, ll. 27, 29.
53 AVPRF, f. 4, op. 32, p. 211, d. 52524, l. 1. Sir Archibald Sinclair reported to Churchill shortly after that Krasin had complained about a higher sum of 50 million francs to form an anti-Bolshevik army headed by Savinkov and members of the Socialist Revolutionary Party. CHAR 16/76/24.
54 GARF, r-393, op. 1A, d. 13, l. 30.
55 Ibid., ll. 5-8.
56 CAB 24/111/67, 91.
57 Churchill, *Great Contemporaries*, 126.
58 Richard B. Spence, 'The "Savinkov Affair" Reconsidered', *East European Quarterly* 24/1 (1990): 27; CHAR 2/111/41-2; CHAR 16/72/14.
59 'Gąsiorowski, 'Poland's Policy towards Soviet Russia', 230.
60 Korbel, *Poland Between East and West*, 105; PSV, ch. II, 106-7.
61 Ibid., 90-2.
62 Lenin, *Collected Works*, vol. 31, 397-403, 408-15, 466.
63 Carole Fink, 'The NEP in Foreign Policy: The Genoa Conference and the Treaty of Rapallo', in Gabriel Gorodetsky (ed.), *Soviet Foreign Policy, 1917-1991: Retrospective* (London, 2013), 12-13.
64 Stalin, *Collected Works*, vol. 4 (Moscow, 1953), 387-94.
65 M. Ul', V. Khaustov and V. Zakharov (eds), *Glazami razvedki. SSSR i Evropa, 1919-1938 gody: sbornik dokumentov iz rossiiskikh arkhivov* (Moscow, 2015), 83-9.
66 GARF, r-393, op. 1A, d. 13, l. 162.
67 See Chicherin's letter to the Politburo from 10 September 1921. AVPRF, f. 4, op. 52, p. 341, d. 55273, l. 22.

68 Borzęcki, *The Soviet-Polish Peace*, 68.
69 Richard K. Debo, 'G.V. Chicherin: A Historical Perspective' in Gorodetsky (ed.), *Soviet Foreign Policy*, 26.
70 For the standout account of the Riga negotiations, see Borzęcki, *The Soviet-Polish Peace*.
71 AVPRF, f. 4, op. 32, p. 209, d. 52482, l. 191; Borzęcki, *The Soviet-Polish Peace*, 161. There was some concern, however, on the Bolshevik side that if Poland did well in the plebiscite this could increase its militancy and the resources of Upper Silesia could be turned to war. PSV, ch. II, 146.
72 SPO, tom 1, 292–3, 310–12, 318–19.
73 Ibid., 355.
74 AVPRF, f. 4, op. 32, p. 209, d. 52482, ll. 172, 184; p. 210, d. 52511, l. 37.
75 Ibid., ll. 64–7.
76 Quoted in Bruski, *Between Prometheism and Realpolitik*, 37.
77 Karski, *The Great Powers and Poland*, 72.
78 AVPRF, f. 4, op. 32, p. 209, d. 52482, ll. 192, 215. The People's Commissariat for Foreign Affairs in Soviet Ukraine received similar material on the changing mood in France, away from intervention. See Rubl'ova and Rubl'ov (eds), *Ukraïna – Pol'shcha*, 98–104.
79 Borzęcki, *The Soviet-Polish Peace*, 170–4.
80 AVPRF, f. 4, op. 32, p. 209, d. 52482, l. 15.
81 AVPRF, f. 4, op. 32, p. 210, d. 52511, l. 13; f. 4, op. 32, p. 209, d. 52482, ll. 50, 56.
82 Michael Jabara Carley, 'Episodes from the Early Cold War: Franco-Soviet Relations, 1917–1927', *Europe-Asia Studies* 52/7 (2000): 1276–7; Jackson, *Beyond the Balance of Power*, 414.
83 Piotr Stefan Wandycz, *The Twilight of French Eastern Alliances, 1926–1936: French-Czechoslovak-Polish Relations from Locarno to the Remilitarization of the Rhineland* (Princeton, 2014), 186, 223.
84 AVPRF, f. 4, op. 32, p. 209, d. 52482, ll. 49, 89.
85 RGASPI, f. 17, op. 86, d. 214, ll. 1–26.
86 Ibid., ll. 27–30.
87 Ibid., ll. 31–5.
88 PSV, ch. II, 171, 176–7; Borzęcki, *The Soviet-Polish Peace*, 195.
89 Karski, *The Great Powers and Poland*, 82.
90 Korbel, *Poland Between East and West*, 107; E.H. Carr, *The Bolshevik Revolution, 1917–1923*, vol. 3 (New York; London, 1985), 346.
91 Wandycz, *The Twilight of French Eastern Alliances*, 8; Korbel, *Poland between East and West*, 107–8; Jackson, *Beyond the Balance of Power*, 368.
92 PSV, ch. II, 172.
93 AVPRF, f. 4, op. 32, p. 209, d. 52482, ll. 26, 60; AVPRF, f. 4, op. 32, p. 210, d. 52511, ll. 12–14; Ungurianu et al. (eds), *Sovetsko-rumynskie otnosheniia*, tom 1, 84.
94 Anna Cienciala and Titus Komarnicki, *From Versailles to Locarno: Keys to Polish Foreign Policy* (Kansas, 1984), 19–20; Jackson, *Beyond the Balance of Power*, 366.
95 Ibid., p. 367; RGASPI, f. 17, op. 86, d. 211, l. 4; Karski, *The Great Powers and Poland*, 83.
96 AVPRF, f. 4, op. 1, p. 490, d. 90, l. 24.
97 Wandycz, *France and Her Eastern Allies*, 221–2; Zara Steiner, *The Lights That Failed: European International History 1919–1933* (Oxford, 2007), 295.
98 Lenin, *Collected Works*, vol. 32, 114–15, 149.

99 PSV, ch. II, 199–202; Borzęcki, *The Soviet-Polish Peace*, 213.
100 PSV, ch. II, 212–13. Ioffe did not discount another war over the longer term. In February he suggested that as part of the settlement with Poland, deliveries of gold and precious stones should be staggered over one to three years to potentially stave off another invasion during this time. TsDAVO, f. 4, op. 1, d. 14, l. 23.
101 RGASPI, f. 17, op. 3, d. 146, l. 1.
102 DiM, tom III, 515; Borzęcki, *The Soviet-Polish Peace*, 215.
103 SPO, tom 1, 392.
104 Ibid., 393. In October 1920, Chicherin had expressed similar confusion to Ganetskii about the nature of French influence on Poland, describing the 'extreme vagueness' and lack of clarity in the situation. Borzęcki, *The Soviet-Polish Peace*, 170–171fn.68.
105 DVP, tom IV, 129. See similar in July, 219–20; Bruski, *Between Prometheism and Realpolitik*, 80.
106 AVPRF, f. 4, op. 32, p. 210, d. 52514, l. 9.
107 AVPRF, f. 4, op. 32, p. 209, d. 52492, l. 19.
108 Lenin, *Collected Works*, vol. 32, 453.
109 AVPRF, f. 4, op. 52, p. 340, d. 55256, ll. 59–60; Pipes, *The Unknown Lenin*, 129.
110 Pepłoński, *Wywiad Polski na ZSRR*, 88.
111 RGASPI, f. 17, op. 86, d. 211, ll. 10; AVPRF, f. 4, op. 32, p. 209, d. 52482, ll. 130, 133; AVPRF, f. 4, op. 32, p. 210, d. 52511, l. 43; SPO, tom 1, 446.
112 RGASPI, f. 558, op. 1, d. 2119, ll. 1–3.
113 Carr, *The Bolshevik Revolution*, vol. 3, 346; Korbel, *Poland between East and West*, 108–9.
114 DVP, tom IV, 354.
115 RGASPI, f. 17, op. 86, d. 208, ll. 15–17.
116 Ibid., l. 24.
117 SPO, tom 1, 469.
118 AVPRF, f. 4, op. 1, p. 490, d. 90, l. 59.
119 For Trotsky's view on Poland not seeking war, from March 1922, see AVPRF, f. 4, op. 32, p. 211, d. 52550, ll. 6, 9, 13.
120 Trotsky, 'Order No. 267: A Fresh Provocation by the Polish Military Clique' (11 November 1921). Available at https://www.marxists.org/archive/trotsky/1921/military/ch73.htm [accessed March 2021]. After reading the draft order, Chicherin suggested adding a line emphasising French hostility. AVPRF, f. 4, op. 32, p. 210, d. 52498, l. 8. In mid-March 1922, the NKID representative in Berlin, Viktor Kopp, in intelligence forwarded to Trotsky by Clara Zetkin, claimed that Piłsudski had agreed to launch a new war against Soviet Russia during a recent trip to Paris. AVPRF, f. 4, op. 32, p. 211, d. 52550, l. 13.
121 Quoted in Carley, *Silent Conflict*, 55.
122 DVP, tom IV, 572–3; 697–706; V. Gostyn'skaia, A. Deryga, A, Zatorskii, G.V. Makarova, P.N. Ol'shanskii, and Ia. Iurkevich (eds), DiM, tom IV, 141, 217, 221–2.
123 RGASPI, f. 558, op. 11, d. 1141, l. 35ob.
124 Lenin, *Collected Works*, vol. 33, 148.
125 *Odinnadtsatyi s'ezd RKP(b): Protokoly* (Moscow, 1936), 637.
126 Kotkin, *Stalin*. Vol. 1, 444.
127 Jackson, *Beyond the Balance of Power*, 415.
128 Steiner, *The Lights That Failed*, 168.
129 Zimmerman, *Jozef Pilsudski*, 377–8.

130 AVPRF, f. 4, op. 32, p. 211, d. 52546, l. 1; Carole Fink, *The Genoa Conference: European Diplomacy, 1921–22* (Chapel Hill, NC, 1984), 106.
131 AVPRF, f. 4, op. 32, p. 211, d. 52550, l. 7.
132 John Hiden, *The Baltic States and Weimar Ostpolitik* (Cambridge, 1987), 111.
133 DiM, tom IV, 144–6; Fink, *The Genoa Conference*, 112.
134 RGASPI, f. 558, op. 1, d. 2326, l. 1.
135 Ul', Khaustov and Zakharov (eds), *Glazami razvedki*, 58.
136 Ibid., 64; RGVA, f. 25899, op. 3, d. 515, l. 118ob.
137 Ul', Khaustov and Zakharov (eds), *Glazami razvedki*, 89.
138 Bruski, *Between Prometheism and Realpolitik*, 194fn.11.
139 RGVA, f. 25899, op. 3, d. 515, l. 20; Steiner, *The Lights That Failed*, 302.
140 Lenin, *Collected Works*, vol. 45, 355.
141 Quoted in Gąsiorowski, 'Poland's Policy towards Soviet Russia', 243; DiM, IV, 177.
142 RGVA, f. 33988, op. 2, d. 533, l. 2.
143 RGVA, f. 25899, op. 3, d. 536, l. 1.
144 RGVA, f. 33988, op. 2, d. 533, l. 29.
145 G.N. Sevost'ianov, *Moskva – Berlin: politika i diplomatiia Kremlia, 1920–1941*. tom 1 (Moscow, 2011), 97–8.
146 Ibid., 106–8.
147 RGVA, f. 25899, op. 3, d. 536, ll. 17, 34ob.
148 Derzhavnyi haluzevyi arkhiv sluzhby bezpeky Ukraïny [hereafter DHASBU], f. 13, ark. 162, tm. 12, ll. 3–4; RGVA, f. 25899, op. 3, d. 536, l. 33; Sevost'ianov et al. (eds), *'Sovershenno Sekretno'*, tom 1, ch. 2, 701.
149 V. Pozniakov, 'The Enemy at the Gates: Soviet Military Intelligence in the Interwar Period and Its Forecasts of Future War, 1921–42', in Silvio Pons and Andrea Romano (eds), *Russia in the Age of Wars* (Milan, 2000), 218.
150 RGVA, f. 25899, op. 2, d. 556, l. 206.
151 DHASBU, f. 13, ark. 162, tm. 12, ll. 3–4; Sevost'ianov et al. (eds), *'Sovershenno Sekretno'* t. 1, ch. 2, 642, 683; A.A. Kol'tiukov et al. (eds), *Russkaia voennaia emigratsiia 20-kh- 40-kh godov XX: Dokumenty i materialy*, t. 4 (Moscow, 2007), 808.
152 Bruski, *Between Prometheism and Realpolitik*, 91. Later in July, the Ukrainian GPU reported on what it claimed to be another Polish Military Organization connected to the Polish diplomatic missions in Kiev and other cities, totalling around 400 people. DHASBU, f. 13, ark. 162, t. 8, ll. 2–6.
153 Ul', Khaustov and Zakharov (eds), *Glazami razvedki*, 100.
154 Karski, *The Great Powers and Poland*, 61.
155 E.H. Carr, *The Interregnum, 1923–1924* (London, 1969), 174; Korbel, *Poland between East and West*, 130.
156 Edouard Herriot, 'A French View of Soviet Russia', *Current History* 17/6 (1923).
157 G.N. Sevost'ianov (ed.), *Moskva – Berlin: politika i diplomatiia Kremlia, 1920–1941: sbornik dokumentov v trekh tomakh* (Moscow, 2011), 100–1; Carley, *Silent Conflict*, 81.
158 Sevost'ianov (ed.), *Moskva – Berlin*, 109.
159 Velikanova, *Popular Perceptions of Soviet Politics in the 1920s. Disenchantment of the Dreamers*, 28–9.
160 RGASPI, f. 588, op. 11, d. 789, l. 2; d. 31, ll. 55–7.
161 Carr, *The Interregnum*, 177–9.
162 Wandycz, *France and Her Eastern Allies*, 279.
163 Korbel, *Poland between East and West*, 132; Jackson, *Beyond the Balance of Power*, 416–17.

164 Ul', Khaustov and Zakharov (eds), *Glazami razvedki*, 108, 115; RGVA, f. 25899, op. 3, d. 536, l. 75; d. 565, l. 120; f. 33988, op. 2, d. 533, l. 89.
165 Wandycz, *France and Her Eastern Allies*, 282; DiM, IV, 238–9; Borzęcki, *The Soviet-Polish Peace*, 270.
166 Bruski, *Between Prometheism and Realpolitik*, 151; Zimmerman, *Jozef Pilsudski*, 388.
167 AVPRF, f. 32, p. 212, d. 52567, l. 153; p. 212, d. 52565, ll. 7–8.
168 *Izvestiia*, 27 June 1923, 1–2.
169 AVPRF, f. 32, p. 212, d. 52565, ll. 2–4, 7.
170 AVPRF, f. 32, p. 212, d. 52567, ll. 156–7.
171 Pierre Broué, *The German Revolution, 1917–1923* (Leiden, 2005), 17, 724; Korbel, *Poland between East and West*, 135.
172 Broué, *The German Revolution*, 756; Aleksandr Vatlin, *Komintern: Idei, resheniia, sud'by* (Moscow, 2009), 111.
173 G.M. Adibekov et al (eds), *Politbiuro TsK RKP(b)-VKP(b) i Komintern. 1919–1943 gg. Dokumenty* (Moscow, 2004), 185–99.
174 Vatlin, *Komintern: Idei, resheniia, sud'by*, 168.
175 Quoted in ibid., 111. On Stalin's position, see RGASPI, f. 558, op. 11, d. 734, ll. 35–6; Haslam, *The Spectre of War*, 48–9.
176 RGVA, f. 25899, op. 3, d. 536, l. 2.
177 V.A. Zolotarev (ed.), *Sovetskoe voenno-promyshlennoe proizvodstva 1918–1936: Sbornik dokumentov* (Moscow, 2005), 283–4.
178 Plekhanov and Plekhanov (eds), *Dzerzhinskii*, 486–7.
179 RGASPI, f. 76, op. 2, d. 17, l. 86.
180 Stone, 'The Prospect of War?', 807; Wandycz, *France and Her Eastern Allies*, 289.
181 Stone, 'The Prospect of War?', 808; AVPRF, f. 4, op. 32, p. 212, d. 52565, l. 70; DiM, IV, 249–50.
182 AVPRF, f. 4, op. 32, p. 212, d. 52565, ll. 52–3, 205–6.
183 RGASPI, f. 17, op. 162, d. 1, l. 12.
184 Stone, 'The Prospect of War?', 804.
185 Ibid.
186 Ibid., 813.
187 Ibid., 811.
188 TsDAVO, f. 2, op. 2, d. 905, l. 8.
189 DHASBU, f. 13, ark. 162, tm. 7, ll. 1–2, 6. For Polish intelligence of Soviet military preparations, RGVA, f. 308, op. 3, d. 39, l. 25.
190 RGASPI, f. 558, op. 11, d. 25, l. 101.
191 Zimmerman, *Jozef Pilsudski*, 390–1.
192 Wandycz, *France and Her Eastern Allies*, 272–4.
193 DiM, IV, 236, 246–7, 256; Bruski, *Between Prometheism and Realpolitik*, 74, 150.
194 RGVA, f. 33988, op. 2, d. 534, l. 108–12, 333–4.
195 Bruski, *Between Prometheism and Realpolitik*, 122, 130.

Chapter 4

1 Silvio Pons, *The Global Revolution: A History of International Communism 1917–1991* (Oxford, 2014), 39–40.
2 Stephanie C. Salzmann, *Great Britain, Germany, and the Soviet Union: Rapallo and After, 1922–1934* (Rochester, NY, 2003), 46.

3   Ibid., 52.
4   In conversation with Moscow journalists in June 1924, head of the Soviet government, Aleksei Rykov expressed hope that the Soviet-French relations would 'quickly improve' with the new French government. He struck a positive tone about new trading opportunities and a revived relationship with French industry. GARF, f. 5446, op. 55, d. 565, l. 6; Jon Jacobson, *When the Soviet Union Entered World Politics* (Berkeley, 1994), 135–6, 39. On the shift in French foreign policy, see Jackson, *Beyond the Balance of Power*, 418.
5   Wandycz, *The Twilight of French Alliances*, 12; Bruski, *Between Prometheism and Realpolitik*, 76; Cienciala and Komarnicki, *From Versailles to Locarno*, 226; Carr, *Socialism in One Country 1924–1926*. vol. 3, part 1 (Basingstoke, 1994), 46; Steiner, *The Lights That Failed*, 306. For Chicherin's remark, see Sevost'ianov, *Moskva – Berlin*, vol 1, 242. In April 1925, Litvinov warned Count Ulrich von Brockdorff-Rantzau that the Bolsheviks could seek better relations with Poland, see 492.
6   Borzęcki, *The Soviet-Polish Peace*, 279.
7   Roman Solchanyk, 'The Comintern and the Communist Party of Western Ukraine, 1919–1928', *Canadian Slavonic Papers* 23/2 (1981): 191; Carr, *Socialism in One Country*. vol 3, part 1, 27.
8   DiM, tom IV, 317.
9   Ibid., 268–70.
10 Solchanyk, 'The Comintern and Communist Party of Western Ukraine', 192. The central committee, in the end, supported the Comintern's position. For Stalin's suggestion, see RGASPI, f. 558, op. 1, d. 2633, l. 1.
11 Velikanova, *Popular Perceptions*, 36.
12 *Trinadtsatyi s'ezd RKP(b): stenograficheskii otchet* (Moscow, 1963), 49, 57.
13 Gabriel Gorodetsky, 'The Soviet Union and Britain's General Strike of May 1926', *Cahiers du Monde russe et soviétique* 17/2,3 (1976): 289.
14 Stone, 'The Prospect of War?', 815.
15 Stalin, 'The Results of the Thirteen Congress of the R.C.P.(B.). Report Delivered at the C.C., R.C.P.(B.) Courses for Secretaries of Uyzed Committees' (17 June, 1924). Available at https://www.marxists.org/reference/archive/stalin/works/1924/06/17.htm [accessed September 2021].
16 Velikanova, *Popular Perceptions*, 37–9.
17 Stalin, 'Concerning the International Situation' (20 September, 1924). Available at https://www.marxists.org/reference/archive/stalin/works/1924/09/20.htm [accessed September 2021].
18 On the interpretation of intelligence, see Sarah Davies and James Harris, *Stalin's World: Dictating the Soviet Order* (New Haven & London, 2014), 100. For the reports on Poland, see RGVA, f. 25899, op. 3, d. 566, l. 88ob; DiM, tom IV, 276–7.
19 RGVA, f, 308, op. 3, d. 39, l. 45.
20 Plekhanov and Plekhanov (eds), *F. E. Dzerzhinskii*, 544.
21 RGVA, f. 308, op. 3, d. 39, l. 61; for more detail on the activity of Polish intelligence in Ukraine and efforts to make useful contacts, see, ll. 81, 101.
22 See the Polish intelligence report in RGVA, f. 308, op. 3, d. 39, l. 95.
23 Bruski, *Between Prometheism and Realpolitik*, 113–14.
24 Zdanovich, *Pol'skii krest sovetskoi kontrrazvedki*, 352–6. On 'M' being a product of Soviet counterintelligence, see Bruski, *Between Prometheism and Realpolitik*, 115.
25 RGVA, f. 308, op. 3, d. 39, ll. 154–5.
26 RGASPI, f. 308, op. 3, d. 39, l. 161.

27 Bruski, *Between Prometheism and Realpolitik*, 117, 296.
28 RGVA, f. 308, op. 3, d. 133, l. 10. Polish intelligence believed some were Soviet provocateurs.
29 RGASPI, f. 17, op. 87, d. 178, l. 80.
30 RGVA, f. 25899, op. 3, d 567, l. 3ob.
31 RGASPI, f. 17, op. 87, d. 178, l. 133.
32 DiM, tom IV, 292-8.
33 Bruski, *Between Prometheism and Realpolitik*, 239.
34 Carr, *Socialism in One Country*. vol. 3, part 1, 443.
35 L.P. Kolodnikova, G.D. Alekseeva, N.M. Peremyshlennikova, A.I. Shishkin, N.E. Bystrova, A.V. Manykin, and T.F. Kariaeva (eds), *'Sovershenno sekretno': Lybianka – Stalinu o polozhenii v strane (1922–1934 gg.)*, tom 3, ch. 1, 1925 (Moscow, 2002), 136.
36 Ul', Khaustov and Zakharov (eds), *Glazami razvedki*, 178. Iagoda was sent a similar report from the head of the Soviet border guards in Ukraine at the end of 1925 that drew attention to funding for anti-Soviet groups from the Polish general staff. RGASPI, f. 76, op. 3, d. 364, l. 6.
37 RGASPI, f. 17, op. 162, d. 2, ll. 148–150.
38 Bruski, *Between Prometheism and Realpolitik*, 178, 228.
39 Ibid., 188.
40 RGASPI, f 76, op.3, d. 364, l. 14.
41 Ibid., l. 12.
42 Bruski, *Between Prometheism and Realpolitik*, 240-1.
43 For Soviet denials, see DiM, tom IV, 325-6.
44 Bruski, *Between Prometheism and Realpolitik*, 242.
45 DiM, tom IV, 353-5.
46 Plekhanov and Plekhanov (eds), *Dzerzhinskii*, 582, 587-8. For a Soviet report noting Polish criticism from the government and in the press, see RGVA, f. 25899, op. 3, d. 566, l. 118; Bruski, *Between Prometheism and Realpolitik*, 249.
47 Ibid., 247; *Materialy 'osoboi papki' Politburo TsK RKP(b)-VKP(b) po voprosu sovetsko-pol'skikh otnoshenii, 1923–1944 gg.* (Moscow, 1997), 12–15. The best account of the raid on Stołpce is David R. Stone, 'The August 1924 raid on Stolpce, Poland, and the evolution of Soviet active intelligence', *Intelligence and National Security* 21/3 (2006): 331–41.
48 See ibid., 337; Bruski, *Between Prometheism and Realpolitik*, 250.
49 *Materialy 'osoboi papki' Politburo TsK RKP(b)-VKP(b) po voprosu sovetsko-pol'skikh otnoshenii*, 12–15; DiM, tom IV, 406–10, 432-3.
50 Steiner, *The Lights That Failed*, 406.
51 Cienciala and Komarnicki, *From Versailles to Locarno*, 227; DiM, tom IV, 380-1.
52 Bruski, *Between Prometheism and Realpolitik*, 116.
53 DiM, tom IV, 389-90.
54 *Materialy 'osoboi papki' Politburo TsK RKP(b)-VKP(b) po voprosu sovetsko-pol'skikh otnoshenii*, 16–17.
55 See article by Feliks Kon, RGASPI, f. 135, op. 1, d. 79, l. 2a. In the following year Kon noted that 'Poland has significance for the Entente only insofar as it can be a supplier of cannon fodder.' RGASPI, f. 135, op. 1, d. 82, l. 10.
56 Steiner, *The Lights That Failed*, 241-2.
57 Pons, *The Global Revolution*, 46.
58 Carr, *Socialism in One Country*. vol. 3, part 1, 28.
59 Ibid., 33-4.

60 Chicherin had first attempted to bring Germany into a Franco-Soviet alliance against Britain but with no success, and then into a stronger Soviet-German alliance in 1925. Jacobson, *When the Soviet Union Entered World Politics*, 156; Karski, *The Great Powers and Poland*, 70–1.
61 Korbel, *Poland between East and West*, 130, 153; Kotkin *Stalin. Vol. 1*, 559.
62 Jacobson, *When the Soviet Union Entered World Politics*, 137; Salzmann, *Great Britain, Germany, and the Soviet Union*, 51; Karski, *The Great Powers and Poland*, 97; Steiner, *The Lights That Failed*, 175, 390, 399.
63 DiM, tom IV, 334.
64 Plekhanov and Plekhanov (eds), *Dzerzhinskii*, 581.
65 DiM, tom IV, 349–50. Chicherin quoted in Jacobson, *When the Soviet Union Entered World Politics*, 139.
66 Carr, *Socialism in One Country*. vol. 3, part 1, 42, 419.
67 Quoted in Carley, 'Episodes from the Early Cold War', 1287.
68 Steiner, *The Lights That Failed*, 294.
69 K.M. Anderson et al (eds), *Reforma v krasnoi armii: dokumenty i materialy 1923–1928 gg.*, kn. 1 (Moscow, 2006), 311.
70 Quoted in Jacobson, *When the Soviet Union Entered World Politics*, 316fn.59. In another report to the Politburo from February on the preparedness of the Red Army and wider country for war, Frunze remarked that the experience of autumn 1923, when the Bolsheviks were increasingly concerned about an imminent war, had revealed 'the complete unpreparedness of our apparatus'. Anderson et al (eds), *Reforma v krasnoi armii*, kn. 1, 324; M.V. Frunze, *Krasnaia armiia i oborona sovetskogo soiuza. Doklad na 3-m s'ezde sovetov SSSR* (Moscow, 1925), 3–37.
71 I.V. Stalin, 'Speech Delivered at a Plenum of the Central Committee of the R.C.P.B' (19 January 1925). Available at https://www.marxists.org/reference/archive/stalin/works/1925/01/19.htm [accessed September 2021].
72 I.V. Stalin, 'The International Situation and the Tasks of the Communist Parties' (22 March 1925). Available at https://www.marxists.org/reference/archive/stalin/works/1925/03/22.htm [accessed September 2021].
73 Stalin, 'Speech Delivered at a Plenum of the Central Committee of the R.C.P.B'.
74 Stone, *Hammer and Rifle*, 21.
75 I.V. Stalin, 'The Results of the Work of the Fourteenth Conference of the R.C.P.(B.). Report Delivered at a Meeting of the Active of the Moscow Organisation of the R.C.P.(B.)' (9 May 1925). Available at https://www.marxists.org/reference/archive/stalin/works/1925/05/09.htm [accessed September 2021]. For similar remarks, see 'Questions and Answers. Speech Delivered at the Sverdlov University' (9 June 1925). Available at https://www.marxists.org/reference/archive/stalin/works/1925/06/09.htm [accessed September 2021].
76 Jacobson, *When the Soviet Union Entered World Politics*, 145.
77 David Crowe, *The Baltic States and the Great Powers. Foreign Relations, 1938–1940* (Boulder, CO, 1993), 9; DBFP, First series, vol. XXV, 845.
78 V.N. Khaustov, V.P. Naumov, and N.S. Plotnikova (eds), *Lubianka. Stalin i VChK-GPU-OGPU-NKVD, ianvar' 1922–dekabr' 1936* (Moscow, 2003), 100; Carr, *Socialism in One Country*. vol. 3, part 1, 443.
79 G. Adibekov, A. Di B'iadzho, F. Gori et al (eds), *Politbiuro TsK RKP(b)-VKP(b) i Evropa, resheniia 'osoboi papki' 1923–1939* (Moscow, 2001), 70, 77. The Politburo believed, in effect, that the British had established an informal protectorate already over Estonia.

80 Shapoval, Prystaiko and Zolotar'ov (eds), *ChK –GPU–NKVD v Ukraïni*, 232; Kate Brown, *A Biography of No Place: From Ethnic Borderland to Soviet Heartland* (Cambridge, MA, 2004), 90.
81 Gl Ul', Khaustov and Zakharov (eds), *Glazami razvedki*, 198–202.
82 Ibid., 179–84.
83 Ibid., 217.
84 RGASPI, f. 76, op. 3, d. 364, l. 21.
85 Lars T. Lih, Oleg V. Naumov and Oleg V. Khlevniuk (eds), *Stalin's Letters to Molotov: 1925–1936* (New Haven, 1995), 85.
86 Anderson et al (eds), *Reforma v krasnoi armii*, kn. 1, 199–204.
87 RGASPI, f. 76, op. 3, d. 364, l. 2.
88 DiM, tom IV, 400–2.
89 Bruski, *Between Prometheism and Realpolitik*, 268.
90 Karski, *The Great Powers and Poland*, 99.
91 DiM, tom IV, 273. On Baltics as staging area, Chicherin made this point to a Polish official in September 1925, see 416–18. On offensive-defensive alliances, see DiM, tom V, 11.
92 Steiner, *The Lights That Failed*, 408.
93 AVPRF, f. 4, op. 32, p. 218, d. 52685, ll. 13–14.
94 'The Fourteenth Congress of the C.P.S.U.(B.)' (18–31 December 1925). Available at https://www.marxists.org/reference/archive/stalin/works/1925/12/18.htm [accessed September 2021]; Kotkin, *Stalin. Vol. 1*, 562–3.
95 Plekhanov and Plekhanov (eds), *F. E. Dzerzhinskii*, 627; Zdanovich, *Pol'skii krest*, 140; Davies and Harris, *Stalin's World*, 101.
96 Carr, *Socialism in One Country*, vol. 3, part 1, 414.
97 R. Craig Nation, *Black Earth, Red Star: A History of Soviet Security Policy, 1917–1991* (Ithaca, NY, 1992), 46; Salzmann, *Great Britain, Germany, and the Soviet Union*, 76. Locarno, moreover, encouraged the Bolsheviks to seek *rapprochement* with France, until it ratified the Locarno treaties in April 1926. Carr, *Socialism in One Country*, vol. 3, part 1, 424; Steiner, *The Lights That Failed*, 405.
98 Karski, *The Great Powers and Poland*, 85–6.
99 RGASPI, f. 76, op. 3, d. 364, ll. 26–8.
100 Ibid., ll. 29–31.
101 Rieber, *Stalin and the Struggle for Supremacy in Eurasia*, 104.
102 Davies and Harris, *Stalin's World*, 101–2; Khaustov, Naumov, and Plotnikova (eds), *Lubianka*, 111–13.
103 'The Fourteenth Congress of the C.P.S.U.(B.)' (18–31 December 1925). Available at https://www.marxists.org/reference/archive/stalin/works/1925/12/18.htm [accessed September 2021].
104 Quoted in Korbel, *Poland between East and West*, 191–2.
105 Shearer, 'Stalin at War, 1918–1953', 193; Carr, *Socialism in One Country*, vol. 3, part 1, 447–8.
106 Zimmerman, *Jozef Pilsudski*, 398–9.
107 SPO, tom 1, 532–3; Bruski, *Between Prometheism and Realpolitik*, 267.
108 Gabriele Simoncini, *The Communist Party of Poland 1918–1929: A Study in Political Ideology* (Lewiston, NY, 1993), 167–8; Carr, *Foundations of a Planned Economy*, vol. 3, part 2 (London, 1976), 564. Dzerzhinskii, for a time at least, saw the rationale in supporting Piłsudski in a struggle between the Polish Socialist Party and the National Democrats, but only to push him towards the Left. RGASPI, f. 508, op. 2, d. 5, l. 31.

109 SPO, tom 1, 535–8; Bruski, *Between Prometheism and Realpolitik*, 267.
110 AVPRF, f. 4, op. 32, p. 218, d. 52688, l. 82.
111 SPO, tom 1, 541–2, 550.
112 Ibid., 544.
113 Ibid., 546.
114 Bruski, *Between Prometheism and Realpolitik*, 268.
115 DVP, tom 9, 199–200.
116 Iu.V. Ivanov, *Ocherki istorii rossiisko (sovetsko)-pol'shikh otnoshenii v dokumentakh. 1914–1945* (Moscow, 2014). 154; Wandycz, *The Twilight of French Alliances*, 49; Bruski, *Between Prometheism and Realpolitik*, 268; Karski, *The Great Powers and Poland*, 87.
117 RGASPI, f. 508, op. 2, d. 5, l. 24. See Zinoviev's explanation of this from June 1926. RGASPI, f. 495, op. 1, d. 95, l. 5.
118 Zdanovich, *Pol'skii krest*, 140–1.
119 Plekhanov and Plekhanov (eds), *F. E. Dzerzhinskii*, 649.
120 Khaustov, Naumov, and Plotnikova (eds), *Lubianka*, 117.
121 AVPRF, f. 4, op. 32, p. 218, d. 52688, ll. 89–90.
122 Wandycz, *The Twilight of French Alliances*, 47.
123 DiM, tom V, 9–10.
124 SPO, tom 1, 574.
125 Bruski, *Between Prometheism and Realpolitik*, 269–70.
126 On this rumour, see Korbel, *Poland between East and West*, 224, 227.
127 SPO, tom 2, 26–8; Carr, *Foundations of a Planned Economy*, vol. 3, part 1, 77.
128 Gorodetsky, 'The Soviet Union and Britain's General Strike', 292.
129 SPO, tom 1, 593–602. On the day following the coup d'état, Radek suggested that Piłsudski was 'linked with England', see Carr, *Foundations of a Planned Economy*, vol. 3, part 1, 76.
130 SPO, tom 2, 39–41; AVPRF, f. 4, op. 32, p. 218, d. 52689, ll. 83–4.
131 Bruski, *Between Prometheism and Realpolitik*, 277.
132 AVPRF, f. 4, op. 32, p. 21, d. 52689, ll. 106–12. Piłsudski reiterated this message again to Voikov in December. SPO, tom 2, 94–5.
133 Timothy Snyder, 'Covert Polish Missions across the Soviet Ukrainian Border, 1928–1933', in Silvia Salvatici (ed.), *Confini: Costruzioni, attraveramenti, rappresentazioni* (Catanzaro, 2005), 56–7.
134 AVPRF, f. 4, op. 32, p. 218, 52689, ll. 148–9.
135 SPO, tom 2, 30–1.
136 Ivanov, *Ocherki istorii rossiisko (sovetsko)-pol'shikh otnoshenii*, 151–2.
137 RGASPI, f. 76, op. 2, d. 58, ll. 156, 185.
138 RGASPI, f. 76, op. 3, d. 364, l. 57. On the Red Army, see Aleksandr Zdanovich, *Organy gosudarstvennoi bezopasnosti i krasnaia armiia: Deiatel'nost' organov VChK-OGPU po obespecheniiu bezopasnosti RKKA (1921–1934)* (Moscow, 2008), 74–5.
139 DHASBU F. 13, ark. 445, l. 1.
140 Bruski, *Between Prometheism and Realpolitik*, 271; Iurii I. Shapoval, 'Vsevolod Balickij bourreau et victim', *Cahiers du Monde Russe* 44/2–3 (2003): 68; Shapoval, Prystaiko and Zolotar'ov (eds), *ChK –GPU–NKVD v Ukraïni*, 254. On war rumours, see Sevost'ianov et al. (eds), *'Sovershenno Sekretno': Lubianka Stalinu o polozhenii v strane*, tom 4, ch. 1, 638 and ibid., tom 4, ch. 2, 718.
141 Zdanovich, *Pol'skii krest*, 357–60.
142 RGASPI, f. 558, op. 11, d. 726, ll. 55–6ob.

143 Plekhanov and Plekhanov (eds), *F.E. Dzerzhinskii*, 665.
144 Bruski, *Between Prometheism and Realpolitik*, 276; Plekhanov and Plekhanov (eds), *F.E. Dzerzhinskii*, 666.
145 Ibid., 667.
146 Ibid., 668.
147 DVP, tom 9, 351–2.
148 SPO, tom 2, 53, 65, 69.
149 Carr, *Foundations of a Planned Economy*, vol. 3, part 1, 78.
150 Bruski, *Between Prometheism and Realpolitik*, 273. Tukhachevskii later gave a press interview and remarked that Soviet Belorussia was most at risk from a Polish attack. See, 274.
151 Korbel, *Poland Between East and West*, 226–7.
152 SPO, tom 2, 65–70.
153 Stalin, *Collected Works*, vol. 8 (Moscow, 1954), 276–7.
154 RGASPI, f. 558, op. 11, d. 824, ll. 50–1.
155 Stone, *Hammer and Rifle*, 20–2.
156 Quoted in N.S. Simonov, 'Strengthen the Defence of the Land of the Soviets': The 1927 "War Alarm" and Its Consequences', *Europe-Asia Studies* 48/8 (1996), 1357.

Chapter 5

1 On Lenin's illness, see Moshe Lewin, *Lenin's Last Struggle* (London, 1975), 31–42.
2 For classic accounts with different emphases, see Leon Trotsky, *My Life* (New York, 1930); Isaac Deutscher, *The Prophet Unarmed: Trotsky, 1921–1929* (London, New York, 1959); Robert V. Daniels, *The Conscience of the Revolution: Communist Opposition in Soviet Russia* (Cambridge, MA, 1960); Robert Conquest, *The Great Terror: Stalin's Purge of the Thirties* (New York, 1968).
3 For more recent, alternate interpretations, see James Harris 'Stalin as General Secretary: The Appointments Process and the Nature of Stalin's Power', in Sarah Davies and James Harris (eds), *Stalin: A New History* (Cambridge, 2005). See also Harris, 'Discipline versus Democracy: The 1923 Party Controversy' in Lara Douds, James Harris, and Peter Whitewood (eds), *The Fate of the Bolshevik Revolution: Illiberal Liberation, 1917–1941* (London, 2020) and Christopher Monty, 'Stalin and the Secretaries of Local Party Organizations, 1921–1927: Subordinates, Clients or Supporters?', *The Soviet and Post-Soviet Review* 45/2 (2018): 183–202.
4 Vladimir N. Brovkin, *Behind the Front Lines of the Civil War: Political Parties and Social Movements in Russia, 1918–1922* (Princeton, 1994), 389–90.
5 Simon Pirani, *The Russian Revolution in Retreat, 1920–24: Soviet Workers and the New Communist Elite* (London, 2008), 55–7; Daniels, *The Conscience of the Revolution*, 137.
6 Lenin, *Collected Works*, vol. 32, 53. For similar comments from Lenin, see ibid., 108.
7 Ibid., 67–169.
8 Daniels, *The Conscience of the Revolution*, 150, 159.
9 T.H. Rigby, *Communist Party Membership in the U.S.S.R.* (Princeton, 1968), 93–4.
10 Lenin, *Collected Works*, vol. 32, 270; Robert H. McNeal, *Stalin: Man and Ruler* (London, 1988), 104–5.
11 Daniels, *The Conscience of the Revolution*, 143.

12 Lenin, *Collected Works*, vol. 32, 241–2.
13 For Dzerzhinskii, see Iain Lauchlan, 'Chekist Mentalité and the Origins of the Great Terror', in James Harris (ed.), *The Anatomy of Terror: Political Violence under Stalin* (Oxford, 2013), 25. Leonid Krasin made similar remarks to the Hands Off Russia! Committee in November 1921. See *Trade with Russia: The Facts; to the Labour Movement of Great Britain* (London, 1921), 3.
14 Lenin, *Collected Works*, vol. 32, 495.
15 Ibid., 505.
16 Daniels, *The Conscience of the Revolution*, 163.
17 Lenin, *Collected Works*, vol. 33 (Moscow, 1973), 322–4.
18 *Protokoly Odinnadtsatyi s'ezd RKP(b)* (Moscow, 1936), 138.
19 Ibid., 603.
20 Daniels, *The Conscience of the Revolution*, 204.
21 *Dvenadtsatyi s'ezd RKP(b) 17–25 Aprelia 1923 goda. Stenograficheskii otchet* (Moscow, 1968), 6. For Kamenev's later comments, see 159.
22 *Dvenadtsatyi s'ezd RKP(b)*, 52.
23 E.H. Carr, *The Interregnum 1923–1924* (Harmondsworth, 1969), 285. See also Daniels, *The Conscience of the Revolution*, 204.
24 Rigby, *Communist Party Membership*, 96–131. For membership figures, see 52.
25 *Dvenadtsatyi s'ezd RKP(b)*, 198–200.
26 Igal Halfin, *Intimate Enemies: Demonizing the Bolshevik Opposition, 1918–1928* (Pittsburgh, 2007), 108.
27 Valentina Vilkova, *RKP(b). Vnutripartiinaia bor'ba v dvadtsatye gody. Dokumenty i materialy. 1923* (Moscow, 2004), 99–101.
28 Ibid., 50–1. For more on Dzerzhinskii's view of factions, see Daniels, *The Conscience of the Revolution*, 216.
29 Adibekov et al (eds), *Politbiuro TsK RKP(b)-VKP(b) i Komintern*, 202.
30 Ian Thatcher, 'Trotsky and the Questions of Agency, Democracy and Dictatorship in the USSR, 1917–1940', in Douds, Harris, and Whitewood (eds), *The Fate of the Bolshevik Revolution: Illiberal Liberation*, 100; Service, *Trotsky*, 308; Geoffrey Swain, *Trotsky* (London, 2006), 148; Daniels, *The Conscience of the Revolution*, 218.
31 Ibid., 147–5.
32 Ibid., 219.
33 Vilkova, *RKP(b). Vnutripartiinaia bor'ba v dvadtsatye gody*, 267.
34 Service, *Trotsky*, 309.
35 Daniels, *The Conscience of the Revolution*, 220–35.
36 Stalin, 'The Party's Tasks' (2 December 1923). Available at https://www.marxists.org/reference/archive/stalin/works/1923/12/02.htm [accessed November 2021].
37 Vilkova, *RKP(b). Vnutripartiinaia bor'ba v dvadtsatye gody*, 268. For Sapronov's view, see *Pravda* (16 December 1923).
38 Vilkova, *RKP(b). Vnutripartiinaia bor'ba v dvadtsatye gody*, 337.
39 Stalin, 'Report on the Immediate Tasks in Party Affairs' (17 January 1924). Available at https://www.marxists.org/reference/archive/stalin/works/1924/01/16.htm [accessed November 2021].
40 Oleg V. Khlevniuk, *Stalin: New Biography of a Dictator* (New Haven, 2015), 791; Kotkin, *Stalin. Vol. 1*, 546–7.
41 Stalin 'Organisational Report of the Central Committee' (24 May 1924). Available at http://www.marx2mao.com/Stalin/TPC24.html [accessed November 2021].
42 Kotkin, *Stalin. Vol. 1*, 564.

43 *Kommunisticheskaia partiia sovetskogo soiuza v rezoliutsiiakh i resheniiakh s'ezdov konferentsii i plenumov TsK* ch. 1 1898-1925 (Moscow, 1953), 913.
44 RGASPI, f. 558, op. 11, d. 8, ll. 54-54ob.
45 RGASPI, f. 76, op. 2, d. 28, l. 12.
46 RGASPI, f. 558, op. 22, d. 726, ll. 55-6ob. Dzerzhinskii was not too wide of the mark. The Polish press reported on the ongoing internal political struggle and the inability of the party majority to handle it. GARF, f. 4459, op. 2, d. 158, l. 45.
47 Stalin 'Once More on the Social-Democratic Deviation in our Party. Report Delivered on December 7' (7 December 1926). Available at https://www.marxists.org/reference/archive/stalin/works/1926/11/22.htm [accessed November 2021].
48 *Pravda* (14 January 1927).
49 Quoted in Samuelson, *Plans for Stalin's War Machine*, 35. For similar comments from other diplomats, see Velikanova, *Popular Perceptions*, 52. The Polish consul in Kiev likewise reported on rumours of war in February, see Bruski, *Between Prometheism and Realpolitik*, 274. For Voroshilov at Osoaviakhim, see Carr, *Foundations of a Planned Economy*, vol 3, part 1, 7.
50 *Pravda*, (14 January 1927).
51 Velikanova, *Popular Perceptions*, 51-2. The new Lithuanian government's relations with Poland worsened, given Voldemaras's intention to take control of Wilno. See Steiner, *The Lights That Failed*, 514.
52 RGASPI, f. 17, op. 162, d. 4, ll. 49-50.
53 DBFP, Series IA, vol. III, 23-5.
54 For these trends, see Velikanova, *Popular Perceptions*, 46.
55 Korbel, *Poland between East and West*, 210.
56 SPO, tom 2, 100, 105; on France, 113; on Piłsudski and Patek, 127-8.
57 Pozniakov, 'The Enemy at the Gates', 220.
58 SPO, tom 2, 118.
59 Ibid., 106; DiM, tom V, 105-7, 112.
60 Ibid., 103-5; SPO, tom 2, 175.
61 Ibid., 118.
62 DiM, tom V, 114-15.
63 In late February, Voikov questioned Zaleski about these reports and was partly convinced by the Polish response, see DBFP, Series IA, vol. III, 66-7. For Voikov's account, SPO, tom 2, 123-5.
64 Carley, *Silent Conflict*, 257; Kotkin, *Stalin. Vol. 1.*, 622-3.
65 RGASPI, f. 17, op. 162, d. 4, l. 42; Samuelson, *Plans for Stalin's War Machine*, 39.
66 Stalin, *Works*, vol. 9, 173.
67 Khaustov, Naumov, and Plotnikova (eds), *Lubianka*, 131.
68 Michal Reiman, *The Birth of Stalinism: The USSR on the Eve of the 'Second Revolution'* (London, 1987), 11.
69 SPO, tom 2, 162-4, 167-8. This had been the view also when the break was anticipated, 161-2; DiM, tom V, 142-3.
70 DVP, tom X, 151.
71 Velikanova, *Popular Perceptions*, 54.
72 AVPRF, f.4, op. 32, p. 218, d. 52689, ll. 46-8. Russian-born French Jew, Sholem Schwarzbard, killed Petliura in Paris and Soviet involvement at some level was likely. Bruski, *Between Prometheism and Realpolitik*, 287-8.
73 For this view from the NKID, see AVPRF, f. 4, op. 32, p. 220, d. 52723, ll. 1-2.
74 RGASPI, f. 588, op. 11, d. 71, l. 2.

75 A.M. Plekhanov, *VChK-OGPU v gody novoi ekonomicheskoi politiki, 1921–1928* (Moscow, 2006), 62, 285.
76 *Pravda* (11 June 1927).
77 Khaustov, Naumov, and Plotnikova (eds), *Lubianka*, 795, fn.56.
78 Quoted in Per Rudling, *The Rise and Fall of Belarussian Nationalism, 19061931* (Pittsburgh, 2014), 285.
79 Carr, *Foundations of a Planned Economy*, vol. 3, part 1, 10; DBFP, Series IA, vol. III, 360-2; Kotkin, *Stalin. Vol. 1.*, 635.
80 Velikanova, *Popular Perceptions*, 51, 77; Reiman, *The Birth of Stalinism*, 15–16.
81 A.Iu. Vatlin, 'Vneshniaia politika i komintern 1921–1929 gg'. in A.N. Iakovlev et al (eds), *Rossiia nepovskaia* (Moscow, 2002), 364.
82 On 14 June, N.D.S. Sokolov reported that Piłsudski assured there had not been a single attempt by the British to push Poland into launching war the Soviet Union. SPO, tom 2, 173, 175.
83 DiM, tom V, 89, 168–70.
84 DVP, tom X, 289, 295–9.
85 AVPRF, f. 4, op. 32, p. 220, d. 52715, ll. 8, 12.
86 DiM, tom V, 166.
87 AVPRF, f. 4, op. 32, p. 200, d. 52723, l. 18.
88 Ibid., ll. 26–7.
89 Simonov, "Strengthen the Defence of the Land of the Soviets', 360.
90 Andrea Romano, 'Permanent War Scare: Mobilisation, Militarisation and Peasant War' in Pons and Andrea Romano (eds), *Russia in the Age of Wars*, 105.
91 TsDAVO, f. 413, op. 2, d. 4, l. 1.
92 RGASPI, f. 63, op. 1, d. 357, l. 61.
93 RGASPI, f. 63, op. 1, d. 357, l. 54; David Brandenberger, *National Bolshevism: Stalinist Mass Culture and the Formation of Modern Russian National Identity, 1931–1956* (Cambridge, MA, 2022), 21–2; V.P. Danilov, R. Manning and L. Viola (eds), *Tragediia sovetskoi derevni: kollektivizatsiia i raskulachivanie: dokumenty i materialy v 5 tom.*, *1927–1938 gg.*, tom 1 (Moscow, 1999–2004), 26.
94 SPO, tom 2, 190.
95 AVPRF, f. 4, op. 32, p. 220, d. 52715, ll. 19–23.
96 SPO, tom 2, 202–3.
97 Velikanova, *Popular Perceptions*, 77.
98 DiM, tom V, 197.
99 Ibid., 203.
100 Stalin, *Works*, vol. 9, 328–69.
101 Danilov, Manning, and Viola (eds), *Tragediia sovetskoi derevni*, tom 1, 25.
102 Stalin, *Works*, vol. 9, 317–18.
103 O.B. Mozokhin (ed.), *Politbiuro i Lev Trotskii, 1922–1940 gg. Sbornik dokumentov* (Moscow, 2017), 139–40.
104 Iu. Fel'shtinskii, *Kommunisticheskaia oppozitsiia v SSSR 1923–1927*. tom 3 (New York, 1988), 96.
105 Danilov, Manning, and Viola (eds), *Tragediia sovetskoi derevni*, tom 1, 25; Velikanova, *Popular Perceptions*, 67.
106 Stalin, *Works*, vol. 9, 336–7.
107 RGASPI, f. 558, op. 11, d. 13, ll. 39ob–40ob.
108 Ibid., ll. 26ob–27.
109 Ibid., l. 5ob.

110 Trotsky, *The Challenge of the Left Opposition 1926-27* (New York, 1980), 322-3.
111 RGASPI, f. 558, op. 11, d. 13, ll. 35-7.
112 Ibid., ll. 71-5.
113 Stalin, *Works*, vol. 10, 62.
114 Trotsky, 'The War Danger – The Defence Policy and the Opposition' (1 August 1927). Available at https://www.marxists.org/archive/trotsky/1937/ssf/sf10.htm [accessed November 2021].
115 Reiman, *The Birth of Stalinism*, 25.
116 Leon Trotsky, 'The "Clémenceau Thesis" and the Party Regime', September 1927. Available at https://www.marxists.org/archive/trotsky/1927/09/cceau.htm [accessed November 2021].
117 Trotsky, 'Platform of the Joint Opposition', 1927. Available at https://www.marxists.org/archive/trotsky/1927/opposition/ch09.htm [accessed November 2021].
118 RGASPI, f. 558, op. 11, d. 1110, ll. 173-4.
119 Stalin, *Works*, vol. 10, 206.
120 Kotkin, *Stalin. Vol. 1.*, 644.
121 Mozokhin (ed.), *Politbiuro i Lev Trotskii*, 198.
122 Reiman, *The Birth of Stalinism*, 33, 126.
123 Mozokhin (ed.), *Politbiuro i Lev Trotskii*, 232-3.
124 Ibid., 264-5.
125 Reiman, *The Birth of Stalinism*, 127.
126 Harvey L. Dyck, 'German-Soviet Relations and the Anglo-Soviet Break, 1927', *Slavic Review* 25/1 (1966): 80; Steiner, *The Lights That Failed*, 540; Oleg Ken, *Collective Security or Isolation? Soviet Foreign Policy and Poland, 1930-1935* (St. Petersburg, 1996), 15.
127 SPO, tom 2, 219-20; Wandycz, *The Twilight of French Alliances*, 97.
128 SPO, tom 2, 222-3; Wandycz, *The Twilight of French Alliances*, 96.
129 *Materialy 'osoboi papki' Politbiuro TsK RKP(b)-VKP(b) po voprosu sovetsko-pol'skikh otnoshenii*, 33; DiM, tom V, 202-4.
130 Brockdorff-Rantzau reported comments from an NKID official along these lines in September, presenting a potentially imminent danger. Dyck, 'German-Soviet Relations and the Anglo Soviet Break', 80.
131 AVPRF, f. 4, op. 3, p. 220, d. 52714, ll. 22-6.
132 SPO, tom 2, 232-3, 236.
133 Stalin, 'Political Report of the Central Committee' (3 December 1927). Available at https://www.marxists.org/reference/archive/stalin/works/1927/12/02.htm [accessed November 2021].
134 Trotsky, *The Challenge*, 248.
135 Ronald Grigor Suny, *Stalin: Passage to Revolution* (Princeton, 2020), 260, 269, 419, 421, 487.
136 For this view, see, for instance, Steiner, *The Lights That Failed*, 536. Alfred G. Meyer, 'The War Scare of 1927', *Soviet Union/Union Sovietique* 5/1 (1978): 1-25; Stone, *Hammer and Rifle*, 43-63; Viola, Danilov, Kozlov, and Ivnitskii (eds), *The Tragedy of the Soviet Countryside: The War against the Peasantry, 1927-1930*: vol 1 (New Haven, 2005), 16-17. Viola and Danilov stated that 'henceforth' Stalin connected domestic discontent to the foreign threat, but we have seen how this predated the 1927 war scare by several years. Likewise, Reiman argued that the Soviet leadership did not give much consideration to war breaking out before 1927, *The Birth of Stalinism*, 13.

137 John P. Sontag, 'The Soviet War Scare of 1926-27', *The Russian Review* 34/1 (1975): 66-77; Hugh D. Hudson Jr., 'The 1927 Soviet War Scare: The Foreign Affairs-Domestic Policy Nexus Revisited', *The Soviet and Post-Soviet Review* 39 (2012): 145-65; Shearer notes that Stalin's 'precise and urgent' demands in pressing the OGPU to steer investigations to reveal evidence of interventions 'makes little sense as a part of a calculated strategy to isolate or discredit political opponents'. 'Stalin at War, 1918-1953. Patterns of Violence and Foreign Threat', 193.

Chapter 6

1 R.W. Davies, 'Industry', in R.W. Davies, Mark Harrison, S.G. Wheatcroft (eds), *The Economic Transformation of the Soviet Union, 1913-1945* (Cambridge, 1994), 132, 137.
2 Davies, *The Socialist Offensive*; Stone, *Hammer and Rifle*; Samuelson, *Plans for Stalin's War Machine*; Davies and Harris, *Stalin's World*, 110.
3 Simonov, '"Strengthen the Defence of the Land of the Soviets"'.
4 Samuelson, 'Mikhail Tukhachevsky and War-Economic Planning: Reconsiderations on the Pre-war Soviet Military Build-Up', *The Journal of Slavic Military Studies* 9/4 (1996): 813; *Plans for Stalin's War Machine*, 34.
5 Ibid., 39-40.
6 Ibid., 70.
7 RGASPI, f. 74, op. 1, d. 388, l. 21.
8 DiM, tom V, 244.
9 SPO, tom 2, 497.
10 Ibid., 266-7. Bogomolov would continue to write about the risk of war against Poland and the speed of its military preparation, see his report from April in Ivanov, *Ocherki istorii rossiisko (sovetsko)-pol'shikh*, 157. On Polish trade, see Eugene Zaleski and Helgard Wienart, *Technology Transfer between East and West* (Paris, 1980), 33.
11 DiM, tom V, 249, 268.
12 SPO, tom 2, 272, 291, 304; DiM, tom V, 292-6. In May, Patek was heard speaking to other diplomats in Moscow, during which he apparently predicted that the Soviet Union would be embroiled in war given its economic 'paralysis' and politic situation 'close to catastrophe' as other powers sought to take advantage. SPO, tom 2, 304.
13 On Piłsudski's health, see Zimmerman, *Jozef Pilsudski*, 415.
14 O.N. Ken and A.I. Rusapov, *Politbiuro TsK VKP(b) i otnosheniia SSSR s zapadnymi sosednimi gosudarstvami (konets 1920-1930-kh gg.): problem, oput, kommentarii* (St Petersburg, 2000), 82.
15 DiM, tom IV, 284-5.
16 Davies and Harris, *Stalin's World*, 109.
17 Samuelson, *Plans for Stalin's War Machine*, 28.
18 SPO, tom 2, 336-41.
19 Ibid., 345.
20 Ibid., 243; Wandycz, *The Twilight of French Alliances*, 100-101.
21 SPO, tom 2, 277.
22 Steiner, *The Lights That Failed*, 543.
23 Kotkin, *Stalin. Vol. II: Waiting for Hitler, 1929-1941* (New York, 2017), 929fn.154; DVP, tom XI, 303.

24 SPO, tom 2, 303. The Bolsheviks were well-aware of the Polish press articles calling for the separation of Ukraine from the Soviet Union. See 319.
25 Ibid., 324.
26 Ul', Khaustov and Zakharov (eds), *Glazami razvedki*, 261; Shearer, 'Stalin at War, 1918-1953', 193-4; Zdanovich, *Organy gosudarstvennoi bezopasnosti i krasnaia armiia*, 385.
27 Alexis Berelovich and Viktor Danilov (eds), *Sovetskaia derevnia glazami VChK-OGPU-NKVD 1918-1939: Dokumenty i materialy v 4 tomakh*, tom 2 (Moscow, 2000), 816.
28 Danilov, Manning, and Viola (eds), *Tragediia sovetskoi derevni*, tom 1, 327.
29 For Voroshilov's speech, see RGASPI, f. 74, op. 2, d. 12, l. 37; for the 1928 harvest, see Davies, *The Socialist Offensive*, 41-2.
30 Quoted in Simonov, '"Strengthen the Defence of the Land of the Soviets"', 1363.
31 Nicholas Werth, 'A State against Its People: Violence, Repression, and Terror in the Soviet Union', in Stephanie Courtois et al. (eds), *The Black Book of Communism: Crimes, Terror, Repression* (Cambridge: Harvard University Press, 1999), 146.
32 Kotkin, *Stalin. Vol. 1*, 676.
33 SPO, tom 2, 359-60.
34 Ibid., 368, 370, 385; Steiner, *The Lights That Failed*, 513.
35 SPO, tom 2, 377-8.
36 RGASPI, f. 74, op. 1, d. 388, l. 21. The head of Polish intelligence was also reported as travelling to Riga and Reval in October. l. 21; SPO, tom 2, 368; Wandycz, *The Twilight of French Alliances*, 111. On trips to Romania, see Zimmerman, *Jozef Pilsudski*, 438.
37 Korbel, *Poland between East and West*, 244.
38 V.P. Danilov, O.V. Khlevniuk, and A.Iu. Vatlin (eds), *Kak lomali NEP: stenogrammy plenumov TsK VKP(b) 1928-1929 gg. v 5-ti tomakh*, tom 3 (Moscow, 2000), 107-9.
39 Plekhanov, *VChK-OGPU v gody novoi ekonomicheskoi politiki, 1921-1928*, 325.
40 DiM, tom V, 333. This followed in the footsteps of Litvinov's declaration for complete disarmament to the international Preparatory Commission on Disarmament at Geneva in November 1927, a proposal that struck other powers as a means of creating division. Jacobson, *When the Soviet Union Entered World Politics*, 236, 246; Steiner, *The Lights That Failed*, 572.
41 Ken, *Collective Security or Isolation?*, 19; Korbel, *Poland between East and West*, 250.
42 On Polish suspicions, see Patek's note to Piłsudski from 3 March 1929. DiM, tom V, 370-1.
43 RGASPI, f. 74, op. 2, d. 15, l. 3.
44 SPO, tom 2, 385.
45 Wandycz, *The Twilight of French Alliances*, 136.
46 Carr, *Foundations of a Planned Economy*, vol 3, part 1, 110-15; Ken, *Collective Security or Isolation?*, 19.
47 A.V. Kvashonkin (ed.), *Sovetskoe rukovodstvo perepiska 1928-1941* [hereafter SKP] (Moscow, 1999), 17, 67-9.
48 SPO, tom 2, 402.
49 RGASPI, f. 74, op. 1, d. 388, l. 1.
50 Ul', Khaustov and Zakharov (eds), *Glazami razvedki*, 270.
51 Ibid., 279-81.
52 Jonathan Haslam, *Soviet Foreign Policy, 1930-1933: The Impact of the Depression* (Basingstoke, 1983), 32.
53 SPO, tom 2, 421-6.

54 Ivanov, *Ocherki istorii rossiisko (sovetsko)-pol'shikh*, 121.
55 Kotkin, *Stalin. Vol. II*, 28.
56 Ibid., 29; Simonov, "'Strengthen the Defence of the Land of the Soviets'", 1362; Samuelson, *Plans for Stalin's War Machine*, 83; RGASPI, f. 17, op. 162, d. 6, ll. 101–2.
57 Samuelson, *Plans for Stalin's War Machine*, 88–9.
58 Pauly, 'Soviet Polonophobia', 178.
59 Haslam, *Soviet Foreign Policy*, 5.
60 Ul', Khaustov and Zakharov (eds), *Glazami razvedki*, 298–9.
61 Shearer, 'Stalin at War, 1918–1953', 194; RGASPI, f. 558, op. 11, d. 184, ll. 45–ob; Kotkin, *Stalin. Vol. II*, 27.
62 Haslam, *Soviet Foreign Policy*, 31.
63 SPO, tom 2, 451, 455. For the Polish press campaign, see Haslam, *Soviet Foreign Policy*, 3. On Sławek, Oleg Ken, *Moskva i pakt nenapadeniia s Pol'shei (1930–1932)* (St. Petersburg, 2003), 6.
64 Karski, *The Great Powers and Poland*, 106.
65 Samuelson, *Plans for Stalin's War Machine*, 135.
66 *Materialy 'osoboi papki' Politbiuro TsK RKP(b)-VKP(b) po voprosu sovetsko-pol'skikh otnoshenii*, 55; Elena Borisenok, *Fenomenon sovetskoi ukrainizatsii: 1920–1930-e gody* (Moscow, 2006), 198.
67 Karski, *The Great Powers and Poland*, 87; Steiner, *The Lights That Failed*, 516, 527.
68 Haslam, *Soviet Foreign Policy*, 28–9.
69 Steiner, *The Lights That Failed*, 515; On Hindenburg, see Korbel, *Poland between East and West*, 24.
70 Karski, *The Great Powers and Poland*, 76.
71 Jacobson, *When the Soviet Union Entered World Politics*, 252.
72 Ken, *Collective Security or Isolation?*, 17.
73 Korbel, *Poland between East and West*, 260.
74 Haslam, *Soviet Foreign Policy*, 55–61.
75 SPO, tom 2, 468, 472.
76 RGASPI, f. 17, op. 162, d. 8, ll. 149–50; Haslam, *Soviet Foreign Policy*, 31; DiM, tom V, 460–1.
77 SPO, tom 2, 470, 473.
78 SPO, tom 2, 475; RGASPI, f. 17, op. 162, d. 8, ll. 165–6.
79 Ken, *Moskva i pakt nenapadeniia*, 6–7; SPO, tom 2, 493.
80 Ibid., 481–2, 496; Pauly, 'Soviet Polonophobia', 179.
81 Ken, *Moskva i pakt nenapadeniia*, 8–9; SPO, tom 2, 517.
82 Ul', Khaustov and Zakharov (eds), *Glazami razvedki*, 319.
83 Lih, Naumov and Khlevniuk (eds), *Stalin's Letters to Molotov: 1925–1936*, 208.
84 Ibid., 196.
85 Adibekov, Di B'iadzho, Gori et al (eds), *Politbiuro TsK RKP(b)-VKP(b) i Evropa*, 240.
86 Davies and Harris, *Stalin's World*, 112.
87 Ken, *Moskva i pakt nenapadeniia*, 7. For Litvinov's account, see SPO, tom 2, 569.
88 DiM, tom V, 473; Ken, *Moskva i pakt nenapadeniia*, 16, 18.
89 SPO, tom 2, 538–9.
90 Ibid., 504–5. For Litvinov's remarks on Poland's inconsistency, see 569.
91 Ibid., 538–9; Ken, *Collective Security or Isolation?*, 19–20.
92 Haslam, *Soviet Foreign Policy*, 69.
93 Samuelson, *Plans for Stalin's War Machine*, 116, 122, 129.
94 Whitewood, *The Red Army and the Great Terror*, 118.

95 Davies and Harris, *Stalin's World*, 113. At the seventeenth party conference in 1932, he warned similarly that the danger of imperialist war was rising, see Kotkin, *Stalin. Vol. II*, 91.
96 Ken, *Collective Security or Isolation?*, 20; Steiner, *The Lights That Failed*, 553; Haslam, *Soviet Foreign Policy*, 68.
97 SPO, tom 2, 569.
98 DVP, tom XIV, 443.
99 Ken, *Collective Security or Isolation?*, 21; Korbel, *Poland between East and West*, 267.
100 DVP, tom XIV, 484-6; SPO, tom 2, 570; Ken, *Collective Security or Isolation?*, 20.
101 Ibid., 22.
102 *Moskva i pakt nenapadeniia*, 26-7; SPO, tom 2, 540-1; DVP, tom XIV, 497.
103 SPO, tom 2, 559.
104 This point is made by Ken, see *Moskva i pakt nenapadeniia*, 32.
105 R.W. Davies, O.V. Khlevniuk et al. (eds), *The Stalin-Kaganovich Correspondence, 1931-36* (New Haven, 1993), 68.
106 Ibid., 93; Ken, *Moskva i pakt nenapadeniia*, 34-6.
107 *Materialy 'osoboi papki' Politburo TsK RKP(b)-VKP(b) po voprosu sovetsko-pol'skikh otnoshenii*, 62.
108 Ken, *Moskva i pakt nenapadeniia*, 41.
109 SPO, tom 2, 565-74.
110 Davies, Khlevniuk et al. (eds), *The Stalin-Kaganovich correspondence*, 93.
111 RGASPI, f. 17, op. 162, d. 11, l. 9.
112 Kvashonkin (ed.), SKP, 161-8.
113 RGASPI, f. 588, op. 11, d. 185, ll. 1-9; Davies and Harris, *Stalin's World*, 115.
114 *Materialy 'osoboi papki' Politburo TsK RKP(b)-VKP(b) po voprosu sovetsko-pol'skikh otnoshenii*, 63; Kvashonkin (ed.), SKP, 161-3.
115 Ken, *Collective Security or Isolation?*, 23; Korbel, *Poland between East and West*, 273.
116 Iu.L. D'iakov 'Neizvestnye dokumenty ob otnosheniiakh SSSR (Rossii) i Pol'shi v XX veke' in E. Durachinski and A.N. Sakharov (eds), *Sovetsko-pol'skie otnosheniia v politicheskikh usloviiakh Evropy 30-kh godov XX stoletiia* (Moscow, 2001), 53, 64; Korbel, *Poland between East and West*, 272.
117 SPO, tom 2, 618; Ken, *Collective Security or Isolation?*, 23.
118 Ibid., 23-4.
119 Ken, *Collective Security or Isolation*, 27.
120 DVP, tom XV, 272-5; Haslam, *Soviet Foreign Policy*, 105.
121 RGASPI, f. 558, op. 11, d. 185, ll. 15-36.
122 RGASPI, f. 558, op. 11, d. 185, ll. 65-70. Doubts about the predicted war appeared elsewhere. In late March, an NKID official in Japan sent Karakhan a message, questioning whether or Poland would launch attacks; the latter, he reported, was more concerned about the rise of the Far Right in Germany. DVP, tom 15, 214-17.
123 Kotkin, *Stalin. Vol. II*, 92fn. 182.
124 Karski, *The Great Powers and Poland*, 109.
125 On the clause in question, see ibid.
126 Shearer, 'Stalin at War, 1918-1953', 196; Snyder, 'Covert Polish Missions', 67; V.V. Kondrashin et al. (eds), *Golod v SSSR. 1929-1934: V 3 t. Tom 3: Leto 1933-1934* (Moscow, 2013), 515.
127 See Sheila Fitzpatrick 'The Foreign Threat during the First Five-Year Plan', *Soviet Union/Union Sovietique* 5/1 (1978), 26-35; Hiroaki Kuromiya, *Stalin's Industrial Revolution: Politics and Workers, 1928-1932* (Cambridge, 1990).

128 Davies and Harris, *Stalin's World*, 74.
129 David Shearer and Vladimir Khaustov, *Stalin and the Lubianka: A Documentary History of the Political Police and Security Organs in the Soviet Union, 1922–1953* (New Haven, 2015) 72; Danilov, Khlevniuk, and Vatlin (eds), *Kak lomali NEP*, tom 1, 348–51; RGASPI, f. 558, op. 11, d. 132, l. 3.
130 Shearer and Khaustov, *Stalin and the Lubianka*, 73–5.
131 Danilov, Khlevniuk, and Vatlin (eds), *Kak lomali NEP*, tom 1, 156–8.
132 Kotkin *Stalin. Vol. 1*, 692, 695.
133 Volodymyr Prystaiko and Iurii Shapoval, *Sprava 'Spilky Vyzvolennia Ukrainy': Nevidomi Dokumenty i Fakty* (Kyiv, 1995) 160, 352. On the SVU trial, see Olena Palko, *Making Ukraine Soviet: Literature and Cultural Politics under Lenin and Stalin* (London, 2020), 160–4.; Pauly, 'Soviet Polonophobia', 178.
134 See, for instance, Borisenok, *Fenomen Sovetskoi Ukrainizatsii*, 198; Sevost'ianov et al. (eds), *'Sovershenno Sekretno': Lubianka Stalinu o polozhenii v strane*, t. 9, 432–45; ibid, t. 8, ch. 2, 1531–47; DHASBU, f. 13, 1068, ll. 1–61; Berelovich and Danilov (eds), *Sovetskaia derevnia glazami VChK-OGPU-NKVD*, t. 3, kn. 1 (Moscow, 2004), 180–9.
135 Liudmyla Hrynevych, 'The Price of Stalin's "Revolution from Above": Anticipation of War among the Ukrainian Peasantry', 5. Available at https://holodomor.ca/wp-content/uploads/2020/04/Hrynevych_TranslatedArticle.pdf [accessed January 2022].
136 DHASBU, f. 13 ark 162, t. 4, ll. 1–3.
137 Snyder, 'Covert Polish Missions', 59.
138 Ibid., 60.
139 RGASPI, f. 17, op. 162, d. 8, ll. 109–10. Lynne Viola, *The Unknown Gulag: The Lost World of Stalin's Special Settlements* (Oxford, 2009), 28; Viola, *The Tragedy of the Soviet Countryside*, 215. Poland carried out repression of its own between September and November when it launched a pacification campaign against Ukrainian nationalists, arresting hundreds. Zimmerman, *Jozef Pilsudski*, 425.
140 Lynne Viola, *Peasant Rebels Under Stalin: Collectivization and the Culture of Peasant Resistance* (Oxford, 1999), 27.
141 Snyder, 'Covert Polish Missions', 65; Berelovich and Danilov (eds), *Sovetskaia derevnia glazami VChK-OGPU-NKVD*, t. 3, kn. 1, 312–27; Sevost'ianov et al. (eds), *'Sovershenno Sekretno': Lubianka Stalinu o polozhenii v strane*, t. 8, ch. 1, 749–58.
142 Snyder, 'Covert Polish Missions', 62; Sevost'ianov et al. (eds), *'Sovershenno Sekretno': Lubianka Stalinu o polozhenii v strane*, t. 8, ch. 2, 1369; DHASBU, f. 13, arkh 177, 17.
143 Berelovich and Danilov (eds), *Sovetskaia derevnia glazami VChK-OGPU-NKVD*), t. 4, kn. 3, 219–20; Hrynevych, 'The Price of Stalin's "Revolution from Above"', 10.
144 Snyder, 'Covert Polish Missions', 64; Sevost'ianov et al. (eds), *'Sovershenno Sekretno': Lubianka Stalinu o polozhenii v strane*, t. 8, ch. 1, 180–1; t. 9, 377–88, 391–6; N.N. Polrovskii et al. (eds), *Politbiuro i krest'ianstvo: Vysylka, spetsposelenie. 1930–1940 gg.* Kn. II (Moscow, 2006), 932–5.
145 D. Nokhotovich and N. Teptsova, 'Raskulachivali dazhe ... inostrantsev. Dokumenty perioda kollektivizatsii' in V.A. Kozlov and S.M. Zav'ialov (eds), *Neizvestnaia Rossiia XX Vek*, II (Moscow, 1992), 333. The British ambassador in Moscow reported similar information in early 1930, noting that some in the Soviet government feared that Poland would 'provoke a quarrel' due to the growing disorder in the Red Army sparked by collectivization. Davies, *The Socialist Offensive*, 260.
146 Ken and Rusapov, *Politbiuro TsK VKP(b) i otnosheniia SSSR s zapadnymi sosednimi gosudarstvami*, 514–15; Sevost'ianov et al. (eds), *'Sovershenno Sekretno': Lubianka Stalinu o polozhenii v strane*, t. 8, ch. 2, 1258–344.

147 Whitewood, *The Red Army and the Great Terror*, 124–6.
148 Romano, 'Permanent War Scare', 118.
149 Ken and Rusapov, *Politbiuro TsK VKP(b) i otnosheniia SSSR s zapadnymi sosednimi gosudarstvami*, 517.
150 Snyder, 'Covert Polish Missions', 70, 76–7.
151 DHASBU, f. 13, ark 124, ll. 32, 115.
152 Ibid., ark 90.
153 Viola, *Peasant Rebels Under Stalin*, 29; SPO, tom 2, 541–2.
154 Whitewood, *The Red Army and the Great Terror*, 128–41.
155 Zdanovich, *Organy gosudarstvennoi bezopasnosti i krasnaia armiia*, 385–7.
156 DHASBU, f. 13, 1068, l. 1. For similar evidence from other arrested officers, see ll. 3–61.
157 Anne Applebaum, *Red Famine: Stalin's War on Ukraine* (New York, London, 2017), 182–3.
158 O.V. Khlevniuk et al (eds), *Stalin i Kaganovich perepiska. 1931–1936 gg.* (Moscow, 2001), 241–2.
159 Applebaum, *Red Famine*, 183–7.
160 Khlevniuk et al. (eds), *Stalin i Kaganovich perepiska*, 273–4.
161 This is Snyder's interpretation, see Snyder, 'Covert Polish Missions', 72–3.
162 Shearer and Khaustov, *Stalin and the Lubianka*, 114.
163 Zdanovich, *Pol'skii krest*, 295–6.
164 Applebaum, *Red Famine*, 188.
165 Yuri Shapoval, 'Vsevolod Balytsky and the Holodomor of 1932–33'. Available at https://holodomor.ca/wp-content/uploads/2016/05/Shapoval-article-translated-BK-ekm-emy-done-1.pdf, 8.
166 DHASBU, f. 13, ark. 180, t. 4, ll. 1, 30, 32, 47, 50, 106; Shearer and Khaustov, *Stalin and the Lubianka*, 163–4.
167 Ibid., l. 92.
168 Pauly, 'Soviet Polonophobia', 181.
169 *Holodomor Studies* 3/1–2 (2011): 189.

Conclusion

1 Stalin, 'Report to the Seventeenth Party Congress on the Work of the Central Committee of the C.P.S.U. (B.)'. Available at https://www.marxists.org/reference/archive/stalin/works/1934/01/26.htm [accessed July 2022].
2 RGASPI, f. 588, op. 11, d. 790, ll. 45–50.
3 Ken, *Collective Security or Isolation*, 92; *Mobilizatsionnoe planirovanie i politicheskie resheniia*, 268; Davies and Harris, *Stalin's World*, 117; RGASPI, 558, op. 11, d. 790, ll. 117–18.
4 Ken, *Collective Security or Isolation*, 83.
5 Davies and Harris, *Stalin's World*, 122; Haslam, *Soviet Foreign Policy*, 36.
6 Davies and Harris, *Stalin's World*, 124–5; RGASPI, f. 558, op. 11, d. 185, 126–32; Sabine Dullin, *Men of Influence. Stalin's Diplomats in Europe, 1930–1939* (Edinburgh, 2008), 97–8; Kokin, Podkur and Rubl'ov (eds), *Sprava 'Pol's'koi Organizatsii Viis'kovoi' v Ukraini*. 192; Ken, *Mobilizatsionnoe planirovanie i politicheskie resheniia*, 271.

7   RGASPI, f. 588, op. 11, d. 187, ll. 79–92, 111–17; Pozniakov, 'The Enemy at the Gates', 222–23.
8   On Lenin's inherent anti-democratic nature, Eric van Ree, 'Dictatorship Unlimited: Lenin on the State, March-November 1917' in Douds, Harris, and Whitewood (eds), *The Fate of the Bolshevik Revolution: Illiberal Liberation*, 17–30.
9   See reports sent to Stalin in December 1935 in Khaustov, Naumov, and Plotnikova (eds), *Lubianka*, 639–8; 705–10; 712–14.
10 James Morris, 'The Polish Terror: Spy Mania and Ethnic Cleansing in the Great Terror', *Europe-Asia Studies* 56/5 (2004): 761.

BIBLIOGRAPHIC ABBREVIATIONS

AVPRF	Arkhiv vneshnei politiki Rossiiskoi Federatsii (Archive of the foreign ministry of the Russian Federation). [Materials used in this book are from the physical archive and its online holdings: http://1917.mid.ru/archives/avprf/]
BRP	A. V. Kashonkin, O. V. Khlevniuk, L. P. Kosheleva and L. A. Rogovaia (eds), *Bol'shevistskoe rukovodstvo perepiska 1912–1927* (Moscow, 1996)
CAB	Cabinet Papers (Cabinet Office, United Kingdom)
CHAR	Churchill Archive, Chartwell Papers
DBFP	*Documents on British Foreign Policy, 1919–1939. First series, Vol I, 1919* (London, 1947)
DGKKA	N. M. V'iunova, N. I. Deeva and T. F. Kariaeva (eds), *Direktivy glavnogo komandovaniia krasnoi armii (1917–1920). Sbornik dokumentov* (Moscow, 1969)
DHASBU	Derzhavnyi haluzevyi arkhiv sluzhby bezpeky Ukraïny (Sectoral state archive of the security services of Ukraine)
DiM	*Dokumenty i materialy po istorii sovetsko-pol'skikh otnoshenii* (Moscow, 1964–)
DVP	*Dokumenty vneshnei politiki SSSR* (Moscow, 1958–)
FRUS	Joseph V. Fuller (ed.) *Foreign Relations of the United States, 1920*, Vol. III (Washington, 1936)
GARF	Gosudarstvennyi arkhiv Rossiiskoi Federatsii (State archive of the Russian Federation)
PSS	V. I. Lenin, *Polnoe sobranie sochinenii* (Moscow, 1974–)
PSV	I. I. Kostiushko, M. N. Chernykh and V. N. Savchenko (eds), *Pol'sko-sovetskaia voina 1919–1920. Ranee ne opublikovannye dokumenty i materialy* ch. 1, 2 (Moscow, 1994)
RGASPI	Rossiiskii gosudarstvennyi arkhiv sotsial'no-politicheskoi istorii (Russian state archive of socio-political history)
RGVA	Rossiskii gosudarstvennyi voennyi arkhiv (Russian state military archive)
SKP	A. V. Kvashonkin (ed.), *Sovetskoe rukovodstvo perepiska 1928–1941* (Moscow, 1999)
SPO	Narinskogo, M. M. and A. V. Mal'gina (eds), *Sovetsko-pol'skie otnosheniia v 1918–1945 gg.: Sbornik dokumentov v chetyrekh tomakh. Tom 1 1918–1926, Tom 2 1926–1932* (Moscow 2017)
TsDAVO	Tsentral'nyi derzhavnyi arkhiv vyshchykh orhaniv vlady ta upravlinnia Ukraïny (Central state archive of supreme bodies of power of the government of Ukraine)

SELECT BIBLIOGRAPHY

Borzęcki, Jerzy, *The Soviet–Polish Peace of 1921 and the Creation of Interwar Europe* (New Haven, 2008).
Bruski, Jan Jacek, *Between Prometheism and Realpolitik: Poland and Soviet Ukraine, 1921–1926* (Krakow, 2016).
Daniels, Robert V., *The Conscience of the Revolution: Communist Opposition in Soviet Russia* (Cambridge, MA, 1960).
Danilov, V.P., R. Manning and L. Viola (eds.), *Tragediia sovetskoi derevni: kollektivizatsiia i raskulachivanie: dokumenty i materialy v 5 tom., 1927–1938 gg.*, tom 1 (Moscow, 1999–2004).
Davies, Norman, *White Eagle, Red Star: The Polish-Soviet War 1919–20 and 'the miracle on the Vistula'* (London, 2003).
Davies, Sarah and James Harris, *Stalin's World: Dictating the Soviet Order* (New Haven, 2014).
Debo, Richard K., *Survival and Consolidation: The Foreign Policy of Soviet Russia, 1918–1921* (Montreal, 1992).
Erickson, John, *The Soviet High Command: A Military–Political History, 1918–1941* (London; Portland, OR, 2001).
Haslam, Jonathan, *Soviet Foreign Policy, 1930–1933: The Impact of the Depression* (Basingstoke, 1983).
Ivanov, Iu.V., *Ocherki istorii rossiisko (sovetsko)-pol'shikh otnoshenii v dokumentakh. 1914–1945* (Moscow, 2014).
Jacobson, Jon, *When the Soviet Union Entered World Politics* (Berkeley, 1994).
Karski, Jan, *The Great Powers and Poland: From Versailles to Yalta* (Plymouth, 2014).
Ken, Oleg, *Collective Security of Isolation? Soviet Policy and Poland, 1930–35* (St. Petersburg, 1996).
Ken, Oleg, *Moskva i pakt nenapadeniia s Pol'shei (1930–1932)* (St. Petersburg, 2003).
Ken, O.N. and A.I. Rusapov, *Politbiuro TsK VKP(b) i otnosheniia SSSR s zapadnymi sosednimi gosudarstvami (konets 1920-1930-kh gg.): problem, oput, kommentarii* (St Petersburg, 2000).
Korbel, Josef, *Poland between East and West. Soviet and German Diplomacy towards Poland, 1919–1933* (Princeton, 1963).
Kotkin, Stephen, *Stalin. Vol. 1: Paradoxes of Power 1878–1928* (London, 2014).
Kotkin, Stephen, *Stalin. Vol. II: Waiting for Hitler, 1929–1941* (New York, 2017).
Pons, Silvio and Andrea Romano (eds.), *Russia in the Age of Wars* (Milan, 2000).
Reiman, Michal, *The Birth of Stalinism: The USSR on the Eve of the 'Second Revolution'* (London, 1987).
Rieber, Alfred J., *Stalin and the Struggle for Supremacy in Eurasia* (Cambridge, 2015).
Samuelson, Lennart, *Plans for Stalin's War Machine: Tukhachevskii and Military-Economic Planning, 1925–1941* (Basingstoke, 2000).
Shearer, David, 'Stalin at War, 1918–1953. Patterns of Violence and Foreign Threat', *Jahrbücher für Geschichte Osteuropas* 66/2 (2018).

Simonov, N.S., "Strengthen the Defence of the Land of the Soviets': The 1927 'War Alarm' and Its Consequences", *Europe-Asia Studies* 48/8 (1996).

Snyder, Timothy, 'Covert Polish Missions across the Soviet Ukrainian Border, 1928–1933', in Silvia Salvatici (ed.), *Confini: Costruzioni, attraveramenti, rappresentazioni* (Catanzaro, 2005).

Stone, David. R., *Hammer and Rifle: The Militarization of the Soviet Union, 1926–1933* (Kansas, 2000).

Stone, David. R., 'The Prospect of War?' Lev Trotskii, the Soviet Army, and the German Revolution in 1923', *The International History Review* 25/4 (2003).

Ullman, Richard H., *Anglo-Soviet Relations, 1917–1921, Vol. 3: The Anglo-Soviet Accord* (Princeton, 1968).

Ul', M., V. Khaustov and V. Zakharov (eds.), *Glazami razvedki. SSSR i Evropa, 1919–1938 gody: sbornik dokumentov iz rossiiskikh arkhivov* (Moscow, 2015).

Velikanova, Olga, *Popular Perceptions of Soviet Politics in the 1920s. Disenchantment of the Dreamers* (Basingstoke, 2013).

Vilkova, Valentina, *RKP(b). Vnutripartiinaia bor'ba v dvadtsatye gody. Dokumenty i materialy. 1923* (Moscow, 2004).

Wandycz, Piotr, *France and Her Eastern Allies, 1919–1925: French-Czechoslovak-PolishRelations from the Paris Peace Conference in Locarno* (Minneapolis, 1962).

Wandycz, Piotr S., *Soviet–Polish Relations, 1917–1921* (Cambridge, MA, 1969).

Wandycz, Piotr S., *The Twilight of French Eastern Alliances, 1926–1936: French-Czechoslovak-Polish Relations from Locarno to the Remilitarization of the Rhineland* (Princeton, 2014).

Zamoyski, Adam, *Warsaw 1920: Lenin's Failed Conquest of Europe* (London, 2008).

Zdanovich, Aleksandr, *Pol'skii krest sovetskoi kontrrazvedki: pol'skaia liniia v rabote VChK-NKVD 1918–1938* (Moscow, 2017).

Zimmerman, Joshua D., *Jozef Pilsudski: Founding Father of Modern Poland* (Cambridge, MA, 2022).

INDEX

1st Cavalry Army 21, 26, 29, 31, 38, 45–7, 55–7, 58, 62
Allied Supreme Council 12, 15, 32, 38–9
All-Russian Cooperative Society 138, 141, 143
American Relief Administration 81
Antonov-Ovseenko, Vladimir 165, 167, 169–70, 173, 179, 181
Aralov, Sergei 80, 119–20
ARCOS (see All-Russian Cooperative Society)
Artuzov, Artur 114, 118, 174

Baldwin, Stanley 103–4, 138
Balitskii, Vsevolod 98, 172, 174, 176, 180–1
Baltic states 4, 42, 83, 90, 102, 104–5, 107, 109, 113–17, 119–20, 136–7, 139, 150, 156, 160, 168
Baranowicze 47–8
Beck, Józef 69
Belarus 9, 10–12, 26, 28, 38, 50, 65, 69, 71, 95–7, 117–19, 135, 140, 179–80
Belorussia (see Belarus)
Berezina River 29, 38
Berzin, Ian 25, 47, 99, 108, 114
Bessarabia 24, 57
Białystok 9, 45, 50
Bogomolov, Aleksandr 151, 155–8, 160, 163–4
Borisov 22–3, 30
Brest-Litovsk 9, 12, 19, 20, 29, 42, 49
Briand, Aristide 78, 83, 105, 161
Britain
    conspiracies about 4–6, 13, 21, 26–8, 30–3, 52, 62, 72, 82, 84, 100, 104–6, 108, 110–12, 114, 116, 118, 135, 137, 139–40, 142–3, 148, 157–8, 160–1, 163, 165, 168, 174, 179, 184–5
    elections in 6, 96, 103
    general strike of 116
    prospects of revolution within 63, 112
    recognition of the Soviet Union 131, 163
    relations with Poland 11–12, 15, 19, 34–5, 39, 63, 77
    relations with the Soviet Union 10, 14–17, 23, 31–3, 40, 42–5, 51, 53, 59, 87, 93–4, 135, 138, 163
    and Wrangel 33, 40–1, 43
British Labour Party 33, 94, 97, 106
Brockdorff-Rantzau, Ulrich von 104, 110, 166
Budennyi, Semen 21, 26, 29, 32, 38, 44, 46–48, 56–9, 62
Bug River 40, 45, 49
Bukharin, Nikolai 38, 42, 46, 86, 89, 125, 133–5, 159, 175
Bułak-Bałakhovich, Stanisłav 66–72, 91, 99, 141

Cartel des gauches 94, 97
Caucasus 15, 18–19, 21, 74, 105, 119
Chamberlain, Austin 138, 144, 146
Cheka (see Soviet political police)
Chicherin, Georgy
    concerns about war 13, 16–21, 24, 42, 71, 109, 157
    conspiratorial thinking of 67–8, 76–7, 80–2, 104–5, 114, 137, 142, 150, 157
    health of 162
    interpretation of intelligence 67, 92
    negotiations with Britain 26, 32–4, 44–5, 51
    negotiations with Germany 104
    negotiations with Poland 23, 34, 47, 54, 67, 70–1, 84, 102, 109, 119, 150, 162
    peace initiatives of 12–14, 22
    realism of 42, 54–5, 59–60, 63, 68, 75, 120, 150, 185

Index

view of international order 78, 87, 112, 140
view of war with Poland 27, 32, 59, 63, 140
Churchill, Winston 12, 14, 16–17, 35, 59, 72–3, 158, 169
Clémenceau, Georges 14–15, 146.
Collectivization 3–4, 7, 153–4, 159, 166, 174, 177–81, 183, 186
Communist International (Comintern) 18, 44, 46, 81, 87, 95, 103, 113, 126, 134, 140, 168
Crimea 26, 29, 32, 40–1, 56
Cuno, Wilhelm 85, 89
Curzon, George 12, 26, 40–3, 46, 52, 60, 73, 87, 96–7
Czechoslovakia 15, 52, 76, 84, 95

D'Abernon, Vincent 1
Dąbski, Jan 68, 70
Danzig 39, 55, 90, 115, 136
Dawes Plan 103
Dekulakization 177, 181
Democratic Centralists 124–5
Denikin, Anton 2, 10–11, 13–15, 17, 30, 35, 38
Dzerzhinskii, Feliks 44, 46, 50–1, 58, 66, 72, 89, 98, 100–1, 104, 108–9, 111–12, 114, 118, 120, 126, 128–9, 134

Egorov, Aleksandr 19, 38, 47, 49, 52, 55, 57, 62–3
Estonia 24, 84, 86, 98, 100, 106–7, 110, 116–17, 137, 143, 162

Ferdinand, Franz 139, 142
Finland 4, 27, 31, 40, 42, 45, 84, 86, 100, 104, 107, 116, 136–7, 140, 143, 150, 173, 180
First World War 9–10, 66, 69, 97, 106, 159, 163–4
Five-year plan 5, 7, 153, 159–61, 164, 175, 186
Foch, Ferdinand 16, 21, 40, 78, 87–8
France
  conspiracies about 4–6, 21, 26, 30–1, 34, 36, 42–3, 72–3, 79, 84–7, 91, 96 100, 108, 124, 126, 135, 140, 157, 160, 165, 168, 170, 174–5, 184–5
  elections in 93, 94, 96

loans of 78, 84, 105
occupation of Ruhr 103
relations with Poland 11–12, 16, 28, 46, 52–4, 63, 76–8, 81–2, 94, 157, 168
relations with the Soviet Union 10, 23, 27, 94, 105, 131, 136, 138, 164, 170, 172, 174
Frunze, Mikhail 84, 99, 101, 105–8, 120–1, 133

Gai, Gai Dmitrievich 47, 60
Galicia 10, 12, 15, 24, 41, 50, 60, 66, 68–9, 79, 95
Ganetskii, Iakov 67, 80
Genoa conference 83–4
German Communist Party 85, 89
Germany
  army of 6, 7, 9, 17, 35
  Bolshevik views of 5, 31, 34, 48, 52, 89
  border disputes of 75
  conspiracies about 35–6, 107, 140, 165, 180–1
  defeat in the First World War 9
  negotiations with the Soviet Union 14, 35, 55, 82, 110–11, 150–1, 166, 170, 173
  position in international order 83, 99, 102–4, 110, 181, 184
  prospect of revolution within 2, 9–10, 96, 130–1, 133
  relations with Poland 80, 104, 135–6, 165–6, 184
  reparations payments of 39, 85, 185
  and the Ruhr crisis 6, 65, 85–93, 95, 127, 129
  transit through 54
  Treaty of Berlin 111, 114
  Treaty of Rapallo 83–4, 93, 104, 111, 166, 174, 183
GPU (see Soviet political police)
Grabski, Władysław 39, 94, 113
Great Terror 5, 187
Grodno 13, 38, 47

Hamburg 90–1
Henrys, Paul 20, 35
Herriot, Edouard 87, 94, 97, 103, 105, 131
Hitler, Adolf 7, 172, 183–5
Hungary 34, 41, 46, 48

Iagoda, Genrikh 100, 108, 118–19, 175
Iampol' 101–2
Industrialization 3–5, 153–4, 159, 174, 181, 183, 186–7
Inter-Allied mission to Poland 1, 40, 60
Ioffe, Adolf 67–8, 75–9, 117
Italy 27, 46, 52, 119, 135

Japan 112, 165, 172–4, 181, 184–5

Kaganovich, Lazar 108, 171–2, 175–6, 179
Kamenev, Lev 41, 51–4, 57, 59–60, 87, 127–9, 132–4, 144, 149
Kamenev, Sergei 18–19, 22, 26, 38, 43–5, 47, 49, 52, 55–7, 62, 73, 84, 86
Karakhan, Lev 69–71, 80, 82, 170
Kellogg-Briand Pact 161–3, 169
Khar'kov 25, 27, 34, 66, 178–9
Kiev 10–11, 18–19, 25–6, 29–30, 39, 57, 60, 66, 71–2, 76, 86, 89, 97, 176, 179
Klyshko, Nikolai 31, 41, 52, 54
Kolchak, Aleksandr 11, 30
Kon, Feliks 43, 63–4
Kopp, Viktor 55, 88, 90, 104
Kowerda, Boris 138–42
KPD (see German Communist Party)
Krasin, Leonid 31–3, 51, 72, 75, 105
Krestinskii, Nikolai 52, 59, 142, 169, 171
Kronstadt 79, 125–6, 134
Kuibyshev, Valerian 133, 164

Łapiński, Paweł 27, 56, 75–6
Latgale 12–13
Latvia 24, 31, 40, 42, 45, 52, 80, 84, 86, 90, 98, 100, 104, 106–7, 110, 116–17, 137, 143, 162, 173
League of Nations 75, 94, 102, 104, 110–11, 113, 119, 135–6, 150, 155, 169, 173
Lenin, Vladimir
  concerns about war 13, 16, 21–3, 29, 73–4, 79, 81, 83–4, 127
  confidence in seizing Warsaw 57–9
  death of 96, 112, 185
  on dictatorship 126, 186
  health of 89, 123, 127–8
  interpretation of the Soviet-Polish war 26, 41, 61–2, 64, 184
  on political unity 124–5, 127
  preparations for war 18, 21
  and revolutionary war 1–2, 6, 9, 13, 21–2, 37, 45–7, 50, 52
  Testament 130, 132
  view of Britain 31–2, 40–1, 52, 56, 59, 61
  view of France 79
  view of the Polish people 26
  on Wrangel 49, 56, 73
Lithuania 9, 11, 26, 40, 43, 50, 52, 80, 86, 90, 100, 104, 110, 113, 119–20, 136, 140, 151, 155, 161, 172
Little Entente 76, 87
Litvinov, Maksim 16, 20, 28, 32, 42, 46, 52–3, 60, 63, 82–4, 87, 135, 137, 141, 150, 162, 166, 169–71, 173, 175–7
Litvinov protocol 162–3, 165–6, 170
Lloyd George, David 15–17, 28, 31–4, 39–40, 44, 51–2, 54, 59–60, 83–4
Locarno, Treaty of 110–13, 115–16, 150, 160
Lublin 55, 57
Lwów 10, 41, 47–50, 55–8, 62

MacDonald, James Ramsay 94, 96–7, 103–4, 131, 163
Mackinder, Halford 24, 28
Manchuria 172, 185
Marchlevsk 100, 180
Markhlevskii, Iulian 13, 44, 50
Menzhinskii, Viacheslav 149, 168, 175
Miasnikov, Gavriil 126–27
Mikaszewicze 11, 13
Millerand, Alexandre 16, 28, 34, 40, 42, 44, 51, 54, 60
Minsk 10, 18, 22, 28, 38, 42, 45, 50, 53, 59–60, 76, 81, 86
Molotov, Viacheslav 82, 139, 144, 146, 159, 168, 170
Muralov, Nikolai 19–20, 22, 29

National Democratic Movement (Polish) 10, 65, 67, 76, 113
National Socialist German Workers' Party 166, 168, 180
New Economic Policy 126, 131, 133, 153, 159–60, 181, 187
Niemen River 45, 60

Nikonov, A.M. 108
NKID (see Soviet foreign ministry)
Northern Taurida 31, 38

Obolenskii, Leonid 88, 90
Odessa 66, 158
OGPU (see Soviet political police)
Ordzhonikidze, Sergo 18, 63, 146

Paderewski, Ignacy 10–12
Patek, Stanisław 12, 15–17, 20, 23, 36, 39, 135–7, 141–3, 155–6, 169–71
Petliura, Symon 11, 24, 66–71, 72, 91, 99, 117, 139, 158, 176
Piłsudski, Józef
    ambitions in the east 11–12, 16–17, 39, 63, 65, 69, 76, 137, 151, 158, 184
    at the battle of Warsaw 2, 57–8
    early life of 10
    and elections 155, 167
    health of 156, 158, 179
    invasion of Ukraine 19, 24–5, 28
    negotiations with the Bolsheviks 11, 20, 22–3, 45, 70, 135–6, 150, 165, 169, 178, 184
    as political outsider 82, 88, 91
    popularity of 26, 75, 77
    return to power 6, 93, 99–100, 109, 112–21, 134, 149, 185
    and Romania 160, 173
    search for allies 24, 38
    subversive operations of 71, 99–100, 117, 141, 167
    and war planning 11–14, 24, 174, 181
Poincaré, Raymond 78, 83, 96–7, 103
Poland
    alliance with France 77–8, 87, 111, 157, 160, 168
    economic position of 77, 84, 86, 113–15, 178
    independence of 9, 14
    intelligence agents of 98–9, 180
    military spending 105
    minorities of 95, 99
    negotiating positions of 20, 22–3, 109–10, 113, 119, 136, 138, 154–5, 170–1, 173
    non-aggression pact with the Soviet Union 7, 173–4, 178, 180, 183–4
    partition of 11–12
    perception within an anti-Soviet coalition 4–7, 14, 16, 74–6, 84, 109, 116, 140, 157
    relations with Baltic states 84, 107, 109–10
    relations with Germany 80, 95, 104, 151, 155, 162, 165–6, 184
    relations with Romania 78, 109–10, 113
    trade negotiations of 82, 155
Polish Bureau (Bolshevik) 16, 18, 23, 142
Polish Communist Party 21, 23, 44, 113
Polish Military Intelligence (see second department of the Polish general staff)
Polish Military Organization 66, 118, 180
Polish People's Party 45, 88
Polish Revolutionary Committee 21, 44, 50, 58
Polish Socialist Party 10–11
Politburo 21, 26, 30–1, 50, 54, 59, 62, 74, 77, 86, 89–90, 99, 101–2, 104, 107, 109, 114, 119, 121, 129, 135, 137–8, 140, 142–3, 145, 149, 154, 156, 164–5, 167–8, 171–2, 184
Polrevkom (see Polish Revolutionary Committee)
Ponikowski, Antoni 82–3
Preobrazhenskii, Evgeny 43–4, 131
Pripet marshes 13, 18
Prussia 9, 50, 60, 85, 90

Radek, Karl 44–5, 58, 60, 66, 73, 88
Rakovskii, Kristian 19, 25, 31, 66, 95, 142, 146, 157
Ransome, Arthur 21, 87
Red Army
    defence of the borders 71
    espionage threat within 118
    failures of 19, 29
    success in the civil war 9
    weaknesses within 1, 6, 13, 21–2, 24–5, 37, 61, 89, 105–6, 109, 121, 154, 164, 178
Red Cross 11, 31
Revolutionary Military Council of the Republic 26, 60, 90

Riga 59–60, 64, 68, 84, 107, 116
    Treaty of 6, 68, 70, 77, 79–82, 88, 90–1, 95, 117
Romania 15, 24, 31, 34, 38, 42–3, 45–8, 52, 57, 63, 76, 81–6, 95–6, 98–9, 102, 105–6, 109, 113, 119, 135, 140, 156, 158, 160–3, 165, 168–70, 172–4, 178
Rotshtein, Fedor 41, 52, 54, 150
Równe 19, 26, 38
Rozwadowski, Tadeusz 36, 49, 60
Rumbold, Horace 17, 20, 24, 39, 48
Russian civil war 1–4, 9, 14–15, 35, 76, 138, 145, 153, 185–6
Russian Revolution 2, 4, 9, 37, 73, 83, 94
Rykov, Aleksei 44, 99, 117, 133, 135, 142, 146, 159, 175–6

Savinkov, Boris 67–73, 75, 91
Second department of the Polish general staff 67, 69–71, 81, 90–1, 98–9, 176, 178, 180
Shakhty trial 175–6
Sikorski, Władysław 19, 57, 69, 88
Skirmunt, Konstanty 69–70
Sklianskii, Efraim 20, 41, 58, 89
Skrzyńsk, Aleksander 102, 115
Skulski, Leopold 12, 39
Sławek, Walery 165, 167
Smilga, Ivar 18, 56, 59, 145
Smolensk 13, 18
Soviet foreign ministry 23, 28, 65, 67–8, 70–2, 75–6, 80–3, 88, 91–2, 97, 99, 101, 104, 110, 112, 114, 116–17, 119–20, 135–6, 138–9, 141, 150, 155–8, 160–7, 169–73, 181, 183–5
Soviet military intelligence 71, 72, 74–5, 78, 84–89, 91, 97, 99, 101, 108, 114, 118, 120, 136, 154, 156, 163–6, 168, 183, 185
Soviet political police 7, 50, 66, 69, 71–2, 78, 82–4, 86, 90–1, 97, 99, 101–2, 108, 114, 118–19, 139–40, 149, 158, 161, 164–5, 175–81, 183–6
Spa conference 39–40
Stalin, Iosif
    and collectivization 178
    criticism of the high command 62
    doubts about Polish revolution 2, 23, 43–4
    and famine in Ukraine 174, 179
    on future war 14, 82, 89, 91, 93, 106, 109, 111–12, 118, 120, 130, 134, 137, 139, 143–4, 165, 168, 181
    on Germany 89, 171, 176
    on grain supply 158–9
    and industrialization 153
    insubordination of 19, 55–6, 62
    Lwów military strategy of 47–8
    and negotiations with Poland 48, 53, 169, 171–3
    on party unity 128, 131–2, 144–8
    on Red Army weaknesses 29
    in the succession struggle 5, 7, 127, 129–32, 176
    view of Britain 52, 139–40, 143–4, 151
    view of espionage 31, 150
    view of international order 74, 87, 96–7, 106–7, 112, 151, 176, 181, 183–4
    view of the war against Poland 27, 30–5, 41, 46
    on Wrangel 32, 35, 38, 41, 48–9, 56–7
Steczkowski, Jan 78, 80
Steklov, Iurii 38, 86
Stomoniakov, Boris 115–17, 136, 143, 150, 155–7, 160, 163, 165, 167, 173, 184
Stresemann, Gustav 110, 140, 166

Teschen 39, 76
Tiutiunnik, Yuriy 71, 91
Tomskii, Mikhail 133, 159, 175
Trotsky, Lev
    criticism of Stalin 63
    expulsions of 99, 133, 149
    on future war 7, 13–14, 17, 19, 21, 23, 29, 86–7, 89, 97
    ill health of 131
    military leadership of 25, 34
    and negotiations with Poland 48–9, 60
    in political opposition 123, 127, 129–33, 144–9, 151, 160, 180, 186
    on political unity 127, 130, 133, 147–8, 151–2
    and propaganda 30, 34, 38–9, 46, 54, 67
    on Red Army weaknesses 21, 29
    on revolution in Europe 27, 42, 44, 63, 89

on Romania 31, 34, 43
view of Britain and France 30, 34, 42, 44–5, 52, 59
on Wrangel 38
Tukhachevskii, Mikhail 26, 28–9, 37, 47, 49–50, 55, 57–60, 62–3, 81, 120–21, 165, 169, 174, 179
Turkey 36, 52, 85, 162, 165, 169

Ukraine
 competition for 11, 65, 69, 71–2, 84, 95, 117, 177–8
 famine in 81, 174–5, 179
 military district of 84, 90
 Polish invasion of 6, 19, 28–9, 32
 security assessments about 86, 97–9, 107–8, 118, 157, 161, 163, 168, 174–81
 Soviet government of 68
Ukrainian People's Republic 68–9, 71, 88, 99, 117, 158, 178
Ul'ianov, Aleksandr 141–3
United States 14, 46, 103, 112, 143, 183
Unshlikht, Iosif 21, 44, 101, 150, 160–1
Upper Silesia 75, 79, 85, 136

Versailles, Treaty of 9, 10, 37, 60, 75, 104, 110, 171, 173
Vistula River 45, 57–8

Voikov, Petr 111–17, 119, 135–6, 138–9, 141–4, 150–1, 156, 166–7
Volhynia 10, 24, 60, 66, 69, 101, 176
Voroshilov, Kliment 45, 47–8, 56, 63, 120, 129, 135, 137, 139–40, 145, 154, 158, 162, 172, 178

Wall Street Crash 154, 164
Warsaw 10, 14, 16, 18, 24, 35, 40, 42, 45, 48, 83–5, 109, 114–15, 138, 141, 168, 174
 Battle of 2, 6, 19, 31, 37, 49–64, 72
White armies 2, 9–11, 13, 18, 25, 63
Wilno 9, 10, 12–13, 26, 39, 50, 68, 72, 110, 115, 119
Witos, Wincenty 45, 82, 88, 90–1, 114–15
Wojciechowski, Stanisław 114–15
Workers' Opposition 124–8
Wrangel, Petr 2, 26, 29–34, 38, 40–43, 45, 48, 51–4, 56, 60, 62, 64, 73, 75–7

Zaleski, August 116–17, 119, 136, 141, 143, 149–50, 155–6, 165, 169, 173
Żeligowski, Lucjan 49, 72, 76
Zhitomir 25, 29–30
Zinoviev, Grigory 18, 42, 46, 87, 89, 95–6, 127–9, 132–4, 144–6, 149
Zinoviev letter 103–4

www.ingramcontent.com/pod-product-compliance
Lightning Source LLC
Chambersburg PA
CBHW071830300426
44116CB00009B/1493